ANALECTA PRAEHISTORICA LEIDENSIA 28

ANALECTA PRAEHISTORICA LEIDENSIA

28

PUBLICATIONS OF THE INSTITUTE OF PREHISTORY
UNIVERSITY OF LEIDEN

INTERFACING THE PAST

COMPUTER APPLICATIONS AND QUANTITATIVE METHODS IN ARCHAEOLOGY CAA95 VOL. I

EDITED BY

HANS KAMERMANS AND KELLY FENNEMA

UNIVERSITY OF LEIDEN 1996

Graphic design: Henk de Lorm

Computer graphics: Peter Heavens

Copy editor: Marianne Wanders

ISSN 0169-7447

ISBN 90-73368-10-3

Subscriptions to the series Analecta Praehistorica Leidensia and single volumes can be ordered from:

Institute of Prehistory
P.O. Box 9515
2300 RA Leiden
The Netherlands

contents

CONTENTS

VOLUME II

Geographic Information Systems I

preface

CAA95, the 23rd annual Computer Applications in Archaeology conference, was held at the University of Leiden from 31st March - 2nd April 1995, and was hosted by the Faculty of Pre- and Protohistory.

The conference was organised jointly by the R.O.B. (State Service for Archaeological Investigations) in Amersfoort, the RAAP Foundation of the University of Amsterdam and the Faculty of Pre- and Protohistory of the University of Leiden.

One hundred and ninety nine people attended the 1995 conference, 44 of which were students. Apart from archaeologists connected with universities and museums, many participants came from local, regional and national government bodies concerned with the management of our cultural heritage.

The geographical distribution of the participants was: United Kingdom 59, the Netherlands 53, France/Spain/Italy/Greece 22, Germany/Switzerland/Austria 20, Norway/Sweden/Denmark 16, Poland/Romania/Slovenia/Hungary/Czech Republic 13, USA/Canada 11, and the Argentine/Japan/Australia 5.

At the conference, a total of 93 papers and 6 posters were presented, while there were 20 demonstrations of systems and applications. The papers were given in four parallel sessions and were grouped into eight different themes, with the following number of contributions: Analysing Ritual 6, Archaeometry 7, Classification 12, Cultural Resource Management 12, Databases 12, Free Range Subjects 13, Geographic Information Systems 19, and Multi Media 12.

For the 1995 proceedings we have regrouped the subjects under six main themes: Database Management, Archaeometry, Statistics and Classification, Geographic Information Systems, Visualisation, and Education and Publication. Reviewing the proceedings of conferences over the last twenty years, one sees that particular fields of research seem to be 'fashionable' at certain times. What does 1995 show us?

Database Management
In the first ten years, most papers presented at CAA conferences fell into two categories, data capture/management and analytical techniques. Database management remains a dominant topic in archaeology, 20-30% of the papers in the last ten proceedings dealt with this subject. With 18% this subject is still well represented this year. Improvements in both hardware and software allow larger and more complex databases. We now have relational databases on sites, combining excavation, curation and site management data, and databases containing nationwide information on archaeological sites and monuments. There are also museum databases, integrating site files, museum catalogues and bibliographic files.

Archaeometry
Until now archaeometry has not been treated as a separate subject in CAA proceedings. It was grouped with, for instance, 'applications of quantitative methods' or 'statistics — methods & techniques'. For our overview we have grouped archaeometry with 'statistics and classification'. We have therefore no history to compare with but the trends described

under 'statistics and classification' apply.

Statistics and Classification

Statistical applications have always been very popular at CAA conferences. Ranging from between 20% (1990) to almost 80% (1980) of the contributions have been on this subject. There has been some decline in popularity in recent years because statistical methods are less popular with 'real world' archaeologists than twenty years ago. Statistical approaches were very much part of 'new archaeology', now called processual archaeology, and post-processualists seem to feel less at ease with this subject. But there are signs that in the near future the pendulum will swing again in the other direction. The application of 'hard science' in archaeology is on its way back. The main reason for this is that much of the funding of scientific archaeological research is by way of 'hard science' projects linked to the environment. We are not sure whether statistical applications in archaeology are part of 'hard science' but they will certainly benefit from this development. In the present proceedings 33% of the articles are devoted to this subject, a fairly low percentage that continues the trend of the last five years. We should, however, expect an increase in future years.

Geographic Information Systems

After a hesitant start with one article in 1986, none in 1987, and two in 1988, GIS has become popular in the CAA proceedings. The proceedings of the conference in Aarhus in 1992 contained already 11 articles on the subject and today GIS is widely used among archaeologists. We suggest, however, that it should not be treated as a separate subject. It is a combination of a (spatial) database management system with a (most of the time rudimentary) statistical package and it creates, often beautiful, pictures. Most of the problems people have with using GIS in a useful manner, stem from the fact that they consider it as something completely new and different. It is not. An often used definition of GIS is that it is a computer assisted system for the capture, storage, retrieval, analysis and display of spatial data. We could do all these things before. All components, database management, graphic applications and statistical analysis were there. New is the integration and the pretty pictures. The picture is, however, not the answer but only the question. A computer can not (yet) replace human thought and analysis. To get at the right question requires study of the tool. In the present volume 23% of the articles are on GIS, the highest score so far!

Visualisation

The number of articles in the CAA proceedings on this theme has varied a lot over the last ten years, from about 5% in 1983 to almost 30% in 1993. In the 1995 proceedings it scores 13%. The main topics in this field are visualisation and the use of CAD, and multi-media seems to be the new buzz word here.

Education and Publication

This has always been a regular topic, usually scoring about 13%. Also in this volume the percentage is 13. Though often enlightning, we have noted that so far the subject of Education has not shown any article explaining why the education in statistical techniques creates so many problems for archaeologists. It does not seem to matter whether you use difficult or simple textbooks, most archaeology students and archaeologists have problems with statistics. Fletcher and Lock speak in this respect of an 'instant mental paralysis in many otherwise competent archaeologists'. We are looking forward to the day when Education in quantitative analysis will solve this problem.

So these proceedings do not really show many changes in the interest of 'computer' archaeologists, but follows the past trend. CAA times are not yet 'a-changin'.

Acknowledgments
The realisation of the conference was made possible by the hospitality and support of the University of Leiden and financial support from the Department of Education, Culture and Science, the Royal Netherlands Academy of Arts and Sciences, and the Leiden University Fund.

Computers for the demonstrations were generously made available by JCN Computer Systems BV and CRI Institute for telecommunication and computer services (University of Leiden), while apparatus for the ARCHIS demonstration was provided by SUN Microsystems Nederland BV.

The State Museum of Antiquities offered the use of the Taffeh hall for a reception on the first evening of the conference which was financially supported by the Committee for the celebration of the 420th anniversary of Leiden University and by Taylor & Francis of London.

We are greatly indebted to Roel Brandt, Monique van den Dries, Jenny Hes, Marianne Wanders, Philippine Waisvisz, Milco Wansleeben, Paul Zoetbrood and the many students who helped before and during the conference.

For the realisation of this book we would like to thank Prof. Dr L.P. Louwe Kooijmans and Prof. Dr C.C. Bakels for their invitation to publish these proceedings in the Analecta Praehistorica Leidensia series, Marianne Wanders for the text editing, Peter Heavens for the computer graphics, Henk de Lorm for the layout and cover design, and of course the reviewers Roel Brandt, Eelco Rensink, Iepie Roorda, Mark Spanjer, Pieter van de Velde, Philip Verhagen, Albertus Voorrips, Milco Wansleeben, Ronald Wiemer, and Paul Zoetbrood for their useful criticism and commentary. We are very grateful to the Foundation for Anthropology and Prehistory for their financial support in the publication costs of this volume.

Hans Kamermans
Kelly Fennema

February 1996

Faculty of Pre- and Protohistory
University of Leiden
P.O. Box 9515
2300 RA Leiden
The Netherlands
e-mail: H.Kamermans@rulpre.LeidenUniv.nl

Data Management

Jens Andresen
Torsten Madsen

IDEA – the Integrated Database for Excavation Analysis

1   Introduction

Archaeology has many diverse appearances. It can degrade to a mechanical manipulation of artefacts with seemingly no theoretical foundation, or it can escalate into wild theoretical digressions with virtually no reference to the archaeological record. One reason for this variability in archaeology is the almost paradoxical epistemological conditions of the discipline: on the one hand the subject matter of contemporary, physical objects, and on the other hand the aim to create a mental construction called the past (Madsen 1994: 31).

In the study of artefacts, during archaeological survey, and last but not least during archaeological excavation, the theories of the researcher are confronted with observations of the real world, and it is through this process that new knowledge is created. This is the reason why archaeological excavations *do not* constitute a mechanical unearthing and subsequent recording of objective facts, an opinion not uncommonly stated in archaeology.

Because of the destructive nature of archaeological excavations, attention is frequently focused on the recording of this activity. It has been customary in recent years to stress the subjective nature of excavation records, an attitude we fully share. However, in their eagerness to point out the biased nature of archaeological doings the critics tend to forget the status of excavation records in archaeology. Although coloured and filtered, these recordings are statements of observations of the real world: one may deliberately select and unwillingly overlook, but one cannot (by the code of the discipline) record something not seen. This is the reason why records from archaeological excavations are to be treated as historical documents and why it makes sense to establish a structured archive of recordings from archaeological excavations.

Still, a major problem in archaeology is to master the inherent complexity, diversity, and quantity of archaeological data. No wonder computer based recording systems for archaeological excavations have been and are continuously being created all over the world. Far the major part of these are either fairly simple flat file systems or hierarchically organised systems (Arroyo-Bishop/Zarzosa 1992; Rains 1995). Flat files and hierarchies, however, are too simple structures to provide a general basis for the description of archaeological reality in all its complexity. As a rule more or less well adjusted *ad hoc* solutions to particular situations become the result (Madsen 1993).

In the late eighties we began to discuss the potentials of relational data modelling applied to archaeological excavation recording, and at the CAA in Southampton in 1990 we presented a paper on the structure of information from archaeological excavations viewed in a relational framework. For various reasons the paper was only published two years later in another context (Andresen/ Madsen 1992). Initial attempts to acquire money for realising our IDEA were not successful either (Madsen 1994: 27), but in late 1993, we finally succeeded. A three year project funded by the Danish National Research Foundation for the Humanities was established (Madsen/ Andresen 1993).

The purpose of the project is to create a general system for recording, analysis and presentation of information from archaeological excavations. The system is intended to serve as an archive of recordings from all types of archaeological excavations, and it shall be able to automate the production of the archival report as a paper-copy. In a next phase of development, not covered by the current funding, the system should develop into an analytical tool for the processing of excavation information.

The core of the system is implemented in a Relational Data Base Management System (RDBMS), naturally. We have chosen Microsoft Access for this purpose because it combines sophistication as a RDBMS with a low cost availability within today's standard PC environment. The advantages are amongst others: low learning curves for the users, high potential for integration with other application software, and upgrading security. Furthermore, the National Museum of Denmark has also chosen Microsoft Access as their development tool for their interface to the Danish central SMR. Using identical development tools should help us to overcome some of the technical obstacles in attempts to integrate data from the excavation archive with SMR-recordings — at least on a national scale.

2   The conceptual model

The basic conceptual model for the system has already been presented and discussed in some detail (Andresen/Madsen 1992, 1994). We will not repeat the discussion here, but only summarise the structure and basic entities of the model.

Fundamental to our model is the acknowledgement of three universal entities into which we can categorize all excavation information. These entities we termed Layers, Objects and Constructs (fig. 1).

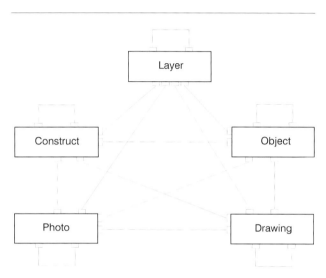

Figure 1. The core of IDEA: five basic entities – Layer, Object, Construct, Drawing and Photo – linked with many-to-many relationships between entities as well as internally between records of the same entity.

A Layer is an entity of deposition separated from its surroundings by its physical and chemical properties. In this sense a layer can be seen as a geological entity, even if often it owns its existence to human activities. Other names for a layer often seen are fill or context (Carver 1985).

Essentially an Object is a subpart of a layer, segregated from this by the actions of the archaeologist. Any part of a layer that an archaeologist sticks a label on, bags, and brings home from the excavation automatically becomes an object, or perhaps as it should be named more correctly, a find or component (Carver 1985).

The Construct is a slightly more controversial entity. In our definition it is any interpretation category that an archaeologist may impose on Layers or Objects, alone or in any combination.[1] In its simplest form an instance of the Construct entity could be something like 'pit', 'post-hole', etc. At the more complex level it could be 'activity area', 'village', 'chronological phase' etc. Traditionally this is what would be classified as cuts, features, structures and beyond (Carver 1985).

In addition to these three universal entities we also defined two documentary entities — Drawings and Photos. These two auxiliary entities are fully interlinked with the archaeological entities. One may question, if it is possible to draw or indeed take photographs of interpretations/Constructs. On the other hand it is customary in archaeological recording systems to refer to interpretation units in the documentary sources, so we have chosen to endorse this practice and allow links between Constructs on the one hand and Drawings and Photos on the other.

This conceptual model may at first glance seem fairly simple, but due to the many-to-many relationships between all five entities and internally within each entity, it is a fairly complex model to implement. Further, there are a number of additional concepts and features that modifies and qualifies the model, adding further complications to the implementation.

One such moderator is the concept of project. In order to be able to handle more than one excavation in the same database, and indeed to be able to handle excavations differently with respect to structure of recordings and classifications of content, we have defined the project as the primary separator of information. Everything within a project is by definition fully comparable. Information from different projects is only compatible and comparable to the extent that the projects share equivalent definitions and classifications of structure and content.

An important, but also a potentially very difficult qualifier to handle is the concept of event. On a fairly simple level it is the ability to record the who and when of a drawing being created by a number of draughtsmen over a period of time at a number of different 'drawing events', or the ability to record information according to a number of different excavation campaigns. On a much more complex level it could be the possibility of recording 'the history' of interpretations of a site. That is, instead of overwriting an interpretative Construct, a substitution takes place with the former Construct being kept as a historical, currently obsolete, piece of information concerning the interpretation. Historical information like this should be hidden, but not forgotten. That is, it should be possible to recall former interpretations on demand.

A full handling of events is truly complicated, and we have decided to take up only the simplest part of the problem relating to different recording events during excavations. Thus, at the moment we are not going to try to solve the problem of event recording in connection with the interpretation of an excavation.

Another very important qualification to the system is the possibility for users to customise the structure of recordings as well as differentiate classifications of their content. In a system where all entities are interlinked, the number of

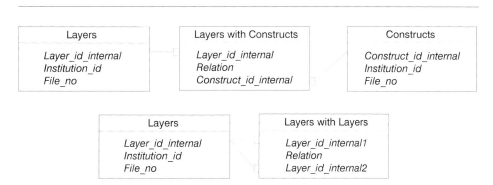

Figure 2. Implementation of many-to-many relationships using link tables. The upper part shows linking between entities, and the lower part linking within entities.

ways to structure the information (by choosing different channels through the web) is high. What particular structure should be used in relation to an excavation is not a programmer's decision. It must be a user decision. The same applies to the classification of items of information, for instance the artefacts. A Stone Age and an Iron Age excavation certainly cannot use the same classification and description system for artefacts. It is the user who should decide the classification system to be used, and the user must be able to tailor the system to fit his or her needs.

3   Implementation of the model

Even though each instance of the database is able to hold data from several excavations — and thus might be maintained by a central authority — the decentralised structure of Danish archaeology (and archaeology in most other countries) demands a decentralised solution. This is one of the reasons why our system is organised into two separate parts: the core data structure in one module and the user-interface in another. This division has several advantages during the phase of software-development. For the end user, one advantage is that by telecommunication channels it will be possible to interface different geographically dispersed data sets. At the same time new versions of the user-interface can be implemented without any side effects on the data part. Indeed, there is the possibility to create multiple user-interfaces to the same set of data, should this be needed.

Another consequence of this architecture is the possibility to separate archaeological from administrative information on the project level. Administrative information dependent on country and institution can be included as tables in the user-interface part. They cannot be separated from their entry forms anyway. Likewise, the structure and layout of reports are also country and institution dependent and thus should be kept entirely in the user-interface module as well.

A disadvantage of this two-level architecture is that uploading of data from one instance of the database to another has to be monitored by a module of specially written code. This we foresee will cause some head-scratching to write. The technical problem is that each entity instance in each instance of the database is given a unique sequential number (key) by the RDMBS. Thus entity instances are very likely to share the same identifiers throughout the various instances of the database. Because these numbers are used as pointers (foreign keys) in the link tables, it is obvious that uploading has to occur as a sequence of multiple, nested transactions in order to maintain integrity of the uploaded database.

The backbone of the implementation consists of five tables corresponding to the five basic entities of our conceptual model. Each of these contain basic information, which subsequently can be tied together using link tables. The link tables are of two kinds (fig. 2). One type consists of link tables interconnecting the five entity tables. There are ten of these, each having the primary keys of each of the two tables they connect as foreign keys, and in addition a field called 'Relation' to hold the type of relation between the two basic tables. Together the three fields of the link table constitute its primary key, and hence a unique entry. The other type of link table is that which connects an entity table to itself. Logically there are five of these, although we have not implemented Photos linked with Photos as we cannot imagine who would use it. This kind of link table is constructed like the former except that both foreign keys refer back to the same primary key in one single table.[2]

The field 'Relation' in link tables between entities is customarily filled in with a 'is linked to' string, but it is currently not used for any purpose, as we have seen no way in which we could make use of different types of relations. Should the need arise, however, the system is prepared for multiple relation types.

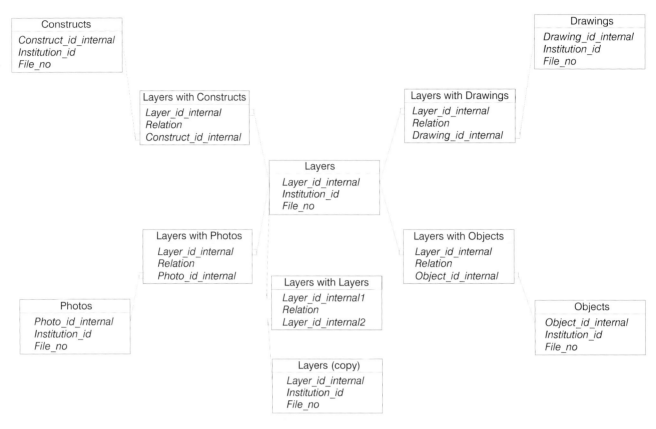

Figure 3. The core of IDEA as seen from one entity (Layers). No other entity is more than one link table away.

In link tables connecting entity tables internally, however, the field holding the relation type in the link table is very useful. Thus in the example shown in figure 2, where Layers are linked to Layers, the field can hold various types of stratigraphic relationships. Had the example been Objects linked with Objects, the relations could have been various types of information on refitting the objects in question.

The implementation of the conceptual model (fig. 1) leads to what looks like a spaghetti junction construction. However, when viewed from any particular entity the structure appears fairly simple. Any entity table is only one link table away, and we have what may be described as a five armed octopus (if that is not too much of a contra-diction) (fig. 3). Four of the arms lead through link tables to the four other entities, while the fifth arm leads through a link table to the entity itself.

In figure 3 we view the structure of the system as seen from the Layers table, but a view from any of the other entity tables would look exactly the same. Any of our five basic entities is thus linked directly to the others as well as to itself. It is our claim that in using this structure we can map most if not all data models for archaeological excavations.

One pre-condition in our implementation of the conceptual model, is that any instance of an analytical or documentary entity has to be uniquely identified. Thus if we want to store information about a specific sherd from a bag find, then this sherd has to be identified separately. Because the user-supplied identification does not enter a key-field in the underlying table, the sherd identified need not be renumbered, that is double-numbering of user-supplied identification is allowed! The key-field for any record in the tables is assigned by the RDBMS automatically as a positive long integer unknown and hidden to the user.

In cases of double numbering the problem for the user of course remains as ever: the difficulty to separate instances with identical identification. The obvious solution is, as it has always been, to number every instance uniquely.

Provided that information has been loaded into the basic entity tables, setting links between the entries in these tables is a fairly simple matter. We have chosen to implement the linking through a form where we can pick any number of items available from the entity you wish to link to, and connect them to the current record of the current entity table. Linking thus always takes its starting point from a specific entity instance, say a layer in the Layer entry form. If we wish to link objects to this layer we call up the linking form by pressing a button at the base of the Layers entry form. This provides us with a form containing two list boxes (fig. 4). The one on the right contains all those finds, if any, already linked to the layer, while the other box contains all recorded finds not linked to the layer. Setting links, or removing already established links is simply a matter of using the arrows between the two list boxes, or by just double clicking the item we want to move.

Figure 4 shows the form used to set links between entries in different entities. As mentioned we do not need to work with different relation types in this case, but if we move to the internal relations (say Layers with Layers) we need to be able to set the type of relation as well. This we do in a form much resembling the one in figure 4, but with the addition of a combo box, where we can choose the type of relation we wish to view and set.

The implementation of the 'project' concept is rather simple. We have created two tables, *Institution* and *File*. An institution may be an archaeological unit, a university, a museum etc. Each institution may house many excavation-projects, each uniquely numbered in the *File*-table. The key-fields of the two tables are included in the five primary tables of the core database and in some auxiliary tables which hold other relevant information.

Further subdivisions within a project may be implemented utilising numbering conventions in the user-supplied identifiers. I.e. area codes and calendar year could be used as suffixes to the identifier of the entity instances. Therefore we can foresee a future demand for a customisation module to take care of project subdivisions and numbering conventions.

4   Customising the system

4.1   IMPLEMENTING A DATAMODEL

At the bottom of each of the entity entry forms (fig. 5) a number of buttons with arrows across opens up link forms to other entities of the type shown in figure 4. However, if we allow users to link as they please we seriously risk that the entries entered will cause inconsistency in the database. Very different structuring of the information can result from unconstrained linking of entity instances.

One way of controlling input is to disallow users to input data to a particular entity, say Objects, unless it is controlled by another entity, say Layer. That is, the only way you will be able to enter Object data is through an input form activated by the Objects button on the Layer entry form. In this case you will not get a link form in response to a press of the button, but an input form setting a pre-defined link as part of the data entry process. At the

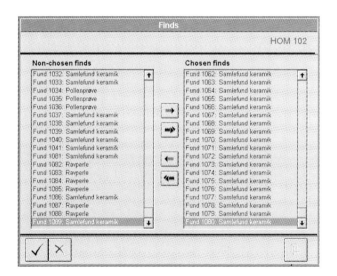

Figure 4. The form used to set relationships between the current record (could in this case be a construct, layer, drawing or photo) and any number of available objects. The list box marked Chosen finds contains those finds already linked to the current record, while those listed in the Non-chosen list box are those finds still available for linking.

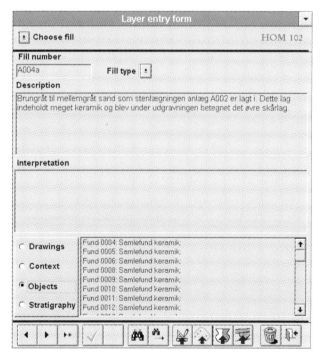

Figure 5. A standard entry form for a basic entity in IDEA (here the entity Layer). Buttons with arrows across call up either link forms of the type shown in figure 4, or other data entry forms with a forced link to the current record.

same time all other buttons leading to a linking of Object information can be disabled, making linking of Objects to Layers the only option available.

Thus by controlling what buttons are available, where and when, and what they will call up, structure can be provided to the recording of excavation information. Different views on the structure of excavation information — that is different data models — can be mapped onto the system by varying the availability of input forms, and not least through the sequence in which these must occur, as well as what possibilities of linking to other entities are available.

Figures 6 and 7 show two examples of data models for excavations. In figure 6 a three-level model is shown. The Construct is seen as the basic entity categorising all observations at the excavation level. That is the excavator has to interpret his observations in the field in terms of structures and features as he proceeds. The Constructs which may well be nested in internal hierarchies are characterised by containing one or more layers or fills, and each layer may contain one or more objects. The principal constraint of this model is that an Object has to be a part of a Layer, which has to be a part of a Construct. Photos and Drawings are seen as independent documentation evidence that may be freely linked to any of the three main entities.

Figure 7 shows a two-level model based on Layers and Objects. A model of this nature, where the Construct entity has been excluded, is widely used in excavations from the old Stone Age, where a geological frame of reference rather than one of man-made structures is prevalent. However, even here the Construct entity is needed. As stated in the paragraph on the conceptual model the Construct covers more than we immediately observe during the excavation. During the post excavation phase or even during the excavation itself we may add interpretations in terms of categorisation of information that goes beyond 'evident structures'. Potentially at any point we can record what has been termed 'latent structures'. Thus in old Stone Age excavations analytical entities like 'living floors' or 'activity areas' are frequently isolated as if they were observable. As a consequence we have to supply forms that allow the entering into the Construct table of latent or inferred structures and the free linking of these regardless of how the model is otherwise structured.

A specific data model should be applied to any excavation to avoid ambiguity in recordings. However, there are reasons why it should be possible to bypass the data model and let experienced operators go into a mode of unconstrained data entry. First of all, if data entry is to occur in a post excavation situation from written lists, it provides far the fastest way of data entry. Secondly, if mistakes occur for one or other reason, it may provide the

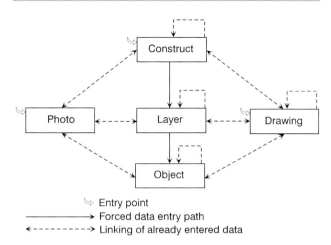

Figure 6. A three-level model for the recording of an excavation with constraints demanding that any object must be part of a layer, which must be part of a construct. 'Entry point' indicates where data input can be initiated.

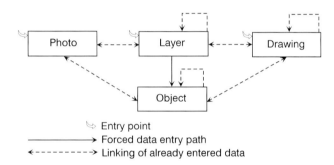

Figure 7. A two-level model, where the Construct entity has been excluded, and where any object must be part of a layer. "Entry point" indicates where data input can be initiated.

fastest way to clear things up. In unconstrained data entry mode the operator has to be very much aware of the model (s)he is dealing with, and use those links only that will give the intended structure.

As demonstrated, it is fully possible to map different data models onto the underlying table structure. However, it is not sufficient for us to have a system where we as programmers can set up different views of the database. It is important that it is the user who can customise the system dynamically.

To make user customisation possible we have created a data model definition module, where it is possible to define how the connections between tables should be presented in terms of optional linking or forced data entry flows. Basically, the customisation is implemented through a full square matrix, where the five basic tables are cross related with each other (fig. 8). A number of possible values for each cell is defined by us, and can be selected by the user in drop down boxes for each cell. A data model may then be defined by setting a combination of the values in the matrix. The choices in each cell include link, no link and (forced) path in the off-diagonal cells and a combination of entry/no entry and link/no link values on the diagonal.

The user can define and select a model. However, we cannot allow this to happen at any time. It is important that there is consistency in recordings throughout any particular excavation. Thus, when initially a project is defined, the user must select the model to be used, and from that moment it is a binding choice for that particular project, not to be changed. Anything else would be an invitation to chaos.

4.2   DEFINITION OF INTERNAL RELATIONS OF ENTITIES

The capability to handle relationships internally between instances of entities makes the system extremely powerful and versatile. It enables users to build up data structures dynamically, and thus removes one of the major weaknesses of most digital excavation recording systems sofar — the predetermined data structures hard coded into the system by the programmer. Thus for the Constructs entity it would in most traditional systems be necessary to operate with a pre-defined hierarchy of features, structures, groups etc. and to stick with these. In our system, however, it is possible to assemble data structures of Constructs dynamically into higher levels of interpretation units to any level and any complexity.

In order to make the use of the internal relations as flexible as possible the users can define the relations they need (fig. 9). Four types of information have to be supplied in the definition form. The domain (i.e. whether the relation is valid for Objects, Layers, Constructs or Drawings), what the relation should be named, the name of the inverse relation, and what abstract data type the specific relation is an instance of. If the relation is symmetric, (i.e. 'same as') one enters the relation name in the inverse relation field as well. In figure 9 an example of defining a parts breakdown is shown: the domain is Constructs, the relation is 'is part of', the inverse is 'contain', and the type of structure is 'hierarchy'.

Following the definition of the relationship the user may use it to relate an instance of a Construct to another instance of a Construct. Thus a specific 'post-hole' may be assigned to a specific 'house' as being 'is part of' that house. Seen from the viewpoint of the house, a 'contain' link to the post-hole will automatically be entered by the system in the same transaction.

The type of structure is selected from a number of types we have defined. Currently we have isolated a set of six

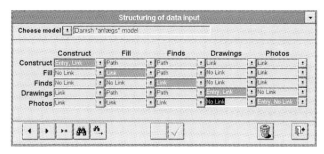

Figure 8. Form used to define a data model. Each cell has a drop down box providing a number of pre-set alternatives.

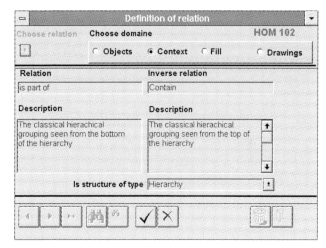

Figure 9. Form used to define internal relationships in entities.

types: Set, Series, Hierarchy, Web, Directed web without loops, and Directed web with loops.

A 'Set' represents an unordered collection of items. The relationship 'same as' is a typical representative of this type. A 'Web' is an unordered collection of items, too. But in contrast to the 'Set', the edges between the items are significant. The relationship 'fits together with' (i.e. used for refitting of sherds) is a typical representative of the 'Web' type. The type 'Directed web with loops' is used if a relationship has an inverse, and if it is possible to return to a specific element when a path through the structure is followed. Currently, we have not come across representatives of this type but we will not exclude their existence, i.e. in complex webs of interpretation.

A 'Series' is an ordered collection of items. The relationship 'is younger than' is a typical representative of this type. A more complex structure is the 'Hierarchy' mentioned above. It is a recursive structure with only one top-node and only one edge pointing to any other node. One may distinguish several variations of 'Hierarchies', but we have found no reason to do so at the moment. A more general structure is the 'Directed web without loops' used, for instance, in stratigraphical relationships. In this structure a node may be pointed at by one or more edges.

Each type represents a characteristic organisation of data (fig. 10), which can be used in the system in different ways. Thus knowing that the structure being defined in figure 9 is of the type 'Hierarchy' we can set up a checking mechanism on data input which prohibit logic failures. I.e. if 'post-hole A' is part of 'house B' then an attempt to record 'post-hole A' as being a part of 'house C' would result in an error, because the entry would violate the constraints of the structure defined.

Another area where the type information can be used is in connection with the presentation of data to the user. As can be seen from figure 10 each type has inherent graphical characteristics that may be utilised in presentation screens (Ryan 1995). Thus we do not need to know the actual content of the recordings, only their type in order to do a proper presentation. Another perspective is that we will be able to combine and display several relationships, as for instance when combining 'same as' and 'lies above'/'lies below' relationships for stratigraphy.

4.3 SETTING UP CLASSIFICATION AND DESCRIPTION SYSTEMS FOR ENTITIES

A further and very important point of user customisation is the possibility to classify and describe the content of the individual records of the entities Constructs, Layers and Objects.

It is of course easy enough to implement a user defined classification, unique within each individual project. However, the critical issue is the varying number of variables relating to each class defined, and their values. We are not yet through with the implementation of this, but we have made some successful proto-typing exercises. The first step is to set up a structure to hold the user defined classification and description system. As shown in figure 11 this can be done in three tables, Object Type, Description Variables and Values of Description Variables linked in that order to each other with one-to-many relationships. This will allow any type to have an unspecified number of variables and any variable to have an unspecified number of potential values.

To use this system in our database we will need at least two tables. The Object table is identical to the one already existing in the database, including a field for the basic classification of the Objects. The other table, linked to the Objects table in a one-to-many relationship, holds the description of the object in terms of the particular variables relevant to the type of the object and the values they exhibit.[3] The two table solution may not, however, be flexible enough. If an object has to be classified as type x

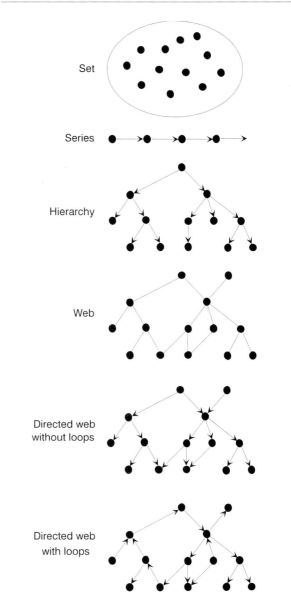

Figure 10. A graphical presentation of the characteristics of six data structures recognised in IDEA.

as well as type y, we need to add an extra table holding the classification exclusively. That is, we will need a table holding the artefact as an object (the one we already have), a table holding one or more classifications of the artefact, and a table holding the descriptions. These three tables are linked of course in one-to-many relationships in the order mentioned.

A possible way to implement the variable description in relation to a classified object is through a pop-up form

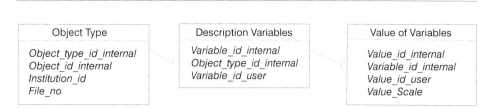

Figure 11. A table configuration for a general object classification system.

(fig. 12). The form works in tight correspondence with the classification tables. The choice of a type for an object, decides which variables will be available in the drop down list of the pop-up form for the variable field, and subsequently the choice of a variable will decide what values are available in the drop down list of the value field. Pressing the buttons of the drop down fields in the wrong order will merely result in a lack of available choices.

4.4   SETTING THE LANGUAGE

An obvious area of customisation is the language presented to the user on the screen. Whereas our documentation of the system is held in a language akin to English (Danelish), the user interface has to be native to the area where it is presented. We have solved this problem by storing all labels, messages, etc. in a special language table, where each language has its own column, and each string to be presented to the user has its own row. Initially we enter all

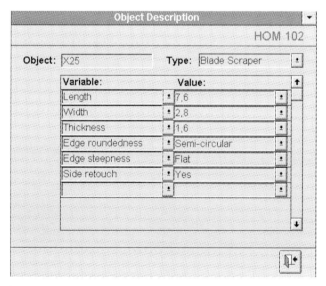

Figure 12. A form for entering a classification and a formal description of an object. Variables available in the drop down boxes will vary according to type chosen, and values will vary according to variables chosen (at the time of writing the classification system has not yet been implemented in IDEA).

strings in this table in Danish and English, the two languages currently supported. Adding a new language is simply a matter of translating the strings in the table and writing the translation in a new column. Selecting a language is a simple choice among the currently available languages in a combo box in the customisation form. The language will change instantly. The currently selected language will be saved to an ini-file, and thus be remembered from session to session until a new language is selected.

5   Programming with a minimum of code

Since the beginning of the project we have placed a lot of effort in making the system as easy and cheap to maintain as possible. We have tried to keep the amount of written code to an absolute minimum, as software development projects producing thousands and thousands of lines of code tend to drown in their own complexity. The result is all too often progressively rising costs in maintenance at best and total failure at worst.

5.1   EVENT PROGRAMMING OF FORMS

The answer of the software industry to the code boom problem, is Object-Oriented Programming (OOP) (Booch 1991). One of the key features of OOP is that objects are self-contained modules, which respond to events. In the case of Microsoft Access, the various objects of the form (i.e. the controls or the form itself) offer the programmer the possibility to write code defining the functionality of an object responding to a particular event. The code itself is not written in an object-oriented language but instead in a Basic dialect. This Basic dialect is able to interact with the so-called DataAccessObjects library.

Using this functionality, the five basic entry forms include only approx. 250 lines of code each, including error-messages. Most of the buttons at the bottom of the forms are enabled and disabled by one global module which contains approx. 150 lines of code. The two forms for setting the internal and external relationships contain approx. 300 lines of code each. Altogether the amount of code is negligible.

5.2   CREATING COMPLEX REPORTS WITH NO CODE AT ALL

One of the areas, where Access really proves its 'fourth generation status' is through its report generator. At first it does not look much. At a second glance you realise that it is very much akin to the forms generator, and indeed has inherited most of its properties from this (Access is indeed object oriented behind the curtains). Finally you realise that a number of features has been added, compared to the forms definitions, making the report generator a truly flexible tool by itself.

One of its stronger features is that reports can be embedded and fully synchronised within reports three levels deep (the same applies to forms). The result is that you can set up a highly complex hierarchical structure involving a number of entities without writing as much as one line of code. In fact for all practical purposes we can handle our rather complex data structure in one code-less construction. Thus without a line of code we can build a list of features from the construct table, where for each feature the layers are listed, and for each layer of the feature, the objects with their descriptions are listed.

In Denmark there is an authorised format for so-called Level II data for the archives (see Carver 1985, fig. 4 for this concept — with reference to the Frere report). This format involves a fair amount of hierarchically organised lists, where especially the lower levels of the hierarchy are cross-referenced to other lists. We have succeeded in implementing this format in the system, and it only takes a press of a button to write out the complete report. Codes are used in two areas only. One is for the creation of an index to the report. The other is to tie parallel parts of the report together in a sequence (in fact we could have avoided this had a fourth level of embedding been available).

6   Future development of the IDEA

What we have achieved sofar is a flexible system for recording traditional textual information from excavations. This is the result of the first year of the project. There is, however, a very long way to go before the IDEA becomes reality.

Next, we have to add full support for the recording of three-dimensional data, not just in terms of a point in space for an Object, a Layer or a Construct, but also in terms of two-dimensional polygons positioned in a three-dimensional space. We have no ambition of achieving a full three-dimensional presentation, since the archaeological recordings in the field in plan and section are — and will always be — ambiguous with respect to a full 3-D representation.

We have characterised the system as an integrated database for excavation analysis, and for very good reasons.

Our primary objective is to create a system which is analytical in its approach to excavation recordings rather than just descriptive. In order to obtain this we will implement analytical methods into the system. These are planned to be of two kinds. One set will be implemented around a GIS-type of interface. Another set will be based on a graph browser type of representation of data. The idea is that we will allow for different types of views on the same set of data, and that any interrogation in one representation is reflected dynamically in others (Ryan 1995).

Providing a system with the ability to handle spatial data, requirements for constraints in the spatial location of entity instances will be created. If for instance a find is assigned to a layer, it is natural that the system should check for consistency in their spatial relationships, that is whether the find location is within the boundaries of the layer. Furthermore it will become necessary to include a quantifier in the various link tables to store information like 'post-hole A' 'is x meters from' 'post-hole B'. The analytical perspective is that the quantifier may serve as a distance operator in descriptions of complex and heterogeneous archaeological objects (Dallas 1992; Dickens 1977).

One set of problems we probably cannot solve within the three year limit of the current project, is the question of user-defined queries and reports. One may foresee the demand for a 'Wizard' (essentially another specialised database) which sets up screen presentations and reports according to the defined model for the project. Furthermore one can foresee a demand for facilities to query multiple projects with different data models, classifications and relationships.

7   Conclusion

In our opening form we have used the Globe as a symbol. By conviction we seek global rather than narrow *ad hoc* solutions to problems. We believe quite simply that by addressing problems in their total complexity we will come up with solutions which in the long run are worth far more than the quick *ad hoc* solutions.

Our project is to run another two years (at the date of CAA95), and we have no guarantee that we will be given money to continue thereafter. It is not however to be an academic project, where the results disappear with the money. We are determined that the destiny of the system is to be used and to be further developed. To ensure this we are very open to cooperation with anybody who can *seriously* contribute to the development of the system. We have already initiated co-operation with different people on various aspects of the system, and it is indeed our hope to be able to widen this co-operation.

notes

1 We coined the word construct because it sounded as a good and meaningful term for the concept. At that time we did not know (shame on us) that Gardin (1980) had used the same word with a very similar meaning.

2 This solution is due to Paul Zoetbrood, generously offered during a very memorable evening at the CAA88 in Birmingham.

3 The idea for this implementation was abducted from a set of tables presented by Lene Rold (1990: 14)

references

Andresen, J.
  T. Madsen
1992 Data Structures for Excavation Recording. A Case of complex Information Management. In: C.U. Larsen (ed.), *Sites & Monuments. National Archaeological Records*, 49-67, Copenhagen: The National Museum of Denmark.

1994 Strukturen af data fra udgravninger, *KARK Nyhedsbrev 1994* 1, 4-27.

Arroyo-Bishop, D.
  M.T. Lantada Zarzosa
1992 The ArchéoDATA System: A Method for Structuring an European Archaeological Information System (AIS). In: C.U. Larsen (ed.), *Sites & Monuments. National Archaeological Records*, 133-154, Copenhagen: The National Museum of Denmark.

Booch, G.
1991 *Object oriented design with applications*. Redwood City, Ca.: The Benjamin/Cummings Publishing Company Inc.

Carver, M.
1985 The friendly user. In: M.A. Cooper/J.D. Richards (eds), *Current Issues in Archaeological Computing*, 47-61, BAR International Series 271, Oxford: British Archaeological Reports.

Dallas, C.
1992 Relational description, similarity and classification of complex archaeological entities. In: G. Lock/J. Moffet (eds) *Computer Applications and Quantitative Methods in Archaeology*, 167-178, BAR International Series 577, Oxford: Tempus Reparatum.

Dickens, P.
1977 An Analysis of Historical House-plans: A study at the Structural Level (Micro). In: D.L. Clarke (ed.), *Spatial Archaeology*, 33-45, London: Academic Press.

Gardin, J.C.
1980 *Archaeological constructs. An aspect of theoretical archaeology*. Cambridge: Cambridge University Press.

Madsen, T.
1993 Archaeology, data structures and computer science. In: J. Pavúk (ed.), *Actes du XIIᵉ Congrès International des Sciences Préhistoriques et Protohistoriques Bratislava, 1-7 septembre 1991*, 269-273, Bratislava: Institut archéologique de l'Académie Slovaque des Sciences à Nitra.

1994 Integrating methods and data: reflections on archaeological research in an IT environment. In: I. Johnson (ed.), *Methods in the Mountains. Proceedings of UISPP Commission IV Meeting, Mount Victoria, Australia 9th - 13th August 1993*, 27-34, Sydney: Sydney University Archaeological Methods Series #2.

Madsen, T.
  J. Andresen
1993 'Den elektroniske gravebog': En informationsteknologisk løsning på udgravnings-registrering og -bearbejdning, *KARK Nyhedsbrev 1993* 3, 7-14.

Rains, M.J.   1995   Towards a computerised desktop: the Integrated Archaeological Database System.
                                In: J. Huggett/N. Ryan (eds), *Computer Applications and Quantitative Methods in
                                Archaeology 1994*, 207-210, BAR International Series 600, Oxford: Tempus Reparatum.

Rold, L.   1990   Databaseteknologi, teori og design. In: C.U. Larsen (ed.), *Arkæologi, statistik og EDB*,
                                København: Københavns Universitet.

Ryan, N.   1995   The excavation archive as hyperdocument? In: J. Huggett/N. Ryan (eds), *Computer
                                Applications and Quantitative Methods in Archaeology 1994*, 211-220, BAR International
                                Series 600, Oxford: Tempus Reparatum.

Jens Andresen and Torsten Madsen
Institute of Anthropology and Archaeology
University of Aarhus
Moesgård
8270 Højbjerg
Denmark
e-mail: farkja@moes.hum.aau.dk
         farktm@moes.hum.aau.dk

Peter Hinge

The Other Computer Interface

1   Introduction

This paper discusses some of the conceptual problems that arise during the implementation of a Relational DataBase Management System (RDBMS). Specifically it focuses on the problems encountered during the implementation and use of the ORACLE RDBMS in a commercial archaeological unit; the Museum of London Archaeological Service (MoLAS) during a one year inter-specialist research project into the Roman London's Eastern Cemeteries (RLEC). The project involved 10 team members with various specialisms, and resulted in the creation of 67 tables, and 17 validation forms. On completion, some 40,000 rows of data have been recorded.

Yet it is not the structure of the RLEC database, the means by which it was interrogated, nor the various techniques developed to help elucidate patterns within the cemetery data sets that is of interest here. Rather it is the interface between the user and the *concept* of relational storage and manipulation that is considered, and how problems in that conception manifest themselves in poorly structured requests, that do not exploit the functionality of the RDBMS. More importantly, such conceptual problems can lead to disillusionment, as the advantage of the new system remains un-apparent, and old conceptual battle-lines between specialist data sets are simply re-drawn in the syntax of a newer technology.

2   Justification

The paper is then about problems, worse still it is about problems with an apparently mundane computing application. The benefits of RDBMSs, seem to be implicitly understood by a CAA audience, as indicated by its casual reference in the manner of a detail within the proceedings; i.e. 'attribute information is stored in an RDBMS while the graphical data is ....' Indeed, this paper also assumes some of that awareness, by not providing an introductory description of RDBMS architecture and mathematical set theory, or data modelling and normalisation.

However, this familiarity is both a bonus and a burden, with the latter becoming apparent during the implementation process when one is both engineer and evangelist. While bringing the good news of dynamic systems to a user

group largely disenfranchised in the rounded interdisciplinary business of archaeological interpretation by inadequate IT, it is easy to forget how ignorant one was before one's own conversion. Users, who for years have dealt with cumbersome data systems offering rudimentary relational capabilities via cryptic procedural syntax, (e.g. most archaeologists at MoLAS) have a theory laden perception of data management which can remain unaffected by the word of Codd (Codd 1970) and the promises of their own computing section. The confounding effect of that perception must not be under-estimated, and is best addressed in an educative dialogue between designer and user. The broad promises of evangelists, must be demonstrated by practical little miracles among the familiar objects of archaeologist's lives.

3   Old Systems And Resident Experts

The conceptual legacies of previous systems, need to be understood and addressed. User-groups who have experienced a gradual implementation of data systems, carried out by various 'resident experts', at various points in time often enjoy an especially rich inheritance of this type. Within archaeology such patterns of implementation are perhaps more common than we would like to admit. The typically idiosyncratic style of systems devised in this manner is understandable, given that the resident expert is generally motivated to design systems to ease her work in her field. Equally the brief of such individuals, if there were one, is unlikely to have been to design for inter-specialist data compatibility, and all that that entails; *i.e.* agreeing referential standards, unique numbering schemes, accepted key-word lists etc. Less excusable, is for such individuals to remain the resident expert, and for the solution they devised not to be shared. The *resident-expert-and-the-bus* problem, (i.e. what would we do if X got ran over by one tomorrow?) is well known, but more subtle, is the question of levels of education and the existence of strategic motivation.

The 'expert' on his or her initiative has provided a solution for an archaeological need that has been inadequately defined. The brief is not for instance, to simply design a system that can record details of animal bones recovered from an excavation and a set of reports that will enable non-(Computing) specialists to print this data out. Rather it is to do these things, and to enhance further analysis through the use of the system, by *explaining* some of its functionality, and the potential it offers. This is not an argument to train further resident experts, for it is unnecessary for users to be able to design relational databases, it is simply to open their eyes and minds to the possibilities. To paraphrase the words of an anonymous sage, the biggest single need for a successful relational database implementation is not for improved recall speed, more rigorous input forms, congenial interfaces or prolonged memory, but for better questions and better use of answers.

The strategic question, is simply that a strategy must be made. A unit must have a policy regarding the utilisation of appropriate IT in general, and the adoption of rationalised systems to store and manipulate the data recovered from an excavation in particular. For archaeological units this is neither as obvious nor as glib a point as it may seem. In such situations the possibility to implement new systems in the manner of the standard System Development Life Cycle (SDLC) with all the steps that process implies (Hussain/Hussain 1991: 215) does not exist. The required time, staff and resources are often unavailable, to allow the necessarily exhaustive process of organising wide blanket development and education to take place. Rather, systems are developed in the manner of prototypes.

'A prototype is a tentative system, a model based on the interaction between analysts and users,.. *(it)* works best for systems that are highly interactive, (have significant human-machine dialogue), and is particularly useful when end users have difficulty specifying their information needs. Typical ad hoc decision support systems meets these requirements. Prototyping is also useful when problems to be solved are unstructured.' (My italics)
                                    Hussain/Hussain 1991: 222.

A prototype system has the advantages of speed of development, and thus cost, it enhances end-user participation in systems development, practically acts as a conversation piece, and often generates a more accurate determination of user requirements. The fact that in archaeological units such prototypes often evolve into the information systems themselves, and therefore that the strict developmental process defined as 'protoyping' is a misnomer, is not a problem in itself. Rather it simply continues the eclectic tradition by which archaeological theory and method has often developed. Yet such gradual modular development can easily mutate to resemble the idiosyncratic efforts of the past resident-expert-specialist, as each user group is focused on in turn. For small

archaeological units, the need for firm strategies to be drawn up and monitored is of the utmost importance, for the very reason that the realisation of those strategies will be a modular, incremental and probably project based process, and one unsuitable to the more rigorous developmental checks that a properly resourced SDLC approach would allow. Organisational as well as interpretative problems will arise if such protoyping is conducted outside a firm policy of implementation, sanctioned by management with the aim of providing a single integrated and rationalised relational system that delivers a communal benefit.

'... the general lesson to be drawn from the relevant management literature is that technological change is likely to influence archaeological organisations and their structures, and the roles of archaeological professionals, very widely.'
                                    Cooper/Dinn 1995: 89.

4   Identifying Changing Needs

Properly implemented and supported, the RDBMS is then an agent of profound change in the conduct of single or multi-site/thematic archaeological enquiries carried out in commercial units for whom such technology is now truly accessible. Misjudging just how profound that change is, will at the very least render the technology impotent in the minds of many.

4.1   SHIFTING TASKS

An appreciation of the degree of this change, is not aided by the classical route of systems analysis, and the stages it involves. Identifying users tasks for instance, allows the designer to characterise the overall purpose of an organisation by considering the components of which it is made. Fundamental questioning of the type What is the task, why is it necessary, what data is required for it, is the task duplicated elsewhere and so forth brings to light poor reasoning of the type *'because we've always done it'*, *'because I was told to'* or the infamous; *'I don't really know.'* The designer understands the individual's role as a component of a larger structure and builds systems to support and ease the data-based tasks those individuals perform. An architectural response is provided for understood business needs, yet how does such an approach fare when the architecture itself is changing the nature, purpose or value of the tasks it is attempting to classify?

For example a finds researcher will identify the pottery from a context, compile lists of the types present and assign a *terminus post-quem* to the assemblage. This list will be passed to the site supervisor who will use it to phase the relative sequence of site development that has been deduced on the basis of structural data. With relationally disciplined tables of find and site data, the task of that finds researcher can and should change. Functionally, the structure makes the conventional 'passing' of data between finds researcher and site supervisor as a single act obsolete. Rather, this occurs at the point and in the manner of the user's choosing, The nature of the intercourse between the two groups also changes as *any* data set they produce is able to use the relational structure in which they exist. For example with access to stratigraphic information, the finds researcher is able to identify residual or intrusive assemblages augmenting their list of tasks and adding value to their role in the whole interpretative process.

The design of systems to support decision making, must begin by understanding the current state of information processing, to identify its weaknesses and strengths. Knowledge of these past modes of organisation however, must not be allowed to inhibit the generation of fresh and innovative solutions and aids to that decision making process. This argument is enforced in the context of archaeological decision making for here necessarily *structured* systems must be designed to record, manipulate and simply cope with large yet notoriously incomplete data sets that are then used to inform us about an *unstructured* phenomena; the past. Our databases have to balance the need for structure and thus intelligibility of data, against the cyclical hermeneutic character of archaeological enquiry that gives that data meaning. Initiatives voiced for an objective post-processual recording methodology, (Hodder 1994) threaten an unworkable imbalance by overfavouring the latter.

4.2   INTERFACES AND UNDERSTANDING

An equally adept means of diverting attention from the profundity of what one is doing when implementing a relational system, is to place too much emphasis on graphical user interfaces and more generally the means by which the system is operated and accessed. Clearly such devices are intrinsic components of a successful implementation. They provide the crucial defence against the accusations of systems disenfranchising the archaeologists as interpreter, by enabling them to interrogate their data without recourse to specialised knowledge.

For RDBMS the Structured Query Language (SQL) requires knowledge of simple fourth generation non-procedural English-like languages. WIMPS based data browsers however, can spare the user even that hardship, as queries are built up from pull down menus of acceptable terms, parameters added and results posted to the screen. The issue here, is that much of the system's potential as an analytical device is dependent on users *conceiving* appropriate questions for the new architecture, which may then be phrased through such congenial object based environments. This point is returned to below.

In summary the conceptual problems that need to be addressed if archaeologists are to realise the potential benefit to their analysis that an RDBMS offers, are subtle, prone to growth without the confines of a strategic plan, and are not dealt with simply by the provision of a cordial interface. Not discussed here, yet equally relevant to the perception of new systems, is the more chaotic world of human emotion and how this is best handled. In this world, such powerful analytical tools which enhance the power of the individual to conduct multi-variable analysis, may also appear to threaten specialist authority, weaken job-security and effect career development. If one is prototyping systems for various user groups, which one shall be chosen first, how will the others feel?; apprehension and scepticism can mingle freely with enthusiasm. (See Cooper/ Dinn 1995 for further discussion of this topic).

5   Some Specific Problems

In the course of the RLEC project introduced earlier, there were three distinct conceptual problems encountered. These were characteristic of users in transition between the older systems described in paragraph four, and the Oracle system they were confronted with. They are now considered.

5.1   INTER SPECIALIST BOUNDARIES

In common with most archaeological units, MoLAS has various basic specialist divisions, environmental, finds and field. These divisions also have sub-divisions, e.g. animal bone analysis, human bone analysis, pottery, building material etc. The divisions correspond to various areas of expertise, and in the initial stages of a project, specialists work in relative isolation, identifying what has been excavated. The extension of these divisions into the interpretative phase, either as an active decision or as a result of inappropriate information technology, will inevitably deny the generation of more holistic interpretations.

Relational database systems enable various archaeological data to be inter-related so that ceramic information may for instance, be related to the stratigraphy to indicate the degree of residually or deposit disturbance within a site. This much is clear, yet it is a bland statement to simply point out the possibility of myriad data relations, and ignore the environment in which such potential is released.

The evolution of recording systems at MoLAS, is a history of balancing the need to record excavations as accurately as possible, (the archaeological incentive) yet as quickly as possible, (the commercial imperative). Non-hierarchical site recording, using various pro-forma context sheets, carried out by archaeologists who are responsible for defining, planning and recording their own contexts, were all in direct response to the requirements of the complex urban rescue environment (Spence 1993). At the interpretative stage, the structural site details would be analysed to provide a frame from which other data sets — once they were available — would be hung, in order to contextualise the structural account. Thus dating information would enable the relative sequence of structural development to be phased.

There are two points here. Firstly that rationalised recording systems are essential if excavations are to be efficiently completed, and secondly the way in which data sets have been related in the past is not *solely* dictated by the adequacies of the information system employed. Thus the use of new systems must be considered within the necessary confines of the interpretative environment. This is not to say that such systems should simply make current practices more efficient, on the contrary there are inevitable consequences for working practices when new systems are implemented. Rather the practical adequacy of each improvement, change and addition to existing empirical techniques must be thoroughly considered relative to the real world in which (in this case) London's commercial archaeology is carried out. A realist stance based on the notion of practical adequacy, (Sayer 1992) is most appropriate to the environment in which MoLAS works, and provides the first line of defence against the use of novel systems and applications on a 'because we could' basis (Huggett/Cooper 1991: 40).

However, in order to provide the right conditions for systems offering improved data relatability to yield innovative solutions, the nature of specialist boundaries, and specifically the means by which 'relatability' will be effected, must be considered. There are two main factors; the architectural and the human.

The purpose of RDB architecture, is to enable relatability between data sets. Therefore table design that enables this functionality through the mechanism of referential integrity is a prerequisite. If properly designed, the relatability of data sets in computing terms is not a problem.

For researchers to adapt to the technology in conceptual terms requires some re-assessment of the forms in which the findings of one specialist group are communicated to another. It is important to point out, that one is interested here in the transmission of database information; an activity that occurs in parallel with the discussions, arguments and debates that occur between the specialists themselves. In the RLEC project, two examples of such reassessment can be given.

Human osteological information on sex and age was determined from some 14 different bone traits, both metric and non-metric. All of these traits are valuable to the specialist, with a final statement of overall age and sex

being the culmination of those observations abetted by a greater or lesser degree of intuition. It is this aggregate decision that is of interest to the team, thus fields for overall age and sex were added to the appropriate osteological tables, enabling other users direct access to appropriate data.

The 2512 small finds recovered from the sites, of themselves, yielded much valuable information to the specialist and some to the rest of the team. But their contribution to the team, was enhanced when finds were grouped into functional categories, (luxury items, items of personal adornment etc.) that were stored as numeric codes in the object index tables. An interpretative, hierarchical judgement was made that built on the specialists work, (i.e. the initial identification of the object) but which enabled that specialist data to relate to the other data sets in a new and possibly more comprehensible way.

5.2   THE SPREADSHEET MENTALITY

A more practical problem, the 'spreadsheet mentality' as it was christened, is characterised by a desire to see all data of interest in a single large table, and by the belief that in order to compare one's data with someone else's, an extra column has to be added to the table and the appropriate data imported. It indicates a belief that data has to be in the same place to be relatable, which is a conceptual legacy traceable to older storage devices, the typical format of familiar reports and published data tables. It is a problem because it indicates that the comparison of traits is perceived as a structural problem and data structures are things that are not easily altered, ergo the potential for any data set to freely interact with any other has not been realised ergo the relational functionality is not used, result: disenchanted users. In this situation, the designer must emphasise two key points; the breaking down of specialist barriers and the importance of retrieval technique.

Excavation is a subjective exercise, and the data it generates is inevitably dependent on the recording procedures employed, and the individual who implements them on site. Yet a good relational structure dictates subsequent interpretation of that theory dependent data as little as possible by storing it in its most disaggregated state, and providing the means by which an aggregated state (of which there will be many) may be reached. One consequence of this is that inter-specialist boundaries are not only unenforced, they cease to be relevant, as the information from the excavation is expressed in terms of common relatable units. Such boundaries are concepts that the database need only be aware of for administrative purposes, a function ably catered for by a systematic table naming conventions. The RDBMS then, by its very nature is not disposed to enforcing incompatibility.

The spreadsheet mentality can also be addressed by emphasising the technique by which data is retrieved from the RDBMS. The user may query the database, and at that point, and in the manner of their choosing, tables are related. Thus querying becomes a more dynamic and slightly different process. Instead of solely analysing a table of data printed by a standard report, users are compelled to expend some time analysing the very form of the table itself. If one is already thinking more systematically about what one really needs from the database, then it is easier to progress to the next stage where the analytical functionality of a system like Oracle is realised.

5.3   THE PILE OF PAPER MENTALITY

This is characterised by general requests for large runs of data with little or no filtering criteria, or grouping. One reason for this is the belief that the computer is hiding information and that a visual check is necessary, another is that analysis is perceived as something that occurs outside the computer. A third is the wholly conceptual one, of data simply needing to be seen in all its exhaustive detail for the researcher to 'get her head around it'. (It could reasonably be argued that this is partly a product of the first two).

The problem is similar to that discussed in the previous paragraph, i.e. the ability of the database to search, verify and summarise data is not realised. Yet it differs, in that it sends a clear signal that the message *access is analysis* has not yet been assimilated (an assimilation that does not take place solely by *providing access*, i.e. an easy to use GUI interface). The volume of data to which access is now possible, and the diminishing resources available to analyse that data, means that it is becoming impractical to approach such resources without some research objective in mind, however insignificant it may be. At a time when project budgets are demanding the most efficient working practices to enable some funds to still be available for the actual analysis of the carefully rescued data, the need to replace mechanisms such as high-lighter pens, hand calculators and visual scans with the targeted search criteria, statistical functions and group operators of the RDBMS itself, is clear.

6   Conclusion

The problems discussed are neither difficult to address, nor are their effects hard to identify; they are however, easy to ignore. If users are to benefit from RDBMS technology in the core area of their profession — the quality and thoroughness of archaeological interpretation — such conceptual problems must be overcome. A poor implementation is that which ignores its own consequences, and for commercial archaeology in the 1990's a proper understanding of the positive benefits that new systems provide, must be recognised for the crucial component of a successful implementation it is. The quality of archaeological interpretation from those working in the commercial sector depends on it.

references

Codd, E. 1970 A Relational Model Of Data For Large Shared Data Banks, *Communications of the ACN* 13 (6), 357-387.

Cooper, M.
J. Dinn 1995 Computers And The Evolution Of Archaeological Organisations. In: J. Wilcock/ K. Lockyear (eds), *Computer Applications And Quantitative Methods In Archaeology 1994*, 89-94, BAR International Series 598, Oxford: Tempus Reparatum.

Huggett, J.
M. Cooper 1991 The Computer Representation Of Space In Urban Archaeology. In: K. Lockyear/S. Rahtz (eds), *Computer Applications And Quantitative Methods In Archaeology 1990*, 39-42, BAR International Series 565, Oxford: Tempus Reparartum.

Hodder, I. 1994 *The Notion Of Objectivity In Recording*. Unpublished paper presented at the Museum of London 9th May 1994.

Hussain, D.
K. Hussain 1991 *Information Systems For Business*. New York: Prentice Hall.

Sayer, A. 1992 *Method In Social Science: A Realist Approach*. London: Routledge.

Spence, C. 1993 Recording the Archaeology of London: the development and implementation of the DUA recording system. In: E. Harris (ed.), *Practices Of Archaeological Stratigraphy*, 23-46, London: Academic Press.

Peter Hinge
Computing Section
Museum of London Archaeology Service
No. 1 London Wall
London EC2Y 5EA
United Kingdom
e-mail: pete@molas.demon.co.uk

Thanasis Hadzilacos
Polyxeni Myladie Stoumbou

Conceptual Data Modelling for Prehistoric Excavation Documentation

1 Introduction

Archaeological method and practice often deals with information that is tentative, liable to change and fuzzy. Data gathered in the field are usually fragmented posing the need to associate between pieces of relevant context. Drawing archaeological knowledge, which is by nature uncertain, from tentative and incomplete information and fragmented data is a formidable task which in itself would justify archaeology being a science (Richards/Ryan 1985; Ross *et al.* 1991).

Traditionally data is kept on paper (including photos and sketches), is organised in a single manner and all non-trivial processing takes place in the archaeologists head. This practice gives rise to problems in sorting and cross-referencing data with related information content. Informatics, or electronic data processing, promised, among others, to facilitate recording and association of excavation data by providing the means to organise and manipulate archaeological information efficiently. This promise has only partially been fulfilled. One reason is that some pieces of computer technology have until very recently been missing (integrating maps, images, text and attribute information in a single system). Another very important reason is the incorrect development of archaeological information systems (lack of methodology, indifference to issues of conceptual data modelling).

Conceptual data modelling of an application is the process of formally describing its static and dynamic properties for purposes of understanding the application's requirements and communication between the application developers and the system's users. This description of the application's properties is done independently of implementation issues and is carried out by use of a certain *conceptual data model*. The outcome of the conceptual data modelling of an application is called a *conceptual schema* and is an abstraction of reality as it is perceived by the intended users of the system, namely the archaeologists.

Computer users express their requirements in natural language — which includes diagrams, images, maps and processes — while computers execute machine code. Applications bridge this gap by executing programs that satisfy users' needs. The transition from user requirements to machine executable code is done by use of intermediate representations which facilitate the implementation of the desired system. One of these representations is produced at the stage of conceptual data modelling (Batini *et al.* 1992; Navathe 1992). Conceptual data modelling aims at the realistic representation of the information content of the application under research, therefore it should not be performed without the co-operation of its users, who are responsible for describing requirements and explaining the meaning of data. The conceptual schema that is produced is understandable to users, so mistakes can be detected at this very early stage. Moreover, the application converges towards the expected result. Furthermore, the designers' choices can be tested and the process of implementation is thus facilitated. Owing to the fact that the conceptual modelling process is independent of implementation details, the conceptual schema produced during the conceptual modelling process can still be used even if the software used at the stage of implementation changes. Lastly, maintenance and transformation of the system (e.g. in the case that application requirements change or are enhanced) are facilitated, because the existence of the conceptual schema of the application eases understanding of its structure and functions.

The *information system* for a specific project (e.g. an excavation documentation system) is a collection of activities that regulate the sharing and distribution of information and the storage of data that are relevant to the project. Information systems' development is a process which follows a series of steps, called the life-cycle of an information system. This life-cycle usually contains the following main stages: requirements analysis, design, implementation and maintenance. An application development methodology is a structured set of procedures, concepts, methods, models and tools covering the whole life-cycle of the system. For data-intensive applications the area of computing technology that leads from problem specification to system implementation is *database design*. Database design is a complex process and can be broken down into conceptual, logical and physical design. The purpose of conceptual database design is to organise data for effective processing by use of a model that is expressively rich and user understandable in order to facilitate implementation. There are several conceptual models that are used in conceptual design. One of them, namely the Entity-Relationship (E-R) model, has emerged as the leading formal structure for conceptual data representation, becoming an established standard. The E-R model is based on only a few modelling concepts and has a very effective and understandable graphic representation. The E-R model is described in detail in section 4 below.

This approach is not sufficient to cope with the special needs of archaeological applications since they deal with information which has three basic dimensions: the *spatial* dimension, which refers to the position of archaeological entities in space (for example the place where certain artefacts were found), the *a-spatial* or *descriptive* dimension (attributes that describe the form of archaeological information, for example the possible uses of artefacts), and also a *temporal* dimension, which refers to objects' location in time. The need for handling sufficient archaeological information as a whole demands a conceptual model enriched with spatio-temporal constructs. Moreover, prehistoric excavations have requirements that are not so evident in other types of excavations. These requirements stem from the fact that there is a vast number of scattered prehistoric excavation data that need to be correlated carefully in order to draw useful conclusions. Since interpretation is the most important task in a prehistoric excavation, the excavation documentation system should be able to provide the means of organising and manipulating archaeological data without eliminating individual observations and interpretative conclusions.

Archaeological information systems have only been developed in recent years (Allen *et al.* 1990; Lock/Stančič 1995), so there is little that can be said about previous work on the subject. While a lot has been accomplished towards the development of predictive modelling for site locations, little work has been done towards conceptual data modelling for excavation information systems. As a result, the excavation documentation systems that have already been developed are inadequate for manipulation of archaeological information and can usually not easily be adapted to satisfy the needs of other archaeological excavations or to handle changes in archaeologists' views and requirements.

The rest of the paper is organised as follows: Section 2 points out the special requirements posed by excavation documentation systems and presents a justification of why a special modelling approach is needed. Section 3 is a description of a prehistoric excavation scenery as viewed by a computer scientist. The archaeological information is analysed and presented, the primary objects are described and the relationships among them are identified. The main contribution of the paper is presented in section 4, which

formally describes the conceptual model that is proposed and used and also explains the approach that was adopted by the authors. Section 5 contains a summary, an assessment of the paper as well as ideas on future research on the subject.

2 Why a specific modelling approach for archaeological applications?

Archaeological information can benefit from a special conceptual modelling approach on the following grounds:

Archaeological information is located in space. As mentioned above, an important aspect of archaeological information is its spatial dimension, the *position* of archaeological phenomena in space as well as their *shape*. The position of an archaeological object is a special attribute in the sense that any change on it affects other objects' positions. This does not usually happen in the case of properties like 'material' or 'use'. For example, a change in the position of a stratum may affect the position of the neighbouring strata. Additionally, the *shape* of an archaeological entity may relate to the shapes of other archaeological entities; consider a set of excavation units with specific shapes 'comprising' a stratum. The conceptual schema must be able to represent such cases.

Archaeological data need also to be 'located' in time. One of the most important features of archaeological data is their time dimension. An excavation documentation system should be able to record information about the dates when the archaeological data were discovered and the dates of their cultural affiliation and, also, to perform temporal queries. Temporal information about the archaeological entities can then be used to view the chronological history of particular phenomena, e.g. the construction phases of a wall. Interpretation itself poses the need for versioning. Consider the case of an artefact. At time A the archaeologist in charge thought that this was an arrow head, whereas at time B the same archaeologist decided that it was the blade of a knife.

Need to handle partially defined objects. Archaeological information about certain finds may sometimes be incomplete or uncertain due to constraints posed by factors such as short time due to lack of funds or construction projects in the area, and destruction of finds by later impositions which can make interpretation rather difficult.

Need to draw useful conclusions from data that do not follow patterns or follow patterns unknown at database design time. Archaeological data are characterised by a variety of form and lack of iteration. That is, archaeological method and practice involve objects that are usually unique and which an archaeologist attempts to classify. In most cases classification poses the need for unique descriptions. Classifying information that does not follow specific

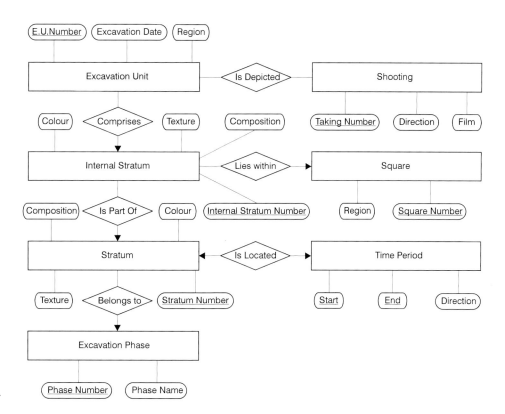

Figure 1. The Conceptual Schema.

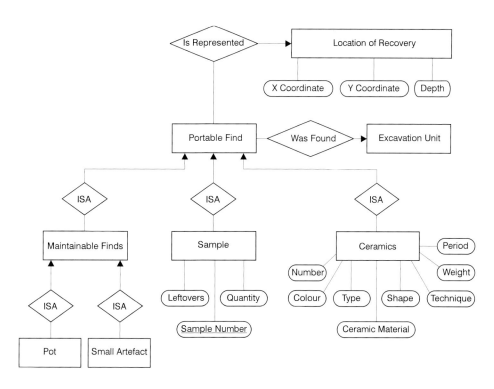

Figure 2. Portable finds.

patterns is a very special kind of decision making, on which interpretation is based. Drawing interpretation in an archaeological project where information does not follow specific patterns from attributes that are not repeated requires a special 'description' attribute in the archaeological database.

3   A layman's description of a prehistoric archaeological excavation

When compared to other kinds of archaeological excavations (e.g. classical or Roman), prehistoric excavations appear to have certain peculiarities that make the excavation practice and interpretation more difficult. Firstly, there is a vast number of prehistoric sites and finds which makes those that are under research only a small sample of the whole. Therefore, a prehistoric excavation cannot be representative of the context of others. An important aspect of a prehistoric excavation is that the information of interest is scattered. Therefore, it is very difficult to associate related pieces (for example finds, walls or hearths) as well as to visualise the excavation scenery as a whole. Moreover, prehistoric finds either have been destroyed by later impositions or are likely to be destroyed during the excavation itself, since excavating is by nature a destructive process. Many destructions are due to the errors and the inexperience of the archaeologists in charge. Therefore, the primary objective of a prehistoric excavation is the reproduction of a prehistoric scenery as well as the association between the elements of the archaeological information. This should be the objective of the excavation documentation system too.

Another important issue in archaeological excavation is *interpretation*. Interpretation is a decision-making process that depends very much on the cultural and scientific background of the archaeologist in charge. In prehistoric excavations, interpretation is very much limited by the findings.

Observation and experiment are very important parts of a prehistoric excavation method and practice. For example, it is possible to construct tools with the methods and techniques which are believed to have been used by prehistoric people. Then, these tools are tested upon use and are compared to finds. Prehistoric excavation itself can be thought of as an experiment, which unfortunately cannot be iterated. Therefore, errors in a prehistoric excavation may be very crucial to the conservation of finds.

Below follows a description of a prehistoric excavation scenery (Andreou/Kotsakis 1991; Andreou *et al.* 1995; Kotsakis *et al.* 1995). This paper presents a specific archaeological method for prehistoric excavations. However, the conceptual data modelling approach that is presented can be easily adapted to suit the needs of other prehistoric excavations.

The excavation site is divided into *squares* (or cuts). The square is the reference point for all archaeological activity that falls within its boundaries. Each find, each excavation unit and each stratum is identified within a certain square. Each square measures 4 × 4 m. The squares are separated from each other by lanes of earth that are not excavated and are called *witnesses*. Each witness is 1 m large. The witnesses are useful in order to study the stratigraphy of the ground in each square.

Most excavation methods use the *stratum* as the basic excavation entity that is located in time. The methods that are used for chronology can be either empirical or absolute (e.g. dendrochronology, chronology with C14). Determining the boundaries between consecutive strata is a very important archaeological decision which relies heavily on the experience of the archaeologist. Stratigraphy usually follows the rule of *overlaying*, which states that strata that are located closer to the surface are associated with more recent time periods than those that are deeper. However, this is not always the case. There are times when strata located in places with different elevations belong to the same chronological period. Since the square is the basic unit that controls the excavation process, strata are usually numbered with regard to the square in which they were identified. Aim of an excavation documentation application is to provide a unified stratigraphy and numbering for the whole of the excavation site. This numbering can take place after the end of the excavation. One must note that it is possible that strata belonging to different cuts are classified as contemporary in the final stratigraphy of the excavation site. Strata are characterised mainly by the colour, the composition and the texture of the soil that they contain.

Strata are usually divided into pieces of undetermined shape and size named *excavation units*. An excavation unit cannot go beyond the boundaries of a stratum and defines a constrained space where finds are distributed. Its fundamental use is to describe the progress of the excavation process.

Chronological period is the main historical product of a prehistoric excavation and provides a reference point for determining chronology for archaeological finds. Since chronological evaluation methods are applied directly to the stratum, the chronology of a certain period is determined by the strata that comprise it. Each period refers to a certain stage in a prehistoric settlement's life. For example, a fire that destroyed the settlement triggers the end of a period and the beginning of another, even if the new settlement is characterised by the same cultural and technological features as the previous one.

Until recently, excavation activities have been recorded on paper on a daily basis. The information that is kept refers to the square, the stratum and the current excavation unit; it describes the activities performed each day. It also contains the positions of artefacts. A large part of these paper manuscripts are in natural language and may also contain sketches, photographs, etc. However, there are some code expressions, for example those that refer to the colour of the ground. The use of code expressions aims at avoiding vagueness in descriptions and at facilitating interpretation. For example, ground samples with the same colour, which is expressed either by use of a code expression or by use of a standard colour set can be easily classified as belonging to the same stratum.

Prehistoric finds may be spatially fixed or not. Finds that are spatially fixed cannot be moved easily, such as walls or floors, hearths, post-holes and pits. All spatially fixed finds have a name or number that uniquely identifies them for the whole of the excavation site. For walls and floors it is interesting to note the material used to construct them (e.g. mud-bricks) and the depth of their foundations. Hearths, post-holes and pits are characterised by the number of their external phases, that is the number of times they were reconstructed or repaired. The phases of hearths, post-holes and pits are different from the phases of the prehistoric settlement.

Finds that are not spatially fixed may be pots, ground samples, seeds, shells and small artefacts that are usually classified with regard to the material used to construct them (stone, metal, bone or clay). Small artefacts, independent of classification, are described by information concerning their dimensions and shape, the material used to construct them, their colour, their type and possible use and are depicted in photographs and sketches. Some artefacts may require additional information recording, for instance concerning their decoration (type of decoration, technique and motif).

4 Modelling archaeological information

4.1 THE ENTITY-RELATIONSHIP MODEL

The *Entity-Relationship* model (E-R) described below is a conceptual data model that is entity-centred since its main objective is to represent entities (the primary objects, their attributes and the relationships in which they participate). The E-R model is a standard conceptual model which offers a very simple but abstractive means for structuring information. Due to its simplicity, it is widely used for the conceptual modelling of applications with very large information spaces. Certain variations and extensions of the model have occasionally been produced and used in order to satisfy the needs of certain applications.

Below follows a description of the fundamental constructs of the model. Each concept is further described by examples from the prehistoric excavation paradigm presented above. Examples are essential to aid understanding of concepts and to differentiate between similar concepts.

4.1.1 Entities

An entity is a thing or object of significance, whether real or imagined, about which information needs to be known or held. An entity represents a type or class of things — not an instance. For example, an entity named Stratum corresponds to the set of strata of a prehistoric excavation. This implies that each stratum identified in the field, for example stratum No 2, is an instance of the entity Stratum. Each entity must be uniquely identifiable. That is, each occurrence (instance) of an entity must be separate and distinctly identifiable from all other instances of that type of entity. In a conceptual schema entities are depicted by rectangles.

4.1.2 Attributes

An attribute is any description of an entity. Attributes serve to identify, qualify, classify, quantify or express the state of an entity. In a conceptual schema attributes are represented diagrammatically by circles which are linked to entities by undirected edges. The entity Stratum, discussed before, may have an attribute called Composition, which refers to the composition of the soil that each stratum in the excavation site contains. A combination of attributes usually serves to uniquely identify an entity. These attributes are then called the *key* for that entity. For example, the stratum number serves to uniquely identify a stratum (the assumption is made that the final stratigraphy of the excavation site consists of strata that are identified by different numbers), therefore an attribute named Stratum Number is the key for the entity Stratum. Attributes that are part of the key for an entity have their names underlined in the conceptual schema.

4.1.3 Relationships

A relationship is a significant association between entities. A relationship definition is one that represents a type of association between entities, to which all instances of relationships must conform. A relationship is represented by a diamond linked to their constituent entities by edges. As an example, consider the relationship which associates the portable artefacts with the excavation units in which they were found. Relationships have a functionality, which may be one of the following:

4.1.3.1 One-to-one

An example of a one-to-one relationship is the association between strata and chronological periods. Each stratum refers to one and only one chronological period. Further-more, each chronological period is associated to one and only one stratum. (It is assumed that contemporaneous strata are merged in the final stratigraphy.) A one-to-one relationship is represented in the conceptual schema by directed edges that point to the entities forming the relationship.

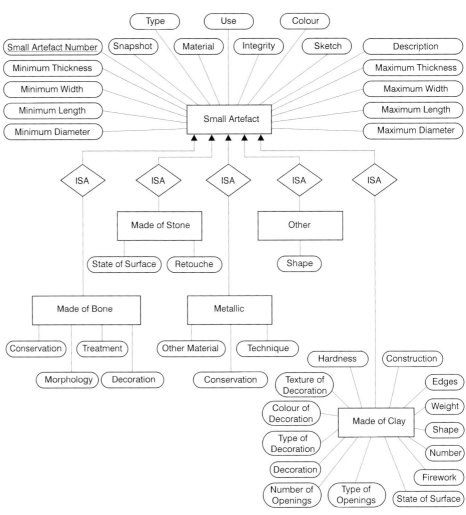

Figure 3. Small Artefacts.

4.1.3.2   Many-to-one

An example of a many-to-one relationship is the association between strata and excavation units. Each excavation unit belongs to one and only one stratum, whereas each stratum may consist of more than one excavation unit. A many-to-one relationship is represented in the conceptual schema by a directed edge that points to the entity which lies in the 'one' part of the relationship and undirected edges pointing to the rest of the entities participating in the relationship.

4.1.3.3   Many-to-many

An example of a many-to-many relationship is the association between spatially fixed finds and strata that surround them. Each spatially fixed find, a wall for instance, may be surrounded by more than one strata, whereas each stratum may surround more than one wall. A many-to-many relationship is represented in the

conceptual schema by undirected edges pointing to the entities that participate in the relationship.

4.1.4   *Isa Relationships*

As we have seen, the Entity-Relationship modelling technique represents the world in terms of Entity Sets (e.g. Artefacts, Sites, Archaeologists) and Relationships among Entity Sets (e.g. 'found at' can be a relationship between Artefacts and Sites). 'Isa' is a special relationship indicating that one Entity Set is a ('Isa') subset of another. For example Archaeologists Isa Persons or Vases Isa Artefacts. The importance of this relationship is that the subset 'inherits' the properties of the superset. For example since Vases Isa Artefacts and Artefacts has the relationship 'found at' with Sites, then Vases also has the relationship 'found at' with Sites and we do not need to explicitly state this; thus when programs will be written we do not need to write a special program to interrogate where a vase was found; the general program written for all artefacts will suffice. On the other hand, if Vases have an additional property, say 'type of clay' but not all artefacts have this property, we do not need to store a field 'type of clay' for all artefacts (and have it with value 'NON APPLICABLE' for all but vases): subsets (Vases in this example) can have additional properties to the ones they inherit from their supersets (Artefacts in this example).

Put another way, Isa relationships serve to declare special cases of entities. These entities implicitly inherit all the attributes and relationships of the entity at the higher level, but they can have attributes and relationships in their own right. For example, consider the case of the entity named Small Artefact. Since a metallic artefact is a special case of a small artefact, there is an Isa relationship between the entities Metallic Artefact and Small Artefact. This means that each occurrence of the entity Metallic Artefact (that is, each metallic artefact) is distinguishable by its identification number (as all small artefacts are) and is described by attributes like Type, Use or Colour. However, a small metallic artefact is further described by attributes of its own, such as Technique, Other Material and Preservation Status. The same holds for small artefacts made of stone, clay or bone.

4.1.5.   Is-part-of and Is-member-of relationships
Is-part-of and Is-member-of relationships are special cases of the Isa relationship often present in some of the extensions of the E-R model. The is-part-of relationship refers to entities that form part of another entity and therefore share some of its properties, whereas the is-member-of relationship refers to an entity that is a member of a set of entities sharing common properties.

4.2   MODELLING ARCHAEOLOGICAL INFORMATION FOR PREHISTORIC EXCAVATIONS
Below follows a presentation of a conceptual schema for the prehistoric excavation presented above. In order to explain choices that were made during the conceptual modelling process, we present briefly the main entities and relationships they participate in. The basic entities of the conceptual schema are the following:

4.2.1.   Excavation Unit[1]
Excavation units are described by their number (unique to the whole of the excavation site), the date they were excavated (it is assumed that an excavation unit corresponds to activities of one day) and the region where this excavation activity took place.

4.2.2.   Square
Squares are identified by their number which is unique to the whole of the excavation site.

4.2.3.   Stratum
The entity Stratum corresponds to strata that belong to the final stratification of the excavation site which is determined at the end of the excavation process. Since prehistoric excavations are usually performed in squares, during the excavation process information is kept for strata that belong to the certain square that is being excavated. Strata that are determined this way may be part of a stratum that expands to more than one square. At the end of the excavation, strata are classified and correlated and thus the stratification of the excavation site is determined. To satisfy the need for storing information about strata during the excavation the conceptual schema contains an entity named Excavation Stratum, which corresponds to the strata that are identified during the excavation of a certain square. Information stored about excavation strata can then be used to help the decision-making process of determining stratification by facilitating the association of strata from different squares that share the same properties. Strata as well as excavation strata are described by their numbers as well as other properties, such as the colour, texture and composition of the soil they contain.

4.2.4.   Phase
A phase is identified by its name (or number) and its description.

4.2.5.   Portable Find
Portable finds may be small artefacts, samples, pots or ceramics. Small artefacts are classified into one of the following categories: of bone, of clay, of stone, Metallic and Other.

4.2.6.   Spatially fixed find
Spatially fixed finds may be walls or floors, hearths, pits or post-holes. All spatially fixed finds are uniquely identified by their name, for example Room A. Like in the case of strata, spatially fixed finds are recorded during the excavation of squares. Therefore, it is possible that parts of houses belong to different squares. Since post-excavation work requires that spatially fixed finds are viewed as a whole, the entity Part of Spatially fixed Find is used in the conceptual schema to suit the need for on-site recording of spatially fixed finds.

The basic relationships are:

1. An excavation unit *comprises* an excavation stratum. This is a many-to-one relationship, since more than one excavation unit comprises an internal stratum and each excavation unit may belong to only one stratum.

2. An excavation stratum *lies within* a square. A many-to-one relationship since each excavation stratum lies within one square exactly whereas each square contains more than one excavation stratum.

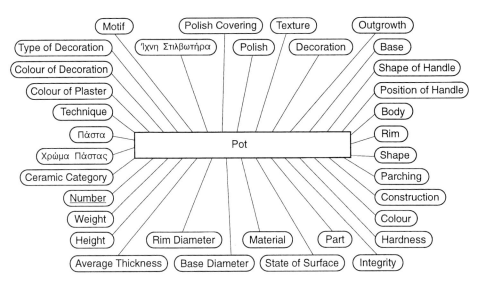

Figure 4. Pots.

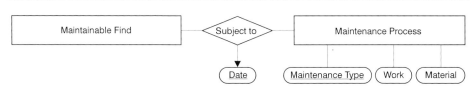

Figure 5. Maintenance of prehistoric finds.

3. An excavation stratum *is part of* a stratum. A many-to-one relationship since each stratum corresponds to more than one excavation stratum and each excavation stratum is part of exactly one stratum.

4. A stratum is *'located'* in a time period. This relationship is one-to-one. Each stratum is located to belong to exactly one time period and each time period corresponds to the chronology of exactly one stratum. It is assumed that strata that belong to the same time period are unified.

5. A stratum *belongs to* a phase. This relationship is many-to-one. Each stratum belongs to exactly one phase and each phase may contain more than one stratum.

6. An excavation unit *is depicted in* a shooting. This is a many-to-one relationship. Each excavation unit is depicted in more than one shooting, whereas each shooting depicts exactly one excavation unit.

7. A portable find *was found in* an excavation unit. This is a many-to-one relationship. Each portable find was found in exactly one excavation unit, whereas each excavation unit could contain more than one portable find.

8. Maintainable finds, samples and ceramics *are (Isa relationship)* portable finds.

9. Small artefacts and pots *are (Isa relationship)* maintainable finds.

10. Artefacts made of clay, stone, bone or metal *are (Isa relationship)* small artefacts.

11. Buildings, hearths, post-holes and pits *are (Isa relationship)* spatially fixed finds.

12. Walls (and floors) *are part of* buildings. A many-to-one relationship since each wall belongs to exactly one building and each building comprises more than one wall.

13. A spatially fixed find *is surrounded by* an excavation stratum. This is a many-to-many relationship. Each spatially fixed find may be surrounded by one or more excavation strata, whereas each excavation stratum may surround more than one spatially fixed find.

14. A spatially fixed find *is located in time* by a stratum. This is a many-to-one relationship. Each spatially fixed find is referenced in time by exactly one stratum, whereas each stratum may be used to chronologically reference more than one spatially fixed find.

15. A maintainable find *is subject to* a maintenance process. This is a many-to-many-to-one relationship. Given a specific date, a maintainable find may have been subject to one or more maintenance procedures. The other way round, given a specific date the same maintenance procedure may have been performed on one or more maintainable finds. What is more, there is only one day where a maintainable find has been subject to a specific maintenance procedure.

16. A portable find *is represented by* a point, the location where it was found. This is the graphical representation needed to map archaeological entities on the map of the excavation site. This relationship is many-to-one.

17. A spatially fixed find *is represented by* a set of solids. A one-to-many relationship. Solids are used to represent 3-dimensional entities in the excavation site and correspond both to the position of entities and to their shape.

18. An excavation unit *is represented by* a solid. A one-to-one relationship.

19. A square *is represented by* a solid. A one-to-one relationship.

20. A stratum *is represented by* one or more solids. A one-to-many relationship.

4.3   THE CONCEPTUAL SCHEMA OF THE ARCHAEOLOGICAL DATABASE

This subsection presents the conceptual design of a database for a prehistoric excavation based on the previous description. The conceptual design, or schema, is presented in a diagrammatic form, known as E-R diagrams, using four symbols: rectangles denote entities; diamonds denote relationships between related entities; attribute names are encircled in oval shapes; underlined attributes are keys, i.e. unique identifiers, of the corresponding entities. Figure 1 is the E-R diagram of the overall excavation relating strata, excavation phases and excavation units. Figures 2, 3, 4, and 5 are the detailed diagrams of the four main types of archaeological finds: spatially fixed ones, portables, small artefacts and pots. Figure 6 is the design of that part of the database which deals with the maintenance of the finds, while figure 7 relates strata and excavation units to space, denoting that it is a 3-dimensional representation we are interested in.

5   Conclusions

Until recently, excavation documentation systems have not been much more than fast archiving systems. What is more, they often have not been correctly and efficiently designed. This paper presents the 'right' way to start developing an excavation documentation system by providing a modelling approach suitable to cope with the needs posed by the

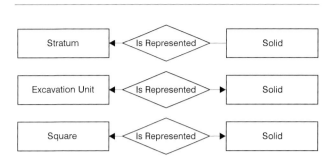

Figure 6. Position of excavation units, strata and squares.

majority of information systems (Hadzilacos/Stoumbou 1994; Hadzilacos/Tryfona 1995). This approach is able up to a limit to deal with a substantial amount of the requirements posed by prehistoric excavations. However, as mentioned above, prehistoric excavations do require special treatment as they present many peculiarities.

In the direction of providing a conceptual model suitable to deal with the special requirements often placed in the case of prehistoric excavation documentation systems, it would be interesting to search among the existing extensions of the E-R model in order to be able to chose the more suitable one for modelling prehistoric excavation information or even design a new extension that would provide the means to efficiently model data from prehistoric excavations.

Acknowledgements
We would like to thank Professor George Hourmouziades who provided the initial stimulus for this work. Professors K. Kotsakis and S. Andreou reviewed presentations of early versions of this work and made fruitful comments; they provided us with relevant material from the prehistoric excavation at Toumba, Thessaloniki. We would like to stress that although the conceptual modelling approach presented in this paper reflects their views on the subject of prehistoric excavation documentation, the authors have full responsibility for any mistakes on understanding the archaeological methodology.

This research was supported by the project GMI (Greek Multimedia Initiative)/STRIDE.

note

1 The excavation unit is an entity that is conceived by the archaeologist in charge of the excavation. Some archaeologists do not use excavation units in practice, while others that agree to the use of excavation units give different definitions to the term 'excavation unit'. The conceptual schema presented here can be easily adapted to cover such cases.

references

Allen, K.
  S.W. Green
  E. Zubrow (eds)

1990   *Interpreting Space: GIS and Archaeology*. London: Taylor & Francis.

Andreou, S.
  K. Kotsakis

1991   The excavation in Toumba, Thessaloniki during 1991, *Archaeological Works in Macedonia and Thrace*, 209-220 (in Greek). Thessaloniki: University of Thessaloniki.

Andreou, S.
  K. Kotsakis
  G. Hourmouziades

1995   The excavation in Toumba, Thessaloniki, 1990-1993. *Egnatia Scientific Annual of the School of Philosophy, Aristotelean University of Thessaloniki* 3 (in Greek).

Batini, C.
  S. Ceri
  S.B. Navathe

1992   *Conceptual Database Design: An Entity-Relationship Approach*. Redwood City, Ca.: The Benjamin/Cummings Publishing Company Inc.

Hadzilacos, Th.
  P.M. Stoumbou

1994   Computer Technology in Archaeological Excavation, *CTI Technical Report* 94.11.54. Patras: Computer Technology Institute.

Hadzilacos, Th.
  N. Tryfona

1995   Logical Data Modeling for Geographic Applications, *International Journal of Geographic Information Systems* 9 (6).

Kotsakis, K.
  S. Andreou
  A. Vargas
  D. Papoudas

1995   Reconstructing a Bronze Age Site with CAD. In: J. Huggett/N. Ryan (eds), *Computer Applications and Quantitative Methods in Archaeology 1994*, 181-187, BAR International Series 600, Oxford: Tempus Reparatum.

Lock, G.
  Z. Stančič (eds)

1995   *Archaeology and Geographic Information Systems: A European Perspective*. London: Taylor & Francis.

Navathe, S.B.

1992   Evolution of Data Modeling for Databases, *Communications of the ACM* 35 (9).

Richards, J.D.
  N.S. Ryan

1985   *Data Processing in Archaeology*, Cambridge: Cambridge University Press.

Ross, S.
  J. Moffett
  J. Henderson

1991   *Computing for Archaeologists*. Oxford: Oxford University Press.

Thanasis Hadzilacos
Computer Technology Institute
University of Patras
P.O. Box 1122
26110, Patras
Greece
e-mail: thh@cti.gr

Polyxeni Myladie Stoumbou
Intrasoft S.A.,
Athens
Greece
e-mail: stoumbou@isoft.intranet.gr

E. Agresti
A. Maggiolo-Schettini
R. Saccoccio
M. Pierobon
R. Pierobon-Benoit

Handling Excavation Maps in SYSAND

1   Introduction

SYSAND is a system to help archaeologists in processing and interpreting excavation data. It has been designed for the excavations of the Gallo-Roman town of Anderitum (now Javols in Lozère, France), but it could be easily adapted to handle data of other sites.

SYSAND records stratification unit (US) cards, checks consistency of physical relationships, and constructs and draws Harris matrices. The archaeologist can visit information related to each unit by navigating in the matrix representation (Maggiolo-Schettini *et al.* 1995a, Maggiolo-Schettini *et al.* 1995b).

To access pictorial and graphical information related to stratification units, SYSAND has been extended with the module SIGMA. In particular, SIGMA inputs maps digitized by means of a scanner. Maps (drawn during the excavation) are given to the scanner in portions. SIGMA reconstructs and stores each map in a stack related to a given year of excavation. The archaeologist has a complete view of the entire site, on a reduced scale, as resulting from the last excavation or from the excavation of a certain year. He can move in on such view, can move to the view related to another year, or can superimpose maps of the same part of excavation but related to different years.

The archaeologist has also at his disposal tools to modify maps by inserting or eliminating elements. For example, he may want to insert hypothetical elements or leave on the map only particular elements, such as walls, and, so store 'particular views' of excavated areas. Moreover, the archaeologist can associate to a line on a map the drawing of a section passing through that line, create links between the card of a stratification unit and maps containing that unit, and, vice versa, and create a link from a point on the map and the card of the related unit. Maps can also be consulted from the cadastral map of the area.

The described system runs on a portable Macintosh Power-book. Both SYSAND and SIGMA are hypertexts realised in a HyperCard environment. Cadastral maps and sections which require a resolution higher than that of maps are manipulated by using the application Photoshop of SIGMA.

The requirement of being able to run the system on a portable computer at the excavation site, together with economic limitations, made us opt for the HyperCard environment rather than other systems such as GIS, that are much more powerful but also require much more powerful machines and incur higher costs.

Two years experience at the Anderitum excavations have shown that the system is efficient and easy to use, also by inexperienced persons.

2   SIGMA

SIGMA (Sistema Ipertestuale per la Gestione di Mappe Archeologiche, that is Hypertextual System for Handling Archaelogical Maps) extends SYSAND with facilities to input and manipulate pictures from the excavation, such as maps and sections (drawn on the site) and photos. SIGMA is implemented in HyperTalk (the programming language of HyperCard), and HyperCard allows to establish links between images and textual information. A consequence of the choice of HyperCard is that images can be handled in two ways: on cards (basic elements of HyperCard for storing text and images) and on external windows. Images on cards may be only bitmap, may have a maximum resolution of 72 dpi, or may be manipulated automatically and manually with HyperCard tools. Images on external windows may be either bitmap or of vectorial type, have no resolution limits, and may be zoomed-in and zoomed-out, but can be modified only with specific graphical applications. We have therefore chosen to have excavation maps on cards, as they do not need a high resolution but may have to be manipulated frequently, whereas sections, photos or cadastral maps of the site are on external windows, as they need a greater resolution but no frequent manipulation.

To input excavation maps, the procedure consists of the following phases:

1. Manual decomposition of each given map into portions suitable for scanning. Maps, drawn by archaeologists, measure 50 × 50 cm (representing 10 × 10 m squares of the excavation). Each map is subdivided into six 16,6 × 25 cm portions.

2. Manual scanning of each portion. Each map is digitized with a resolution of 72 dpi and then saved on disk.

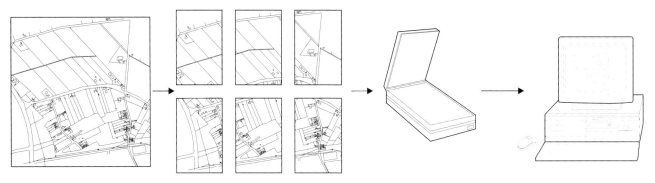

Figure 1. Phases of input procedure.

3. Automatic reconstruction of the original map with a 50% reduction. Such a map is stored in a sequential stack with information needed to view it in its real position in the planimetry.

The entire procedure is illustrated in figure 1.

Experiments suggest that 5 minutes are required to accomplish the first two phases. The third phase takes about 2 minutes (for a precise evaluation see Agresti/Saccoccio 1994).

With sections, photos and cadastral maps, phase 1 differs from the one described for excavation maps because sizes are variable, while in phase 2 a resolution of 300 dpi is chosen. Phase 3 is not automatic, the sections, photos and cadastral maps are reconstructed by the user, piece by piece, by means of a graphical application, such as Photoshop or Canvas.

3   Visualising and navigating in the excavation planimetry

Characteristic of hypertext is the possibility of linking pieces of information according to an ideal arrangement, possibly independent of how they are stored in reality. For excavation maps, the ideal arrangement is the planimetry of the site. One may therefore want to be able to move horizontally on the planimetry in a particular direction. As one has a planimetry for every excavation year, one may also want to move vertically from a map of a certain year to the corresponding map of another year.

Each excavation map has an associated map number. A map number is a sequence of integers: the last integer representing the position of the map in a 10 × 10 map array, the last but one representing the position of this array in an array whose elements are arrays like the one considered, and so on.

From the map number the system can compute numbers of adjacent maps (in four directions) in the planimetry, and

let the user view these maps (the user has a palette at his disposal to accomplish this).

Apart from the described horizontal navigation in the planimetry, a vertical navigation along excavation years is also offered. It may well be possible that the planimetry of a given excavation year is incomplete, for instance, the map for one particular square of one particular year may be missing. But as there are maps available of that square from different excavation years, the planimetry is automatically completed by inserting a map from a different year.

Single maps of the planimetry can be accessed in three ways (fig. 2):

1. going through the stack of map cards;
2. starting from the cadastral map;
3. through an 'interface', namely a reduced view of the most recently created planimetry.

Let us first describe the stack of map cards. Each card contains a reduced view of a single map, together with information such as among others the square number which identifies the map, the list of US numbers contained in the map itself, and a flag which is set on if there are drawings of sections of the represented square. From the map card one can access the related map, and may do a number of search operations; for instance, one can view, in a sequence, all maps containing a given stratification unit.

Secondly the cadastral map. It is a square, measuring 1 × 1 m, which offers a global view of the area comprising the excavation site. The archaeologist can inspect this cadastral map by exploring it continuously. By means of a single click he gets the number of the map of the selected location, by means of a double click he can visualise this map.

And finally, the 'interface' is a stack of cards, each containing a reduced view of fifty maps of the excavation (corresponding to 50 × 100 m in the real world). It is also possible to access one single map from the 'interface'. One can also go back and forth between the 'interface' and maps.

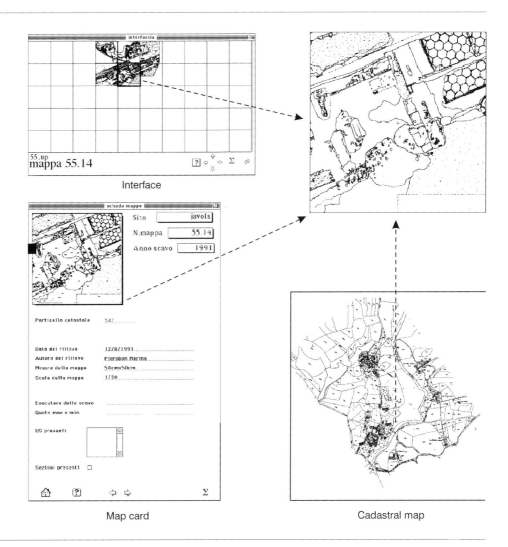

Interface

Map card

Cadastral map

Figure 2. Ways of accessing planimetry.

The main difference between accessing maps through the cadastral map and accessing them via the 'interface', is that, in the latter case, one can also access non existing maps obtained by joining parts of the real maps. We call these 'intermediate maps' and we shall give more details about them later. Maps of the interface will also be automatically updated when a new map is added so that one always gets a view of the most recent map of an area, unless a particular excavation year is specified.

4 Tools for consulting and interpreting excavation maps

In the horizontal navigation in the planimetry one normally moves discretely with one map step. Thanks to the intermediate maps mentioned earlier, one can view a map consisting of pieces of scanned maps. Note that this map is obtained by patching maps belonging to different years if

maps of the same year are not found. The user should be warned that consulting intermediate maps is rather costly.

As an aid to archaeologists, the possibility is provided of superimposing either the altimeter curves or a grid on the maps. The archaeologist may also want to superimpose maps of different years for two purposes: joining parts that are complementary (thus giving an updated view of the entire area) and showing the temporal evolution of the excavation.

To a map the archaeologist can associate drawings of sections. A sign on the map indicates the existence of a section; by a single click on this sign the direction of the section is represented on the map, by a double click the section itself is shown.

The archaeologist may also want to zoom out maps in order to have a more comprehensive view. This is not possible if maps are stored in HyperCard cards, as in our

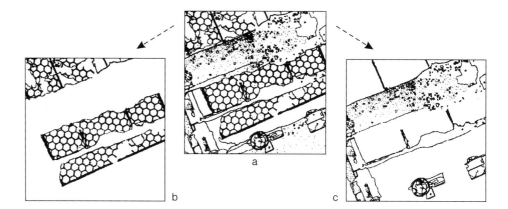

Figure 3. (a) A general view,
(b) A view with only mosaic,
(c) A view with only walls.

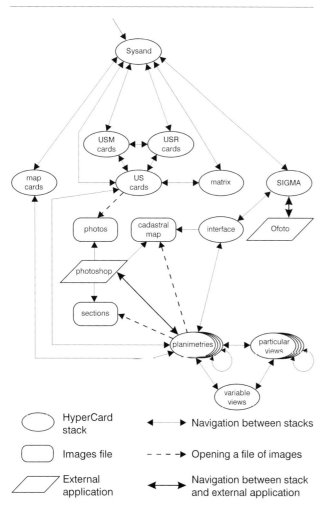

Figure 4. Scheme of links.

case, but it can be simulated. The archaeologist may wish to view m times n maps together, with m being an integer up to 10 and n an integer up to 5. This requires the creation of a card in which the desired maps, suitably reduced, are patched together. Once created, these cards, called 'variable view', can be stored for future consultation.

As an aid to interpretation, it may be useful to add information to or remove information from a given map. For instance, one may want to leave on a map only information representing walls, or one may want to complete a map with hypothetical elements. This is achieved by supplying the archaeologist with tools for modifying a map, that, once modified, can be stored as a 'particular view'. A planimetry of these particular views can be created and navigated upon (fig. 3). All facilities for such a navigation are also supplied.

5   Moving around in SYSAND

In previous sections we have described the modules of the system. By modules we mean stacks of programs, such as SYSAND and SIGMA, stacks of US cards, USM cards (cards that detail information of the US cards when the stratigraphic units are walls), USR cards (cards that detail information of the US cards when the stratigraphic units are pavements of tiles, mosaic, etc. or plasters, frescoes, mosaics, etc.), map cards, map 'interface', planimetries, particular views, variable views, files of images such as pictures, sections, and cadastral maps, and, finally, external applications such as Ofoto and Photoshop.

We have already mentioned a number of links created between cards in a stack (such as those that allow the visualisation of excavation maps as a planimetry) or between stacks, like those between planimetries.

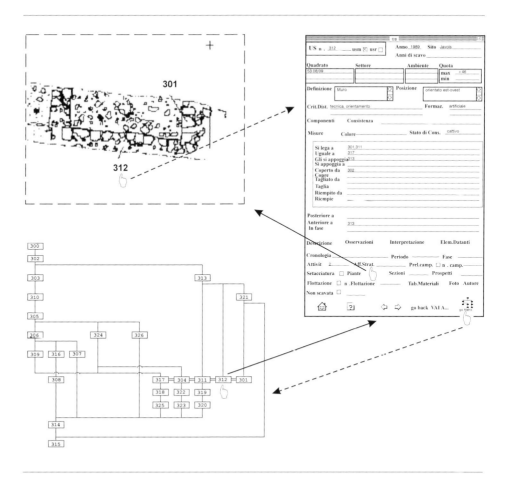

Figure 5. Navigating among US
card, matrix and map.

We will now describe other links, both static ones, which are established by the programmer, and dynamic ones, which are created by the user.

Such links appear in the picture in figure 4. Circles denote HyperCard stacks (e.g., SYSAND, US cards), squares denote images files (e.g., photos, sections), and rhomboids are external applications (e.g., Ofoto). Double arrows between two modules indicate that one can navigate between the two; we distinguish navigation between stacks of HyperCard, represented by a double thin arrow, and between navigation between a stack of HyperCard and an external application, represented by a boldface double arrow. Simple dotted arrows represent the possibility of opening a file of images from an external application or from a stack (e.g. a cadastral map either from a planimetry or from Photoshop). Note that this case differs from that of navigation between, for instance, a planimetry and 'interface', where the stack of a planimetry is left to go into the interface stack. When opening the cadastral map from a planimetry, the stack of the planimetry is not left, the cadastral map is only consulted and can be used to navigate between the cards of the planimetry.

The usual way to access the system is from SYSAND. One can also enter US, USR, USM stacks and either consult them or introduce new cards. In this case one may reconstruct the new stratigraphy. The already computed stratigraphy may be viewed either starting from SYSAND or from any US (USR, USM) card. From SYSAND one may also consult map cards (that are created by SIGMA when maps are inserted into the system).

With SIGMA one can digitise a new map, calling Ofoto, reconstruct the map from the digitized portions, and consult planimetries via 'interface'.

One has the possibility of opening a US card from the related node of the matrix, and, from the US card, consult maps, photos and cards of materials found in that US (to be done) (fig. 5, the path indicated by dotted links). Links between US cards and maps are established by the archaeologist, who has a suitable tool to sensitise an area on the map to which the US number is associated, so that by clicking on this area the relative card is opened. One can, therefore, also go from a map to a US card and from this card to the matrix (fig. 5, the path indicated by solid links).

6   Future work

At present, our work is concentrated on integrating into SYSAND a relational data base system of material found on the excavation site.

For each stratification unit a card gives a general description of Common pottery, Fine pottery, Small objects, Miscellaneous material, all associated with the unit. To each such card, detail cards will be associated with a precise description of each piece. The archaeologist should be able to query the data base, to ask for statistics and to create thematic maps.

references

Agresti, E. R. Saccoccio	1994	*Un sistema per la gestione di mappe di scavo.* Master Thesis in Computer Science, University of Pisa, December 1994.

Maggiolo-Schettini, A.
    P. Seccacini
    C.D. Serratore
	1995	Computation and Representation of Stratigraphic Sequences in a System for Archaelogical Data, *Archeologia e calcolatori* 6: 109-121.

Maggiolo-Schettini, A.
    P. Seccacini
    C.D. Serratore
    R. Pierobon-Benoit
    G. Soricelli
	1995	SYSAND: A System for the Archaelogical Excavations of Anderitum. In: J. Huggett/ N. Ryan (eds), *Computer Applications and Quantitative Methods in Archaeology 1994*, 229-233, BAR International Series 600, Oxford: Tempus Reparatum.

E. Agresti
A. Maggiolo-Schettini
R. Saccoccio
Dipartimento di Informatica
Università di Pisa
Corso Italia 40
56125 Pisa
Italy
e-mail: maggiolo@di.unipi.it

M. Pierobon
Centre J. Bérard
Via F. Crispi 86
80121 Napoli
Italy

R. Pierobon-Benoit
Dipartimento di Discipline Storiche
Università Federico II
Via Porta di Massa 1
80133 Napoli
Italy

Alaine Lamprell
Anthea Salisbury
Alan Chalmers
Simon Stoddart

An Integrated Information System for Archaeological Evidence

This paper reports on an ongoing programme to provide a tailor-made database facility including linkage to stratigraphic analysis and automated procedures for the visualisation of principle classes of artefacts.

1   Introduction

The Xaghra Brochtorff Circle site in Malta was excavated for seven seasons (1987-1994) resulting in the recovery of many artifacts including thousands of human bones (Evans 1971; Malone 1986; Malone *et al.* 1988; Stoddart *et al.* 1993). The archaeologists now face the daunting task of characterising, quantifying and analysing these finds. A system is under development at the University of Bristol to computerise this procedure, and provide an integrated framework for visualising and analysing the multitude of archaeological evidence from this important site.

The foundation for the system is a detailed database of the information. Constructed on top of this database is an interface to allow archaeologists to use established tools such as a Harris Matrix package, as well as new facilities which have been developed to enable the location of the bones and artifacts to be viewed in a three-dimensional volume. The Harris Matrix program establishes the relationship between different contexts in an archaeological site as a two-dimensional hierarchy (Harris 1989). As there are more than 1500 contexts within the Brochtorff Circle, such a computerised hierarchy is essential to gain an easy understanding of the contexts. The three-dimensional volume visualisation of the bones may be used to determine spatial relationships between the contents of a spit, distinctive bones from an area, or the orientation of the bones within the site.

2   The System

Data gathered at a site currently is recorded on paper forms. (The growing availability of inexpensive portable computers could enable this data to be directly entered into the computer.) To minimise errors, the data entry interface resembles the paper version as closely as possible. The individual records have a unique identifier, so once entered, they can be selected, amended or deleted. Some records which in previous years had already been entered into an alternative database format can be added to the system using the file conversion interface so the database is complete. The Harris Matrix Analysis Program and the Graphical Display of Bones use these stored records.

2.1   User interface

The User Interface is a series of windows. Movement between the windows is either by pressing the highlighted key, clicking on the button using the mouse or by moving to the choice using the Tab key and pressing Return. Figure 1 shows the screen used for capturing all the necessary information concerning the bone finds.

The design of the data entry screens was based on the paper forms filled in at the site to aid the transfer of the data. The form is split into four parts, each containing its own fields. When data entry for a field is completed, pressing tab moves the cursor to the next field. The final field in each window is a button allowing the user to move to the next part of the form. The order of tab movement is based on the number identification used on the paper forms. Creating a new form or exiting from the data entry screens will save the data to a file. Individual forms can be retrieved by typing in the context number, the unique identifier for each form. This also serves as an error detector so that no form can have the same context number.

There are four entities in the database: Common, Stratigraphic, Interpretation and Small Finds. The Context Number field is the primary key of the Common entity and the foreign key for all the other entities, so that the four parts of the one form can be retrieved together. The system provides, via the Stratigraphic entity, an automated interface between the database and a widely available Harris matrix program.

2.2   Harris Matrix Analysis

A Harris Matrix Diagram is a simple way in which relationships between stratigraphic sections can be viewed on a single diagram, as shown in figure 2. It describes the stratigraphic sequence of the site as found during excavation, no matter how complex the individual sequences may be and helps to clarify the relative chronology. The Bonn Harris Matrix Analysis Program

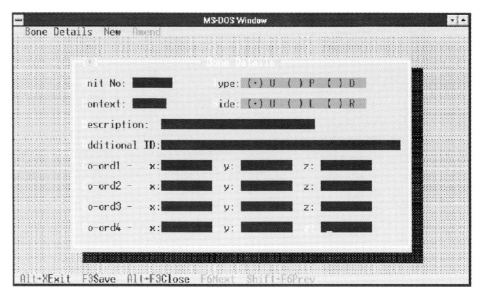

Figure 1. Bone information capture screen.

provides a computer-aided method of stratigraphic analysis (Harris 1989).

The Harris Matrix Program provides a file converter called Harconv. This converts an ASCII file for use by the Harris Matrix program. On choosing this option, the program generates the ASCII file, passes it to Harconv and runs the Harris Matrix program. On start up the Harris Matrix program asks the user for the data set to be used. By entering the name of the file created from file conversion the user will be able to carry out analysis on the data.

3   Visualising the Bones

A substantial number of human bones have been recovered from the site in Malta. There is thus an enormous amount of data that needs to be incorporated within the system. The bone visualisation facilities within the system can be split into three main areas: recording the information about each bone, obtaining analysis details from the user and displaying the results graphically.

There is an individual record within the database for a single bone, identified by a unique bone number. This number is assigned by the archaeologist during data preparation. The details recorded for each bone include:

– Four sets of (x, y, z) coordinates to specify the three dimensional location of the bone with respect to a reference point; and,
– the bone type, side, proximal/distal, additional identification, context, age and method used, sex and method used, measurements, pathology, conservation, related units and any remarks.

In setting up the database the archaeologist is required to enter such details for every bone recovered from the site. Hence a data entry screen with all such fields is presented to the user to enable each bone record to be created. Additional options to assist this process are display, amend and delete. The creation of the full database of bones is expected to be carried out prior to any analysis, as incomplete data may affect the results produced, which in turn could lead to an incorrect assessment of such results. This will, however, be a lengthy process due to the large amount of data.

3.1   OBTAINING ANALYSIS DETAILS

The main body of the system consists of a series of pull-down menus that the user is able to manipulate to enter all the details required for the analysis. The options available for entering data are:

– rotation: enter degree and axis
– scaling: enter 'factor' and 'focus'
– sectioning: enter axis and coordinate value to define partitioning line
– grid squares: indicate whether to add or remove
– bone details: enter new bone type
– bone details: enter bounding coordinates (x_1, y_1, z_1) and (x_2, y_2, z_2) for a particular area

These latter two forms of data entry result in the search for and retrieval of all matching bones from the bones database. The first of the two finds all bones of the specified type, setting up a new temporary data structure in main memory recording bone unit number and the four sets of coordinates for each match. The latter sets up a similar structure for all bones recovered from the specified area. The user is able to enter a maximum of ten types to be used in the analysis at any one time, but only one area can be specified. In addition to entering such data, the user is also able to display and delete bone types, and display the full records (i.e. all relevant details stored in the database of bones) of those bones which satisfy the specifications entered.

A final option offered is to display the site, either the whole site with the bone types specified, or the specified area of the site with all bones recovered from that area. The results of these options are outlined in the following section.

3.2   DISPLAYING THE RESULTS

The three-dimensional visualisation facility of the system uses computer graphics techniques to manipulate the large database of bone finds. The initial display on screen depends on the choices made by the user as outlined in the previous section. Whatever the choice, however, the user is presented with a representation of either the whole or part of the site, containing all relevant bones. At present, the 'whole' site is not actually the whole of the site in Malta, but a specific area of it, namely that enclosed within 98E to 102E, 108N to 114N, and 135.4 m up to 137 m vertically. Thus the representation of the whole site on screen is a cuboid with dimensions $4 \times 6 \times 1.6$ m. Similarly, when only part of the site is displayed, a cuboid of the relevant dimensions is constructed on screen. Such cuboids are labelled with the relevant world coordinates in order to aid analysis and avoid confusion.

The bones within the representation of the whole site are the 4 sets of coordinates from the bones database linked by coloured lines, where each colour represents a different type. A key is displayed on screen to relate these colours to the actual type descriptions. When a particular area is displayed, the bones are again the 4 sets of coordinates linked by lines, but this time no colours are used as there are likely to be too many types displayed on screen to enable a colour coding scheme to be used effectively. Hence, if an area is chosen from which many bones have been recovered, the display is simply a mass of lines on the screen. The only way this display can be improved is to introduce a more sophisticated method of graphical display, such as scanning the bones in or producing a set of accurate illustrations for all possible bones. Then the display would consist of detailed representations of all bones recovered from an area, each of which could be identified by the archaeologist from the shape alone, with perhaps an accompanying list to detail all bones displayed.

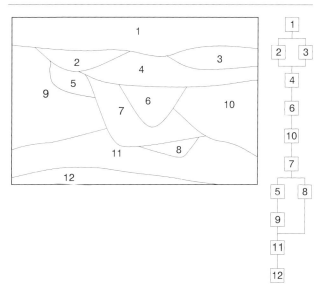

Figure 2. Sample Harris Matrix Analysis.

One of the problems encountered in producing even such simple graphical displays on the screen was the representation of a three-dimensional image in a two dimensional environment. Perspective projection was used in the solution of this problem, as this converts world coordinates into screen points in such a way as to enable the user to perceive depth in a two-dimensional image, namely by displaying distant lines as shorter than lines of the same length that are closer. Perspective projection is achieved by firstly choosing a view reference point (VRP) which is the point from which the site is viewed, and the distance (d) of the object plane away from the viewpoint. These were determined during the design stage of the project to produce images that would represent those seen from an observer located centrally, standing a couple of metres away from the site. Then, for each of the world coordinates (both of the site and the bones) the screen point is calculated by the following algorithm:

– translate the point so the VRP becomes the origin (i.e. subtract VRP from world coordinate);
– set two-dimensional coordinate x to world coordinate x multiplied by d and divided by world coordinate z;
– set two-dimensional coordinate y to world coordinate y multiplied by d and divided by world coordinate z;
– reposition and scale to produce image of required size in required area on screen.

Hidden surfaces also had to be considered in the display of the site and bones: those on the site are displayed as dotted lines on the screen, to prevent any confusion; the bones are sorted before display into order of depth, from those furthest away to those closest, thus any that are hidden will not be seen unless the site is rotated.

In addition to the initial display of the site and bones on screen, facilities to rotate, scale and section the site are available to the user. These use the data entered by the user as in the previous section, and enable the user to view any section of the site from any angle, to any degree of magnification.

The rotation facility enables the user to rotate the site (and all bone types displayed within it) about any axis (x, y or z) by the required degree (1 - 359). The standard rotation equations below were incorporated into the system to produce the rotation effect:

About the x-axis (θ degrees):
$$x' = x$$
$$y' = y\cos(\theta) - z\sin(\theta)$$
$$z' = y\sin(a) + z\cos(a)$$

About the y-axis (θ degrees):
$$x' = x\cos(\theta) + z\sin(\theta)$$
$$y' = y$$
$$z' = z\cos(\theta) - x\sin(\theta)$$

About the z-axis (θ degrees):
$$x' = x\cos(\theta) - y\sin(\theta)$$
$$y' = x\sin(\theta) + y\cos(\theta)$$
$$z' = z$$

The centre of the site was chosen as the most logical coordinate to fix as the point about which to rotate the site. When carrying out the rotation, it is necessary to rotate the world coordinates of the site (including bone types) to produce new world coordinates, which are then converted to points on the screen by perspective projection and scaling.

The scaling facility enables the user to 'zoom in' to the site representation at a particular point to the required magnification. These two pieces of information, referred to as the 'focus' and the 'factor' respectively, are specified by the user as required. The effect is achieved in implementation by:

1. taking the focus to be the origin, thus translating all world coordinates appropriately;
2. scaling all the coordinates by the factor;
3. translating all coordinates so that focus returns to its original position; and finally,
4. converting the world coordinates to screen points as outlined earlier.

A 'zoom out' facility is also provided to the user to reverse any enlargement of the display. This is achieved in implementation by the same procedure as 'zoom in' but with the focus being replaced by its reciprocal.

Finally, the sectioning facility enables the user to divide the site into two separate cuboids by specifying a line to act as the partition (i.e. x = a, y = b, or z = c). Both cuboids are displayed on the screen at the same time, with each occupying half the area used to display the full site. The rotation and scaling facilities are applicable to both representations, though the user is required to specify which cuboid. This is achieved by using the same procedures as outlined earlier, but with two different sets of world coordinates. Clipping is also required for any bones that may cross the boundary line used to partition the site.

4 Future Developments

The system developed so far has proved to be a useful prototype for analysing bone finds from Malta. There are several areas of the system that will be developed in the future to enhance the existing facilities. For example, the visualisation of the site could include some of the natural and cultural features, such as the surrounding rock, and the central stone bowl discovered at the site. These features would aid the archaeologists, as they would be able to incorporate them within their analysis of the site. The graphics display of the bones could also be improved to provide a more detailed and accurate illustration of bones recovered. The Archaeology Department would also like to see some statistical displays as part of the system – e.g. all femurs, skulls, etc. found within a certain area plotted on a histogram.

references

Evans, D.J.   1971   *The prehistoric antiquities of the Maltese islands*. London: The Athlone Press.

Harris, E.C.   1989   *Principles of Archaeological Stratigraphy*. New York and London: Academic Press.

Malone, C.A.T.   1986   *Exchange systems and style in the Central Mediterranean*. PhD thesis, University of Cambridge.

Malone, C.A.T.   1988   A house for temple builders: recent investigations on Gozo, Malta, *Antiquity* 62, 297-301.
   S.K.F. Stoddart
   D. Trump

Stoddart, S.K.F.   1993   Cult in an island society: Prehistoric Malta in the Tarxien period, *Cambridge Archaeo-logical Journal* 3 (1), 3-19.
   A. Bonanno
   T. Gouder
   C. Malone
   D. Trump

Alaine Lamprell
Anthea Salisbury
Alan Chalmers
Department of Computer Science
University of Bristol
Bristol BS8 1TR
United Kingdom
e-mail: alan@compsci.bristol.ac.uk

Simon Stoddart
Department of Classics & Archaeology
University of Bristol
Bristol BS8 1TR
United Kingdom
e-mail: s.k.stoddart@bristol.ac.uk

Jon Holmen
Espen Uleberg

The National Documentation Project of Norway – the Archaeological sub-project

1   Introduction

The National Documentation Project of Norway is a cooperative project between the Faculties of Art in the Norwegian universities, and is now in its fourth year. The main purpose of the project is to convert information from paper based archives to electronically readable media in order to make the archives more accessible. The project has been working with what can be called the 'collection departments', like the Department of Lexicography, the Department of Folk Music and the university museums with Archaeological and Numismatic collections. The aim is to create a national database for language and culture, where it will be possible to do multidisciplinary studies, combining material from all Norwegian universities.

2   Project organization

The project has its base at the University of Oslo. It uses hand-picked, previously unemployed persons to convert the information (Ore 1995: 278). The workforce is organized in a number of small groups in southern Norway, and four larger groups in northern Norway. The different groups are assigned to different part projects. The people converting the archaeological data do not necessarily have any previous experience with archaeology, but through supervision they are given sufficient education to be able to perform the required text analyses and encoding.

The aim is to create a system that integrates information from several disciplines. Because of this, it is not sufficient to create computerized versions of today's archives. One of the most important aspects when building such a data model, is to have a fruitful dialogue between programmers and professionals in the different disciplines. There is of course no one solution as to how this system should be made, but it is vital that the system is not dramatically different from what is in use today. The cooperating institutes need systems that they feel comfortable with, so that the computerized versions will be of use and will be used by all staff members.

3   Using the data

The resultant information will eventually be more readily accessible to researchers, students, people working with Cultural Resource Management and the general public. Information from the different sections of the project will be combined, so that studies concentrating on a certain area will retrieve information from all the different sources. These sources, (fig. 1) Archaeology, Runes, Old Norse, Modern Norwegian, Dialects, Syntax/semantics, Place names, Folklore and Folk Music will all be connected through the variables Time, Location and Word. This will be accessible for enquiries from Government Planning Agencies, Norwegian Archaeological Authorities, the National Archives, people interested in local history, the Norwegian Mapping Authority, and the Norwegian Language Council. It will be useful in connection with dictionary production, as a writing assisting tool and for primary education.

Combining these sources with an incremental database structure, the system makes it possible to look at an area in a time perspective (fig. 2). Textual information is combined with drawings, photos, maps and sounds to create a Geographical Information System which will eventually include all of Norway. It will be possible to make queries about language development, place names and archaeo-logical sites and finds. The potential inherent in the combination of different sources is especially useful to synthesizing disciplines like archaeology and history.

4   The archaeological sections of the Documentation Project

Norway has five archaeological museums. They are situated in Oslo, Bergen, Trondheim, Tromsø and Stavanger, and with the exception of the latter, all are university museums. Norway does not have a central museum, although the museum in Oslo tends to take a leading role, being situated in the capital. All five museums started as private collections and gradually developed into regional museums. Each museum has a collection of items from its own district. However, previously the geographical division between the museums was not so rigid, resulting in the different museums having artefacts from other museum districts. This means that it is necessary to combine information from all museums to get as complete a picture as possible of the known artefacts.

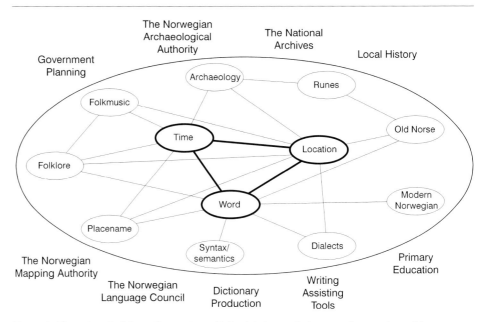

Figure 1. The university information system with its data types, their connections and possible use. (After Ore 1995: 278).

Comprehensive archaeological surveying has been conducted by the Land Use Mapping Agency based at the archaeological museums since 1963 (Larsen 1990: 48). Through this, large parts of the country have already been surveyed. All the resultant information from Oslo university museum, Oldsaksamlingen's district is now stored on computer in a 'free text' database called SIFT (Boaz/Uleberg 1993: 178-179).

The archaeological sections of the Documentation Project are presently limited to the universities in Oslo, Bergen and Tromsø. Work in Bergen started with converting information on sites, and is continuing with the artefact catalogues. Tromsø has just started, beginning with the artefact catalogues. At the Oslo university museum, the Oldsaksamlingen, the work within the Documentation Project started with conversion of information related to archaeological sites. Since 1993, it has also focused on the artefact catalogues. The artefact catalogues have been converted to machine readable format, and Standard General Markup Language (SGML) is used as a tool to make them more readily accessible.

5   Ongoing Projects

In addition to the work with the existing archives, the Documentation Project cooperates with ongoing rescue excavation projects. At the moment we are actively collaborating with three projects. One of which has mainly Stone Age excavations, one with Bronze Age/Iron Age

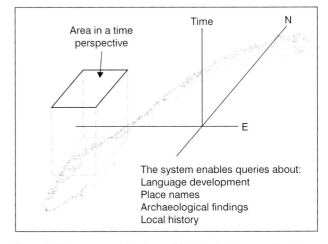

Figure 2. The system makes it possible to look at an area in a time perspective. (After Ore 1995: 281).

excavations, and one is an excavation in a Medieaval town.

Materials from the Stone Age excavations offered the possibility to develop a Geographical Information System to be used on a small scale – to study the artefact spread within one site.

The Bronze/Iron Age excavations gave us a possibility to develop systems to increase the accuracy and efficiency when exposing large areas, and the Medieval town gave the entanglements of a multilayer site. The methods developed, allows the excavator to have a constant overview over the different structures that are found, both by viewing them on screen, and by printing out distribution plots.

Perhaps the most important aspect is that the data capturing devices that are in use during the excavation make it possible to use the information immediately during the excavation and not just in the final stages of analysis. In addition, the preparation of the final reports can be conducted much more efficiently when the complete data are readily at hand at the end of the field season.

6   The database model

The conceptual model of the database is object oriented, and consists of a number of different relational bases. The concept of an event is a crucial element in the model. An event has been defined as 'something that takes place in time and space, perhaps on account of 'someone' or 'something'' (Rold 1993: 215). There are basically two types of events: internal and external. In this context, all internal events takes place at the museum, external ones out in the field. Internal events include cataloguing, conservation work, etc. Examples of external events are surveying, describing and excavating sites.

The event allows us to make the system incremental, adding a historical depth to the database. It is not a relational database with only the updated information. Every time an action is undertaken, there will be information added to the base. All events will create documents such as artefact catalogues, excavation reports, plan- and profile drawings, photographs, surveying reports and test results. The documents will be in the form of free text, hypertext, bitmap files, scanned documents and pictures. All events will be connected to either an artefact, a site or both. The event makes it possible to retain the information from the original cataloguing as well as incorporating the information from magazine revisions and researcher's special studies on selected artefacts.

All original names are kept when transferring the original artefact descriptions. This means that there will be outdated names on artefacts as well as on places. Lengthy discussions commonly surround the terminology of artefacts. We have avoided this discussion, and will later add standardized artefact names on a higher level, using a meta-language to select for all objects of a particular type, originally given different names in the catalogue. The meta-language will interpret the data without changing the original data (Rold 1993: 218). This will solve problems in cases where old and new terms define the same artefact classes. However, in cases where there is only partial overlap, where one old type now is defined as several new

ones, the database will not give precise answers to a query. This situation will gradually be resolved in the future as researchers reclassify these artefacts, and their results are added to the base.

Standard General Markup Language (SGML) is used as a tool to make the converted texts more readily accessible. The SGML is based on formatting a text through adding tags showing the type of information following the tag. In the archaeological artefact catalogues, there are tags for location, material type, artefact type, decoration, dating, and so on. This makes it easier and faster to search in a text, and it also creates a link between a relational database and the free text. In this way, the SGML is a means for structuring a text. One might say that while a database is putting text into tables, SGML is putting a table on a text. The text structure is outlined in a Data Type Description (DTD).

Since a number of different people have written the catalogues at the museum, there are at least as many text structures. A very tight SGML system will give ample opportunity to check that the text is consistent with the DTD, but it will not be possible to incorporate all texts. A system that covers all possible types of text structures, will have become so loose that it is not a structure any more. The final DTD must be somewhere in between these two possibilities.

7   Geographical information

The relation between an artefact and a place needs special consideration in two ways. First, we have to know the present-day equivalent of the old place name, since the original catalogue texts are always used. A problem arises because boundaries between administrative units have changed, and in many cases objects do not have an exact provenance. Because of this, every place name must be associated with a chronological date, indicating what geographical area is covered by that place name.

Secondly, we must decide what to do with artefacts without an exact provenance — perhaps only the parish, county or even just the country is known. One solution is to let the artefact's position be a point somewhere within an area corresponding with the most accurate provenance data. When looking for artefacts from a smaller area, like a group of farms, there is a possibility that artefacts only related to a larger area, like the county, could actually come from that smaller area. Therefore, one must also be able to search for artefacts with a possible provenance within a specified area. This means, that an artefact that cannot be attributed with certainty, should have a geographical location as a point included in a surface area. When users search for artefacts from a certain geographical area, they should obviously retrieve all artefacts where the area of the artefact coincides with or is contained within the search area. In addition, they should also retrieve the artefacts where the search area is contained within the artefact area, as well as the artefacts whose area intersects with the search area.

8   Conclusion

The National Documentation Project creates a system where databases from different institutions can communicate through the Internet, forming a national database for language and culture. A user will be able to access a client section which will be designed according to the users' needs and use privileges. The databases can be aware of each other, send queries according to a predefined protocol, and interpret the resulting data according to the predefined data models.

The system will allow individual users to create their own interfaces. One such interface can be created in connection with the preparation of an exhibition. Information from different archives related to the exhibited items can be put together in an application running in the exhibition rooms.

There are three major assets of the National Documentation Project of Norway. Firstly, it is an effective system for converting large amounts of data in a relatively short time. Secondly, it promotes a dialogue which is vitally important between system developers and professionals from different disciplines. This ensures the development of effective systems that are sufficiently familiar to be used by all staff members.

A third and final aspect is the increased availability of vast amounts of data. This opens up possibilities, not only for researchers and students, but also for teachers and for the interested public. Most people want to know their local history and what is found at or near their homes. The day is soon at hand when an interested member of the public can turn to the computer in their library to obtain access to information concerning them.

references

Boaz, J.S.
  E. Uleberg
1993   Gardermoen Project – Use of a GIS system in antiquities registration and research. In: J. Andresen/T. Madsen/I. Scollar (eds), *Computing the Past, Computer Applications and Quantitative Methods in Archaeology CAA92*, 177-182, Aarhus: Aarhus University Press.

Larsen, J.H.
1990   *Om desimering av våre fornminner. Noen resultater av arbeidet med registrering av fornminner for det Økonomiske kartverket i 1980-årene.* Universitetets Oldsaksamlings Årbok 1989/1990:47-60.

Ore, C.E.
1995   Making an Information System for the Humanities, *Computers and the Humanities* 28, 277-282.

Rold, L.
1993   Syntheses in object oriented analyses. In: J. Andresen/T. Madsen/I. Scollar (eds), *Computing the Past, Computer Applications and Quantitative Methods in Archaeology CAA92*, 213-220, Aarhus: Aarhus University Press.

Jon Holmen and Espen Uleberg
The Documentation Project
Faculty of Arts
University of Oslo
P.O. Box 1102
Blindern
0317 Oslo
Norway
e-mail: jon.holmen@dokpro.uio.no
        espen.uleberg@iakn.uio.no

Irina Oberländer-
Târnoveanu

Statistical view of the Archaeological Sites Database

1 Introduction

When CIMEC — Information Centre for Culture and Heritage — initiated a database for sites and monuments in 1992, using existing lists in order to gather, within a short time, a core of information regarding our immovable heritage, the attempt raised a chorus of 'don't do it', accompanied by arguments such as: 'not enough information', 'wrong information', 'wait until a site form will be designed', 'there are other institutions more capable of creating a national record'.

We nevertheless proceeded. We had ten years experience with the National Database of movable heritage — over 700,000 records — and seriously needed to have references for the field 'place of discovery'. The Ministry of Culture agreed to finance our project. In the last three years, while various commissions debated over a site card — with no final conclusions yet — while the organisations and people responsible for the monuments changed several times and the law for the protection of cultural heritage is still being debated — we recorded the existing information regarding the sites and monuments proposed for protection, using a core data standard. Thus, with modest resources and much perseverance, we have sofar gathered over 16,600 records which are proving to be a valuable source of information. And a reason for the Ministry of Culture to decide this year to finance the expansion of the initial project at CIMEC. It would seem therefore that we were right to proceed, instead of to wait.

2 The source of information: from paper list to computer record

The Romanian Archaeological Sites and Monuments Database has 3,900 records of sites and 12,700 records of monuments proposed for protection. The main source of information — a national list compiled manually in 1991 by the Historical Assemblies, Monuments and Sites Direction (DMASI) — still remains to be checked and updated and no new list has been forthcomimg for the last four years.

The formal distinction between a 'site' and a 'monument' was based on the position — under or above ground level, on the chronological period — 'monuments' are mostly late medieval and modern, while 'sites' are prehistoric to early

medieval, and on its condition — ruined versus roofed over. We maintained this formal grouping of the list, as is traditional in Romania. There is also a special chapter for buildings with a memorial value — very confusing in fact, as there are many buildings with both an architectural and a memorial value.

Because the list we used to record the information from was often ambiguous, both in content and in form, as well as difficult to read, we had to analyse, check with other sources and interpret the information.

Descriptive information regarding location, period and finds was separated into multiple fields but the data content still requires improvement. We also tried to normalise the terminology by compiling terminology lists for periods, cultures and site types. The present information in the database therefore closely follows that in the list, while being much more structured and thus suitable for analysis.

The list of protected sites and monuments was based on proposals sent in by county museums. The list is richer for those counties where archaeological excavations have a longer tradition and were a significant number of archaeologists are involved in the area (around the university centres, such as Cluj and Iaşi, for instance, or in Dobroudja). We had no information regarding archaeological sites in Bucharest and consequently, our statistical data will not include Bucharest. Although there will certainly be archaeological areas underrepresented, the selection is a sample of present knowledge in the field. Only a systematic survey will bring more light in the future. Part of the recorded sites are not excavated and there is no guarantee that the periods and the site types indicated for them are correct.

Nevertheless, for the first time, we have a core of data for analysis. We have tried to look at the distribution of sites by period, archaeological culture, site type and location. Our software is Paradox 4.0 (Borland) on PC.

3 Statistical view of the database

Statistical analysis is very exciting for the researcher. As soon a number of records have been gathered, the temptation to try various ways of sorting, counting and grouping is overwhelming. First, you get hundreds of data from thousands of records. Very interesting, but still

Table 1. The distribution of sites by location.

region		%	number of sites
Moldavia	(eastern part of the country, 19.4% of the territory)	16	654
Dobroudja	(southeastern part, 6.5%)	14	550
Walachia	(southern part, excluding Bucharest city, 19.8%)	19	755
Oltenia	(southern part, 12.3%)	8	334
Banat	(southwestern part, 7.2%)	6	225
Transylvania	(central part, 23.9%)	32	1,278
Crişana & Maramureş	(northwestern and northern parts, 10.9%)	5	193

difficult to follow or to graph them. Then, you realize that you have to group the information in larger classes in order to make some sense out of it:

– administrative divisions (40 counties), in historical regions (8);
– site types, in categories (for instance, various types of settlements grouped as 'settlement');
– various periods and archaeological cultures, in larger chronological divisions.

During this preliminary processing, you must take care not to alter the basic information through artificial grouping. Yet, you realize that if you want to identify dominant features or trends by periods or geographical areas that you should ignore low frequency data (site types mentioned only once in a period and county, for instance) and establish a limit beyond which you consider the data for comparison.

As much as you find the figures obtained fascinating, they are boring for a reader, the more so if he or she hardly knows the geography or the history of the territory. I therefore want to present fewer figures and more what they said to me.

3.1 GENERAL VIEW
The database contains 3,900 site locations. Among them, 63% are declared single-level sites while 37% are complex, multilevel sites. Among the two thirds of sites identified by only one period or site type, future research will certainly reveal more complex situations.

The entity 'site' is defined by place, site type and period. For 3,900 locations, we entered over 4,500 records of site types, 6,000 records for periods and 4,800 records for archaeological cultures. For each record we have entered location (county, town/village, place, location details), single or complex site, site type, name, period, culture, date, finds, and references.

3.2 THE DISTRIBUTION OF SITES BY LOCATION
The distribution of the sites by location is shown in table 1 and figure 1. Central and southeast Romania — that

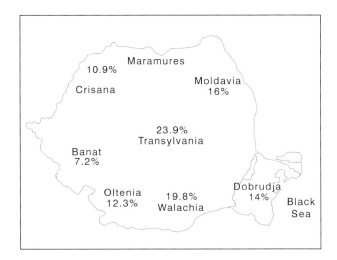

Figure 1. Distribution of sites by region.

is, Transylvania and Dobroudja — have the highest site density related to their surface. The density of the sites in those areas indicates a long tradition of habitation due to geographical and environmental conditions.

The counties with the largest number of sites (over 100) are, in descending order: Cluj (325), Constanţa (288), Tulcea (262), Dâmboviţa (217), Bistriţa-Năsăud (190), Iaşi (184), Sălaj (168), Caraş-Severin (128), Buzău (124), Prahova (120), Mureş (114).

The high number of sites for a single period in a county can show the dominant archaeological feature of that area. For the Roman Period, the greatest number of sites is in the area of the former Province of Dacia (Cluj county – 124 Roman sites on a surface of 6,650 square km; Bistriţa-Năsăud – 92 Roman sites etc.) and in the former province of Moesia Inferior and Scythia Minor (Tulcea county – 121 Roman sites and Constanţa county, 118 sites for the same period). For the Medieval Period, the area around the former capital of Moldavia, Iaşi, has the highest number of protected medieval sites – 94. For the Bronze Age, Dâmboviţa county has 83 sites.

Table 2. The distribution of sites by period.

period	until	%	number of sites
Prehistoric Period including Palaeolithic			
Neolithic, Bronze Age, Hallstatt	the 5th c. B.C.	40	2,546
Palaeolithic	6 millennium BC	1	69
Neolithic	2nd millennium BC	12	766
Bronze Age	12th century BC	14	869
Hallstatt	6 - 5th century BC	12	767
Greek	7th c. BC-1 c. AD, Dobroudja	1	40
La Tène	4th c. BC-1 c. AD	13	1,312
Roman Period	1st-late 3rd/ 4th c. AD	21	1,312
Early Byzantine and Migrations period	4th-12th c.	9	572
Medieval	13th-late 18th c.	16	1,053
Various periods	uncertain	1	63

With the exception of the Neolithic Period and the end of the La Tène (2nd-1st centuries BC), during all the periods the greatest density of human remains were found in the hill areas, on both sides of the Carpathians Mountains.

3.3   THE DISTRIBUTION OF SITES BY PERIOD
The distribution of the sites by period is given in table 2 and figure 2. Of the prehistoric archaeological culture, in descending order of frequency, more than half are Geto-Dacian sites (53%), followed by the great Neolithic cultures of Cucuteni (14%), Gumelniţa (5%) and Starčevo-Criş (3%), which represent together 21% of the sites with a known culture. The Bronze Age culture has 19%: Monteoru (5%), Noua (5%), Suciu de Sus (5%), Tei (4%).

3.4   SITES BY PERIOD AND BY REGION
The *Palaeolithic* is best represented in Northern Moldavia: (Iaşi 9 sites and Botoşani 2), the Southwest (Hunedoara 7 and Timis 5) and the South Carpathian Hill Region (Vâlcea 5, Argeş 4, Gorj 3).
The *Neolithic Period* — more evenly spread: (Cluj 70, Iaşi 69, Vrancea 35, Botoşani 32, Buzău 32, Giurgiu 31).
The *Bronze Age*: (Dâmboviţa 103, Cluj 60, Maramureş 53, Buzău 52, Sălaj 46, Vrancea 36, Vâlcea 34).
Hallstatt: (Bistriţa-Năsăud 51, Iaşi 42, Cluj 31, Buzău 30, Vâlcea 26).
La Tène: (Iaşi 98, Tulcea 57, Călăraşi 46, Bistriţa-Năsăud 42, Vâlcea 41).
The Roman Period: (Cluj 124, Tulcea 141, Constanţa 132, Bistriţa-Năsăud 92, Sălaj 67, Caraş-Severin 58, Mureş, Sibiu, Vâlcea).
The *Medieval Period*: (Iaşi 154, Dambovita 53, Constanţa 49, Tulcea 66).
    The high number of archaeological sites in an area is in part a sign of demographic growth for a certain period but also a consequence of the continuous movement of the

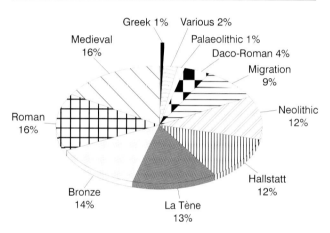

Figure 2. Distribution of sites by period.

population over a territory, a phenomenon encountered from Prehistoric times until the Early Middle Ages. Some of the sites are temporary settlements.

3.5   SITES BY SITE TYPE
The settlements represent about two thirds of the number of sites (60%), followed by cemeteries (15%) (fig. 3). The number of settlements could be inflated due also to the fact that any uncertain site is often classified as 'settlement'. Also the fortifications which appeared as early as the Neolithic Period, and became significant in the Bronze Age, built as they were on high peaks and with complicated defence systems, led archaeologists to classify them as a 'fortress' rather than as a 'settlement' or fortified settlement. The sites designated as fortresses cover 8% of the sites. We also found over 90 records for barrow areas, period not indicated.

Table 3. Site types by period. In brackets number of sites.

	Neolithic	Bronze Age	periods Hallstatt	La Tène	Roman	Medieval
settlements	84% (530)	83% (724)	71% (334)	74% (650)	50% (528)	59% (620)
occupation layers	6% (39)					
Tell	4%					
fortifications	2% (26)	3% (24)	8% (33)	12% (109)	24% (254)	16% (164)
cemeteries	2% (15)	8% (68)	11% (52)	8% (73)	8% (90)	11% (120)
mines				1% (1)	1% (3)	
salt mines	1% (2)					
vestiges	10% (6)					
isolated burials		<1% (3)				
isolated structures				1% (1)	% (88)	8% (84)
undetermined		6% (54)	10% (49)	5% (40)	9% (99)	6% (69)

3.6 SITES BY SITE TYPE AND BY LOCATION

I wanted to look at the distribution of the main site types by county, taking into consideration only the counties with more than ten sites of the same type. The settlements Iaşi, Dâmboviţa, Bistriţa-Năsăud, Buzău, Giurgiu, Prahova, Tulcea, and Vâlcea have the highest number of locations, in hill areas and along river valleys. Areas undergoing frequent movements of populations have also a large number of barrows, cemeteries, and isolated burials: Buzău, Cluj, Tulcea, Constanţa, Prahova, and Caras-Severin. In the border areas — along the Danube —, in Tulcea and Constanţa, along the Carpathian Mountains, on the Transylvanian side — Harghita and Covasna, and at the Northern border of Dacia — Cluj and Bistriţa-Năsăud, the number of fortifications is the highest.

3.7 SITES BY SITE TYPE AND BY PERIOD

Site types by period show more or less the same characteristics, with a greater variety of site types for the Roman and Medieval Periods, when the social structure and economic activity became more complex (table 3).

4 Conclusions

A statistical analysis of the distribution of sites can reveal the degree to which the protection list properly reflects the field reality, and is not a subjective personal selection.

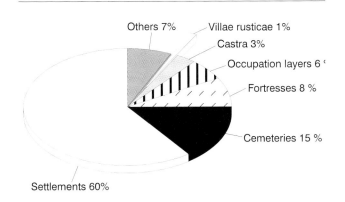

Figure 3. Distribution of sites by categories.

It clearly indicates the need for a systematic survey, with modern investigation methods, for the proper recording of the sites to be protected. Until then, we can try to find further answers to our questions through statistics.

Irina Oberländer-Târnoveanu
CIMEC - Centrul de Informatică şi Memorie Culturală
Piata Presei Libere 1
71 341 Bucharest
Romania
e-mail: Irina@cimec.sfos.ro

Nigel D. Clubb
Neil A.R. Lang

A Strategic Appraisal of Information Systems for Archaeology and Architecture in England – Past, Present and Future

1 Introduction

The growth of the available literature on sites and monuments records in central and local government in England has been notable, especially in publications arising from CAA. These contributions have mainly been submitted from the perspective of one of the three major interested parties, in local government, the county sites and monuments records (SMRs) and in central government, English Heritage (EH), as the national body concerned with conservation management, and the Royal Commission on the Historical Monuments of England (RCHME) as the national body of survey, record and dissemination. While these papers have made valuable inputs to the development of information systems, and have made reference to the links between systems, a published strategic overview of their inter-relationships, both in theory and in practice, has been lacking.

In a European and international context, the heritage record systems in England can appear confusing. This paper attempts to address the current synergy between these local and national bodies. It examines advancement in the context of the current initiative of the government's organ of heritage policy, the Department of National Heritage, to coordinate certain aspects of the operation of national heritage records, particularly in relation to records of statutory protected buildings. The paper also makes reference to progress made in developing national, European and international coordination of data standards. Our discussion will be measured against the likely future potential of the technology and the future requirements for providing access to information including the needs of conservation management.

In a provocative paper delivered to the CAA conference in 1994, Booth argued that archaeology had 'missed out' on the information age (Booth 1995b). He suggested that, despite the extensive use of information technology in a wide number of application areas within the heritage community — museums, cultural resource management, excavation and survey — this has not extended to the major media of dissemination. He concluded that this lack of dissemination through digital techniques risks making archaeology and, by implication, the built heritage, more marginal than it presently is in the public consciousness, reducing the potential for public participation in the heritage, because of a general failure to embrace electronic means of presenting information, whether as text, images or sound.

Although Booth's argument was not exclusively directed towards monument records systems, these were included in some detail as part of his review. It is therefore a pertinent component of his paper and one to which we shall return. To commence, we present a model of the information relationships between the various heritage bodies and related functions in England at the levels of policy, data and function. We then look in detail at the historical inter-relationships of these systems, and finally assess progress towards an idealised model and the extent to which these heritage information systems have transcended Booth's thesis. The paper also presents a new and comprehensive bibliography of the available literature on monuments records in England.

2 Information Frameworks in England

Figure 1 provides a model of the current policy frameworks within which the three principal heritage information systems operate. This functional model reflects the policy roles of the Department of the Environment (DoE) and the Department of National Heritage (DNH) and the executive functions of EH and RCHME. The DoE is responsible for setting planning policy for both central and local government and does not itself create heritage information. It does, however, manage records at a regional level. The DNH is responsible for heritage policy. This is subsequently executed by English Heritage (EH) for conservation management, and by the RCHME through its role in surveying, recording and disseminating information. Within local government, conservation and record functions for archaeology operate mainly at the county level and for the built heritage, primarily at a more local, district level. The current review of local government in England (1994-1995) is set to create further urban, and some rural unitary (single tier) authorities, augmenting the urban unitary authorities set up in the local government review of 1985/1986. To some extent, this will erode the current two tier

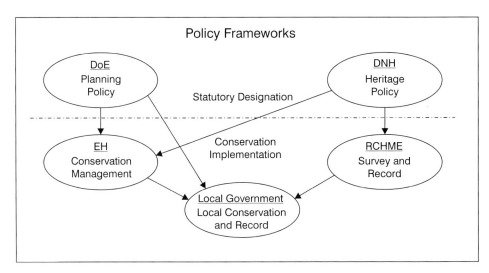

Figure 1. Policy Frameworks.

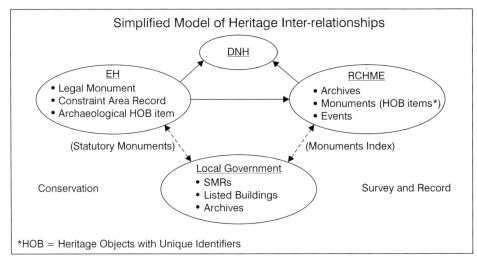

Figure 2. Simplified model of heritage inter-relationships.

system of local government comprised of counties and districts.

Figure 2 illustrates in summary form the principal data relationships between the information systems of the main holders of heritage information. EH information systems are oriented towards the automation of the conservation processes, including statutory protection and casework and RCHME systems towards the automation of recording, curation and dissemination processes. In local government are the county SMRs, complemented by records of historic buildings, largely held at district level for management purposes. In central government, EH is the government's adviser on designation for statutory protection, and RCHME

the national body of survey, record and dissemination. These three records systems share several common interests in recording information on the historic environment and also have interests related to the functions of the host body.

The EH records system (mainly comprising statutory and management records) and the RCHME National Monuments Record MONARCH database (which includes both statutory and non-statutory records and associated data and archive for dissemination) have in common the concept of a 'heritage object', providing a close intellectual link between them. The National Monuments Record (NMR) of the RCHME and local SMRs are less formally connected, but a model (unpublished) agreement forged in September

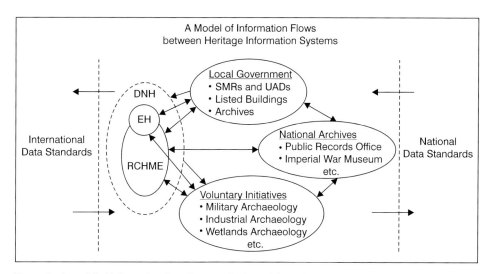

Figure 3. A model of information flows between heritage information systems.

1994 provides for the exchange of information between the two bodies at the level of a core index. This provides for information on the location, period, site type, form, condition and a basic reference for the site or monument. At a national level, it will provide the means to concord information on a thematic basis, and identify gaps in both local and national records. At a local level, it will ensure that all information on sites is registered as a constraint within the local planning process by SMRs.

A model of the information flows between the principal heritage information bodies is given in figure 3. At a national level, the combined records of RCHME (including its SMRs index), EH and DNH comprise the national heritage data set. Within local government, other, sometimes more detailed records are held primarily for the implementation of local management. Both interface with archives held locally (through County Archive Services) and nationally (for example, through the Public Record Office). Partly outside of this framework of public administration, there are also a growing number of 'voluntary' initiatives creating substantial databases concentrating on a theme, period or region. Many of these have received support in kind or through grant aid from the DNH, EH and RCHME. Each of these bodies contributes, in some respect, to the development of data standards, though contributions to international standards initiatives have tended to come almost exclusively from central government.

The next four sections of the paper look in more detail at the development of systems in local government, and RCHME and at the operation and impact of the Department of National Heritage at the policy level.

3   Sites and Monuments Records in local government

The English system of SMRs held in local government are unusual in a European context, where the norm is for unitary national records (see for example Hansen 1993). The situation has recently been further complicated by the development of SMRs at a district level, and by the creation of Urban Archaeological Databases, centred on the 30 or so most important historic urban centres in the country (EH 1992b).

While local government SMRs have benefited from a considerable degree of central government funding, they have maintained a singular independence, expressed both at the level of their national body, the Association of County Archaeological Officers (ACAO) and through the individual constitutional status of their host bodies.

Local government SMRs are a discretionary function of local government. The first were established as manual systems in the late 1960s (Benson 1974). The development of local sites and monuments records in the last 21 years has been an impressive phenomenon, in parallel with the growth of the RCHME National Monuments Record (see below). In 1973, when ACAO was first set up, there were just 5 members, and only one county had considered a programme of computerisation of its SMR records. The nearest equivalent to a national archaeological record at that time was the index records and maps held by the Archaeology Division of the Ordnance Survey, Britain's National Mapping Agency, which was then an entirely manual system. All SMRs in England have to some extent been founded on this card index, which was transferred to the RCHME in 1983.

Despite these modest origins, the importance and potential of local SMR record systems was recognised from an early date. In 1974, a working party on archaeological records was set up by the Council for British Archaeology, at the request of RCHME, which published a joint report in 1975 (CBA 1975). While this did not lead to the adoption of the common standards which many had hoped for, it did make the important distinction between the compilation of 'intensive' and 'non-intensive' records at national and local levels, and this has been influential in the development of records ever since.

The Survey of Surveys, undertaken by the RCHME in 1978 (RCHME 1978) urged the establishment of compatibility and standardisation of local records, a theme to which we shall return. It noted the extent of non-conformity, but recommended that 'County-based sites and monuments records should be the major, detailed archive for their areas'.

The significant investment in the development of computerised SMRs in the mid 1980s by EH, in part to assist its Monuments Protection Programme, built rapidly on these earlier foundations and helped to create the information base and architecture of 'cultural resource management' in English local government as we know it today.

In 1989, the RCHME was given the task of coordinating local SMRs, a responsibility confirmed in its new Royal Warrant of 1992. It has assisted developments through the production of joint data standards (RCHME 1993b), a review of SMRs (RCHME 1993a), and the development of the MONARCH for SMRs product, which is currently being piloted in four sites, and is likely to be used by at least a quarter of the SMRs in England.

4 English Heritage – the national conservation body

4.1 BACKGROUND

English Heritage (EH) is sponsored by the governments Department of National Heritage (DNH) to undertake statutory responsibility for preserving England's architectural and archaeological heritage and for encouraging the enjoyment of the historic environment. It advises the government on statutory protection such as the scheduling of monuments and the listing of buildings and gives grants towards conservation generally. It manages and markets nearly 400 historic properties in the care of the state, including world-famous sites such as Stonehenge, parts of Hadrian's Wall and the Iron Bridge at Coalbrookdale. Many of the records it creates for operational purposes also form part of the permanent public national archive curated within the NMR of the RCHME.

EH was established in 1986 and most of the functions assumed at that date had been undertaken previously by the Department of the Environment. There has been a long tradition of heritage computing within the Department and EH, including applications for scientific analysis (for example see Jones *et al.* 1980) and archaeological excavation and other investigations (Hinchcliffe/Jefferies 1985; Jefferies 1977), but this paper concentrates on information systems which support monument records. The key areas are the scheduling of monuments and listing of buildings with their associated processes and spatial and graphic requirements.

4.2 SCHEDULING OF MONUMENTS

The history of the DoE/EH record of scheduled monuments is described in Booth 1988a. Computerisation began in 1980, using a suite of programmes originally developed for recording excavations and known subsequently as 'Version 1 Software'. By 1984, facilities for on-line data entry, editing and interrogation were required and Southdata's Superfile package was selected. From 1986, EH began to plan an enhanced programme of scheduling known as the Monuments Protection Programme (Darvill *et al.* 1987). It became evident that the record would no longer be a relatively static Inventory of monuments and that a new system would be required to manage the data and to automate much of the scheduling process (involving among other things the writing of around 50 letters for each of the monuments scheduled), and to provide a dynamic system for the management of monuments. The system, known as the Record of Scheduled Monuments (RSM) was designed during 1986-1989 and implemented for the automation of the scheduling process in 1991 (Clubb 1991a, 1991b; Clubb/Startin 1995).

Also in preparation for MPP, EH implemented in 1987 a computer mapping system providing for the management of 6,000 'raster' images of Ordnance Survey maps of England and the vectorised outlines or constraint areas of monuments (Clubb 1988). This system has fulfilled every expectation, but is now (1995) looking old-fashioned in its functionality and is reaching the end of its useful life.

4.3 LISTING OF HISTORIC BUILDINGS

The computerisation of listed buildings has a different history. Problems in securing funding for the computerisation of listed buildings records (Clubb 1995) led to the introduction of a partial interim solution to support the listing process within EH (Clubb/White 1990). Following a review of the cycles of activity and flows of data relating to the listing process, a Clipper compiled version of dBASE was established for the processing of listed buildings recommendations to DNH since 1990, but this holds merely a small proportion of the total number of buildings listed. The mapped representation of listed buildings at a national level has remained as a manual system.

The first strategic review of information systems within EH took place in 1991-1992 (for details see Clubb/Startin 1995) and confirmed at a corporate level some of the concepts developed in the RSM, particularly the relationships between the monument and building records and their associated procedures and case-work and the requirement for flows of information from and to other bodies, including DNH, RCHME and local SMRs. It is understood that subsequent strategic analysis at EH has focused on the requirements for spatial and geographic information and on detailed data modelling and definitions.

A major achievement of EH activity on monument records has been the development of the complex model which embraces archaeological items, monuments as legally defined and areas of land (constraint areas) which do not necessarily have a one to one relationship (fig. 2 above). These have different attributes associated with them and different management implications.

5   Royal Commission on the Historical Monuments of England – the national body of Survey, Record and Dissemination

RCHME is also sponsored by DNH and was established in 1908 to investigate and report on the historical monuments of England (prior to 1992, it was sponsored by DoE). Its record and archive functions have expanded in recent years with the assumption of responsibility for the National Buildings Record (1963), the archaeological records section of the Ordnance Survey (1983) and the national library of air photographs (1984), all now managed and disseminated within the unified National Monuments Record (NMR). The NMR also provides an access point for certain records created by EH in the course of its operations. The first major computer implementation was the archaeological record from 1984, as the permanent national public database for buildings and monuments (Aberg/Leech 1992; Beagrie 1993; Grant 1985; Hart/Leech 1989; Lang 1995).

A strategic review of requirements was carried out in 1990 and this recommended the development of a unified data-base to replace the original archaeological data-base and a number of other archaeological and architectural data-bases, again using Oracle. The new system (MONARCH) was developed in 1991-1992 and implemented in 1993 (Beagrie 1993). However, its major contribution to the development of monument records is undoubtedly the analysis and implementation of the complex model which relates monument records, activities/event records, archive and bibliographic recording and the roles of individuals and institutions (fig. 2 above). Two other significant advances are the development of a sophisticated thesaurus module

and a general enquiry mechanism which provides powerful retrieval facilities to individuals with little or no programming experience. Recent strategic analysis within RCHME has focused on the requirements for spatial and geographic systems, in parallel with similar EH initiatives.

In 1989, government gave RCHME a lead role for the coordination of local SMRs in England (RCHME 1990b). In 1993 RCHME published a review of local SMRs (RCHME 1993a) which seeks to establish a new partnership between local records and the national record.

It is worth considering here the degree of co-operation achieved by RCHME and EH to date. As stated above, both organisations recognise the concept of the 'heritage object', an entity which may have a one-to-many or a many-to-one relationship with physical space (such as constraint areas or land parcels) which is at the heart of their information systems. Both also agree on the concept of 'core' data, a sub-set of the record system defining type, location, status and source authority ('references') for monuments as the basis for compatibility of information at national and international levels (see section 8 below; Clubb/White 1990; Bold 1993b; Grant 1990b). They have cooperated in data standards (Booth 1988b; RCHME 1993b). EH and RCHME have produced joint publications on thesaurus terms for monument and building type (RCHME; EH 1989, 1992, 1995). There has been co-operation on relationships with local SMRs (RCHME 1993a). The decision by EH to adopt Oracle software for the RSM implemented in 1990-1991 was influenced directly by its use in RCHME and the potential for sharing expertise between staff and the requirement for flows of information between DNH, EH, RCHME and local SMRs. Most recently, there has been cooperation in the context of the DNH's proposal for a heritage management database.

6   The Department of National Heritage and the Heritage Management Database

The main role of the Department of National Heritage is to help foster the ideas, creativity and skills which help generate new heritage work and which care for the inheritance of England's past. Its role is thus essentially one of policy rather than direct involvement with operational issues.

Many of the functions of DNH resided with the Department of the Environment prior to 1993. The DoE as sponsoring body for EH and RCHME and, indeed, with an interest in local SMRs through its oversight of the planning process, did not intervene significantly in heritage records matters. One exception was that it supported EH in 1988 on the choice of Oracle for the RSM system on the grounds of compatibility with RCHME. However, the DoE were reluctant to take a proactive role between 1986 and 1993 in encouraging the computerisation of the statutory lists of historic buildings which were still a major omission from the national record (see above; Clubb 1995). Ten major studies (and several lesser studies) were produced between 1986 and 1993, but funding for the work remained elusive until 1994, given the costs of retrospective computerisation (around £ 2 million), until the present Heritage Management Database initiative was launched.

6.2   THE HERITAGE MANAGEMENT DATABASE

The various studies and initiatives carried out by RCHME and EH attempted to deal with the requirements of other bodies, including SMRs, as well as their own needs. A significant new development coincided with the transfer of heritage sponsorship responsibilities from the DoE to the new Department in 1993. In particular, the new Department showed greater interest in coordinating certain aspects of the information strategies of its sponsored heritage bodies. The situation had changed following a report in 1992 by the Audit Office which commented on the lack of computerisation of the lists of the 500,000 or so listed historic buildings in England (National Audit Office 1992). The new Department of National Heritage decided to act on an earlier internal Information Systems Planning Framework report within the Heritage Division, then still part of the Department of the Environment, which recommended that a feasibility study was needed to determine the requirement for a National Heritage Management Database. In 1993, the Department of National Heritage commissioned consultants Ernst & Young to carry out a feasibility study into the National Heritage Management Database (Ernst & Young 1993).

The substantive project began in Autumn 1994 including the generation of indexes by RCHME to the agreed data standard. The development of the data standard for listed buildings is based on existing initiatives. The list is due to be fully computerised by 1996, with well-developed links to the RCHME MONARCH system. There is an appreciation of the requirement to link the listed building record with other data, both images of the buildings and spatial/ geographical information, although these are not currently funded.

6.3   THE IMPACT OF THE HERITAGE DATABASE ON RCHME AND ENGLISH HERITAGE

The project is intended to reflect the operational roles of RCHME (recording, curation and dissemination) and EH (conservation management). As stated last year (Clubb 1995), two main issues continue to be of interest; the proposal for two main computer platforms, and the tripartite management arrangements between DNH, EH and RCHME which will govern how the proposals work out in detail,

given the medium to long term problems to be solved in coordinating the information systems strategies of organisations which may have different priorities and different cycles for budgeting and planning. The Ernst & Young proposal for the computing platforms is set out in summary form in Clubb and Startin (1995). One computing platform hosted by EH is planned to support the new heritage management database and maintain the records of statutory constraints such as listed buildings and scheduled monuments. This platform is linked closely to the DNH and EH systems which support the process of listing and scheduling on the one hand and their case management systems on the other.

In parallel with the new platform is the RCHME National Monuments Record (MONARCH) system, already in place, which, under the proposals of the study, is set to contain an updated copy of the publicly-accessible sections of the heritage database (in effect, a record of statutory constraints) as a sub-set of the total national record to be disseminated. Links to the local authority sites and monuments records are provided through the 'extended' National Monuments Record (see also RCHME 1993a).

The listed buildings project represents a significant development in monument records at national level. Not only has there been a more proactive policy role on the part of the sponsoring government department, but the potential, if funding permits, that a similar approach might be adopted for future developments such as spatial/geographic systems and imaging/multi-media services means that the information system strategies of the three bodies would need to be finely tuned to each other for the foreseeable future, at least in respect of records of monuments/buildings with statutory protection and their dissemination. This would have both advantages and potential problems at an operational level.

7   Data standards and European/international cooperation

7.1   INTERNATIONAL DATA STANDARDS

While DNH, EH and RCHME have all taken an interest in data standards and co-operation at European and international levels, as have the equivalent bodies for the rest of the UK, RCHME has taken a lead role in these areas in England as the national body of survey and record. Data standards begin at national level and the role of RCHME in conjunction with EH and local SMRs has been described above. At European and international levels co-operation has been initiated on the basis of both architectural and archaeological documentation. The concept of a European core data standard for the documentation of the architectural heritage was first discussed at the Council of Europe Round Table in London in 1990, organised under the architectural documentation programme of the Cultural Heritage Committee in cooperation with RCHME (Council of Europe 1990a) and developed further at a European colloquy organised by the Council of Europe and the French Directeur du Patrimoine in Nantes in 1992 (Council of Europe 1993). Proposals for the core data index are set out in Bold 1993b and approval of the representatives of the participating governments of the Council of Europe is anticipated very shortly.

The major international development on core data standards for archaeological sites has been carried out under the auspices of the International Documentation Committee (CIDOC) of the International Council of Museums (ICOM). The Archaeological Sites Working Group is chaired by Roger Leech of RCHME and is well advanced in preparing a standard due to be made available in draft at the triennial ICOM meeting at Stavanger, Norway, in June/July 1995. This standard is intended to be compatible with the European core data index for architectural documentation. It is being developed as a European initiative under the auspices of the Council of Europe for discussion at an international conference on archaeological heritage documentation to be held at Oxford in September, 1995. Both architectural and archaeological standards are compatible with the core standards recommended for use in the UK and employed by DNH, EH and RCHME.

Finally, within the context of terminology control, several multi-lingual thesaurus projects have been initiated. For architectural records, the International Terminology Working Group, sponsored by the Getty Art and Architecture Thesaurus (AAT), includes the AAT, the L'Inventaire Général, the Royal Institute of British Architects and the RCHME, and liaises with the Council of Europe. For archaeology, a pilot project under the auspices of the Council of Europe is working towards a multi-lingual glossary of monuments for the European Bronze Age (Council of Europe 1995).

7.2 LOCAL GOVERNMENT DATA STANDARDS IN ENGLAND

Notwithstanding the significant level of agreement at national and international levels, traditionally, local SMRs have not concerned themselves greatly with data standards. A modicum of communality has been achieved through the promotion of standards by the Department of the Environment and EH (DoE 1981), and more recently, through the jointly developed Data Standard for the extended national archaeological record between the ACAO and RCHME (1993b), although the latter is too recent to have yet made a major impact. Commonly agreed local authority standards for the recording of standing structures are, if anything, even less well established, although RCHME has provided

guidance for buildings recording conventions (RCHME 1990c, 1991).

Although the original support provided by the Department of the Environment and EH for SMR development was coupled with suggested data fields, adherence to this structure was not mandatory, and was viewed as being of secondary importance compared with the political imperative to establish a local SMR network. Recording instructions, where developed, were not coordinated. Hence, between local recording bodies, many of the problems of consistency and compatibility, highlighted in previous reviews, remain (e.g. Chadburn 1989; Lang 1992; RCHME 1993c). Indeed, in some instances, local SMRs have preferred to make a fresh start on their record, using data from the RCHME National Monuments Record as the basis of their system as the most cost-effective option for achieving consistency in data compilation.

Standards work has not been prominently exploited by local government SMRs, though valuable contributions have been made both through the efforts of individual sites, and through input to national fora (for example, the ACAO and RCHME Data Standards Working Party, which led to the publication of the Data Standard for the Extended National Archaeological Record (RCHME 1993b)).

To the extent that local authority SMR staff are often fully committed to case work as opposed to records maintenance, the growth of developer funded archaeology in the last five years has meant that SMRs have become a victim of their own success. The increasing demands of development control-related duties threaten, in many Counties, to undermine the continued development of the very record providing the basis for planning decisions. The RCHME's SMR Review (RCHME 1993a) highlighted the staff shortages and growing recording backlogs in many SMRs. These shortcomings are exacerbated by the shortage of available funding to adhere to published standards, and to migrate from some of the older database management systems, which are now coming to the end of their useful lives.

Data modelling has been less prominent in the development of local government SMRs, but significant progress is being made in some counties in the development of spatial information systems. Some of these are currently in advance of developments in either of the two national bodies, predominantly, though not exclusively, because of difficulties in negotiating an affordable national mapbase.

8 An idealised model of information relationships

Following on from the above assessment of existing national and local systems in England, it is possible to describe an idealised model of information relationships

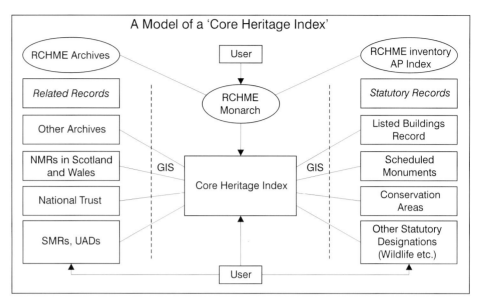

Figure 4. A model of a 'core heritage index'.

between these systems. The physical mechanisms behind
this model are beyond the scope of this paper (whether
through a physical network or through use of a smart meta-
data set), but in either case, the underlying principles may
be applied. The system we have in mind would be
accessible through a national publicly accessible spatial
index, which could interrogate a core heritage record
common to all of the three information systems we have
previously described (fig. 4).

It is suggested that the RCHME is the logical body for
the management of such an index given its national role in
survey, record and dissemination, its lead role for SMRs
and its substantial data bases and archives which add
significant value to the index concept. RCHME's archive
and inventory, both retrievable through its MONARCH
information system, provides a substantial base in combination with statutory records of archaeology, architecture
and ecology and related non-statutory records held by other
bodies for a powerful spatial database of the historic
environment.

We would envisage that further information held in
addition to the core index could be made available for
public dissemination via the custodian body as the intensive
disseminator of that information, or supplied on a more
restricted basis to other custodians of information within the
network (for example, where confidential management
implications apply). The model would assume there will be
at least some elements of a physical (or meta-physical)
network between participating bodies enabling data sharing
and dissemination, and that satisfactory agreements would
exist covering ownership, copyright, security and standards

issues. While not wishing to diminish the difficulties
attendant on turning this model into reality, it may be
suggested that the foundations for its deployment are in
large part in place.

9   Conclusions

In the first section of this paper, we referred to Booth's
hypothesis (1995b) that archaeology had missed out on the
information age. In the light of the above, in relation to
heritage information systems, this thesis seems to us to be
one requiring further qualification.

We have attempted to demonstrate in this paper that
significant steps *have* been taken towards establishing
compatible information systems within archaeology and
architecture. There has been progress in the development of
data standards, controlled vocabulary and reference data
both at national and international levels. In England,
developments in geographical and spatial information
systems, imaging and multi-media have often been more
feasible at a local rather than a national level. Nonetheless,
the data standards and models already established provide a
springboard for future national development. We would
therefore contend that significant progress is being made
towards a coordinated approach, leading to a coherent
information network embracing not merely our national
interests, but with the rapid potential to expand to our
European colleagues, and indeed to operate within a truly
international framework.

Information systems for the historic environment in
England have been developed originally without a central
model guiding their deployment. In RCHME and EH,

significant progress has now been made on data modelling. Robust systems now exist in the EH RSM, governing the relationship between archaeological items, constraints and legislative processes and in the RCHME MONARCH system, governing the relationship between events, monuments and archives. Support for the processes of scheduling of ancient monuments, listing of buildings and monument recording is generally well developed and effective, underpinned by the key concepts of the 'heritage object', 'core data', data standards initiatives and the integrated archaeological and architectural thesaurus. Archival recording is perhaps less well established, but through the development of the archive module of the RCHME MONARCH system during 1995-1996 significant progress may be expected over the next year. Issues of funding, however, still dampen progress with spatial and multi-media projects associated with these models at a national level.

These, then, are some necessarily tentative thoughts on the inter-relationships of the principal archaeological and architectural information systems in England, and their current relationship to complementary systems abroad. We would welcome seeing more papers from our colleagues in other countries setting out the relationships between their respective heritage information partners. The more explicit documentation of the inter-relationships of heritage information systems in Europe may help us move perceptibly closer towards truly integrated systems.

Notwithstanding this, Booths's assertion concerning the compatibility and retrievability of data does raise significant concerns, which must be addressed through much greater investment in developing communal and compatible interfaces to information systems, or rigorous meta-data routines. Ultimately, these should enable our systems to communicate with one another, in effect, in a common language. This would seem to be a pre-requisite for the widespread digital dissemination of monument record information. There is, thus, some truth in Booth's suggestion that heritage data is still not disseminated effectively in England to the wider heritage community and beyond. Issues of protecting monuments against metal detector abuse and buildings against architectural thefts still require resolution in terms of the free supply of information (for example, see ACAO 1991, 1992; Council of Europe 1990b; Stine/Stine 1990). However, the essential models for the effective management and dissemination of heritage data are now in place. The European heritage and traditions are shared and valued by millions throughout the world, and can only gain strength and vitality through fostering an accessible, commonly understood medium of interchange.

Acknowledgements
This paper is based on existing published literature but, of course, the analysis remains our responsibility. The ideas will undoubtedly require further development and refinement in the light of further analysis of the strategic and business requirements of the local, national and international heritage community and the public. We are grateful to many colleagues in EH, RCHME and local government, and in central government in Europe and the United States for stimulating a debate over a period of some years which has made this paper possible.

bibliography

Aberg, A.	1986	Computer data in archaeology. In: J.D. Richards (ed.), *Computer Usage in British Archaeology*, 9-11, IFA Occasional Paper No. 1, Birmingham: Institute of Field Archaeologists.
Aberg, F.A. R.H. Leech	1992	The national archaeological record for England. Past, present and future. In: C.U. Larsen (ed.), *Sites and monuments. National Archaeological Records*, 157-169, Copenhagen: National Museum of Denmark.
Allden, A.	1986	The use of computers for sites and monuments records. In: J.D. Richards (ed.), *Computer Usage in British Archaeology*, 33-37, IFA Occasional Paper No. 1, Birmingham: Institute of Field Archaeologists.
Allen, K.M.S. S.W. Green E.B.W. Zubrow (eds)	1990	*Interpreting Space: Geographical Information Systems and Archaeology*. London: Taylor & Francis.
Andresen, J. T. Madsen	1993	Data structures for excavation recording. In: J. Andresen/T. Madsen/I. Scollar (eds), *Computing the past, Computer Applications and Quantitative Methods in Archaeology CAA92*, 49-70, Aarhus: Aarhus University Press.
Andresen, J. T. Madsen I. Scollar (eds)	1993	*Computing the past, Computer Applications and Quantitative Methods in Archaeology CAA92*. Aarhus: Aarhus University Press.
Ashmore, P.	1992	Coping with Diversity through Harmonisation. In: C.U. Larsen (ed.), *Sites and monuments. National Archaeological Records*, 217-219, Copenhagen: National Museum of Denmark.
Association of Conservation Officers	1990	*Context*, Journal of the Association of Conservation Officers, March 1990.
	1992	*Context*, Journal of the Association of Conservation Officers, 1992.
Association of County Archaeological Officers	1978	*A guide to the establishment of Sites and Monuments Records*. London: Association of County Archaeological Officers.
	1990	*Sites and Monuments Records: Some Current Issues*. (M. Hughes ed.). Hampshire: Association of County Archaeological Officers.
	1991	*Sites and Monuments Records. Access and Charging* (1st edition). Birmingham: Association of County Archaeological Officers.
	1992	*Sites and Monuments Records. Access and Charging* (2nd edition). Birmingham: Association of County Archaeological Officers.
Baker, D.	1985	The national/local interface – a County View. In: I. Burrow (ed.), *County Archaeological Records: Progress and Potential*, 64-67, London: Association of County Archaeological Officers.
Baker, D. I. Sheperd	1993	Local authority opportunities. In: J. Hunter/I. Ralston (eds), *Archaeological Resource Management in the UK: An Introduction*, 100-114, Stroud: Allan Sutton/Institute of Field Archaeologists.
Beagrie, N.	1993.	The computerisation of the National Archaeological Record, *Revue Informatique et Statistique dans les Sciences humaines*, 1-4, 9-16.

	this volume	Excavations and Archives: Alternative Aspects of Cultural Resource Management.
Beagrie, N. D. Abercromby	1992	The archaeological site type thesaurus, *Thesauri for Museum Documentation*. Museum Documentation Association Occasional Paper 18, 43-52.
Bearman, D.	1990	*Archive and Museum Data Models and Dictionaries.* Technical Report 10. Pittsburgh: Archives and Museum Informatics.
Benson, D.	1974	A Sites and Monuments Record for the Oxford Region, *Oxoniensia* 37 (1972), 226-237.
Benson, D.G.	1985	Problems of data entry and retrieval. In: I. Burrow (ed.), *County Archaeological Records: Progress and Potential*, 27-34, London: Association of County Archaeological Officers.
Benson, D.G. J.S. Jefferies	1980	Microprocessors and Archaeological Records. In: J.D. Stewart (ed.), *Microcomputers in Archaeology*, MDA Occasional Paper 4, 5-12.
Biek, L.	1988	Is this a record? Judgement on Domesday: the first year in archaeo-archiving. In: S.P.Q. Rahtz (ed.), *Computer Applications and Quantitative Methods in Archaeology 1988*, 543-550, BAR International Series 446 (ii), Oxford: British Archaeological Reports.
Biggs, J.	1992	A Little List, *Context* 36, Journal of the Association of Conservation Officers.
Bold, J.	1993a	The Documentation of the Architectural Heritage in Europe, *Architectural Heritage: inventory and documentation methods in Europe 1993*, 11-15. Strasbourg: Council of Europe.
	1993b	The Core Data Index: Summary and Proposals, *Architectural Heritage: inventory and documentation methods in Europe 1993*, 149-152. Strasbourg: Council of Europe.
	1994	Defining and Recording the Resource: the built environment. In: R. Harrison (ed.), *Manual of Heritage Management*, 79-84, Oxford: Butterworth-Heinemann.
Booth, B.K.W.	1984	The changing requirements of an archaeological database. In: J.G.B. Haigh (ed.), *Computer Applications in Archaeology 1983*, 23-30, Bradford: University of Bradford.
	1986	Computing at English Heritage. *Archaeological Computing Newsletter* 6, 3-4.
	1988a	The SAM Record – past present and future. In: S.P.Q. Rahtz (ed.), *Computer Applications and Quantitative Methods in Archaeology 1988*, 379-388, BAR International Series 446, Oxford: British Archaeological Reports.
	1988b	*Site specific data – a standard for data transfer.* (Unpublished). London: English Heritage.
	1993	A high resolution imaging system for the photographic archive at the National Railway Museum, York. In: J. Andresen/T. Madsen/I. Scollar (eds), *Computing the past, Computer Applications and Quantitative Methods in Archaeology CAA92*, 457-461, Aarhus: Aarhus University Press.
	1995a	Developing an information strategy for the National Museum of Science and Industry. In: J Wilcock/K. Lockyear (eds), *Computer Applications and Quantitative Methods in Archaeology 1993*, 95-99, BAR International Series 598, Oxford: Tempus Reparatum.
	1995b	Has archaeology remained aloof from the information age? In: J Huggett/N. Ryan (eds), *Computer Applications and Quantitative Methods in Archaeology 1994*, 1-12, BAR International Series 600, Oxford: Tempus Reparatum.

Booth, B.K.W.
S.A.V. Grant
J.D. Richards (eds)

1989   Computer usage in British Archaeology (2nd edition). Birmingham: Institute of Field Archaeologists.

Bowler, J.

1985   Computerising Northamptonshire's sites and monuments record, *Archaeological Computing Newsletter* 5, 4-8.

Brand, V.

1988   *Buildings at Risk Register*. (Unpublished Paper). London, English Heritage. Reproduced in Yakub, 1992.

1990   Buildings at Risk, *Context* 25, March, 1990, Journal of the Association of Conservation Officers.

Burnett, J.
I. Morrison

1994   Defining and recording the resource. In: R. Harrison (ed.*), Manual of Heritage Management*, 117-124, Oxford: Butterworth-Heinemann.

Burrow, I. (ed.)

1985a   *County Archaeological Records: Progress and Potential*. London: Association of County Archaeological Officers.

1985b   The history of the sites and monuments records system. In: I. Burrow (ed.), *County Archaeological Records: Progress and Potential*, 6-15, London: Association of County Archaeological Officers.

Byrne, K.F.

1993   Information systems at RCAHMS. In: *Monuments on Record, RCAHMS Annual Review 1992-3*, 14-16.

Castelford, J.

1992   Archaeology, GIS and the time dimension: an overview. In: G. Lock/J. Moffett (eds), *Computer Applications and Quantitative Methods in Archaeology 1991*, 95-106, BAR International Series 577, Oxford: Tempus Reparatum.

Chadburn, A.D.B.

1988   A review of approaches to controlling archaeological vocabulary for data retrieval. In: S.P.Q. Rahtz (ed.), *Computer Applications and Quantitative Methods in Archaeology 1988*, 389-397, BAR International Series 446, Oxford: British Archaeological Reports.

1989   Computerised county sites and monuments records in England. In: S.P.Q. Rahtz/ J.D. Richards (eds), *Computer Applications and Quantitative Methods in Archaeology 1989*, 9-17, BAR International Series 548, Oxford: British Archaeological Reports.

Charles, D.

1986   Computers in the National Monuments Record, *Archaeological Computing Newsletter* 9, 2-4.

Chartrand, J.
J. Richards
B. Vyner

1989   Bridging the urban-rural gap: GIS and the York Environs Project. In: S.P.Q. Rahtz/ J.D. Richards (eds), *Computer Applications and Quantitative Methods in Archaeology 1989*, 9-18, BAR International Series 548, Oxford: British Archaeological Reports.

Cheetham, P.N.

1985   The archaeological database applied: North Yorkshire County Council Sites and Monuments Record at the University of Bradford. In: E. Webb (ed.), *Computer Applications in Archaeology 1985*, 49-56, London: University of London Institute of Archaeology.

Cheetham, P.N.
J.G.B. Haigh

1992   The archaeological database-new relations. In: G. Lock/J. Moffett (eds), *Computer Applications and Quantitative Methods in Archaeology 1991*, 7-14, BAR International Series 577, Oxford: Tempus Reparatum.

CIDOC

1995   *Draft International Core Data Standard for Archaeological Sites and Monuments Records*. International Documentation Committee, International Council of Museums. Paris: ICOM.

Cleere, H.   1984   Only Connect. In: R. Martlew (ed.), *Information Systems in Archaeology*, 9-20, Stroud: Allan Sutton.

Clubb, N.   1988   Computer mapping and the Scheduled Ancient Monument Record. In: S.P.Q. Rahtz (ed.), *Computer Applications and Quantitative Methods in Archaeology 1988*, 399-408, BAR International Series 446, Oxford: British Archaeological Reports.

                              1989   Investment appraisal for information technology. In: S.P.Q. Rahtz/J.D. Richards (eds), *Computer Applications and Quantitative Methods in Archaeology 1989*, 1-7, BAR International Series 548, Oxford: British Archaeological Reports.

                              1990a   Records of buildings and monuments, *Context* 25, March, 1990, Journal of the Association of Conservation Officers.

                              1990b   English Heritage and County-based Sites and Monuments Records – Technical Developments. In: Association of County Archaeological Officer 1990: *Sites and Monuments Records: Some Current Issues*, (M. Hughes ed.), Hampshire: Association of County Archaeological Officers (unpaginated).

                              1991a   Procuring medium-large systems. In: K. Lockyear/S.P.Q. Rahtz (eds), *Computer Applications and Quantitative Methods in Archaeology 1990*, 81-84, BAR International Series 565, Oxford: Tempus Reparatum.

                              1991b   The operational requirement for a medium to large-scale System – the Experience of the English Heritage Record of Scheduled Monuments. In: K. Lockyear/S.P.Q. Rahtz (eds), *Computer Applications and Quantitative Methods in Archaeology 1990*, 85-91, BAR International Series 565, Oxford: Tempus Reparatum.

                              1995   Computerising the lists of historic buildings in England – a historical case study on initiating a national project. In: J. Huggett/N. Ryan (eds), *Computer Applications and Quantitative Methods in Archaeology 1994*, 193-202, BAR International Series 600, Oxford: Tempus Reparatum.

Clubb, N.   1989a   Digital mapping at English Heritage, *Mapping Awareness* 3 (2), 18-21.
  D. Hilder

                              1989b   Mapping system for English Heritage, *AM/FM International European Division, Proceedings of Conference V, Montreux, Switzerland*, 183-188.

Clubb, N.   1985   A computer record for Greater London's Heritage, *London Archaeologist* 5, 38-9.
  P. James

Clubb, N.D.   this   Learning from the achievements of Information Systems – the role of the Post-
  N.A.R. Lang   volume   Implementation Review in medium to large scale systems.

Clubb, N.D.   1995   Information systems strategies in national organisations and the identification, legal
  W.D. Startin   protection and management of the most important sites in England. In: J. Wilcock/ K. Lockyear (eds), *Computer Applications and Quantitative Methods in Archaeology 1993*, 67-73, BAR International Series 598, Oxford: Tempus Reparatum.

Clubb, N.D.   1990   Towards a minimum standard level of information for recording historic buildings. In:
  P.R. White   *Proceedings of a Council of Europe Round Table of Experts on Architectural Heritage, New Technologies in Documentation, 1989*, Council of Europe Architectural Heritage Reports and Studies, No. 19.

Cooper, M.A.   1985   Computers in British Archaeology: the need for a national strategy. In: M.A. Cooper/ J.D. Richards (eds), *Current Issues in Archaeological Computing*, 79-92, BAR International Series 271, Oxford: British Archaeological Reports.

| | 1985 | *Current Issues in Archaeological Computing.* BAR International Series 271. Oxford: British Archaeological Reports. |

(eds)

| | 1995 | *Managing Archaeology.* London: Routledge. |

J. Carman
D. Wheatley (eds)

Coopers & Lybrand Deloitte   1991   *Royal Commission on the Ancient and Historical Monuments of Scotland: Information systems strategy, 1991.* (Unpublished report to the Royal Commission on the Ancient and Historical Monuments of Scotland).

   1992   *Historic Buildings Maps Computerisation Project.* (Unpublished report to English Heritage). July, 1992.

Copeland, J.   1982   *A survey of record retrieval systems in archaeological units, planning departments and museums* (unpublished).

   1983   Information retrieval systems for archaeological data. In: J.G.B. Haigh (ed.), *Computer Applications in Archaeology 1983*, 39-46, Bradford: University of Bradford.

Council for British Archaeology   1952   Standard Record Card. *Council for British Archaeology Annual Report 1951-52,* Appendix III. London.

Council of Europe   1990a   *Architectural Heritage, New Technologies in Documentation 1989.* Council of Europe Architectural Heritage Reports and Studies, No. 19. Strasbourg: Council of Europe Press.

   1990b   *Council Directive of 7 June 1990 on freedom of access to information on the environment, 90/313/EC.* Official Journal of the European Communities, 23 June 1990, No. L 158, 56-58, Strasbourg.

   1993   *Architectural Heritage: Inventory and Documentation Methods in Europe.* Cultural Heritage 28, Strasbourg: Council of Europe Press.

   1995   *European Bronze Age Monuments. A Multi-Lingual Glossary of Archaeological Terminology. A draft covering Denmark, France, The Netherlands, the Republic of Ireland and the United Kingdom.* Amersfoort: Council of Europe Glossary SS7, May 4th, 1995.

Darvill, T.
W.D. Startin
A. Saunders   1987   A question of national importance: approaches to the evaluation of ancient monuments for the monuments protection programme in England, *Antiquity* 61, 393-408.

Department of the Environment   1972   *Field Monuments and Local Authorities.* London: Department of the Environment Circular 11/72, 1972.

   1981   *Advisory Note No. 32.* Ancient Monuments Records Manual and County Sites and Monuments Records. London: Department of the Environment.

   1990   *Planning Policy Guidance Note 16: Archaeology and Planning.* London: HMSO.

Department of the Environment and Department of National Heritage   1994   *Planning Policy Guidance Note 15: Planning and the Historic Environment.* London: HMSO.

English Heritage   1992a   *Buildings at Risk: a sample survey.* London: English Heritage.

   1992b   *Managing the urban archaeological resource.* London: English Heritage.

Ernst & Young   1993   *Heritage Database Feasibility Study. Business Case.* (Unpublished Report to the Department of National Heritage). April, 1993.

Evans, D.M.   1984   A national archaeological archive – computer database applications. In: S. Laflin (ed.), *Computer Applications in Archaeology 1984*, 112-118, Birmingham: University of Birmingham Centre for Computing and Computer Science.

Evans, D.   1985   Computerisation of sites and monuments records: the development of policy. In: E. Webb (ed.), *Computer Applications in Archaeology 1985*, 62-74, London: University of London Institute of Archaeology.

Farley, M.   1985   The contents of sites and monuments records. In: I. Burrow (ed.), *County Archaeological Records: Progress and Potential*, 35-41, London: Association of County Archaeological Officers.

Foard, G.   1978   *The Northamptonshire Sites and Monuments Record. Part 1: Archaeology. A guide to the structure, purpose and use of the archaeological record.* Northampton: Northamptonshire County Council.

Fowler, P.   1985   The national/local interface: a view from RCHM. In: I. Burrow (ed.), *County Archaeological Records: Progress and Potential*, 56-63, London: Association of County Archaeological Officers.

Fraser, D.   1985   Sites and Monuments Records: the state of the art. In: I. Burrow (ed.), *County Archaeological Records: Progress and Potential*, 47-55, London: Association of County Archaeological Officers.

                        1986   The role of archaeological record systems in the management of monuments. In: M. Hughes/L. Rowley (eds), *The Management and Presentation of Field Monuments*, 17-26, Oxford: Oxford University, Department of External Studies.

                        1993   The British Archaeological Database. In: J. Hunter/I. Ralston (eds), *Archaeological Resource Management in the UK: An Introduction*, 19-29, Stroud: Allan Sutton/Institute of Field Archaeologists.

Grant, A.   1994   *Spectrum: The UK Museum Documentation Standard.* Cambridge: Museum Documentation Association.

Grant, S.   1985   Computing the past and anticipating the future. In: E. Webb (ed.), *Computer Applications in Archaeology 1985*, 152, London: University of London Institute of Archaeology.

                        1986a   Summary and recommendations. In: J.D. Richards (ed.), *Computer Usage in British Archaeology*, 13-31, IFA Occasional Paper No. 1, Birmingham: Institute of Field Archaeologists.

                        1986b   A note on the IFA/RCHME working party on computer usage in archaeology, *Archaeological Computing Newsletter* 6, 13-14.

                        1990a   Promoting a national record, *Context* 25, March, 1990, Journal of the Association of Conservation Officers.

                        1990b   Compatibility of information. In: Council of Europe 1990: *Architectural Heritage, New Technologies in Documentation 1989*. Council of Europe Architectural Heritage Reports and Studies, No. 19, Strasbourg: Council of Europe Press.

Griffin, J.   1994   Strategic linkages and networks In: R. Harrison (ed.), *Manual of Heritage Management*, 43-53, Oxford: Butterworth-Heinemann.

| | 1990 | The rewards of a year's hard slog, *Context* 25, March, 1990, Journal of the Association of Conservation Officers. |

| :d.) | 1983 | *Computer Applications in Archaeology 1983*. Bradford: University of Bradford. |

| Hansen, J.H. | 1993 | European archaeological databases: problems and prospects. In: J. Andresen/T. Madsen/ I. Scollar (eds), *Computing the past, Computer Applications and Quantitative Methods in Archaeology CAA92*, 229-237, Aarhus: Aarhus University Press. |

| Harris, T.M. | 1986 | Geographic information system design for archaeological site information retrieval. In: S. Laflin (ed.), *Computer Applications in Archaeology 1986*, 148-161, Birmingham: University of Birmingham Centre for Computing and Computer Science. |

| | 1988 | Digital terrain modelling in archaeology and regional planning. In: C.L.N. Ruggles/ S.P.Q. Rahtz (eds), *Computer and Quantitative Methods in Archaeology 1987*, 161-172, BAR International Series 393, Oxford: British Archaeological Reports. |

| Harris, T.M. G.R. Lock | 1990 | The Diffusion of a New Technology: A Perspective on the Adoption of Geographic Information Systems within UK Archaeology. In: K.M.S. Allen/S.W. Green/ E.B.W. Zubrow (eds), *Interpreting Space: GIS and Archaeology*, 33-54, London: Taylor & Francis. |

| | 1992 | Towards a regional GIS site Information retrieval system: the Oxfordshire Sites and Monuments Record (SMR) Prototype. In: C.U. Larsen (ed.), *Sites and monuments. National Archaeological Records*, 185-199, Copenhagen: National Museum of Denmark. |

| Harrison, R. (ed.) | 1994 | *Manual of Heritage Management*. Oxford: Butterworth-Heinemann. |

| Hart, J. R. Leech | 1989 | The national archaeological record. In: S.P.Q. Rahtz/J.D. Richards (eds), *Computer Applications and Quantitative Methods in Archaeology 1989*, 57-67, BAR International Series 548, Oxford: British Archaeological Reports. |

| Hedges, J. | 1985 | The role of the sites and monuments record in historical conservation. In: I. Burrow (ed.), *County Archaeological Records: Progress and Potential*, 16-26, London: Association of County Archaeological Officers. |

| Hinchcliffe, J. J.S. Jefferies | 1985 | Ten years of data processing in the Central Excavation Unit. In: M.A. Cooper/ J.D. Richards (eds), *Current Issues in Archaeological Computing*, 17-22, BAR International Series 271, Oxford: British Archaeological Reports. |

| House of Commons | 1987 | *First Report from the Environment Committee – Historic Buildings and Ancient Monuments*. London: HMSO. |

| | 1993 | *29th Report from the Committee of Public Accounts – Protecting and Managing England's Heritage Property*. 29th Report. London: HMSO. |

| Huggett, J. N. Ryan (eds) | 1995 | *Computer Applications and Quantitative Methods in Archaeology 1994*, BAR International Series 600. Oxford: Tempus Reparatum. |

| Hughes, M. L. Rowley (eds) | 1986 | *The Management and Presentation of Field Monuments*. Oxford: Oxford University, Department of External Studies. |

| Hunter, J. I. Ralston (eds) | 1993 | *Resource Management in the UK: An Introduction*. Stroud: Allan Sutton/Institute of Field Archaeologists. |

| Inspectorate of Ancient Monuments | 1984 | *England's Archaeological Resource. A rapid Quantification of the National Archaeological Resource and a Comparison with the Schedule of Ancient Monuments*. London: Department of the Environment. |

Iles, P.D.
  M. Trueman
1989   SUPERFILE – a user's view. In: S.P.Q. Rahtz/J.D. Richards (eds), *Computer Applications and Quantitative Methods in Archaeology 1989*, 19-26, BAR International Series 548, Oxford: British Archaeological Reports.

Jefferies, J.S.
1977   *Recording Systems in use by the Central Excavation Unit*. Department of Ancient Monuments and Historic Buildings Occasional Paper No. 1, HMSO.

Jones, H.
1989   The Greater London Sites and Monuments Record – a case study. In: S.P.Q. Rahtz/ J.D. Richards (eds), *Computer Applications and Quantitative Methods in Archaeology 1989*, 33-38, BAR International Series 548, Oxford: British Archaeological Reports.

1990   The Greater London Sites and Monuments Record, *Context* 25, March, 1990, Journal of the Association of Conservation Officers.

Jones, J.
1990   The Clwyd approach, *Context* 25, March, 1990, Journal of the Association of Conservation Officers.

Jones, R.T.
  S.M. Wall
  A.M. Locker
  J. Maltby
  J.M. Coy
1980   *Computer based osteometry. Data capture user manual (1)*. First supplement to AML Report No. 2333, Technical Report 3342. London: Ancient Monuments Laboratory.

Kvamme, K.
1992   Geographic Information Systems and Archaeology. In: G. Lock/J. Moffett (eds), *Computer Applications and Quantitative Methods in Archaeology 1991*, 77-84, BAR International Series 577, Oxford: Tempus Reparatum.

Laflin, S.
1973   Computer systems for county gazetteers, *Science and Archaeology* 9, 26-28.

1984   *Computer Applications in Archaeology 1984*. Birmingham: University of Birmingham Centre for Computing and Computer Science.

1986   *Computer Applications in Archaeology 1986*. Birmingham: University of Birmingham Centre for Computing and Computer Science.

Lang, N.A.R.
1989   Sites and Monuments Records in historic towns. In: S.P.Q. Rahtz/J.D. Richards (eds), *Computer Applications and Quantitative Methods in Archaeology 1989*, 41-50, BAR International Series 548, Oxford: British Archaeological Reports.

1990a   Sites and Monuments Records and historic buildings, *Context* 25, March, 1990, Journal of the Association of Conservation Officers.

1990b   Sites and monuments records: some current issues. In: M. Hughes (ed.), Association of County Archaeological Officers 1990: *Sites and Monuments Records: Some Current Issues*, Hampshire: Association of County Archaeological Officers (unpaginated).

1992   Sites and Monuments Records in Great Britain In: C.U. Larsen (ed.), *Sites and monuments. National Archaeological Records*, 171-183, Copenhagen: National Museum of Denmark.

1993a   From model to machine: procurement and implementation of Geographical Information Systems for County Sites and Monuments Records. In: J. Andresen/T. Madsen/I. Scollar (eds), *Computing the past, Computer Applications and Quantitative Methods in Archaeology CAA92*, 167-176, Aarhus: Aarhus University Press.

1993b   Air Photography and Sites and Monuments records: some observations. *AARG News, the newsletter of the Aerial Archaeology Research Group*, February, 1993.

| | 1995 | Recording and managing the national heritage. In: J. Wilcock/K. Lockyear (eds), *Computer Applications and Quantitative Methods in Archaeology 1993*, 75-80, BAR International Series 598, Oxford: Tempus Reparatum. |

Lang, N.A.R.
  S. Stead
1992   Sites and monuments records in England – theory and practise. In: G. Lock/J. Moffett (eds), *Computer Applications and Quantitative Methods in Archaeology 1991*, 69-76, BAR International Series 577, Oxford: Tempus Reparatum.

Larsen, C.U. (ed.)
1992   *Sites and monuments. National Archaeological Records.* Copenhagen: National Museum of Denmark.

Lavell, C.
1985   Information: Are we retrieving it? In: I. Burrow (ed.), *County Archaeological Records: Progress and Potential*, 42-45, London: Association of County Archaeological Officers.

Leech, R.
1986   Computerisation of the National Archaeological Record. In: S. Laflin (ed.), *Computer Applications in Archaeology 1986*, 29-37, Birmingham: University of Birmingham Centre for Computing and Computer Science.

1990   RCHME and Sites and Monuments Records. In: M. Hughes (ed.), Association of County Archaeological Officers 1990: *Sites and Monuments Records. Some Current Issues*, Hampshire: Association of County Archaeological Officers, (unpaginated).

1991   The Computerized National Archaeological Record for England – its development and future potential for Medieval Studies, *Literary and Linguistic Computing* 6 (1).

1993a   Recording Englands Historic Resource. In: H. Swain (ed.), *Rescuing the Historic Environment*, 35-40, Hertford: RESCUE, the British Archaeological Trust.

1993b   The Computerised National Archaeological Record for England – its development and future potential for Roman burial studies. In: M. Struck (ed.), *Römerzeitliche Gräber als Quellen zu Religion, Bevölkerungsstruktur und Sozialgeschichte*, 433-441, Mainz: Universität Mainz.

1993c   Data standards for archaeological site records in England – RCHME initiatives. In: D.A. Roberts (ed.), *European Museum Documentation Strategies and Standards*, 159-162, Cambridge: The Museum Documentation Association.

1993d   Sites and monuments: National Archaeological records, *Journal of European Archaeology* 1.2, 200-204.

1993e   Documentation Standards for European Archaeology, *Newsletter of the European Association of Archaeologists* 1, 4.

Leech, R.
  (with G. Soffe)
1994   Cistercian Houses in England: the Construction of the National Inventory and the European Context. In: L. Pressouyre (ed.), *L'espace cistercien*, 295-310, Paris: Comité des travaux historiques et scientifiques.

Lock, G.
  T. Harris
1991   Integrating spatial information in computerised SMRs. In: K. Lockyear/S.P.Q. Rahtz (eds), *Computer Applications and Quantitative Methods in Archaeology 1990*, 165-174, BAR International Series 565, Oxford: Tempus Reparatum.

Lock, G.
  J. Moffett (eds)
1992   *Computer Applications and Quantitative Methods in Archaeology 1991*, BAR International Series 577. Oxford: Tempus Reparatum.

Lock, G.R.
  Z. Stančič (eds)
1995   *Archaeology and Geographic Information Systems: A European Perspective.* London: Taylor & Francis.

Lockyear, K.
  S.P.Q. Rahtz (eds)
1991
Computer Applications and Quantitative Methods in Archaeology 1990, BAR International Series 565. Oxford: Tempus Reparatum.

Martlew, R. (ed.)
1984
Information Systems in Archaeology. Stroud: Allan Sutton.

Martlew, R.
  B.L. Creaser
1989
Sites and Monuments Records of the East Midlands. In: S.P.Q. Rahtz/J. D. Richards (eds), *Computer Applications and Quantitative Methods in Archaeology 1989*, 51-54, BAR International Series 548, Oxford: British Archaeological Reports.

Middleton, R.
  D. Winstanley
1993
GIS in a landscape archaeology context. In: J. Andresen/T. Madsen/I. Scollar (eds), *Computing the past, Computer Applications and Quantitative Methods in Archaeology CAA92*, 151-158, Aarhus: Aarhus University Press.

Miller, A.P.
1995a
The York Archaeological Assessment: Computer Modelling of Urban Deposits in the City of York. In: J. Wilcock/K. Lockyear (eds), *Computer Applications and Quantitative Methods in Archaeology 1993*, 149-154, BAR International Series 598, Oxford: Tempus Reparatum.

1995b
How to Look Good and Influence People: Thoughts on the Design and Interpretation of an Archaeological GIS. In: G.R. Lock/Z. Stančič (eds), *Archaeology and Geographic Information Systems: A European Perspective*, 319-333, London: Taylor & Francis.

Moffett, J.C.
1984
The Bedfordshire County Sites and Monuments Record database management system. In: S. Laflin (ed.), *Computer Applications in Archaeology 1984*, 101-109, Birmingham: University of Birmingham Centre for Computing and Computer Science.

Murray, D.M.
1992
Towards Harmony: A view of the Scottish Archaeological Database. In: C.U. Larsen (ed.), *Sites and monuments. National Archaeological Records*, 209-216, Copenhagen: National Museum of Denmark.

1995
The management of Archaeological Information – a Strategy. In: J. Wilcock/K. Lockyear (eds), *Computer Applications and Quantitative Methods in Archaeology 1993*, 83-86, BAR International Series 598, Oxford: Tempus Reparatum.

National Audit Office
1992
Protecting and Managing England's Heritage Property. London: HMSO.

North Yorkshire County Council
1982
Archaeological Record System. Northallerton: North Yorkshire County Council Computer Services.

Oppenheim, C.
1984
Online information retrieval, data-bases and records. In: R. Martlew (ed.), *Information Systems in Archaeology*, 90-98, Stroud: Allan Sutton.

Pannell Kerr Forster Associates
1990
Project landmarks: a report on the marketability of computerised listed buildings records. (Unpublished report to the Royal Commission on the Historical Monuments of England, English Heritage and the Department of the Environment). May, 1990.

Petersen, T.
1993
Collaborative Efforts Toward Multi-Lingual Versions of the AAT. *International Documentation Committee, International Council of Museums Newsletter* 4, July 1993. CIDOC: 57-61.

Petrie, L.
  I. Johnson
  B. Cullen
  K. Kvamme
1995
GIS in Archaeology. An Annotated Bibliography. Sydney University Archaeological Methods Series 1, 1995.

Pressouyre, L. (ed.)
1994
L'espace cistercien. Paris: Comité des travaux historiques et scientifiques.

Rahtz, S.P.Q. (ed.)   1988   *Computer Applications and Quantitative Methods in Archaeology 1988*, BAR International Series 446, Oxford: British Archaeological Reports.

Rahtz, S.P.Q.
   J.D. Richards (eds)   1989   *Computer Applications and Quantitative Methods in Archaeology 1989*, BAR International Series 548. Oxford: British Archaeological Reports.

Redknap, M.
   L. Emptage   1986   Marine archaeological surveys: mapping the underwater cultural heritage. In: S. Laflin (ed.), *Computer Applications in Archaeology 1986*, 49-58, Birmingham: University of Birmingham Centre for Computing and Computer Science.

Reilly, P.
   S.P.Q. Rahtz (eds)   1992   *Archaeology and the Information Age. A global perspective.* One World Archaeology 21. London: Routledge.

Richards, J.D. (ed.)   1986   *Computer Usage in British Archaeology*, IFA Occasional Paper No. 1, Birmingham: Institute of Field Archaeologists.

   1991   Terrain modelling, deposit survival and urban archaeology. In: K. Lockyear/S.P.Q. Rahtz (eds), *Computer Applications and Quantitative Methods in Archaeology 1990*, 175-182, BAR International Series 565, Oxford: Tempus Reparatum.

Roberts, D.A. (ed.)   1993   *European Museum Documentation Strategies and Standards.* Cambridge: The Museum Documentation Association.

Robinson, H.   1993   The archaeological implications of a computerised integrated national heritage information system. In: J. Andresen/T. Madsen/I. Scollar (eds), *Computing the Past. Computer Applications and Quantitative Methods in Archaeology CAA92*, 139-150, Aarhus: Aarhus University Press.

Rowley, T.
   M. Breakell   1975   *Planning and the Historic Environment.* Oxford: Oxford University, Department for External Studies.

   1977   *Planning and the Historic Environment II.* Oxford: Oxford University, Department for External Studies.

Royal Commission on Historical Monuments (England)   1960   *A matter of time.* London: HMSO.

   1975   *Report of the Working Party on Archaeological Records.* London: Council for British Archaeology and the Royal Commission on Historical Monuments.

   1978   *Survey of Surveys.* London: Royal Commission on the Historical Monuments of England.

   1986   *Thesaurus of Archaeological Terms* (1st edition). London: Royal Commission on the Historical Monuments of England.

   1990a   *A Guide to the National Monuments Record.* London: Royal Commission on the Historical Monuments of England.

   1990b   RCHME lead role for SMRs. *British Archaeological News* 5, 23.

   1991   *Recording Historic Buildings: A Descriptive Specification* (2nd edition). London: Royal Commission on the Historical Monuments of England.

   1993a   *Recording England's past: A review of national and local sites and monuments records in England.* London: Royal Commission on the Historical Monuments of England.

   1993b   *Recording England's Past: A data standard for the extended national archaeological record.* London: Royal Commission on the Historical Monuments of England.

Royal Commission on Historical Monuments of England and English Heritage	1989	*Revised Thesaurus of Architectural Terms*. London: Royal Commission on the Historical Monuments of England.
	1992	*Thesaurus of Archaeological Site Types* (2nd edition). London: Royal Commission on the Historical Monuments of England.
	1995	*Thesaurus of Monument Types: A Standard for Use in Archaeological and Architectural Records*. Swindon: Royal Commission on the Historical Monuments of England.
Ruggles, C.L.N. S.P.Q. Rahtz (eds)	1988	*Computer and Quantitative methods in archaeology 1987*, BAR International Series 393. Oxford: British Archaeological Reports.
Ryan, N.S.	1992	Beyond the relational database: managing the variety and complexity of archaeological data. In: G. Lock/J. Moffett (eds), *Computer Applications and Quantitative Methods in Archaeology 1991*, 1-6, BAR International Series 577, Oxford: Tempus Reparatum.
Sanders, D.	1994	Building Equivalencies to Architectural Terms in the AAT, *Art and Architecture Thesaurus Bulletin* 22, 13, Massachusetts: The Art History Information Programme.
Savage, S.H.	1990	GIS in Archaeological Research. In: K.M.S Allen/S.W. Green/E.B.W. Zubrow (eds), *Interpreting Space: GIS and Archaeology*, 22-33, London: Taylor & Francis.
Startin, D.W.A.	1988	The Integrated Archaeological Database. In: C.L.N. Ruggles/S.P.Q. Rahtz (eds), *Computer and Quantitative Methods in Archaeology 1987*, 279-284, BAR International Series 393, Oxford: British Archaeological Reports.
	1992	The Monument Protection Programme: archaeological records. In: C.U. Larsen (ed.), *Sites and monuments. National Archaeological Records*, 201-206, Copenhagen: National Museum of Denmark.
Stead, S.D.	1985	Computerisation of Lincolnshire's sites and monuments record, *Rescue News* 36, 12.
	1990	The logical data structure of the Record of Scheduled Monuments. (Unpublished paper, presented at CAA 1990, Southampton).
Stewart, J.D. (ed.)	1980	*Microcomputers in Archaeology*. MDA Occasional Paper 4.
Stine, L.F. R.S. Stine	1990	GIS, Archaeology and Freedom of Information. In: K.M.S Allen/S.W. Green/E.B.W. Zubrow (eds), *Interpreting Space: GIS and Archaeology*, 54-64, London: Taylor & Francis.
Struck, M. (ed.)	1993	*Römerzeitliche Gräber als Quellen zu Religion, Bevölkerungsstruktur und Sozialgeschichte*. Mainz: Universität Mainz.
Swain, H. (ed.)	1993	*Rescuing the Historic Environment*. Hertford: RESCUE, the British Archaeological Trust.
Todd, R.	1994	*The Role of Computerised Databases in Conservation*. (Unpublished MSC Dissertation). Oxford: Oxford Brookes University.
Van Leusen, P.M.	1995	GIS and Archaeological Resource Management: A European Agenda. In: G.R. Lock/Z. Stančič (eds), *Archaeology and Geographic Information Systems: A European Perspective*, 27-41, London: Taylor & Francis.
Walsh, D.	1969	*Report of the Committee of Enquiry into the Arrangements for the Protection of Field Monuments 1966-68*. Chairman Sir David Walsh. Command 3904. London: HMSO 1969, reprinted 1972.

Wansleeben, M.	1988	Applications of Geographical Information Systems in Archaeological research. In: S.P.Q. Rahtz (ed.), *Computer Applications and Quantitative Methods in Archaeology 1988*, 435-451, BAR International Series 446, Oxford: British Archaeological Reports.
Webb, E. (ed.)	1985	*Computer Applications in Archaeology 1985*. London: University of London Institute of Archaeology.
Wheatley, D.	1995	The impact of Information Technology on the Practice of Archaeological Management. In: M. Cooper/A. Firth/J. Carmen/D. Wheatley (eds), *Managing Archaeology*, 163-174, London: Routledge.
Wilcock, J. K. Lockyear (eds)	1995	*Computer Applications and Quantitative Methods in Archaeology 1993*, BAR International Series 598. Oxford: Tempus Reparatum.
Wood, J.	1989	Using dBase for county SMRs: the Humberside experience. In: S.P.Q. Rahtz/ J.D. Richards (eds), *Computer Applications and Quantitative Methods in Archaeology 1989*, 27-29, BAR International Series 548, Oxford: British Archaeological Reports.
Yakub, H.	1992	*Buildings at Risk Registers: Their Influence in Reducing Risk of Dilapidation*. (Unpublished PhD Thesis), Oxford: Oxford Brooks University.

Nigel D. Clubb and Neil A.R. Lang
Royal Commission on the Historical Monuments of England
National Monuments Record Centre
Kemble Drive
Swindon SN2 2GZ
United Kingdom

Nigel D. Clubb
Neil A.R. Lang

Learning from the achievements of Information Systems – the role of the Post-Implementation Review in medium to large scale systems

1 Introduction

In the last decade, a number of papers on information systems supporting heritage records in English local and central government have been published. Several of these have stressed the considerable financial value accruing to these information systems, which may often be disguised by the relatively modest initial investment in the basic technology to sustain them. The purpose of all information systems, whether large or small, is to support the business of their parent organisation, and the process of managing these projects seeks to ensure their cost-effective and timely delivery to meet the business objectives. Regular reviews during the life cycle of the information system are an essential process to ensure these objectives are achieved.

For central government in England, Clubb (1989) has already described the Investment Appraisal process, which may govern a decision to initiate a new information system. In this paper, the authors seek to describe the logical conclusion to an implementation — the Post-Implementation Review (PIR). It is an important phase in the life cycle of all IT projects, although it is often overlooked, or paid scant attention. This paper places the PIR in the context of the systems development process, sets out potential areas of risk to projects and considers four English cases studies, of which the authors of the paper have first-hand experience:

- the English Heritage Record of Scheduled Monuments (RSM),
- the Royal Commission on Historical Monuments of England (RCHME) National Monuments Record, MONARCH,
- the Greater London Council/English Heritage Greater London Sites and Monuments Record,
- the West Midlands Sites and Monuments Record.

The implementation of all new computing systems requires, to some degree, a process of learning. Heritage computing will only progress if we are all willing to share the knowledge derived from this process, both good and otherwise. We are grateful that colleagues in the organisations mentioned in this paper have been willing to share their experiences in this way.

2 The system development process and areas of risk to the success of information systems projects

Large information systems projects usually require to be managed through a series of discrete stages, sometimes called the system development process or project life cycle. A typical project life cycle will follow some or all of the following stages illustrated in figure 1 (not necessarily in the order shown, since certain processes may run concurrently).

The PIR occupies a critical role in the system development process in reviewing the system as implemented against the original assumptions and preparing the way for future developments. Before embarking on a major system, it is worth examining in advance some of the areas of potential risks. These should be anticipated in the Investment Appraisal (Clubb 1989) which should include both an appraisal of risk and the testing of the sensitivity of the investment to changes in the fundamental assumptions inherent in a project.

2.1 AREAS OF RISK:

All information systems are susceptible to a number of areas of risk. These may include some or all of the following:
- lack of clearly defined objectives and benefits,
- lack of user commitment or system 'ownership',
- failure to improve data/procedures *before* developing new systems,
- lack of formal project management/development methodologies,
- lack of clearly defined project rules,
- failure to define acceptance criteria and testing protocols
- failure to estimate adequate resource, including training and documentation,
- failure to assess hardware/software capacity,
- failure to establish formal disaster recovery plans and security standards,
- lack of legal/contractual advice on relationships with suppliers,
- lack of documentation.

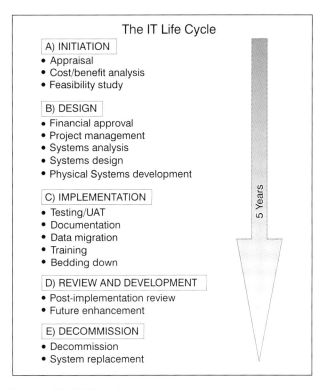

The IT Life Cycle

A) INITIATION
- Appraisal
- Cost/benefit analysis
- Feasibility study

B) DESIGN
- Financial approval
- Project management
- Systems analysis
- Systems design
- Physical Systems development

C) IMPLEMENTATION
- Testing/UAT
- Documentation
- Data migration
- Training
- Bedding down

D) REVIEW AND DEVELOPMENT
- Post-implementation review
- Future enhancement

E) DECOMMISSION
- Decommission
- System replacement

5 Years

Figure 1. The IT life cycle.

Those responsible for managing an information project should ideally have the necessary experience to anticipate risks and act to minimise them.

2.2   THE ROLE OF THE POST-IMPLEMENTATION REVIEW

In the system development cycle, the PIR performs a critical role in assessing the achievements of a system against the original expectations which justified the decision to invest in its development. If an organisation does not conduct reviews, then it is likely that its information systems will not be properly managed. Money will be wasted because it is likely that:

– information systems will not be fully aligned with the business objectives of the organisation,
– the organisation which has funded the initiative will have no means of knowing whether its investment is providing value for money,
– benefits management will not be effective and the benefits predicted in the business cases will not be realised,
– the costs and risks to the enterprise will not be minimised,
– generic lessons, of use to future implementations within the organisation and to others will not be assimilated.

The PIR is normally initiated when the new system is fully implemented and when the users are fully conversant with its features and facilities. The timing of the review needs careful judgement. For micro-systems, normally, about three months after implementation is appropriate. For larger scale systems, the review would normally be conducted between six and twelve months after implementation. If the review takes place too soon, then it may attach undue importance to what are no more than short-term technical issues and this may lead to erroneous conclusions. The focus of the review should, in the main, be on the medium to long term and the degree to which the system supports the business activity. It is particularly important that the timing of the review adequately covers any cyclical features, such as quarterly, bi-annual or annual tasks which the system is expected to perform.

In summary then, the primary purpose of the review is to determine whether:

– events have proved the validity of the planning assumptions,
– the claimed savings and/or benefits have been achieved.

The scope of a PIR will be governed by the size and the complexity of the project to which it relates. For simple micro-systems, this may be a very brief document, but this in no way lessens the desirability of holding the review. For larger systems, PIRs can often be extensive documents, and consideration should be given to the adoption of a formal review methodology such as MEVIOS (Method for Evaluating the Impact of Office Systems, CCTA 1989).

Information for the PIR can be gathered from:

– interview or the circulation of questionnaires to those operating and using the system,
– examining system documentation such as project minutes, user and training documentation, testing protocols, system maintenance logs and computer resource accounting packages,
– observations on the business and IT operations,
– feedback from external clients of the system, where appropriate.

The PIR may be undertaken as an in-house review, or by an external consultant. As one of its final actions, the IT project board overseeing the project should have set up the terms of reference for the review. The key issue is to ensure that the process is undertaken as objectively as possible. This usually means that the report should be prepared by someone not directly involved with the project, either as developer or user.

A formal methodology for risk assessment, such as CRAMM (Computer Risk Analysis and Management

Models, CCTA 1988) and general security issues should be undertaken periodically after any significant new change to a system.

Against this background, the authors would like to examine four case studies, two drawn from central government records systems, the Record of Scheduled Monuments, operated by English Heritage, and the National Monuments Record application (MONARCH) run by the RCHME, and two at a local level, the Greater London Sites and Monuments Record (SMR), now managed by English Heritage, and the West Midlands SMR, run by the West Midlands Joint Data Team, a jointly sponsored body established to service strategic information systems requirements by the seven metropolitan district councils of the West Midlands County.

All four systems are substantially successful, but they all provide lessons for their host organisation, as well as for others.

3   English Heritage – Record of Scheduled Monuments

3.1   OBJECTIVES OF THE SYSTEM

The objectives and implementation of the English Heritage RSM are well documented elsewhere (Clubb 1991a, 1991b; Clubb/Startin 1995). The system curates the national database of scheduled monuments and automates the complex processes involved in the identification, legal protection and management of the most important archaeological sites in England.

3.2   IMPLEMENTATION HISTORY

A cost-benefit analysis carried out in 1988 concluded that the costs of the system of £ 605,380 over a 7 year period would represent savings over a range of alternative ways of meeting the requirement. The investment appraisal associated with the decision to develop the system is discussed in Clubb 1989 and included an element of both risk analysis and sensitivity testing. The system was developed during 1990-1991 using the Oracle relational database.

3.3   POST-IMPLEMENTATION REVIEW

The PIR was carried out by external consultants and completed in April 1992. The system was undoubtedly a success in terms of automating the procedures of scheduling monuments. The PIR identified strengths in the project implementation as follows:

– significant financial savings achieved,
– systems liked by staff,
– system analysis, design and programming handled well,
– reliable application software,

– meets original design specification, administrative activities and data storage requirements,
– choice of Oracle software will facilitate links with RCHME systems and sharing of expertise between English Heritage and RCHME.

3.4   CONCLUSION

The PIR also concluded that some lessons could be drawn from the project. Although system analysis, design and programming had been handled well, it was noted that system testing, user acceptance and data take-on experienced delays. It was also noted that without the dedication and sheer tenacity of key members of staff, several aspects of the project would have been unlikely to have been successfully implemented. It recommended that the English Heritage information technology system development standards provided a good basic framework, but required strengthening. It also commented on the need for formal project management methodologies. Other recommendations identified the need for regular planning exercises on hardware capacity and for English Heritage to review the balance between local information technology support and the need for a large central support and maintenance team.

4   Royal Commission on Historical Monuments (RCHME) – National Monuments Record (MONARCH) system

4.1   OBJECTIVES OF THE SYSTEM

The objectives of the MONARCH system are discussed elsewhere (Beagrie 1993). It sought to unify a number of existing computer databases within the RCHME, provide a single point of entry to RCHME information systems for external users and staff and to offer a number of other benefits of convenience, speed and scope of coverage. The system presents a new model of the relationships between monuments and their associated archives and events.

4.2   IMPLEMENTATION HISTORY

The first major computer implementation in RCHME was the National Archaeological Record (NAR) from 1984 (Aberg/Leech 1992; Beagrie 1993; Grant 1985; Hart/Leech 1989; Lang 1995). A strategic review of future requirements was carried out in 1990 and this recommended the development of a unified database to replace the original NAR database and a number of other archaeological and buildings databases. The key elements of the new system were Monument Recording, Activities/Event Recording, Archive and Bibliographic Recording and persons/organisation. This system was developed in 1991-1992 and implemented in 1993.

4.3 POST-IMPLEMENTATION REVIEW

The PIR was carried out by a senior member of RCHME staff who was independent of the MONARCH system development process and reported in December, 1994. The system undoubtedly broke new ground in analysing the relationship between monuments and their sources. The PIR identified strengths in the project implementation as follows:

– underlying philosophy and architecture excellent,
– opened internal communication and discussion of harmony of working procedures,
– considerable range and complexity of retrieval mechanism,
– successfully handles large quantities of complex data,
- links, associations and cross-references a major development in concept and functionality.

4.4 CONCLUSION

The PIR also concluded that some lessons could be drawn from the project. The decision to proceed with the system was based on the corporate benefits of a unified database which should have been underpinned by a formal cost-benefit analysis. This would make it much easier to assess the strengths and weaknesses of the new system against the original assumptions. Most of the other issues raised relate to the need to develop project management methodologies and to ensure proper training and involvement of staff. The PIR also examined the timing of the introduction of a new system. Sometimes a project may act as a catalyst for corporate improvements in existing working arrangements and procedures. It is debatable whether a more effective approach is to review existing working practices and procedures *before* system development is undertaken. These are issues on which an organisation must exercise judgement in devising an implementation plan.

5. Greater London Council/English Heritage – The Greater London Sites and Monuments Record

5.1 OBJECTIVES OF THE SYSTEM

Details of the original objectives and implementation of the Greater London SMR have been published (Clubb/ James 1985; Jones 1989). The objectives are similar to those of the West Midlands SMR (discussed below), although there was a greater emphasis on historic buildings as well as archaeological sites and monuments. This reflected the original sponsor of the SMR, the Historic Buildings Division of the Greater London Council (GLC), which worked in close association with the museums and archaeological services for London in developing the project.

5.2 IMPLEMENTATION HISTORY

The Greater London SMR was first developed in the period 1984-1986 on an ADABAS database on the GLC main-frame. On the abolition of the GLC in 1986, the project was transferred to the London Region of English Heritage with a privatised computer bureau service provided by Hoskins plc. The costs of the bureau service were considerable, nearly £ 100,000 pa and following a consultants' report in November 1987 it was decided to re-develop the computer system using Oracle as an in-house facility. This was estimated to cost £ 200,000, but the lower running costs subsequently were expected to ensure that there were significant financial advantages in the proposal, as well as benefits in the migration from ADABAS to the Oracle relational database. The transfer took place in 1991-1992.

5.3 POST-IMPLEMENTATION REVIEW

The PIR was carried out by external consultants and completed in March 1993. The project is undoubtedly a success in providing a better, less expensive system. The PIR identified significant strengths in the project implementation. These are summarised below:

– project delivered on time and on budget,
– successful migration from old to new system,
– system testing was effective,
– improved functionality,
– good change control procedures,
– significant financial savings achieved (about £ 37,880 pa).

5.4 CONCLUSION

The PIR also considered that some lessons could be drawn from the project. Although it should be regarded as successful in terms of the original objectives, the success was due to the natural ability of those concerned and relied heavily on the abilities of those individuals. The consultants concluded that any degree of risk to the project could have been minimised by the use of a structured project manage-ment methodology and with associated project management tools. They also recommended that project managers should be trained in project management. Of some interest is the suggestion that the envisaged benefits from the system should not just have centred on the benefits of an outside bureau versus an in-house operation but should have re-visited the SMR from first principles and considered the total cost of the system against the benefits rather than just the savings.

6 West Midlands SMR

6.1 OBJECTIVES OF THE SYSTEM

Details of the organisational objectives and implementation of the West Midlands SMR have been published (Lang

1989; Lang/Stead 1992). In essence, these were to establish a computerised inventory of archaeological and architectural sites and monuments to provide for more effective management and planning control of this resource, though the details of how the system would support these functions were not established prior to implementation.

6.2   IMPLEMENTATION HISTORY

The West Midlands SMR was developed as a stand-alone computerised system from 1987 onwards on a PC using Superfile database management system software. It closely followed the standard of DoE Advisory Note 32 (DoE 1981). In common with many SMRs, the initial capital set-up costs were very low, amounting to around £ 4,000. However, by the end of the four year strategic plan for its development, investment in the system, including data entry costs, amounted to some £ 75,000. In 1989, on transfer to the West Midlands Joint Data Team, an organisation of around 40 information professionals providing information processing and analytical services for the 7 West Midlands District Councils, it was decided to develop a new system to improve data handling, development control, and cartographic manipulation. Although resources for the SMR were scarce, by combining this initiative with other requirements within the Data Team, it was possible to justify the investment. Following an extensive evaluation, a solution using a relational database and GIS software (INGRES and Genamap) was selected and prototype systems were constructed.

6.3   POST-IMPLEMENTATION REVIEW

In common with the majority of SMR systems established in local government, no formal process of review was required either by the host authority or by English Heritage, as the initial grant aiding body (although monitoring of data entry rates was conducted throughout the period of grant aid, see below). The strengths of the systems development may be summarised as follows:

– development costs were shared with other functions within the organisation,
– the operational requirement was clearly established and the procurement was carefully controlled,
– there was close integration of database and spatial GIS elements of the system,
– it met its principal requirement -development control- both through the SMR and in support of archaeological development control functions elsewhere,
– the analysis for the system broke new ground through defining generic groupings of related monument types,
– the system provided both tangible and intangible benefits through enhanced functionality.

6.4   CONCLUSION

There were also some areas where the review indicated improvements could have been made. The main areas of weakness were in underestimating resource requirements for the development. In common with most local government SMRs, the conflicting pressures of development control-related work, and maintenance of the existing system, meant that development work could not be reliably programmed and progress was slower than anticipated. This could have been avoided through including external technical consultancy in the development of the system, though, given the constraints of local government funding, it is not certain whether this could have been better resourced. Finally, the project was (perhaps inevitably in such a small team) closely identified with a single member of staff. The subsequent departure of that member of staff has caused considerable delays to the full implementation of the system as originally envisaged.

7   Conclusions

Post-implementation reviews are an essential mechanism for minimising risk in IT systems, and should be seen as an integral and indispensable part of the overall review process within the life cycle of an information system. The examples quoted above provide solid examples of the benefits derived from a formal review, and also point to some of the dangers in failing to measure system performance against the original expectations of the system, as opposed to the performance of individuals as processors of data. They also stress the need for formal methodologies and the potential risk of depending on a small number of individuals.

In central government, PIRs are an expected part of all significant IT projects, and for major initiatives, these are normally conducted by external consultants. Post-implementation reviews are also accepted practice in local government computing, but do not tend to be applied as a formal requirement in quite the same way. In the case of local authority SMRs, very few have been subject to a formal review process, with, in many cases, adverse consequences.

The original justification for computerised local SMRs was made largely by the Department of the Environment (and later by English Heritage) at a central government level. English Heritage took responsibility during the 1980s for the extensive 'pump-priming' of local government SMR systems, having a considerable influence over the choice of software systems used in over half of the 46 County SMRs. While local government officers took up the development of these systems with considerable enthusiasm, the responsibility for ensuring the effective initial implementation of these systems through the review process must rest with central government.

The initial supervision of local SMR implementations was made almost entirely by the Department of the Environment Ancient Monuments Inspectorate (English Heritage after 1986), which consisted of archaeological professionals who were not necessarily 'computer literate'. Their concern rested largely with the achievement of data entry rates as a key performance indicator, rather than with the quality of the system developed, the integrity of records being entered or the testing of assumptions about the ability of these systems to answer questions in the furtherance of central and local government objectives. These were regarded as local matters, although as early as 1984, one member of the Inspectorate was lamenting that there had been no formal analysis of the operational requirement and functionality for SMRs (Inspectorate of Ancient Monuments 1984).

In local government as a whole, SMRs are generally considered to be peripheral IT systems. It may be argued that the case for making these more robust would be enhanced through the adoption of formal review methodologies. Following the establishment of a lead coordinating role for local authority SMRs, RCHME is helping to support audits of sites and monuments records considering taking the PC version of the MONARCH database. Although these are not intended as PIRs, much of the information provided through the audit could be used, with minimal further translation, to form the basis for a PIR, and are being used to make the case for further IT development.

In general, the required investment in technical development and maintenance of local SMR systems has been substantially underestimated, with only a minority having defined the resources for formal development. Nonetheless, the majority of local SMRs report that their systems *do* successfully support their internal functions qualitatively, but their ability to provide statistics for national programmes has often been found to be more limited.

The lack of formal management methodologies in IT planning for local SMRs means that further investment is now required to maximise the benefits from these systems, including the establishment of efficient protocols for digital data exchange with the RCHME National Monuments Record and other relevant bodies. This is not simply a question of providing resources to support data preparation and input (though both should be covered in IT planning). It is equally a question of the need to review and to measure performance against original objectives. These are areas where the RCHME, as the lead co-ordinating body for SMRs, should, perhaps, develop a more proactive role in the future, in the light of experience of PIRs of their own systems.

Our companion paper in this volume (Clubb/Lang 'A Strategic Appraisal of Information Systems') includes an extensive bibliography, with relevant additional literature to that specifically cited in the text. The paper seeks to achieve a strategic appraisal of monuments records in England and PIRs have a critical role to play in helping to refine this process.

bibliography

Aberg, F.A.
R.H. Leech
1992 The national archaeological record for England. Past, present and future. In: C.U. Larsen (ed.) *Sites and monuments. National Archaeological Records*, 157-169, Copenhagen: National Museum of Denmark.

Beagrie, N.
1993 The computerisation of the National Archaeological Record, *Revue Informatique et Statistique dans les Sciences humaines*, 1-4, 9-16, Liège.

CCTA
1988 CRAMM (Computer Risk Analysis and Management Models).

1989 MEVIOS (Method for Evaluating the Impact of Office Systems, IT Series No. 6).

Clubb, N.D.
1989 Investment appraisal for information technology. In: S.P.Q. Rahtz/J.D. Richards (eds), *Computer Applications and Quantitative Methods in Archaeology 1989*, 1-7, BAR International Series 548, Oxford: British Archaeological Reports.

1991a Procuring medium-large systems. In: K. Lockyear/S.P.Q. Rahtz (eds), *Computer Applications and Quantitative Methods in Archaeology 1990*, 81-84, BAR International Series 565, Oxford: Tempus Reparatum.

1991b The operational requirement for a medium to large-scale System – the Experience of the English Heritage Record of Scheduled Monuments. In: K. Lockyear/S.P.Q. Rahtz (eds), *Computer Applications and Quantitative Methods in Archaeology 1990*, 85-91, BAR International Series 565, Oxford: Tempus Reparatum.

Clubb, N.
P. James
1985 A computer record for Greater London's Heritage, *London Archaeologist*, Vol. 5, 38-9.

Clubb, N.D.
W.D. Startin
1995 Information systems strategies in national organisations and the identification, legal protection and management of the most important sites in England. In: J. Wilcock/ K. Lockyear (eds), *Computer Applications and Quantitative Methods in Archaeology 1993*, 67-73, BAR International Series 598, Oxford: Tempus Reparatum.

Department of the Environment
1981 *Advisory Note no. 32*. Ancient Monuments Records Manual and County Sites and Monuments Records. London: Department of the Environment.

Grant, S.
1985 Computing the past and anticipating the future. In E. Webb (ed.), *Computer Applications in Archaeology 1985*, 152, London: University of London Institute of Archaeology.

Hart, J.
R. Leech
1989 The national archaeological record. In: S.P.Q. Rahtz/J. Richards (eds), *Computer Applications and Quantitative Methods in Archaeology 1989*, 57-67, BAR International Series 548, Oxford: British Archaeological Reports.

Inspectorate of Ancient Monuments
1984 *England's Archaeological Resource. A rapid Quantification of the National Archaeological Resource and a Comparison with the Schedule of Ancient Monuments*. London: Department of the Environment.

Jones, H.
1989 The Greater London Sites and Monuments Record – a case study. In: S.P.Q. Rahtz/ J. Richards (eds), *Computer Applications and Quantitative Methods in Archaeology 1989*, 33-38, BAR International Series 548, Oxford: British Archaeological Reports.

Lang, N.A.R.
1989 Sites and Monuments Records in historic towns. In: S.P.Q. Rahtz/J. Richards (eds), *Computer Applications and Quantitative Methods in Archaeology 1989*, 41-50, BAR International Series 548, Oxford: British Archaeological Reports.

Lang, N.A.R.   1995   Recording and managing the national heritage. In: J. Wilcock/K. Lockyear (eds),
                                    Computer Applications and Quantitative Methods in Archaeology 1993, 75-80, BAR Inter-
                                    national Series 598, Oxford: Tempus Reparatum.

Lang, N.A.R.   1992   Sites and monuments records in England – theory and practise. In: G. Lock/J. Moffett
    S. Stead   (eds), *Computer Applications and Quantitative Methods in Archaeology 1991*, 69-76,
                                    BAR International Series 577, Oxford: Tempus Reparatum.

Larsen, C.U. (ed.)   1992   *Sites and monuments. National Archaeological Records*. Copenhagen: National Museum
                                    of Denmark.

Lock, G.   1992   *Computer Applications and Quantitative Methods in Archaeology 1991*, BAR International
    J. Moffett (eds)   Series 577, Oxford: Tempus Reparatum.

Lockyear, K.   1991   *Computer Applications and Quantitative Methods in Archaeology 1990*, BAR International
    S.P.Q. Rahtz (eds)   Series 565, Oxford: Tempus Reparatum.

Rahtz, S.P.Q.   1989   *Computer Applications and Quantitative Methods in Archaeology 1989*, BAR International
    J. Richards (eds)   Series 548, Oxford: British Archaeological Reports.

Webb, E. (ed.)   1985   Computer Applications in Archaeology 1985. London: University of London Institute of
                                    Archaeology.

Wilcock, J.   1995   *Computer Applications and Quantitative Methods in Archaeology 1993*, BAR International
    K. Lockyear (eds)   Series 598, Oxford: Tempus Reparatum.

Nigel D. Clubb and Neil A.R. Lang
Royal Commission on the Historical Monuments of England
National Monuments Record Centre
Kemble Drive
Swindon SN2 2GZ
United Kingdom

Neil Beagrie

Excavations and Archives: Alternative Aspects of Cultural Resource Management

1 Introduction

In this paper I would like to explore how some issues of cultural resource management are beginning to affect the collection of information about excavations and the management of archaeological archives in England. I would like to focus on four main issues:

1. The rapidly increasing volume of archaeological documentary and finds archives and the need for long-term curation and storage.
2. Access to information on excavations and archives for cultural resource managers.
3. The analysis of trends in archaeological fieldwork and its contribution to our interpretation and management of the past.
4. The contribution of national computerised databases and analytical tools to these areas, using examples from the MONARCH database of the Royal Commission on the Historical Monuments of England.

I am conscious that I will be talking solely about England and that the volume of archaeological fieldwork and the organisational structures of archaeology vary greatly across Europe but the issues raised should also be of interest to colleagues outside England.

2 The Development of the RCHME's Database Information on Archaeological Events and Archives

There has been an increasing trend in recent years in England to re-examine archaeological databases and to begin to distinguish between information on sources and primary investigation and secondary interpretation. This has proved to be particularly important in urban areas with complex and fragmentary deposits and this distinction has been fundamental in the development of Urban Archaeological Databases in England. This distinction has also been fundamental to MONARCH.

I now wish to explain to you the background to how the RCHME began to collect discrete database information on archives and excavations and related archaeological issues.

In England there has been a diverse and thriving network of individuals and local, regional and national bodies, undertaking archaeological work, several hundred museums and other institutions in which this material has been deposited, and almost as many newsletters, journals and monographs in which this work could be published.

Growing concern in the 1970s over the very large backlog of publication in England, the safekeeping of documentary archives and finds, and the need to improve awareness and access to them has led the RCHME to actively compile information on archaeological excavations and archives as one of its core activities.

3 The Management of Archaeological Archives in England

There have been a number of fundamental shifts in British Archaeology in recent years with funding being increasingly derived from developers rather than government and an increasing emphasis on small-scale evaluations and use of the planning system rather than large excavation projects.

A recent article in British Archaeological News shows that the rapid increase in excavations and volume of archive being deposited in museums is now an issue in England, particularly in major urban centres such as London (Council for British Archaeology 1994).

The existence of a national database with discrete and retrievable information on excavations and archives can provide quantification and analysis of such issues, which extend beyond any one locality or region. To illustrate this, I would like to look at information held on archaeological collections in museums in England by the RCHME, and present some national quantification of the resource derived from information on excavations and archives held in MONARCH.

We have only recently completed the updating and expansion of our information on archaeological events. However, I think the value of a national dataset on archaeological interventions is already apparent (fig. 1). The scale of the increase in excavation in England since the early 1800s, and by implication, its impact on museum collections, can now be seen from the data we have

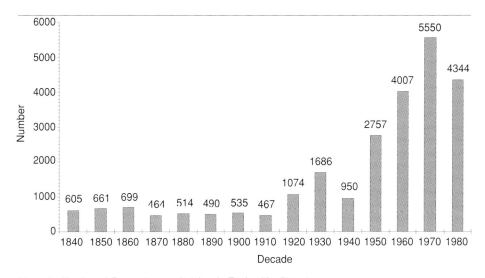

Figure 1. Number of Excavations undertaken in England by Decade.

collected. Figure 1 shows the number of excavations which have taken place in England in each decade since 1840.

From the outset we have aimed for comprehensive national coverage and have recorded excavations of any date, on sites of all archaeological periods, including sites from the industrial revolution, and excavations which have recorded negative as well as positive results. We have collected information on excavations undertaken by early antiquarians in the nineteenth century, through to the growth in excavations between the two world wars and the major surge in excavations from the 1960s onwards. As you can see, there were over 5,500 excavations in England in the 1970s alone.

This information has recently been updated to include all excavations up to 1992/1993 and we have added information on evaluations and watching briefs, and finally surveys funded by English Heritage or its predecessors since 1960.

As of March 1995 we have recorded:

– 28,777 excavations,
– 7,482 evaluations and watching briefs,
– we have located the documentary archives for 53% and the finds for 54% of the total excavations recorded.

For a session on the future of archaeological archives at the Institute of Field Archaeologists conference in England in April 1994, MONARCH was used to provide a broad quantification of the scale of the likely archive and publication problems facing the profession (fig. 2).

The period 1940-1980 was selected to cover the archives being tackled in post-excavation backlogs. 1980 was chosen as a cut off date as information on the late 1980s was still being entered onto MONARCH when these figures were compiled.

Over 13,000 excavations were recorded for the period 1940-1980. Final reports had been published for 37%, while for 11% there was no known publication at all. Substantial post-excavation and publication programmes are in progress which will reduce these backlogs, but much will remain unpublished: this emphasises the growing importance of the archives as repositories of original data. The cost of publication and the consequent trend towards summary publication reports supported by a publicly accessible archive will also emphasise the importance of the archive.

Documentary archives and finds had been located for 65% of the excavations over this period. Of the documentary archives located, 51% were in museums, 17% with individuals, and 32% in other locations (principally units and local societies). For the finds located, 72% were in museums, 9% with individuals, and 19% in other locations.

I should emphasise that these statistics should be regarded as best estimates as they cover 2/3rds of the archives for excavations undertaken between 1940-1980; the remaining 1/3rd, for which we have no information on the archive, may not follow an identical pattern.

These figures provide some insight into the growth of archaeological collections, the potential transfers to repositories in the next decade and pressures on resources, which may arise in England. Without central collection and computerisation of information on excavations and archives such an analysis would have been impossible.

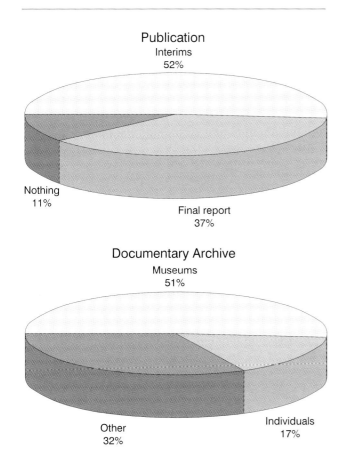

Publication

Interims
52%

Nothing
11%

Final report
37%

Documentary Archive

Museums
51%

Other
32%

Individuals
17%

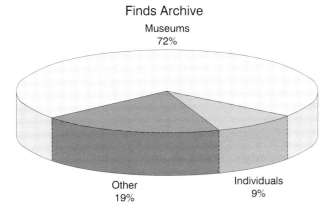

Finds Archive

Museums
72%

Other
19%

Individuals
9%

Figure 2. Publication and Archive Locations for Excavations undertaken in England between 1940 and 1980 (as of March 1994).

4   Access to Information on Excavations and Archives

The great diversity of organisations undertaking archaeological work, the range of publications and archive locations, combined with the increase in small-scale evaluations published in limited circulation copy, make access to primary data very difficult for researchers. I think there can be no doubt that archaeological collections can be an under-utilised resource.

In 1991 the Society of Museum Archaeologists undertook a survey covering access to museum archaeological collections in Britain. The survey found that requests to view collections were disappointingly small. 12% of museums, mostly those with very small archaeological collections, had received no requests to view the collections over the previous 12 months. Just over half (53%) received up to 10 requests a year. Only 3 museums received over 100 enquiries a year — and this figure may have been doubtful because some museums did not distinguish between archaeological and non-archaeological enquiries.

Overall a picture emerged of few individual requests to view collections, which were most likely to be restricted to specialist researchers (Merriman 1993).

Several years have passed since the SMA survey was undertaken and hopefully a similar survey undertaken today would show that the position has improved considerably. However there can be little doubt that locating material and gaining access to it can still be difficult and that computerisation of finding aids for archaeological finds and documentary archives has great potential for improving this situation.

The ability to identify collections of excavated material by period or site type is a valuable tool for regional or national research. MONARCH will not give detailed finds lists, but can provide a high-level index to what is in which museum or other repository. For example The Medieval Ceramics Studies Group requested a printout giving details of repositories and publications for several thousand excavated medieval sites in England as part of the Survey of Medieval Ceramics Studies in England, the results of which have recently been published (Mellor 1994).

An example of the difficulty of locating material recently appeared in the newsletter of the Prehistoric Society concerning the archives of Benjamin Harrison (Cook/Jacobi 1994). Harrison, who was born in 1837 and died in 1923, was a collector and recorder of archaeological finds of all periods in the county of Kent in Southeast England. In 1890 he excavated a site at Oldbury, which is still Britain's only significant open-air site of the Middle Palaeolithic. He donated the finds from this site to the British Museum. Recent research on this collection has highlighted the necessity of locating any of Harrison's surviving records and British Museum staff appealed for information through the newsletter of the Prehistoric Society.

A search of the archive records in the RCHME's database identified records from Harrison in several different institutions in Southern England, including the Pitt Rivers Museum in Oxford, Maidstone Museum, Croydon Natural History and Scientific Museum, the Guildhall

Museum in Rochester, the Tunbridge Wells Museum and
Art Gallery, and the Surrey Archaeological Society collections at Guildford. Computerisation has allowed our
information on the location and nature of Harrison's
archives to be extracted quickly and this information has
now been passed to staff at the British Museum and a brief
note published in PAST (Sargent 1995).

Benjamin Harrison's archive demonstrates how widely
dispersed records of any one individual or site can become
and our own systematic surveys of excavations and other
archaeological archives show how this pattern can be
repeated for most sites of regional or national significance
in England.

It also demonstrates some of the current problems with
access to information, particularly for those involved in
cultural resource management working within the time
constraints imposed by developers or the planning system.
For many the option of writing to a newsletter editor or any
traditional form of gathering primary information is just too
slow.

In many cases I suspect computerisation and online
access to museums, regional and national databases is the
only means by which this data will become widely
available and used. I would expect online access to the
RCHME's information on monuments, archives and
excavations and to similar resources such as the British
Archaeological Bibliography or regional databases to
provide a significant increase in the use of such resources.

5   Trends in Archaeological Fieldwork

The growth of developer funded work in recent years and
changes in planning guidance, particularly the introduction
of PPG 16, have led to increasing discussion on research
frameworks and research to monitor new trends in
archaeological fieldwork. In England research has been
commissioned into the growth and effectiveness of
archaeological assessments (English Heritage forthcoming),
and funding bodies are beginning to compile database
information on projects and research objectives to monitor
achievements against policy objectives and improve
strategic planning (an example of this is the Management
Information System being developed by the Archaeology
Division of English Heritage).

The structure of MONARCH and our database
information on events and archives as well as monuments
are beginning to allow us to examine some of these trends
in archaeological fieldwork.

Research 'fashions' in Bronze Age studies and their
impact on our knowledge of the period were examined in
1992 in an article in Antiquity by Michael Morris based
substantially on analysis from the excavations data in
MONARCH (Morris 1992).

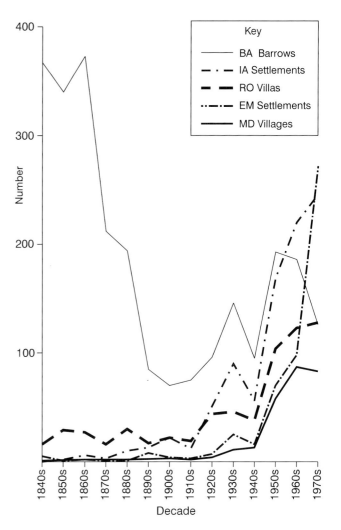

Figure 3. Number of Excavations for Specific Site Types by Decade
between 1840 and 1980.

It is possible to examine trends for any period, site or
intervention type utilising data in MONARCH. Figure 3
shows excavation trends in England from the early 1840s for
specific monuments types and periods, namely Bronze Age
barrows, Iron Age settlements, Roman villas, Anglo-Saxon
and other Early Medieval settlements, and Medieval villages.

Comparison with figure 1 shows how these partly reflect
broader national trends in excavation, particularly the growth
in excavations between the wars and the exponential increase
from the end of World War II through the 1970s. However,
there are some significant differences. The most marked of
these is the very different trend in the excavation of Bronze
Age barrows, with sharp falls in the number of excavations
undertaken in the late nineteenth century and again in the
1960s and 1970s. This reflects the late nineteenth century
trend away from barrow digging; the development of a more

systematic and therefore more intensive approach to excavation of individual barrows; and the government sponsored programme of barrow excavation in response to destruction by agriculture in the 1950s and early 1960s, which was subsequently curtailed. The post World War II intensification of research on Iron Age, Early Medieval and Medieval sites is also apparent. The excavation of Early Medieval settlements and Medieval villages reflects other aspects of data retrieval from MONARCH and research trends, as the term settlements covers both rural and urban site types which have been excavated whilst the term villages does not. The trend line for the excavation of Early Medieval settlements therefore includes the large number of excavations started in the 1960s on historic urban centres such as York, Southampton and Winchester.

6   Conclusion

In conclusion I hope I have demonstrated to you the value of computerised data at a national level on excavations and archaeological archives, and of database structures which can link this information to monuments but which also allows them to be analysed as discrete datasets.

I have concentrated on MONARCH, England's national database and examples from archaeology in England but hope that you will also find that these examples have relevance elsewhere and for local or regional databases as well as databases at national level.

7   Access to the NMR

The MONARCH database on which this article is based can be consulted by contacting NMR Customer Services, National Monuments Record Centre, Kemble Drive, Swindon SN2 2GZ (Telephone 44 (0)1793 414600 or Fax 44 (0)1793 414606)

Acknowledgements

I would like to thank Suzanne Ferguson and Andrew Sargent for assistance in compiling this article.

references

Council for British Archaeology	1994	Unhappy Museums, *British Archaeological News*, New Series 19, 6-7.
Cook, J. R. Jacobi	1994	Where are they now, *PAST: The Newsletter of the Prehistoric Society* 18, 9.
English Heritage	forth- coming	*Planning for the Past: A review of archaeological assessment procedures in England 1982-1991.*
Mellor, M.	1994	*Medieval Ceramic Studies in England: A review for English Heritage.* London: English Heritage.
Merriman, N.	1993	The use of collections: the need for a positive approach, *The Museum Archaeologist* 18, 10-17.
Morris, M.	1992	The rise and fall of Bronze Age studies in England 1840-1960, *Antiquity* 66, 419-426.
Sargent, A.	1995	Where are they now – some answers, *PAST: The Newsletter of the Prehistoric Society* 19, 8-9.

Neil Beagrie
Royal Commission on the Historical Monuments of England
Kemble Drive
Swindon SN2 2GZ
United Kingdom

Mark Bell
Nicola King

The MARS Project – an interface with England's past

1   Introduction

The full title of the MARS Project is the Monuments at Risk Survey. This project is funded by English Heritage, the national body responsible for archaeology in England. In response to a number of studies carried out during the 1980s which underlined the need for quantified, nationwide information (Darvill 1987; English Heritage 1991; IAM 1984; RCHME 1993), this three-year project was commissioned to undertake a large-scale, but rapid, survey of the condition and potential of England's archaeological resource. The purpose is to establish a baseline for the future. The results may stimulate work on national and regional scales to identify further the threats to England's archaeology, and to develop cultural resource management techniques. MARS is not an attempt to identify particular monuments under extreme threats, nor is it an attempt to identify particular areas under special risk. MARS is attempting to understand the national picture, the range of threats, the impact on groups of monument classes; for example, what proportion of upland sites are threatened by changes in agricultural activity; and whether prehistoric sites are being greatly affected by urban growth.

The history of MARS dates back to a pilot study, also funded by English Heritage, undertaken in the county of Wiltshire during 1989-90, in which methods of data collection and techniques of data analysis were tested. The project designs of both the pilot study and MARS have been open to consultation by professional archaeologists, and a considerable period of review and discussion was allowed between the presentation of the results of the pilot study and the commencement of MARS (Darvill 1991).

One aim of MARS is to provide information about the state and potential of England's archaeological resource. This includes identifying the scale and nature of the resource; the range of methods of recording archaeology, and the levels of recording for single monuments, archaeologically defined landscapes, and historic urban areas. This kind of information is not routinely gathered on a national scale, the last attempt was in 1984 (IAM 1984), but it is essential in order to develop any strategy for the future management of sites and monuments on a national scale. The simple questions MARS is aiming to answer

include identifying how many monuments are recorded in England, and which periods they are from. Some of the problems relating to the concept of a national database for England are discussed by Fraser (Fraser 1993).

MARS has three main research and data collection areas. The most labour intensive is the combined efforts of field survey and aerial photographic teams which are examining the current and previous condition of the recorded sites and monuments within a 5% random sample of the land area of England. This is an area of 6500 km^2 which is thought to contain around 20,000 known archaeological sites. A 5% sample was chosen after analysis of the results of the Wiltshire-based pilot study (Darvill 1991: 123-126). A 5% sample is needed to obtain a sufficient number of sites with information from aerial photographs from the last 50 years. The efforts of the aerial photographic team are concentrated on the last 50 years because the aerial photographs from before the 1940s are not widespread enough to give a coherent picture of change to the archaeological resource. These two strands are supported by a survey of the recorded resource, generating data to support the sampled part; and by case study research into the effects of monument and landscape type on the value of data retrieved by archaeological methods. This section is best described as a national survey of sites and monuments records.

Enough has been suggested above to indicate that MARS is utilising the computerised resources of many bodies; the individual county, district, borough, and city sites and monuments records (SMRs), and the resources of the Royal Commission on the Historical Monuments of England (RCHME). MARS makes extensive use of computers for the manipulation, analysis, and the recording of data. All of the MARS computers run Windows for Workgroups as the operating system. The data generated by each part of MARS is stored in a Paradox for Windows database. The relational nature of Paradox is essential to allow recording of information from different SMRs in the same database. The information about sites is held in a variety of ways by the various SMR databases. The data from SMRs is organised to a standardised Paradox format so that the field surveyors can enter data directly into laptop computers, saving time and rewriting. Being part of a university has advantages and disadvantages: large discounts are available for some types of hardware and software, but there are some restrictions as to the packages we may use, and in-house technical support is not necessary targeted towards areas which concern the project.

2   The National Survey: an 'audit' of the recorded resource

The National Survey is attempting to understand the development of England's recorded resource. The first public records were those of local societies and museum indexcs. However, the most important as a national record was the data systematically collected by the Ordnance Survey after 1948. The Ordnance Survey material later formed the backbone of many of the SMRs in England. The report of the Walsh Committee recommended that 'A consolidated record of all known field monuments should be held by the County Planning Authorities so that they may be aware of all such monuments in their areas.' (Walsh 1969: § 7). As a result of this report registers and records have been developed since the 1970s on a local scale by counties, districts, boroughs and cities to index archaeology (Burrow 1985). Fifty-six were identified in 1994 as being the current holders of definitive records for specific areas; whilst it was recognised that some museums and private bodies hold extensive archaeological indexes these have been excluded, largely because the information they contain is included within the local authority managed systems. A pro-forma questionnaire was developed to 'audit' the contents of these public records. The first question is to ask how many records are held by each organization. MARS acknowledges that records are generated in a variety of forms which do not necessarily reflect archaeological sites and monuments as such; the majority of records are in the form of information relating to land parcels, archaeological events, and archaeological entities, this does not affect the gross counting of records (see Fraser 1993 for further discussion). This is perhaps the most useful measure of how much change has occurred within the record since 1984 (IAM 1984). In 1984 an average of 2.32 per km^2 was recorded, by the end of March 1995 MARS had identified that this density had risen to around 5.20 per km^2, although not all results had been processed. The number of records may have almost doubled, but has the quality of the records changed? The National Survey is also studying the monuments sampled for the field survey in an attempt to understand the kinds of changes which have occurred within the records held in SMRs and whether measures to control quality are evident within these individual records.

Whilst the form of the record may vary, the information held may be of several types. MARS is asking questions about major types of record; monuments, archaeological landscapes, archaeological urban areas, stray finds, and miscellaneous records. Currently there is a ratio of two records referring to monuments to one record of another type. In the future this may change, perhaps towards more archaeologically-defined landscapes which combine monument records; or towards record systems which combine archaeological and environmental data. There are some issues of consistency to be raised when discussing record types because data-standards are always subject to some interpretation by the individual compiling the record or curating the systems. The ratio of monuments to other records, and sub-groups of buildings records, and the numbers of records per period are being used as a comparison to the information retrieved for the field survey and aerial photographic work. These data-fields appear to be fundamental to all systems, and if not completed consistently between systems, are at least completed on most. There is a wide degree of variation for information on more complex issues, for example condition and survival appear to be recorded solely for monuments which have been examined as part of the Monuments Protection Programme (MPP) of English Heritage in many counties, although there are rare exceptions which can generate data for most, if not all, of their recorded monuments. The MPP is the overhaul of the list of scheduled monuments through-out England and it includes the collation of information on the condition of these monuments of national importance so that the resource requirements for future preservation, and the priorities for action can be assessed (Darvill *et al.* 1987).

3   Field Survey: the challenge of the data

England supports 56 SMRs, all using slightly different computerised systems, all interpreting data standards to suit their individual needs. All 46 counties now have SMR databases, the remaining 10 included in the MARS survey are district, borough or city records. This is not a static position, and new databases, particularly those for urban areas are continually being developed in England. Funding for SMR activities comes from a number of sources, the majority currently being funded by the local authorities and supported by English Heritage and RCHME for particular enhancement projects or activities. It is expected that this situation will change as the effects of local government review are felt in England (see also Fraser 1993). Infor-mation from the SMRs is exchanged with RCHME who curate the National Archaeological Record (NAR), but because of the diverse methods of record accumulation, the information held by the RCHME is now simply an index to more widely held information. One of the most challenging problems MARS has faced is the extraction of data from

SMRs. One county record is still based on record cards with supporting maps and bibliographic materials, several others are semi-computerised, the computer acting as an index to cards or other materials. One mainframe computer still figures in the curation of archaeological records; while the remainder use a diverse range of software and hardware configurations (table 1 lists the software systems identified). The provision of information about the archaeological remains recorded in the sample for the field survey thus varies from photocopies of handwritten cards, to computer print-outs, to partial and full data sets. The format of information supplied on disk file varied from ASCII text to various database file formats. Thankfully, the dBASE file format has become an accepted standard, easing data transfer between database packages. All of these data sets have to be manipulated to fit into the Paradox database developed for MARS. This has involved hand-typing, some optical character recognition scanning, and the writing of bespoke programs to manipulate data. Supplementary information, for example the location of sites known from aerial photographic evidence, has been gathered from the SMRs by MARS staff. A lot of knowledge is in the form of 'wetware', stored in the heads of SMR officers. This is a very volatile form of storage because people leave jobs, retire, or forget things. It is, however, very important for connecting the basic information held on computer with the written sources and other indexed material that all SMRs hold in addition to their basic list of sites and monuments.

Table 1. Frequency of software programs used for SMR databases in England.

Database system	Frequency of use
Superfile	18
(Paper index)	6
	(1 county and 5 districts)
Oracle (various versions)	6
dBASE IV	4
dBASE III+	4
File Tab	2
FoxPro (2 versions)	2
Monarch	2
PI Open	2
Other software (one each of 13 systems)	13

MARS has learned by experience a lesson it had hoped to avoid, that SMRs can be difficult to use as analytical tools. Currently they are collections of sometimes ambiguous data, which is of varying quality, almost all of which is forced into flat file structures which are not suitable for storing information about archaeological sites and monuments. However, it is complex questions that

professional archaeologists, researchers, students and other individuals want answered. We are eager to know how many sites exist in certain types of landscape, and estimates of their condition. These questions were first posed in the 1980s (Burrow 1985: 10), but in many cases we are no closer to having answers. The answers may still be compiled through accumulation of data and site visits, but not yet at the touch of a few buttons. MARS will begin to show the national trends, but local research will be needed to identify sites most in need.

4   Field Survey: methods and results

Field survey teams record measurements and descriptions of the recorded sites as they appear in the field today. In total some 26 key variables are being recorded for each site. These range from monument form and class, through to assessments of survival and decay and perceived threats to monument condition. Each team is provided with summary information about each site from the SMR sources in a database file on a laptop computer, together with printed reports and SMR 1:10,000 map information. Data generated in the field is directly input into the computer system, except during bad weather when laminated paper is used instead. The technological challenge of MARS is to reassemble this information into a central database where it can be related to the information recorded by the aerial photographic team. Computer training has played an important element in MARS, even people with previous experience need time and support to learn and understand new systems.

Results from one of the first areas to be surveyed may be used to illustrate some of the questions which MARS is studying. The Isle of Wight is a small county, 380 km^2 in area, four sample transects were located on the island, and they contained 166 monuments. When the land type is identified it can be seen that the majority of monuments are on land classified as either agricultural buildings or as field crops. When classified by form, it can be seen that the majority of the monuments are standing buildings (fig. 1). This accords with the analysis of the SMR by the National Survey which identified that almost 80% of the monuments recorded within the SMR were buildings, that is, over 65% of the entire SMR. Major impact on the monuments is either widespread or localized, that is all over a monument, or only on a part of a monument. Little peripheral impact, that is around the edges or in the neighbourhood of a monument which may present a long-term threat, is recorded for sites on the Isle of Wight. Only 1% of sites are without any impact at all (fig. 2). The major causes of damage are agriculture and building alterations, (not surprising as most of the sites are buildings) (fig. 3). The significance of the data from the Isle of Wight will

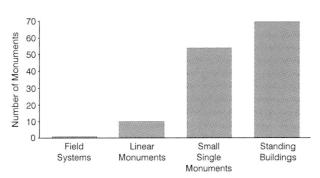

Figure 1. Isle of Wight - breakdown of monuments by form.

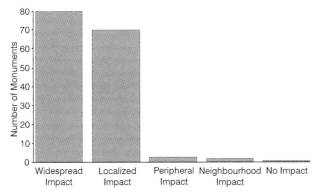

Figure 2. Isle of Wight - breakdown of monuments by impact.

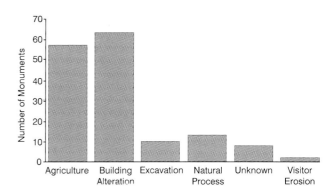

Figure 3. Isle of Wight - breakdown of monuments by cause of impact.

only become apparent when it is analysed with data from other counties on a regional level, and with England as a whole.

5   The future of MARS

The project is aiming to complete data collection during 1995, after which will come a period of intense validation and analysis. The results of MARS will be made available during 1997, and it is hoped that a variety of publications will result, aiming to communicate these results to both professional archaeologists, and others in related disciplines, as well as to students and anyone with an interest in the future of archaeology in England.

references

Burrow, I.	1985	The history of the sites and monuments record system. In: I. Burrow (ed.), *County Archaeological Records: Progress and Potential*. 6-16. Somerset: Association of County Archaeological Officers.
Darvill, T.	1987	*Ancient monuments in the countryside: An archaeological management review* (= Historic Buildings and Monuments Commission for England Archaeological Report 5). London: English Heritage.
	1991	*England's archaeological resource: The survival assessment programme. Report on the Wiltshire pilot study*. London: English Heritage typescript report.
Darvill, T. A. Saunders B. Startin	1987	A question of national importance: approaches to the evaluation of ancient monuments for the Monuments Protection Programme in England, *Antiquity* 61, 393-408.
English Heritage	1991	*Exploring our past: Strategies for the archaeology of England*. London: English Heritage.
Fraser, D.	1993	The British archaeological database. In: J. Hunter/L. Ralston (eds), *Archaeological Resource Management in the UK: An Introduction*. Stroud: Institute of Field Archaeologists, 19-29.
IAM	1984	*England's archaeological resource: A rapid quantification of the national archaeological resource and a comparison with the schedule of ancient monuments*. London: English Heritage.
RCHME	1993	*Recording England's past. A review of the national and local sites and monuments records in England*. London: RCHME.
Walsh	1969	*Report of the committee of enquiry into the arrangements for the protection of field monuments 1966-8*. Chairman Sir David Walsh. Command 3904. London: HMSO.

Mark Bell and Nicola King
Department of Conservation Sciences
Bournemouth University
United Kingdom
e-mail: mbell@bmth.ac.uk

Archaeometry

M.J. Baxter
H.E.M. Cool
M.P. Heyworth

Detecting Unusual Multivariate Data: An Archaeometric Example

1 Introduction

There has been much recent interest in the statistical literature concerning the detection of outliers and other unusual cases in multivariate data. This has arisen, in part, because developments in computing power have made possible the application of methodology that is iterative and computer-intensive in nature.

Methods of chemical analysis, such as inductively coupled plasma spectroscopy, increasingly generate large multivariate data sets, of artefact compositions for example, that are subjected to 'standard' methods of statistical analysis such as cluster analysis, principal component analysis (PCA) or discriminant analysis (Baxter 1994).

The performance of these analyses can be affected by unusual cases, such as outliers, in the data. It is good practice to screen the data in advance of applying such methods in order to identify cases that may affect their performance. How cases that are unusual are treated will depend on the context of a study, but it is often sensible to remove unusual cases from subsequent analyses, in order to study the structure in the bulk of the remaining data.

The present paper has arisen as part of a wider programme of study looking at approaches to the statistical analysis of large archaeometric data sets. Here we look selectively at a number of approaches for identifying unusual cases in such data sets, with a view to raising questions about aspects of some of the methodologies that are available.

The data used are the chemical compositions of 250 specimens of glass found in a single post-Roman context in excavations at Winchester. Most of the glass is window glass, mainly light blue-green in colour but including other more distinctive pieces representative of other colours in the assemblage of several thousand specimens. Some samples that were possibly vessel glass were also selected for comparative purposes. For the purpose of this paper the major and minor oxides only, based on the elements Al, Ca, Fe, K, Mg, Mn, Na, P and Ti, will be used. It was postulated, in advance of chemical analysis, that most of the glass would be reasonably homogeneous with respect to such oxides. We have also looked statistically at analyses

based on nine trace elements, and on the full set of eighteen variables, and will refer in passing to some of the results of these analyses.

The glass had not previously been analysed statistically and, as part of an experiment, was studied typologically independently of the statistical analysis. The aim was to see whether unusual cases detected statistically were also typologically unusual, without the interpretation of the statistical analysis being affected by a knowledge of the typology.

In the next section a brief review of some approaches to detecting unusual multivariate data is given. We have not attempted a comprehensive review, and refer the reader to the original publications and references given there for technical details. The application of some of the methodologies to the data set described above, and its relationship to the typological analysis, is then discussed.

The concluding discussion, rather than attempting to reach definitive conclusions about the structure of this particular data set, is more concerned to raise issues about how unusual data should be identified and handled. We wonder to what extent fairly 'simple' approaches will often suffice for practical purposes. This is not a question that can be answered without more practical experience of the methodologies discussed here, and others that 'compete' with them.

2 Detecting unusual data

Approaches to detecting unusual multivariate data include the following.

1. Univariate and bivariate data inspection.
2. Inspection of the first and last few principal components from a principal component analysis (PCA) (e.g. Hawkins/ Fatti 1984).
3. Influence analyses to identify those cases that have the greatest effect on some specific technique such as PCA (e.g. Brooks 1994).
4. Cluster analysis.
5. The use of Mahalanobis distance, d_j, for the j'th case, where the square of d_j is given by

$$(x_j - \bar{x})^T S^{-1} (x_j - \bar{x})$$

and $\bar{x}$ and S are the multivariate mean and covariance matrix of the $n \times p$ data matrix X of which $\mathbf{x_j}$ is the j'th row. Large values of d_j are intended to identify points remote from the bulk of the data.

Many other statistics have been proposed for detecting unusual data, but Mahalanobis distance, or variants of it, has received the most attention in practice. Its major disadvantage is that $\bar{x}$ and S are themselves affected by unusual observations so that d_j is affected by the cases it is designed to detect, and may fail to do so. Principal component analyses, which are based on an eigen-analysis of S, possibly after standardising the data, suffers from a similar problem.

This has led to a variety of proposals for robust analyses in which estimates of $\bar{x}$ and S are determined, usually iteratively, that are unaffected by outliers. There are two broad ways in which this can be done, either by defining weighting schemes that downweight extreme cases, or by identifying a subset of data uncontaminated by extremes and basing calculations on this. This last idea forms the basis of the paper by Atkinson and Mulira (1993), whose approach is used here. The Atkinson/Mulira approach is similar in spirit to other approaches that have been proposed while being simpler and more practical. It is aimed at the detection of multivariate outliers, rather than directly at the robust estimation of S. Other approaches, not discussed here, aim to estimate S robustly, and then use the estimate in a principal component analysis to detect outliers, for example. The basic idea is as follows.

1. Select p + 1 observations and calculate $\bar{x}$ and S using these.
2. Calculate d_j, increment the sample size by some small integer k, and select a new sample to consist of those cases with the smallest values of d_j.
3. Use the new sample to recalculate $\bar{x}$ and S and then repeat stage 2, selecting $(p + 1 + sk)$ cases at stage s, until the data set is exhausted.
4. Identify and display results for a suitable choice of s.

Reference can be made to Atkinson and Mulira (1993) for a discussion of methods of displaying the results. Here we shall use an index plot of d_j, where calculations for S are based on about 80% of the data. The results we give are not sensitive to variation about this value of 80%, and were virtually the same for several different choices of initial sample, including one specifically designed to include the most obvious outliers. Atkinson and Mulira (1993) suggest statistical guidelines for identifying outliers that assume that the sample from which S is calculated is multivariate normal. As shall be seen this turns out to be far from the case with our data, and we have interpreted the plots subjectively.

3 Analysis

Using the 250×9 data set described in the introduction, box-and-whisker plots and dot-plots were used to identify 'obvious' univariate outliers. Let H denote the inter-quartile range; then such outliers were defined to be points more than 3H from the upper or lower quartiles and visibly separate from the rest of the data. This last criterion was imposed to avoid identifying as outliers points in the tail of a long-tailed distribution. According to this definition the following points clearly stand out.

1. (87, 127, 179, 232) with high Ca and Ti;
2. (18, 31, 93, 118) with high Fe;
3. 98 with high Mn and Ti;
4. (141, 234) with low Ca.
5. Additionally it was noted that 20 cases, of which (225, 242) were most prominent, lay in the tails of Mg, K and P, which all had long tailed distributions. These were not designated as outliers but form a distinct cluster of points. The question of whether or not the data should have been transformed prior to analysis is raised by this observation, and we return to it in the final section.

Figure 1 shows two index plots of d_j, the upper plot using S calculated from all the data, and the lower plot using the (hopefully) uncontaminated 80% of the data determined by the Atkinson/Mulira procedure. The lower plot quite clearly suggests 9 cases as unusual and these correspond to the first 9 cases identified by univariate inspection above. The upper plot, which is affected by the unusual data is less clear cut and less easy to interpret.
Note that values of d_j for the unusual cases are much more extreme in the lower diagram.

A plot of the 4'th and 5'th principal components of standardised data also clearly identified the same 9 cases as unusual. An average-link cluster analysis of standardised data with Euclidean distance as the measure of dissimilarity, shown in figure 2, if 'cut' at about 6, separates out the 11 points noted in 1 to 4 above from the rest. If cut at 5 the majority of the cases noted in 5 above are also separated out.

The 9 'obvious' unusual points were removed from the data set and analyses repeated. Cases 141 and 234 then stood out, particularly on the second principal component, and were also removed.

Figure 3 shows the principal component analysis plot for the first two components, undertaken after this removal, and suggests some clustering of the data, with 242 as possibly unusual. The cases in the cluster to the lower right of the plot all belong to the group noted in 5 above.

In summary the Atkinson/Mulira approach, tailored to the identification of multivariate outliers, identifies much the same points as a simple univariate analysis or a cluster

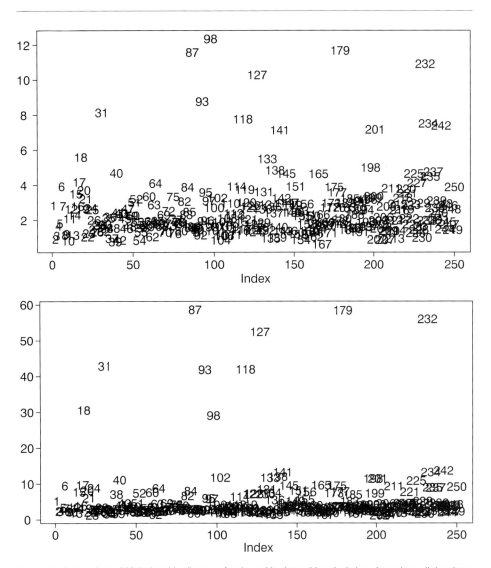

Figure 1. Index plots of Mahalanobis distance for the oxide data with calculations based on all the data (upper figure) and 80% of the data identified by the Atkinson/Mulira procedure. Points are labelled by their index for convenience of identifications.

analysis for these data. Additionally, the apparent clustering in figure 3 suggests that there is not a single homogeneous group against which other specimens can be judged to be 'unusual'. This raises a number of issues about the utility of the multivariate methodology to which we will return after briefly noting the relationship of the statistical analysis to the typological analysis.

4   Typological analysis

The statistical and typological analyses were initially carried out independently of each other. This is not recommended as a general practice but, in the present case,

it was of interest to see whether or not the two approaches produced compatible results.

Three of the first group noted previously, (87, 127, 179), are Roman vessel or bottle glass while 232 is heat-affected so a clear identification is not possible. That is three, if not all four, of these cases are typological outliers, compared to the bulk of light blue-green post-Roman window glass.

The same is true of 98, which is an unusual specimen of vessel glass, possibly of Mediterranean origin. The other group of four, (18, 31, 93, 118), is also highly distinctive in terms of colouring (emerald) and stands out from all other specimens.

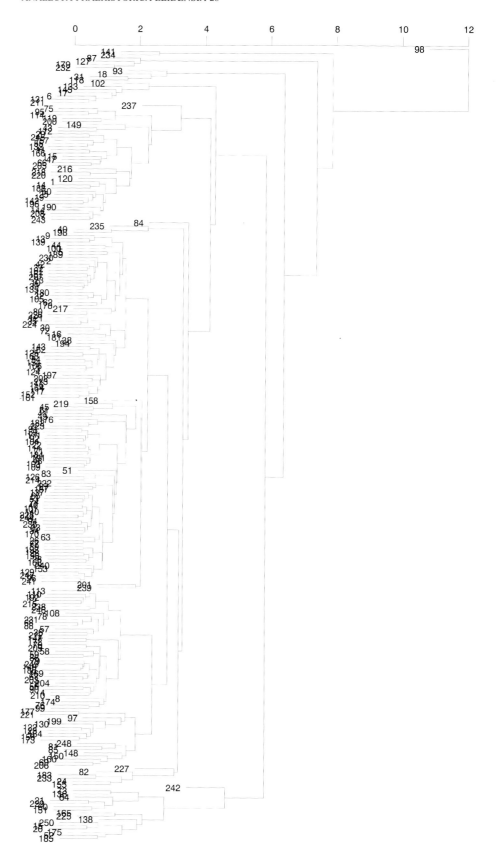

Figure 2. Average link cluster analysis of oxide data.

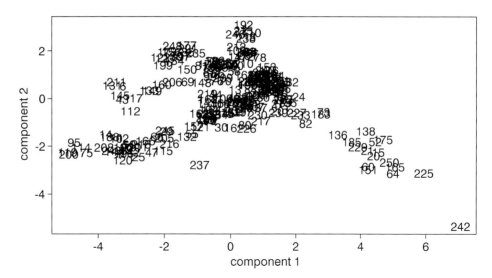

Figure 3. Principal component plot of the first two components using standardised data, after removal of the 11 clearest outliers identified in the text.

Cases (141, 234) were not originally singled out as typologically distinct. On re-inspection they are clearly window glass but the colouring, pale lime-green, is quite unusual.

The 20 or so specimens with high Mg, K and P, which were noted in the univariate and PCA analyses were also not identified as distinctive on a first examination. On re-inspection it appeared that they were mostly more 'bubbly' than other specimens, and this may reflect the interaction between composition and aspects of furnace technology connected with the speed at which the glass was heated.

The typological analysis also identified other cases that were either atypical (because they were Roman and/or non-window glass), or which formed small, distinctively coloured, sub-sets of the sample. Though not identified by an analysis of the major/minor oxides the majority of such cases were identified by a similar analysis of the trace elements.

5   Discussion

The work reported here is part of a broader programme that is examining approaches to the analysis of large archaeometric data sets. Only one data set has been discussed and any conclusions drawn from this can only be suggestive. What follows draws on this, and work as yet unreported. It is intended to suggest areas of study which would benefit from further research, and general guidelines that may help in the analysis of large and complex data sets.

1. The statistical analyses reported, and those conducted on the trace elements, have done rather well in identifying typologically unusual cases. It is also the case that most of the unusual data was identified using the simple univariate approaches, or 'standard' approaches such as PCA.

   Identification of unusual multivariate data is a technically challenging problem. The simpler techniques identify the really obvious univariate and bivariate outliers, and it may be sensible to omit these from the data before attempting to identify genuine multivariate outliers. In the present example the simpler methods are all that is needed.

2. Cluster analysis can be bad at identifying clusters in archaeometric data, in the sense that the results are often method-dependent. It may, however, be quite good at suggesting outliers. It uses information on all pairs of distances between cases, rather than the distance of a case from the centroid of a sample of data so perhaps this is not surprising.

   In the version of this paper presented at the CAA95 conference it was suggested that cluster analysis, though not as 'exciting' as the development of new methodology, could be more widely used for the detection of multi-variate outliers. Some discussants noted that, in their experience, it was widely used for this purpose but rarely reported. Commonly, cluster analysis is used to detect clusters, and any outliers detected in the process are noted *en passant*. If cluster analysis is indeed used directly, and often, for multivariate outlier detection its wider reporting would be welcome. We have seen references to the use of single-link, complete-link and average-link cluster analysis as suitable for outlier detection, but know of no systematic study comparing their merits. In particular a comparison with some of the newer methodology that is being proposed would be of interest.

3. The Atkinson/Mulira approach is easy to apply but, like other approaches based on Mahalanobis distance, assumes that a majority of the data form a coherent reference group against which the 'unusual' nature of other data may be judged. Ideally this reference group will have a multivariate normal distribution.
Identifying the reference group, which may then be used as a basis for robust analyses, is an aim in some of the literature. A theoretical ideal in some cases is that methodologies should be able to deal with up to 50% (almost) of cases that are outlying or unusual with respect to the reference group. In practice, outside of the context of simulated data, the idea of 50% of data being 'unusual' does not seem very realistic, and 20% or so may be a more reasonable limit. Leese and Main (1994), suggest a similar limit in their paper on the detection of outliers using probability plotting methods. They deal with the problem of detecting outliers relative to a known reference group, and such known grouping is not assumed in this paper.
The presence of grouping, unknown in advance of analysis, is a problem in the application of the Atkinson/ Mulira and similar approaches, as suggested by figure 3. Real data are frequently clustered, rather than the bulk forming a coherent group. As a hypothetical example, if we had three equal sized, equally dispersed, and equidistant groups of data in multivariate space there is not a natural reference group against which unusual data may be judged. The outcome of the application of the Atkinson/Mulira method in this case is dependent on the initial choice of cases from which Mahalanobis distance is calculated. One possible way round this difficulty might be to identify any distinct groups in the data, in the first instance, and then identify those cases which are outlying relative to all the groups so identified. This is not a trivial task and also raises the question of sample sizes.

4. The issue of sample size has not been mentioned so far, but is a non-trivial one. Even in ideal circumstances (i.e. a single multivariate-normally distributed set of data) the ratio n/p should be in the region of 3-5 or more

for techniques of the kind discussed here to 'work'. (Recommendations vary according to context.) Analytical techniques now available will often produce data sets with $p > 20$, and obtaining samples with large n may be costly. If the samples that are obtained have a clustered structure, and so need to be broken down into smaller sub-samples in order to apply methods for multivariate outlier detection, this will exacerbate the problem.

5. The important issues of variable selection and data transformation have been ignored for the purposes of this paper. We have, in fact, looked at the analysis of different variable subsets and logarithmic transformation of the data and found that they give rise to different results in terms of the unusual cases identified. In general none of these results are 'wrong'; it is simply that, depending on the data treatment, different 'unusual' cases are being identified. For example, analysis of the trace elements identifies small and highly coloured groups rich in Cu and Ni, that are not distinctive with respect to the major and minor oxides. Whether such specimens are to be regarded as unusual will depend on the objectives of the research; those cases just noted are unusual in terms of their appearance but not in terms of their major/minor oxide composition.

We offer one further thought here. Data transformation, to normality, is often advocated as desirable without discussion. For some of our analyses this would down-weight the visual impact of specimens in the tail of a distribution, since if the transformation is successful then the specimens will lie in the tail of a normal distribution, and not be worthy of note. However, such specimens may be of distinct archaeological interest (e.g. the 'bubbly' group noted earlier) but may be less evident in analyses where the data have been transformed. The 'bubbly' group is much more evident on a PCA of the untransformed data than on one where the data are log-transformed, for example, but this is another story.

Acknowledgements
The British Academy is thanked for funding the analyses through the Fund for Applied Archaeological Science; Caroline Jackson is thanked for the sample preparation; Dr J.N. Walsh at Royal Holloway and Bedford New College, University of London, is thanked for providing the analytical data; and Katherine Bibby is thanked for undertaking some preliminary data analyses.

references

Atkinson, A.C.
  H.-M. Mulira   1993   The stalactite plot for the detection of multivariate outliers, *Statistics and Computing* 3, 27-35.

Baxter, M.J.   1994   *Exploratory multivariate analysis in archaeology*. Edinburgh: Edinburgh University Press.

Brooks, S.P.   1994   Diagnostics for principal components: influence functions as diagnostic tools, *The Statistician* 43, 483-494.

Hawkins, D.M.
  L.P. Fatti   1984   Exploring multivariate data using the minor principal components, *The Statistician* 33, 325-338.

Leese, M.N.
  P.L. Main   1994   The efficient computation of unbiased Mahalanobis distances and their interpretation in archaeometry, *Archaeometry* 36, 307-316.

M.J. Baxter
Dept. of Mathematics
Statistics and OR
Nottingham Trent University
Clifton Campus
Nottingham NG11 8NS
United Kingdom
e-mail: mat3baxtemj@nottingham-trent.ac.uk

H.E.M. Cool
Archaeological consultant
16 Lady Bay Road
West Bridgford
Nottingham NG2 5BJ
United Kingdom

M.P. Heyworth
Council for British Archaeology
Bowes Morrell House
111 Walmgate
York YO1 2UA
United Kingdom
c-mail: m.heyworth@dial.pipex.com

Jon Bradley
Mike Fletcher

Extraction and visualisation of information from ground penetrating radar surveys

1   Introduction

The analysis of ground penetrating radar (GPR) data is, for a variety of reasons, an imprecise and time consuming activity. Manual evaluation of the data involves a high level of experience and takes an inordinate amount of time. It often requires that subjective decisions be made by the analyst, and this leads to the introduction of bias (both systematic and non-systematic) into the final results.

Computer analysis of GPR data has, until now, tended to focus either on the use of complex signal processing algorithms in an attempt to remove all sources of distortion from the image (Daniels *et al.* 1988: 298-303), or on simple image enhancement techniques to make the image easier for the analyst to understand (Blake 1995; Daniels *et al.* 1988: 297-298). The former approach, whilst effective in simple scenarios, tends to fall down on more complex sites, whilst the latter fails to remove the subjectivity from the process.

The objective of this paper is to outline and demonstrate an alternative, statistically based, approach to the extraction of information from GPR data. Such an approach requires some measure of the level of *radar activity* at each point of a radar image. Two possible solutions are discussed in this paper — *the sum of squared errors (SSE)* and the *k* measures.

The basic implementation of the technique yields a plan view of the site, which is useful as a first stage of interpretation. The drawback is that it contains no depth information, but a simple elaboration of the analysis allows rudimentary depth information to be extracted from the data in the form of horizontal 'slices' through the site.

In order to illustrate the practical application of the techniques outlined in this paper, two case studies are examined. They are based on survey work done at Worcester Cathedral and at a Bronze Age ring cairn at Stapeley Hill near Welshpool (Stratascan 1994).

2   Activity measure analysis

An analyst might manually examine radar data with the intention of picking out features of interest. The criteria which decide whether a feature is of interest may be very varied. Factors influencing the choice include contrast, coherency, size and shape of features. The interest/no interest decision is obviously a subjective one, hence the need for a high level of expertise, and any way of introducing objectivity into the process would therefore be of benefit in terms of reliability of results. A simple way of addressing this problem is the use of activity measures. Their function is to provide an objective, quantitive assessment of the degree of interest in a chosen region of the radar image. The criteria on which this value is based varies with the particular measure chosen. This paper discusses two of the simpler possibilities.

2.1   ACTIVITY MEASURES

Two statistically based activity measures were developed for use with the technique.

The *sum of squared errors (SSE)* measure quantifies the degree of deviation away from the mean intensity of the image. It is given by

$$SSE = \sum_{i=1}^{n} (x_i - \bar{x})^2 \qquad (1)$$

where x_i is the intensity of the ith pixel, $\bar{x}$ is the mean pixel intensity and n is the number of pixels under consideration.

The k measure combines the SSE measure discussed above with second order information on the abruptness of change in the image. It is normalised between 0 and 1 and is given by

$$k = 4SSE/naC \qquad (2)$$

where n is the number of pixels under consideration, a is the sum of the pixel intensities and C (total change) is given by

$$C = \sum_{i=1}^{n-1} |x_i - x_{i+1}| \qquad (3)$$

2.2   IMAGE PREPROCESSING

Before analysis of the radar survey can take place certain preprocessing steps have to be taken. Firstly the images must be cropped to remove any scrap data caused by the antenna unit standing still at either end of the transect (fig. 1). Then the image is scanned to establish the positions of the

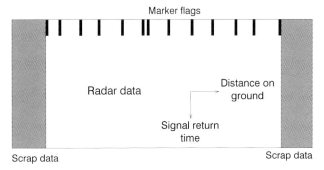

Figure 1. Features of a typical radar image.

ground distance marker flags. These correspond to intervals of one metre on the ground and are inserted manually by the antenna operator. Because the antenna unit is dragged at a non-constant rate (particularly on rough terrain), the markers in the image are generally unevenly spaced.
In order to allow an accurate plan of the survey to be constructed, these irregularities must be removed prior to processing. This is done using simple linear interpolation techniques to rescale all intervals to a standard, pre-determined width. Once the horizontal rectification process has been performed on all of the images, they will be of a standard horizontal scale, and the analysis can continue.

2.3   ACTIVITY PROFILING, MAPPING AND VISUALISATION
The objective of the analysis is to reduce each survey transect (a two-dimensional image) to a single string of values — *an activity profile*. Each value in what is now a one-dimensional string of data represents the level of activity below that point of the transect *for the full depth of the survey*. Activity values are calculated at predetermined

intervals along the transects and once profiles have been generated for each transect, the data can be used to build a plan of the activity over the survey area.

The surveying in both of the case studies was carried out along orthogonal transects to produce grids of squares. Three approaches to visualising the activity of the survey area were tested. A problem arises here in deciding which of the two possible activity values at transect intersections to use. Differences in the measured activity values for differently oriented transects could arise for various reasons including calibration drift, asymmetries of the radar beam geometry and random effects caused by terrain and operator error. So far no work has been done to investigate these problems quantitatively. For the sake of simplicity the approach adopted in this paper was to use the higher of the two activity values.

The first method, *the activity grid*, represents each transects activity profile as a grey level strip arranged in a grid on a black background. An example of this technique is shown in figure 2a. Although useful as a preliminary visualisation tool, this approach proves unsatisfactory in one important respect; the use of linear grey level strips on a monotone background can sometimes deceive the eye into seeing spurious linear features in the data.

This potentially serious drawback is overcome by the use of a *simple activity map*, an example of which is given in figure 2b. Here the data is presented as a colour coded map (with the option of contours or pseudo-surface representation). To achieve this a second order surface is fitted to the square grid of points formed by the transect intersection points. The drawback of this approach is that it makes minimal use of the available information. The sampling rate along survey transects is extremely high, but this approach uses only a tiny fraction of the sampled points.

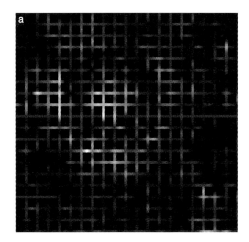 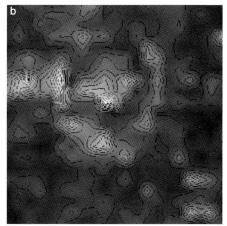

Figure 2. An activity grid and the corresponding simple activity map.

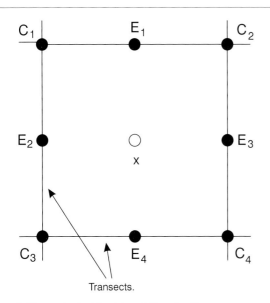

Figure 3. The scale-doubling interpolation algorithm.

The third and more sophisticated approach, *the interpolated activity map*, goes some way to addressing the problem of utilization of data. The interpolation is a two stage process. The basis for the first stage (which effectively doubles the scale) is shown in figure 3 and equation (4)

$$x = 0.5 \sum_{i=1}^{4} E_i - 0.25 \sum_{i=1}^{4} C_i \qquad (4)$$

where x is the unknown value, C is the activity value at each transect intersection and E is the activity value

midway between transect intersections. This interpolation step produces a square grid at twice the resolution to that used by the simple activity map. The second interpolation step is then identical to that in the previous technique, but produces a map on double the scale.

2.4   CASE STUDIES

The following two case studies are used to illustrate the potential of the new technique. For the sake of brevity only the *interpolated* results of the *SSE* analysis are presented. The k analysis appears, on the basis of these two studies, to produce similar results with only subtle differences in contrast between the two.

2.4.1   *Stapeley Hill ring cairn*

Stapeley Hill (OS Ref. SO 313 991) is a small ring cairn of supposed Bronze Age origin. Topographical surveying carried out on the site (Fletcher/Spicer 1990; Spicer 1991), has confirmed the presence of ridge and furrow and field walls. A lit three-dimensional surface representation of the topography of the site from a more recent survey (Stratascan 1994) is shown in figure 4. The vertical heights are exaggerated by a factor of three to emphasise features. Note the edge of a wide ridge in the foreground of the image caused by the remains of an ancient field wall, and behind it the obvious ring structure with a small central mound. Ridge and furrow are also in evidence to the left of the ring cairn (although not so obviously). The scale of the site is 20 m square, north is to the top left.

Radar surveying was carried out at the site in May 1994 using a 500 MHz antenna on a two directional 1 m grid. An

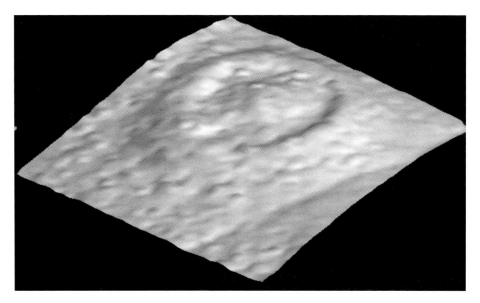

Figure 4. Stapeley Hill - topography.

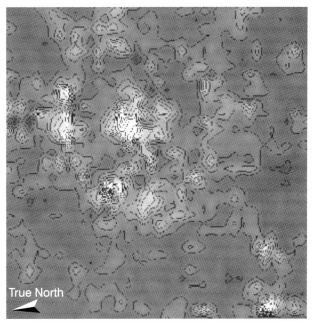

True North

Figure 5. Stapeley Hill - radar activity (SSE).

interpolated activity map of the SSE values for the site is shown in figure 5.

The activity map reveals a rough ring shaped area of enhanced radar activity (top centre of image) with an irregular central feature. A further area of high activity lies at the bottom right of the image and is probably associated with field wall remains. Superimposition of the radar activity map on the topography (fig. 6) reveals good correspondences between radar and topographical evidence for field wall remains, between the positions of the circular bank of the ring work and the circular feature on the radar map, and between the central mound and the central radar feature.

This evidence probably points to the presence of a large proportion of stony material in the circular bank. The activity strength of the bank is weaker on the SE side of the ring. This may be due to the topography of the site (fig. 7) or to possible removal of stone associated with the ridge and furrow or with the field wall. The greater strength and degree of coherency of the central feature may point to the presence of a large, coherent mass of stone — possibly a cist.

2.4.2   *Worcester Cathedral*
The second case study is based on a survey conducted at Worcester Cathedral which was expected to reveal traces of foundations from a previous structure. The survey covered a rectangular area of approximately 280 square metres and was done on a regular 1 m grid in two directions, again at 500 MHz. The SSE analysis results are shown in figure 8.

The results are not as revealing as those for Stapeley Hill. The most obvious feature is the area of high activity in the top left of the survey. This feature is possibly the high activity end of a linear region of enhanced activity extending from top left to bottom right of the map, though this is by no means certain. This may correspond to the path of an old drainage channel which still retains some moisture. Some regular features can also be discerned at bottom centre and bottom left, and it is tempting to associate these with building foundations.

3   Retrieval of depth information
3.1   SIMPLE STRATIFICATION
The approach as it stands at this point yields only two-dimensional information in the form of a plan view of the radar activity levels over the survey site. This should, in many cases, provide a coarse indicator of the *presence* of features of interest, but it may be that a more comprehensive, three-dimensional picture of the site is required.

Accurate extraction of three-dimensional information from radar data is a problematic process. Various factors including surface topography and lateral inhomogeneities in the electro-magnetic properties of the soil matrix cause vertical distortions in the data which cannot be easily rectified. A first step towards the extraction of depth information from a survey is to simply 'stratify' the radar images and to analyse each layer separately. It should be emphasised that vertical distance on the radar images does not correspond directly to vertical distance below the ground surface but to the signal return time of the radar emissions. This means that what is produced by this process is a series of activity maps which, *approximately* speaking, depict the activity at different distances below the ground surface. Theoretically, the simpler the site, the better this approximation will be.

This approach is similar in nature to that taken by Milligan and Aitkin (Milligan/Aitken 1993: 26-39), but with several distinct advantages. The approach adopted by Milligan and Aitken is limited in scope in that the horizontal (signal return time) slices are produced by direct extraction of pixel values from a *uni-directional* set of parallel radar images. No 'interest' values such as the activity values developed herein were employed and no interpolation was attempted since interpolation from a uni-directional survey tended to result in spurious linear features at right angles to the transect direction.

3.2   CASE STUDIES
3.2.1   *Stapeley Hill*
The results of applying the stratification process to Stapeley Hill are interesting. Examination of the images in figure 9 shows that the NE side of the ring shows up clearly only on

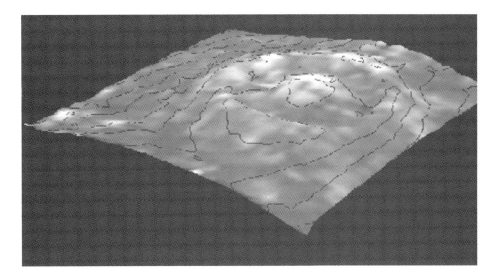

Figure 6. Stapeley Hill - radar activity superimposed on topography.

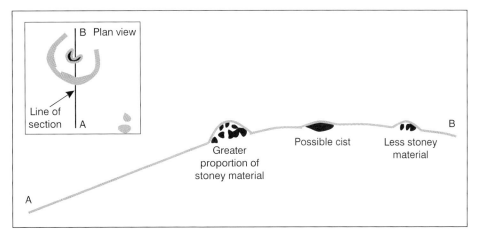

Figure 7. One possible explanation for the discontinuous nature of the radar activity in the bank of the ring cairn.

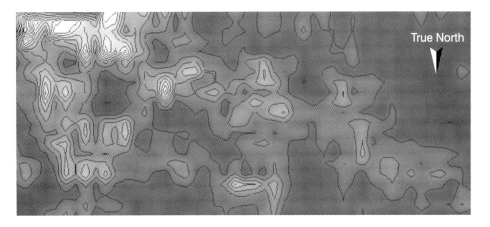

Figure 8. Worcester Cathedral - SSE results.

the first (shallowest) map, whilst the rest of the structure shows up on all of the maps. This lends support to the conclusions that the ring is more substantially constructed on the down slope (NW and W) sides. The central structure does not show up at all in (a), appears very strongly in (b), fades away again in (c), then makes a reappearance in (d). This lends support to the hypothesised presence of a structured central feature i.e. a cist. A further feature of

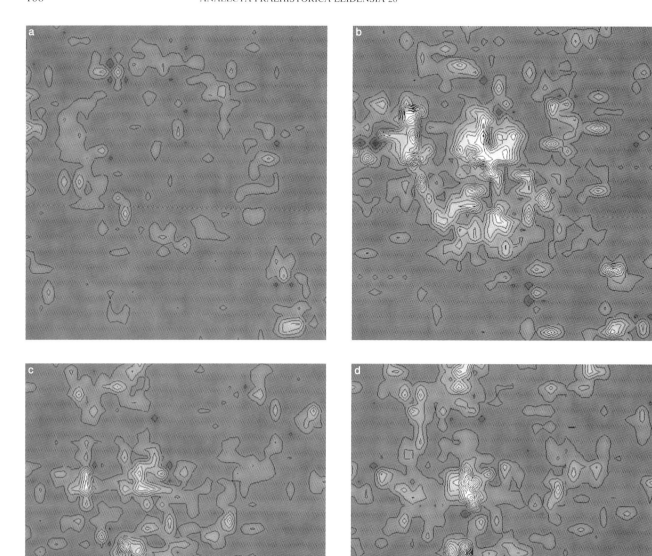

Figure 9. Four consecutive SSE slices through Stapeley Hill.

possible interest is a large anomaly which shows up very strongly in the NW side of the ring at greater depths (in maps (c) and (d)). The radar signatures associated with the field wall appear concentrated mainly at intermediate to shallow depths (map (b)). This would appear consistent with the supposed later origins of the wall.

3.2.2   Worcester Cathedral

The use of the simple stratification method on the Worcester Cathedral data is very revealing. The sequence of maps (fig. 10) going from (a) the shallowest, to (e) the deepest, clearly confirm the presence of the suspected linear feature. This provides a good example of how problems caused by overlapping features in successive strata can be easily and effectively overcome.

4   Further work

4.1   IMAGE FILTERING AND DEPTH INFORMATION

In order to progress further certain issues need to be addressed. The results obtained thus far, although interesting, are flawed in that the presence of detectable objects in the upper layers of the site tends to affect the activity levels calculated for areas of the radar image which lie below. This is due to the fact that the radar pulse produced by the apparatus is not instantaneous in nature, but consists of a decaying wave train. This leads to a periodic *echoing* effect where 'ghosts' of objects appear in the radar image below the main object signature.

Because these effects are periodic, they should prove amenable to manipulation by frequency domain techniques such as Fourier analysis. The main problem here is that the removal of the unwanted 'ghosting' is not simply a matter of detecting the echo frequency and filtering it from the image. Although this would have the desired effect, it would also mean that the primary signal is filtered out. Further investigation of the problem is obviously necessary.

4.2   IMPROVING DATA UTILIZATION

Data points are available at very small intervals along the transects (so much so in fact, that the data can almost be considered to be continuous). Some attempt has been made to use interpolation techniques to make better use of the available data (section 2.3). In spite of this there is still a great deal of room for improvement, perhaps by treating the data as irregular xyz values and using routines which can deal with this type of data.

5   Conclusions

This paper shows that it is possible to produce simple, quick and, most importantly, objective routines for analysing data from ground penetrating radar surveys. Two statistical measures of radar activity — the SSE and k values — have been developed. Other measures, possibly relying on frequency domain information, have yet to be examined.

A simple extension of the basic technique allows some appreciation of the three-dimensional structure of the survey site to be obtained. As has been demonstrated, this often allows extra inferences and conclusions about the site to be drawn. An initial evaluation detailed in the case studies examined above, indicates that this technique may prove to be an extremely useful tool, but much work still needs to be done in this area in order to iron out difficulties caused by the radar ghosting effect detailed in section 4.1.

It is not possible to say at this stage which measure of activity produces the better results, and work using a known 'model' site is necessary in order to test them.

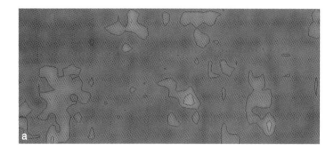
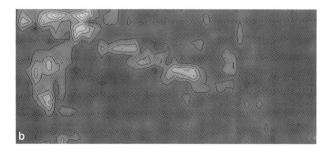
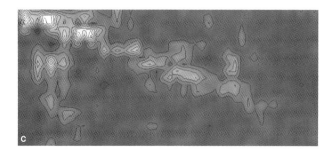
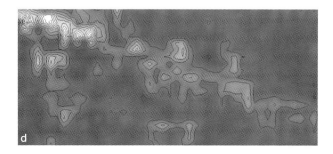
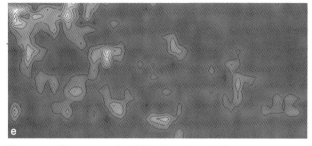

Figure 10. Five consecutive SSE slices through Worcester site.

references

Blake, V.S. 1995 Image processing and interpretation of ground penetrating radar data. In: J. Huggett/ N. Ryan (eds), *Computer Applications and Quantitative Methods in Archaeology 1994*, 175-180, BAR International Series 600, Oxford: Tempus Reparatum.

Daniels, D.J. 1988 Introduction to subsurface radar, *IEE Proceedings* 135 (4), 278-320.
D.J. Gurron
H.F. Scott

Fletcher, M. 1990 Ridge and furrow – regression and fourier. In: P. Reilly/S.Rahtz (eds), *Communication in*
R. Spicer *archaeology: a global view of the impact of information technology. vol. 3: late papers,* 31-44, The World Archaeological Congress.

Milligan, R. 1993 The use of ground-probing radar within a digital environment on archaeological sites. In:
M. Aitken J. Andresen/T. Madsen/I. Scollar (eds), *Computing The Past, Computer Applications and Quantitative Methods in Archaeology CAA92*, 21-32, Aarhus: Aarhus University Press.

Spicer, R.D. 1991 *Applications of graphical techniques in archaeology and their implications on methodoly.* PhD Thesis, School of Computing, Staffordshire University, Beaconside.

Stratascan 1994 A report for the University of Staffordshire on a geophysical survey carried out at Stapeley Hill.

Jon Bradley
Staffordshire University
School of Computing
Beaconside
Stafford
United Kingdom
e-mail: J.C.Bradley@soc.staffs.ac.uk

Mike Fletcher
Staffordshire University
School of Computing
Leek Road
Stoke
United Kingdom
e-mail: M.Fletcher@soc.staffs.ac.uk

Gayle T. Allum
Robert G. Aykroyd
John G.B. Haigh

Restoration of magnetometry data using inverse-data methods

1   Introduction

Magnetometry has become one of the most popular techniques for the geophysical prospection of archaeological sites. Modern instruments are reliable, easily portable, convenient in use, and reasonably inexpensive. The data are logged automatically and can readily be transferred to a small computer for subsequent processing. Anyone who has received proper training in the operation of field magneto-meters can expect to survey a considerable area of ground each day and, provided that conditions are favourable, be able to present the results in an archaeologically meaningful form.

A typical opportunity for magnetometry occurs when ancient ditches or pits have been cut into inert soil, but have subsequently been filled in with material which is magnetically active. The locations of the features can then be detected as induced magnetic anomalies relative to the earth's main field. The response of the magnetometer to such an anomaly is somewhat complicated, presenting a positive lobe along the southern side together with a negative shadow towards the north (Linington 1964). The relative sizes of the positive and negative lobes depend on the mode of operation of the magnetometer (gradiometer or single mobile detector), on the survey's location on the surface of the planet, and on the depth of the archaeological features below the modern ground surface.

Some care has to be taken in interpreting the results of a magnetometer survey, because the actual position of the anomaly corresponds neither to the positive lobe nor to the negative lobe, but is close to the junction between them. This may not be important when the survey reveals only a limited number of well spaced features, but it may cause crucial difficulties if there are many features, overlapping each other at different depths.

The data logged by the magnetometer provide, in effect, a digital image of the site. Such an image differs from more familiar electronic images, such as those derived from conventional photography, only in that it contains both positive and negative readings, whereas in most cases only positive intensities are permitted. Many different methods of image restoration have been developed over the years, and the majority are still valid when applied to images containing a mixture of positive and negative values.

Standard methods of image restoration include spatial filtering, for smoothing and edge enhancement, Fourier transform methods, and construction of the inverse response function. In recent years a number of alternative methods have been developed, based upon statistical estimation techniques, such as the EM algorithm which is discussed in this paper. Such techniques model the distribution of the survey data, on the basis of the known magnetometer response. The magnetic intensity is then estimated from the data, taking into account any reasonable prejudice about the nature of the anomalies. These techniques are known collectively as 'inverse-data methods'.

The aim of our project is to apply suitable inverse-data methods to various types of archaeological magnetic data, and to appraise their success in comparison with standard techniques of image restoration. Some preliminary results are presented in this paper.

2   Outline of this project

Recognising that the analysis of full-scale archaeological field data presented formidable problems, because of both the size of the problem and the complexity of the response function involved, it was decided that the project should be developed in three distinct stages, each progressing towards the ultimate objective.

Stage I
The analysis of digitised measurements of magnetic susceptibility over the length of earth cores from archaeological sites. These measurements arise from a project undertaken by the Department of Archaeological Sciences at the University of Bradford with the aim of determining the location and depth of the magnetically active regions of a site. Earth cores, extracted from several locations over the site, are passed through a detector coil which allows the susceptibility to be measured continuously along the core; the readings are recorded digitally.

Since the detector coil is sensitive to the susceptibility over a considerable length of the core, its effective response function to the susceptibility of any point in the core has very long tails (fig. 1a). In consequence, the curve of the continuous measurements shows very broad, smooth peaks,

(a)

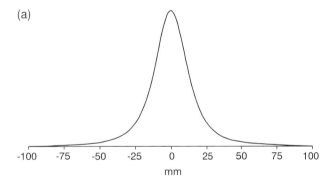

(b)

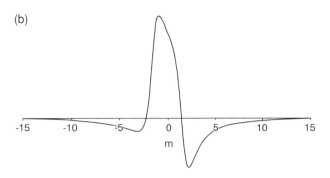

Figure 1. Theoretical response functions for (a) measurements of core susceptibility and (b) line magnetometer measurements.

and responses from different regions of the core may overlap very strongly. Our aim is to account for the broad spread of the response function and to allow the measured susceptibility to be attributed to sharply defined regions of the core, representing distinct epochs in the development of the site.

Since the restoration of susceptibility values is a line problem, it requires relatively little computing power. Furthermore the response function does not possess the positive and negative lobes which normally appear in magnetometry work. Consequently this should provide a fairly straightforward problem on which to test our techniques.

Stage II
Gradiometer measurements along a line transecting linear features. Rather than progress straight to full survey over an extended area of ground, we first look at data from a survey along a line transecting some linear feature, such as a long straight ditch. Here the ground is modelled as a collection of magnetised prisms of rectangular cross-section, and infinite in length in the direction of the feature. The response function has positive and negative lobes, and may vary with location on the planet, the depth of the feature,

and the strike (or transection) angle (fig. 1b). Nevertheless the problem is more manageable than full area field survey at Stage III.

Stage III
Gradiometer measurements from area surveys. This type of problem usually involves a large data set and a more complex response function than either of the earlier stages. Hence it is only to be tackled when we have gained considerable experience of the methodology during the earlier stages.

3   Techniques tested during Stage I, using
         susceptibility data
Two forms of susceptibility data were used for testing restoration methods. The first form was entirely simulated, by convolving a known pattern of susceptibility with a suitable response function, and finally adding some Gaussian noise. The second form came from actual measurements, but made on blocks of material of known susceptibility fabricated to resemble earth cores, rather than on true earth cores. The advantage of using 'phantom' data of this type is that the expected answer is known, and therefore the accuracy of the results may be judged.

All the techniques worked much as we would have predicted with the simulated data. The straight Fourier method and the direct calculation of the inverse response function tended to give fragmented results in the presence of noise, for reasons discussed below, but the other methods worked well enough. We therefore decided to concentrate on the 'phantom' data, since these should give a fairer indication of how the various techniques would perform in practice.

3.1   FOURIER TRANSFORM METHODS
It is possible to calculate the (discrete) Fourier transform of the response function, to find its exact inverse, which can then be used to calculate the restored susceptibility. In fact the results are extremely disappointing and have little resemblance to the 'known' pattern of susceptibility. The reasons for this poor performance are well known. The response function used here is very smooth and has long tails; consequently its Fourier transform has very small amplitude in the high-frequency components. Hence the inverse of the Fourier transform has very large amplitude in those components. Furthermore, since the observed data represent a convolution which includes the smooth response function, they should have very small high-frequency components; any significant component in those frequencies is almost certainly associated with noise. One effect of dividing by the transformed response function is to exaggerate components arising from noise, which often gives rise to unsatisfactory results.

One technique to counteract the exaggeration of noisy components is the use of the Wiener filter (Gonzalez/Wood 1992). The basis of this method is an analysis of the frequency spectrum resulting from the noise, but in practice it is often interpreted as the simple addition of a small positive constant Φ to the denominator of each component of the inverse of the transformed response function. The constant Φ prevents division by near-zero, but it is difficult to provide a prescriptive formula for its optimum value; a suitable value is usually found by subjective trial and error.

3.2   CONSTRUCTION OF INVERSE RESPONSE FUNCTION

It is possible to construct the inverse response from a set of simultaneous equations derived from a precisely constrained problem (Tsokas *et al.* 1991). The results are effectively equivalent to the straight Fourier method, and have similar deficiencies. Better results may be obtained by setting up an over-constrained problem, which is solved by minimising a sum of squares. This takes account of the presence of noise in the data and leads to results which are qualitatively similar to those from the application of the Wiener filter in Fourier transforms. Singular value decomposition provides a more stable and more controlled approach to the over-constrained problem, but the results are not markedly improved.

3.3   MAXIMUM LIKELIHOOD ESTIMATION

Our initial trial of inverse-data methods was based on the well established Metropolis-Hastings algorithm (Hastings 1970; Metropolis *et al.* 1953). The calculations proved to be extremely slow and the final results did not show any significant improvement over those discussed above. These conclusions are not entirely surprising since the algorithm was devised in order to solve non-linear problems, whereas the problems of fitting the magnetic data are linear ones. As a result of these observations we abandoned the Metropolis-Hastings method in favour of an alternative statistical technique which has proved to be successful in other imaging applications.

3.4   THE EM ALGORITHM

This algorithm was published by Dempster *et al.* (1977) as a summary of various earlier methods, one of the best known of which is the Lucy-Richardson method (Lucy 1974; Richardson 1972). We offer a brief description of the algorithm here, with the intention of publishing more of the mathematical detail elsewhere.

Suppose that the susceptibility profile along the core is divided into m discrete elements, that x_j is the 'true' susceptibility of element j, and that $\hat{x}_j$ is some estimate of x_j. Suppose also that data are observed at n locations, and that y_i is the observed value at location i, whereas μ_i is the expected value when the 'truth' is convoluted with the response function.

Then

$$\mu_i = \sum_{j=1}^{m} h_{ij}x_j \qquad \text{and} \qquad y_i = \sum_{j=1}^{m} z_{ij}$$

where h_{ij} is the response function coupling location i to element j, and z_{ij} is the contribution to observation i from element j. The values z_{ij} may be envisaged as 'unobservable' data whose expected values are $h_{ij}x_j$. The introduction of such 'missing' or 'unobservable' data is an essential requirement of the EM algorithm.

The algorithm defines two separate steps:

E step: (Expectation), where z_{ij} is estimated by its conditional expectation, given the data:

$$z_{ij} = E\left[z_{ij} \mid y_i\right] = h_{ij}x_j + \frac{1}{m}\left(y_i - \mu_i\right)$$

M step: (Maximisation), where the value $\hat{x}_j$ is found to maximise the log-likelihood, or minimise the error sum of squares, assuming that the z_{ij} are observed data.

The E and M steps may be combined to give a revised estimate of x_j:

$$\hat{x}_j^{new} = \hat{x}_j^{old} + \sum_{i=1}^{n} (y_i - \mu_i)h_{ij} \bigg/ m \sum_{i=1}^{n} h_{ij}^2$$

This equation provides an iterative process where the estimate of each 'truth' element is decoupled from the estimates of the other elements.

Since this simple implementation of the EM algorithm is based on minimising an error sum of squares, the results are essentially similar to those from the Wiener filter or the other least squares methods. In consequence there is a choice of methods leading to similar results:

EITHER The normal equations are set up for a least squares calculation, or the equivalent Fourier transforms are used, both of which involve very large arrays, so that the calculation is *memory intensive*;

OR The EM algorithm may be used as described above, which results in a very slowly convergent iterative process, and hence is *processor intensive*.

The true advantage of the EM algorithm only becomes apparent when the expected results are influenced by pre-existing concepts of their pattern.

3.5   THE EM ALGORITHM WITH PENALISED LIKELIHOOD

There are likely to be many different solutions in the region close to the optimum defined by a maximum-likelihood procedure. The solution defined as strictly optimal is unlikely to conform to our prejudices, so preferred solutions are selected by introducing a penalty which favours restorations felt to be more appropriate to the problem.

In the case of the susceptibility, restorations are expected to show features with clearly defined boundaries, and a smooth variation of intensity elsewhere. The EM algorithm can be modified to take account of such a penalty, but strictly leads to a set of non-linear simultaneous equations. A linear approximation may be obtained, however, by replacing the value $\hat{x}_j^{new}$ in the penalty term by the value $\hat{x}_j^{old}$ obtained from the last iteration step. This is known as the OSL approximation (one step late), and has been shown to be valid provided that convergence to the required solution is reasonably slow (Green 1990).

The E step remains the same as in the previous subsection, but a penalised likelihood is introduced into the M step. On combining the two steps, the OSL approximation gives the following iterative formula for the estimated susceptibility:

$$\hat{x}_j^{new} = \hat{x}_j^{old} + \frac{1}{m \sum\limits_{i=1}^{n} h_{ij}^2} \left[\sum\limits_{i=1}^{n} (y_i - \mu_i) h_{ij} - \beta\sigma^2 \frac{\partial\varphi}{\partial x_{ij}}\bigg|_{\hat{x}_j^{old}} \right]$$

The function φ, differentiated in the right-hand term, defines the nature of the penalty and is often referred to as the *potential function*; apart from this term, the equation is identical to the pure EM algorithm. The value σ^2 is the assumed variance of noise in the data and the coefficient β defines the strength of the penalty. The larger the value of $\beta\sigma^2$, the more likely is the restoration to conform to our prejudices, at the expense of goodness of fit to the data.

One significant advantage of the EM algorithm with the OSL approximation is that it is possible to introduce a penalty without greatly increasing the computational expense. This is not the case with other methods known to us.

4 Results from Stage I

The calculations described in the last section were applied to two sets of *phantom* susceptibility data (fig. 2). The observed data are shown as a solid line, and the underlying 'truth' as a dashed line; the 'truth' line is repeated in subsequent figures.

The Wiener filter was first applied to both sets of data (fig. 3); the solid line represents the answer returned by the calculation. When distinct blocks of susceptibility are well separated their locations are predicted quite well, but their shapes are entirely wrong, since they are quite smooth and contain no sharp edges. There is no meaningful information to enable us to separate the three adjacent blocks in the upper diagram. The side-lobes visible at the edges of the main peaks are a characteristic feature of Fourier analysis. The methods based on maximum-likelihood procedures, including the simple EM algorithm, gave such similar results to the Wiener filter, that we have not illustrated them here.

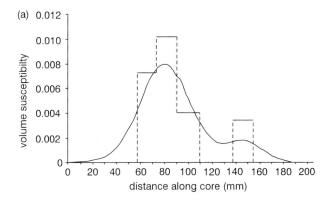

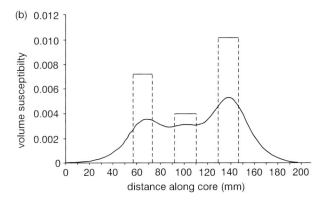

Figure 2. Two sets of 'phantom' susceptibility data (solid lines), measured from synthetic cores constructed from material of known susceptibility (dotted lines).

Using the EM-OSL algorithm for penalised likelihood estimation, we experimented with several different types of potential, of which two were found to give good results. Following the suggestion of Besag (1989), our first choice for the potential function φ was the absolute difference between the values of x_j and its neighbouring elements, so that the penalty was the sum of such differences. A suitable value for the constant $\beta\sigma^2$ was determined by experimental investigation; the final choice was made on the basis of a subjective balance between goodness of fit and the anticipated form of the results (fig. 4).

The separated blocks are more clearly defined than they were with the Fourier and maximum likelihood methods, but there is some filling of the intervals between them. The triple block is not resolved and has the appearance of a broad single block. All the blocks have sloping sides rather than the sharply defined vertical edges shown in the 'truth', indicating that they are made up of a succession of small steps rather than one large step.

In an attempt to eliminate this last problem, we introduced a second potential φ which incorporates a cut

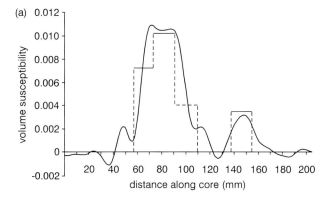

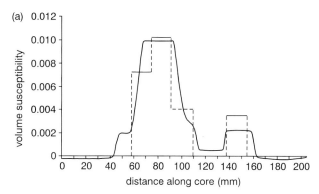

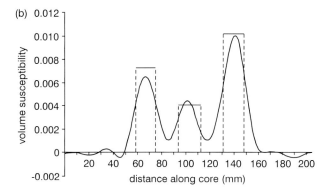

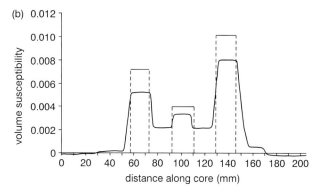

Figure 3. Restored susceptibility (solid lines) from the Fourier method with Wiener filter applied to the data of figure 2.

Figure 4. Restored susceptibility (solid lines) from the EM-OSL algorithm applied to the data of figure 2; the potential function is the absolute difference between neighbouring elements.

off, so that a single large step is penalised less heavily than an equivalent series of small steps. In this case, it was necessary to find suitable values not only for the constant $\beta\sigma^2$ discussed above, but also for the parameter defining the cut-off. The blocks are now very sharply defined, with nearly vertical sides (fig. 5). The positions and widths of the blocks are largely coincident with the 'truth', but there is still some filling-in of the intervals between the blocks, and smaller blocks seem to appear on the edges of the main blocks. The triple block is now partially resolved (fig. 5a), but has not been fully accounted for along its left-hand edge.

Of the various methods described above, it is clear that the EM-OSL algorithm seems to produce the most realistic results, particularly when used with the potential function φ which incorporates a cut-off. The general agreement between the results and the assumed truth is excellent, apart from the small blocks on the side of the main blocks and the filling-in of the intervals between blocks. Since the data used here are actual measurements, the precise mathematical nature of the response function is uncertain to an extent.

It is possible that the small additional blocks may arise from minor errors in the response function that was used in the modelling.

5   Results from Stage II

Following the successful application of the EM-OSL algorithm at Stage I, using the cut-off penalty function, it was also tested at Stage II. Because of difficulty in locating suitable field data, we decided to work entirely with simulated data, creating various models in which the magnetised features were prisms of infinite length and rectangular cross section, each located at the same depth below the soil surface.

A typical simulation from our tests comprised a large prism of low magnetic intensity juxtaposed with a smaller prism of higher intensity. This magnetic distribution was convolved with the response function (appropriate to the depth below the soil surface, the location of the model on the planet's surface, and the strike angle between the line of survey and the line of the feature) and a reasonable measure of Gaussian noise was added to give the simulated data

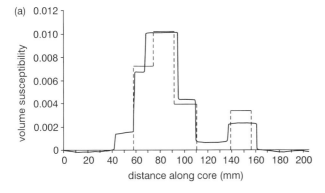

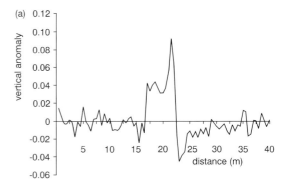

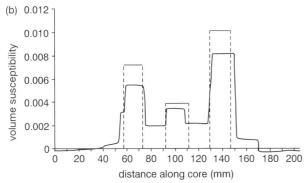

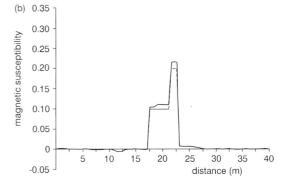

Figure 5. Restored susceptibility (solid lines) from the EM-OSL algorithm applied to the data of figure 2; the potential function incorporates a cut-off, penalising a single large step less than an equivalent series of small steps.

(fig. 6a). The result of applying the EM-OSL algorithm to the data can be seen to be in remarkable agreement with the original model (fig. 6b).

Working with simulated data, we were confident that the response function used in the restoration was precisely the same as the one used to create the data. This might be an unrealistic situation in practice, given the wide variation in form of the magnetometer response function. We repeated the restoration of the same data, but deliberately using inappropriate response functions, first a response function which assumed that the magnetic features were above their true level (fig. 6c), and then one which assumed the features were below their true level (fig. 6d). It can be seen that the location and general shape of the simulated feature are recovered reasonably well, but nowhere near as accurately as with the correct search depth. There is also a fair amount of spurious background activity.

In order to test the noise model, whose specification is somewhat problematic for magnetometry data, we repeated the whole simulation, doubling the magnitude of the noise. The signal from the feature is now substantially hidden by the noise (fig. 7a). The general shape of the feature is still recovered by the EM-OSL algorithm, but the details are not

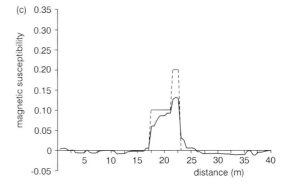

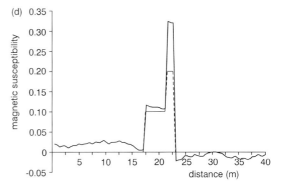

Figure 6. (a) Simulated line magnetometry data restored with EM-OSL algorithm using response functions that assume (b) the correct depth of the feature, (c) too shallow a depth for the feature, and (d) too great a depth for the feature.

as accurate (fig. 7b); there is a fair amount of spurious activity in the background. The results from the searches at the incorrect levels still give some indication of the location of the feature, but are generally inaccurate in other respects (figs 7c, 7d).

6   Questions to be answered

We have shown that the EM-OSL algorithm, maximising the penalised likelihood, produces good results at both Stage I and Stage II, with the 'phantom' susceptibility data and the simulated data for linear traverses. The results suggest that it is now worthwhile to set up the more complicated calculations at Stage III, so that the algorithm may be applied to data from magnetometer surveys over areas of land. Before moving to Stage III, however, a number of questions should be answered.

a. How should the parameter β (or the product $\beta\sigma^2$) and the cut-off parameter in the penalty function be chosen? We have experimented with various combinations of values until finding a set which appeared to give a near optimal restoration. Although the results are relatively insensitive to the choice of these parameters, it is clear that a more objective approach is desirable.

b. How can it be ensured that the response function is appropriate to the physical conditions of the survey? We have shown that the choice of response function for the simulated magnetometry data makes a considerable difference to the quality of the results. This is a critical consideration when moving into 3-dimensional modelling at Stage III, where the response functions are more complicated than those at Stage II.

c. What noise model is appropriate to the data? We have experimented with simple Gaussian models at Stage II, using two different levels of noise, in order to see how the amount of noise affects the quality of the results. The choice of noise model for actual magnetometer survey is problematic, since the signal from features close to the surface is often regarded as noise.

d. Is it possible to predict the vertical depth of restored features as well as horizontal location? The response function from magnetised features differs with depth, as is clearly shown by our experiments in attempting to restore data using the wrong depth. The question is whether it is possible for the EM-OSL algorithm to detect the difference between the response functions sufficiently clearly to attribute a feature to the correct depth. Our experiments suggest that it may be possible, but the results are far from conclusive; further experiments are needed at Stage II, before any depth analysis is tried at Stage III.

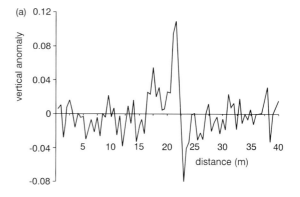

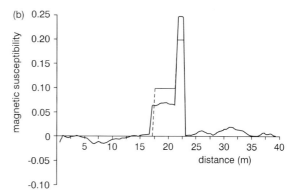

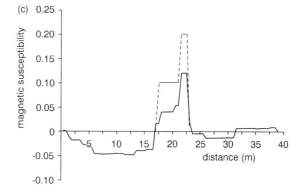

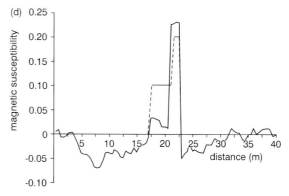

Figure 7. Similar to figure 6, except that noise of doubled intensity has been incorporated into the simulated data.

e. Can a large data set be divided into manageable
'chunks' for calculation? Although each iterative step
of the EM-OSL algorithm is calculated quite swiftly,
it may still become burdensome if m and n (the number
of model elements and the number of observations) are
both large. Since a data set at Stage III may contain
several hundred thousand readings, it would be more
efficient to work with small subsets. It would then be
necessary to ensure that the results at the edges of each
portion matched correctly with those of neighbouring
subsets.

7   Prospects for Stage III

The good progress through Stages I and II of the project
has encouraged us to move on to Stage III as rapidly as
possible. It is at Stage III that the project will become
widely useful to archaeological geophysicists, allowing
access to plenty of field data on which to test our mathematical methods. One important aspect of the usefulness of
the techniques is their likely computational cost, which we
now consider. With around 80 items of line data, the EM-
OSL algorithm requires about 2000 iterations to converge to
its final answer, taking about two minutes of processor time
on a Sun 4 workstation. It is likely that similar computation

times would be achieved on personal computers equipped
with the current Pentium processors.

Extrapolating to larger data sets for Stage III, we expect
the computational time to be roughly proportional to the
size of the data set, although allowance must be made for
the more complicated response functions of the 3-dimen-
sional model. A typical field data set of 400 readings over a
square grid might take 10 minutes to process on a fast
personal computer. If this estimate proves to be reasonable,
then it should be possible to process data as rapidly as it
can be produced from the field survey.

We conclude that the EM-OSL algorithm is capable of
providing the basis for a practical method to restore
magnetometry data. We are confident that satisfactory
answers to the questions of the previous section will be
found, allowing a useful implementation of the technique in
general archaeological field survey.

Acknowledgements

We gratefully acknowledge the advice and technical co-
operation of Dr Arnold Aspinall and Dr Armin Schmidt,
both of the Department of Archaeological Sciences,
University of Bradford; in particular, we thank them for
providing the susceptibility data.

references

Besag, J.	1989	Towards Bayesian image analysis, *Journal of Applied Statistics* 16, 395-407.
Dempster, A.P. N.M. Laird D.B. Rubin	1977	Maximum likelihood from incomplete data via the EM algorithm, *Journal of the Royal Statistical Society* Series B 39, 1-38.
Gonzalez, R.C. R.E. Wood	1992	*Digital Image Processing*. Reading, Massachusetts: Addison-Wesley.
Green, P.J.	1990	Bayesian reconstruction from emission tomography data using a modified EM algorithm, *Institute of Electrical and Electronic Engineers Transactions on Medical Imaging* 9, 84-93.
Hastings, W.K.	1970	Monte Carlo sampling methods using Markov chains and their applications, *Biometrika* 57, 97-109.
Linington, R.E.	1964	The use of simplified anomalies in magnetic surveying, *Archaeometry* 7, 3-13.
Lucy, L.B.	1974	An iterative technique for the rectification of observed distributions, *The Astronomical Journal* 79, 745-765.

Metropolis, N.
  A.W. Rosenbluth
  M.N. Rosenbluth
  A.H. Teller
  E. Teller
    1953   Equations of state calculations by fast computing machines, *Journal of Chemical Physics* 21, 1087-1092.

Richardson, W.H.
    1972   Bayesian-based iterative method of image restoration, *Journal of the Optical Society of America* 62, 55-59.

Tsokas, G.N.
  C.B. Papazachos
  M.Z. Loucoyannakis
  O. Karousova
    1991   Geophysical data from archaeological sites: inversion filters based on the vertical-sided finite prism model, *Archaeometry* 33, 215-230.

Gayle T. Allum
Department of Statistics
University of Leeds
Leeds LS2 9JT
and
Department of Mathematics
University of Bradford
Bradford BD7 1DP
United Kingdom
e-mail: x11032@bradford.ac.uk

Robert G. Aykroyd
Department of Statistics
University of Leeds
Leeds LS2 9JT
United Kingdom
e-mail: robert@amsta.leeds.ac.uk

John G.B. Haigh
Department of Mathematics
University of Bradford
Bradford BD7 1DP
United Kingdom

W. Neubauer
P. Melichar
A. Eder-Hinterleitner

Collection, visualization and simulation of magnetic prospection data

1   Introduction

The majority of our archaeological heritage is buried in the ground and archaeologists are interested in the exploration of the landscape for remains of past human activity. For non-intrusive location of archaeological structures magnetic prospection is an appropriate technique. It is a fascinating discipline under continuous development and has become an important tool of research in Austrian archaeology (Melichar 1990; Melichar/Neubauer 1993; Neubauer 1990). Especially in Lower Austria, we know many archaeological sites easily prospectable by magneto-metery. They are mainly situated in homogeneous loess with low susceptibilities ($\kappa \approx 10 - 20 \cdot 10^{-5}$). Sites are commonly close to the surface and are known due to the last twenty years of systematic aerial photography (Doneus 1994; Fenster zur Urzeit 1982). The archaeological features in the landscape generally have geometric properties different from those of the natural surrounding. Most monuments discovered by aerial photography are being steadily and rapidly destroyed by erosion. Those sites cover areas of many hectares. For precise measurements of large areas in a short time we had to develop both apparatus and techniques. High speed, highest achievable accuracy and spatial resolution are required for an efficient collection of magnetic data. Optically pumped magnetometers have proved to be the appropriate instruments for archaeological prospecting. During the last seven years a cesiumgradiometer with automatic position control and data acquisition has been developed and improved continuously. Site surveys have been carried out systematically on various sites all over Austria.

2   Measuring Device and Data Collection

In a cooperation between the Austrian Central Institute for Meteorology and Geodynamics and the Institute for Prehistory we developed an automatically recording cesiumgradiometer device. The magnetic scanning system ARCHEO PROSPECTIONS® used in Austria is mounted on two completely unmagnetic wooden wheelbarrows. The main wheelbarrow carries the two alkali vapour sensors. The two cesiumsensors are fixed in a plexiglas tube for gradiometer array, measuring the difference of the total magnetic field. In this tube the sensors can be positioned at several heights resulting in different gradients. The first sensor at 50 cm and the second at 2 m above groundlevel is the commonly used gradiometer array. To ensure a vertical gradient the tube is able to swing like a pendulum. For this movement in all directions we constructed a kardan. The gradiometer system operates with a specified accuracy of 0.05 nT. With the optically pumped cesiummagnetometer, being an oscillator at a relatively high frequency, 11 readings can be taken per second. To reach a maximum measurement speed in the field, the gradiometer system is connected to an automatic positioning and data recording system. Thus the survey can be carried out continuously without limitations of the apparatus. The data logger and the gradiometer readout unit are mounted on a second wooden wheelbarrow which is connected to the first one by a 50 m long cable. The automatic position control is realized by optical detection of the wheels rotation. The measuring process is controlled by two audio signals.

For the survey the area of interest is divided into rectangles by using a theodolite and fixed by absolute coordinates. The rectangles themselves are normally measured with 50 or 25 cm grid spacing driving in zigzag. Because the terrain is not always smooth, the count of position impulses from the rotating wheel is varying. To reduce these errors a test line is measured for every rectangle and the count of position impulses is used for calibration. The system is operated by three persons. Under normal conditions about 8 000 square meters can be easily prospected in one day, that means a recording of up to 64 000 readings per day with a spatial resolution of 0.5 × 0.25 m. Sofar the system has recorded about four million readings.

3   Visualization and data processing

In the field the magnetic data are stored in binary format on a laptop computer. Every measured rectangle is represented by one binary data file and an information file for optional corrections. All data files are arranged by their coordinates to compose the resulting image by using a special grid description file. For visualization of the data various data formats are produced by the developed image composer.

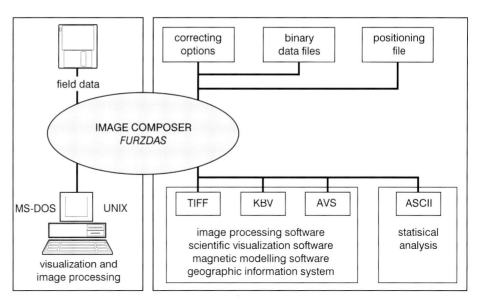

Figure 1. Visualization as a digital image.

TIFF-files can be imported by almost all available digital image processing software for MS-DOS or Windows. Other formats are necessary for input to image processing and scientific visualization software under UNIX on work-stations (see fig. 1).

Every single reading in the field is represented by one pixel on a high-resolution screen. The range of the greyscale is 0 to 254 using 8 bits for representation of one value. For visualization of the mostly very weak archaeological anomalies every 0.1 nT has to be represented by one grey tone. In that way only a range of -12.7 to 12.7 nT can be displayed. Zero nT is therefore given the medium grey tone 127, values bigger than -12.7 nT become white, values smaller than 12.7 nT get black. This is enough because almost all the anomalies of archaeological interest lie in a range of +/- 5 nT. Although the magnetic device operates with high reliability, due to the rough conditions of field-work, several systematic and unsystematic errors occur during data collection.

The first step in data processing is the correction of errors looking like spikes (fig. 2). These single spikes are due to failures of one sensor caused by low batteries, high temperatures (above 35° C) or physical shocks. They are detected in the image and replaced by the median of a 3×3 pixel surrounding. Variations in the height of the sondes above the surface are visible as line shifts. They are mainly due to surface roughness of ploughed soil or traces of tractors. Correction is done by detection of shifted lines and following equalization of the running line average.

Another kind of distortion is due to positioning errors of the moving sensors on the lines and appear as stripes (fig. 3).

These dislocations are conspicuous in the results of nearly all magnetic prospecting teams and with our equipment and measuring process they occur in a maximum range of 0.25 - 0.75 m. They can be corrected by moving or stretching every second line up and down and computing a correlation measure. The final position of a column is reached at the minimal correlation measure. The result of this correction is a visible improvement of the image quality. These corrections are done automatically during the production of the image file. There are many reasons for these distortions and therefore we developed several methods of correction for the demands of the different range of positioning errors.

For further analysis the picture is inverted to get the anomalies of interest in dark grey tones. The next step uses the histogram of the displayed data to produce a higher contrast. For image enhancement the greyscale is stretched over the frequent data values. After the correction of the greyscale, brightness and contrast are tuned manually to improve visibility of the structures of interest. To reduce noise a median filter can be useful. Experience showed, however, that the corrected raw data without any filtering provide the best representation for the archaeological interpretation. Filtering always results in a loss of small archaeological details.

4 Evaluation of magnetic data

A method for the detection of anomalies by image processing is interactive thresholding. The following use of a contour tracing algorithm points out the anomalous zones. Yet, an interpretation only done by image processing techniques is not satisfying for archaeological purposes.

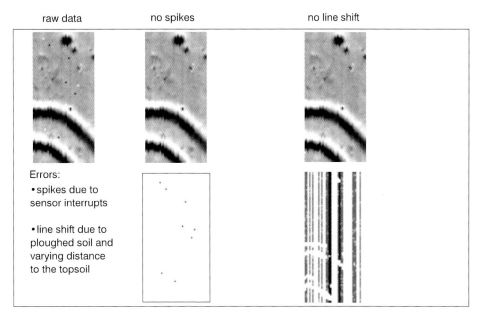

Figure 2. Correction of single spikes and the line shifts.

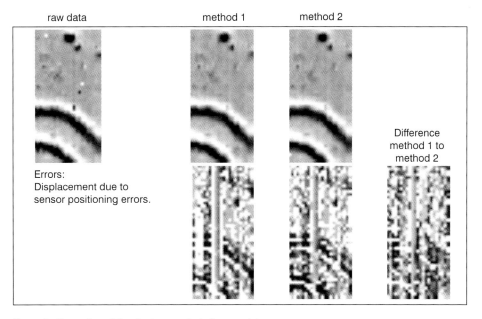

Figure 3. Correction of the displacements in the raw data.

An experienced interpreter is able to line out the archaeological features in a preprocessed image by mental comparison with excavated features. These features are frequently quite complex in shape and often have pronounced geometric forms. Superpositions of anomalies from different sources complicate the interpretation.

The boundaries of detected anomalies of archaeological significance are lined out on the screen overlaying the magnetogram. For the different features detected in the image we create various layers in different colours. Different thematic maps can be easily created from the interpretation layers. The mapped archaeological features

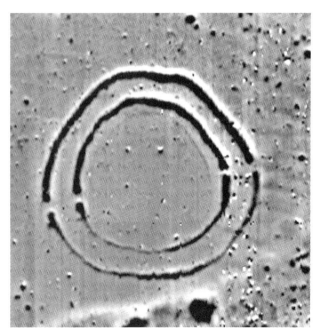

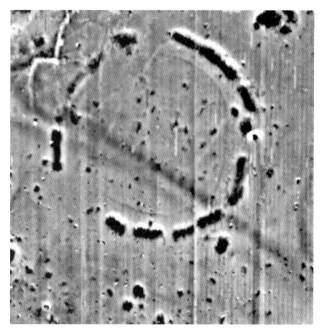

Figure 4. Magnetogram of Puch 1, corrected raw data, range [-7,3,2,7] nT → [white,black].

Figure 5. Magnetogram of Puch 2, corrected raw data, range [-5.3,2.7]nT → [white,black].

are then combined with the existing geodetic data by using CAD software (fig. 7). A primary requirement of the archaeologists with regard to geophysical prospection is to produce a presentation of the evaluated data which is understandable to anyone. The output as an interpretation map is a first step to reach this goal. Thus the end product is a map containing geographical information such as field boundaries, roads and contour lines together with the interpreted archaeological features from magnetic surveys. Later on excavation results are easily integrated into the general site context. For the high-resolution output of the magnetogram we use a 35 mm digital film recorder. The maps containing the interpretation are plotted on a A0 ink jet plotter. The produced maps are the most important basic information for the planning of consecutive excavations. In the following we will present three examples of magnetic surveys on large neolithic sites.[1]

4.1   PUCH 1

The first example of a magnetic survey is a circular ditch system from the Middle Neolithic, from about 6500 years before present. The monument is known from aerial photographs (Fenster zur Urzeit 1982). The position and orientation of the entrances to the enclosure are of high interest. In the aerial photos they are fairly visible and for Puch 1 the interpretation assumed four entrances (Trnka

1991a). In the summer of 1994 an area of 120 × 120 m was magnetically prospected on a grid of 0.5 × 0.5 m.

In the processed magnetogram of Puch 1 (fig. 4) the two circular ditches are shown up very clearly. The magnetogram of the circular ditch delineates the feature outlines and shows many unknown details. Only two entrances were found in the east and west which are clearly visible. In the northern part of the interior a slight concentric anomaly can be detected. These are the last remains of a wooden palisade inside the enclosure. In the southern part of the magnetogram a decrease in the intensity and width of the ditch anomalies is an obvious sign of a bad state of preservation. Topsoil was removed from this area in modern times and filled into a washed-out river bed. The traces of the refilling are visible in the south of the surveyed area. Small anomalies all over the magnetogram are due to iron debris in the ploughed layer.

4.2   PUCH 2

Only 160 m away from Puch 1 another circular ditch system is known from aerial photography (Fenster zur Urzeit 1982; Trnka 1991a). The second ditch system looks quite different from the other known monuments of the middle neolithic period and Puch 2 (fig. 5) was therefore thought to belong to a badly preserved Bronze Age settlement. In the spring of 1994 an area of 160 × 160 m was surveyed with a spatial resolution of 0.5 m.

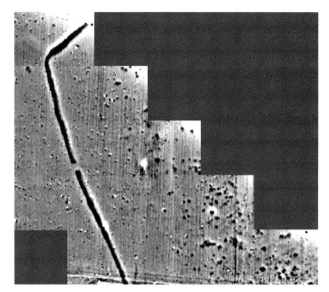

Figure 6. Magnetogram of Weinsteig, corrected raw data, range [-7.3,2.7]nT → [white,black].

The magnetogram shows an interrupted circular ditch. The concentric slight anomaly of a wooden palisade and new excavation results of other monuments underline a neolithic datation also for this ditch. Further research has to provide more information on that specific type of circular ditch systems. Around and inside the enclosure many pit structures were detected. Other anomalies are of geological origin or are due to the boundaries of the old fieldsystem before changing the orientation. These field boundaries respond as filled ditches.

The cross-sections of excavated circular ditch systems are triangular. That is the typical V-shape always observed with middle neolithic circular ditches. The excavated monuments showed that those ditches can be up to 6 m deep and up to 8 m wide. All have at least two and up to 6 entrances in specific orientations. Only well-preserved enclosures show concentric wooden palisades in the interior. Normally the posts were put into a small ditch. The filling of the ditches contains polychrome painted pottery (Lengyel) of high quality, animal bones and sometimes female statuettes. The enclosures must have been of cult use, for all kinds of rituals or meetings. Some have burial pits in the centre or pits with deer burials in the entrances. Because of the orientation of the entrances and lines of posts several prospectors and archaeologists suggest that they were also used for astronomical observations. Anyhow, these circular ditches represent the oldest and largest monumental structures known in European archaeology. Magnetic prospection is the most suitable method for the archaeological exploration of the 35 circular

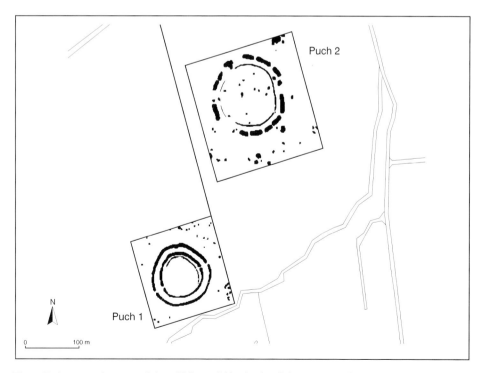

Figure 7. Interpretation map of the middle neolithic circular ditch systems at Puch.

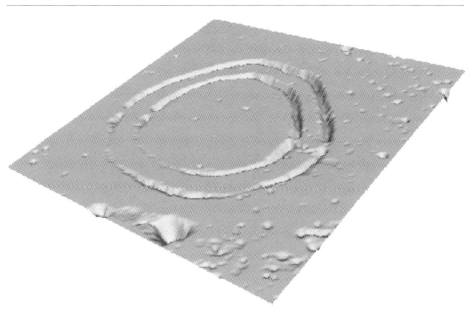

Figure 8. 3-D model of the reconstructed ditches and pits of Puch 1.

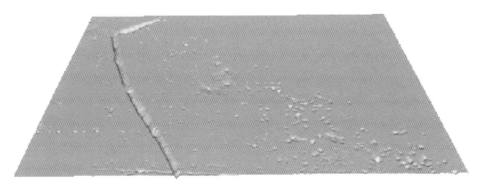

Figure 9. 3-D visualization of the reconstructed ditch and pits of Weinsteig.

ditch systems known in Austria (Melichar/Neubauer 1993; Trnka 1991a).

4.3 WEINSTEIG

Weinsteig is a fortified settlement known again from aerial photography (Fenster zur Urzeit 1982). The habitation is surrounded by a ditch of rectangular plan view with large dimensions of 725 × 350 m (Trnka 1991b). A first survey in the summer of 1994 (fig. 6) covered the northwestern part of the site with an area of 2.72 ha. The ditch is again clearly visible in the magnetogram and a first entrance could be discovered. Many structures, mainly pits can be seen inside the fortification. At this site massive erosion could be detected in the slopes. Only the flat top of the hill where the site is situated shows traces of habitation. Surface

findings suggest an early neolithic datation for the extended monument (probably Late Bandkeramik). 3-D modelling of the ditch showed a U-shaped ditch (fig. 9) which seems to be typical of early neolithic fortifications. The surveys will be continued in the next few years.

5 Simulation and 3-D modelling

To understand the development of the prehistoric cultural and economic activities archaeologists try to obtain as much relevant information as possible. For this purpose, large numbers of similar sites must be identified, normally by aerial photography. Evaluation of further details can be done by non-destructive magnetic surveys prior to any excavation. Excavations are always coupled with an irreversible destruction of the investigated archaeological

Figure 10. Aerial photography of Puch combined with a plan view of the modelling of Puch 1 and the magnetogram of Puch 2.

structure. It is also the most expensive way of evaluating archaeological data. Therefore it is desirable to try and build a model of a monument including all relevant and known information prior to any excavation. In our case magnetic prospection data offers the possibility of reconstruction by modelling the subsurface. A model of the basic physical phenomena is constructed and changed until the measured data are accounted for with minimum error (Eder-Hinterleitner 1994). Prior to that, heuristics are used to separate components of the measurements due to archaeological sources from other than natural or modern origins. This is done by a classification algorithm which outputs a probability for each reading. The probabilities are used to separate archaeologically relevant anomalies from others.

The reconstruction algorithm is able to handle a survey of hundreds of thousands of readings at a calculation time of a few hours on modern workstations. The final result is a 3-D model (fig. 8) of the surveyed monument in a resolution of at least the used grid spacing. By input of a 3-D model, a magnetogram can be simulated. Variations of the primary model and the produced magnetograms can be

used for training interpreters. The different outputs of magnetometry can also be combined with the aerial photography. In this example (fig. 10) we integrated the magnetogram of Puch 2 and a plan view of the 3-D modelling of the double ditch system of Puch 1.

6   Archiving

The ultimate goal of archaeological prospection is the generation of a visual information system based on all archived prospection data (Scollar 1990). Therefore, all relevant information including aerial photographs has to be digitized. For practical considerations we prefer orthophotos for archiving which are produced by combining digital elevation models and scanned images.

The digital terrain or elevation model (DEM) is measured directly from the aerial photograph with an analogue stereo-interpretation device (Kern DSR14) or with an automatic recording tachymeter in the field. The elevation data is rendered and combined with the outlined interpretations of archaeological features or is used as input to the orthophoto software. Scenic views can be produced by mapping the orthophoto on a perspective view of the digital elevation model. With this technique virtual views of monuments of thousands of years old again become available to archaeologists.

All data together form the basic information material of a database, *the prospection archive* of the Institute for Prehistory at the University of Vienna. For the realization of the already mentioned visual archaeological information system we use GIS-technology (ARC/INFO). From this information system the archaeologist can obtain results by searching either geographically, by type of site or by period. The information from the database and the evaluated aerial photographs or geophysical measurements can then be treated by methods of spatial statistics. That permits the analysis of associations between sites of similar and different types or periods, time or spatial trends and the significance of geographical distribution. Our ultimate aim is the realization of a visual geographic information system which can be used by anyone interested in the study or protection of the buried remains of our past.

note

1 These surveys were supported by the Austrian Scientific Foundation under grant P9242-HIS.

references

Doneus M.   1994   Datenbestände des Luftbildarchivs am Institut für Ur- und Frühgeschichte der Universität Wien, *GeoLISIII, Österreichische Zeitschrift für Vermessung und Geoinformation* 1+2, 119-124.

Eder-Hinterleitner A.   1994   Ein robustes Rekonstruktionsverfahren zur Bestimmung der Form von Gräben für die archäologische magnetische Prospektion. In: W.G. Kropatsch/H. Bischof (eds), *Tagungsband Mustererkennung 1994*, Informatik Xpress 5, 532-539.

Fenster zur Urzeit   1982   Katalog zur Sonderaustellung im Museum für Urgeschichte in Asparn an der Zaya. *Katalog des niederösterreichischen Landesmuseums*, Neue Folge 117.

Melichar P.   1990   Eine geomagnetische Prospektionsmethode im Dienst der Archäologie, *Aerial Photography and Geophysical Prospection in Archaeology, Proceedings of the second international Symposium Brussels 8-XI-1986*, 176-182.

Melichar P.
   W. Neubauer   1993   Magnetische Prospektion von Kreisgrabenanlagen in Niederösterreich, *Archäologie Österreichs* 4/1, 61-68.

Neubauer W.   1990   Geophysikalische Prospektionsmethoden in der Archäologie, *Mitteilungen der anthropologischen Gesellschaft in Wien*, Bd 120, 1-60.

Trnka G.   1991a   Studien zu mittelneolithischen Kreisgrabenanlagen, *Mitteilungen der prähistorischen Kommission*, 124-126.

              1991b   Neolithische Befestigungen in Ostösterreich, *Mitteilungen der anthropologischen Gesellschaft in Wien*, Bd. 121, 137-155.

Scollar Irwin   1990   Archaeological Prospecting and Remote Sensing. *Topics in Remote Sensing* 2, Cambridge 1990.

W. Neubauer
Institute for Prehistory
Dept. Geophysical Prospection
University of Vienna
F. Kleingasse 1
1190 Vienna
Austria
e-mail: Wolfgang.Neubauer@univie.ac.at

P. Melichar
Central Institute for Meteorology and Geodynamics
Dept. of Geophysics
Hohe Warte 38
1190 Vienna
Austria

A. Eder-Hinterleitner
Inst. f. Automation
Dept. f. Pattern Recognition and Image Processing
Technical University of Vienna
Treitlstr. 3/1832
1040 Vienna
Austria
e-mail: ahi@prip.tuwien.ac.at

A. Eder-Hinterleitner
W. Neubauer
P. Melichar

Reconstruction of archaeological structures using magnetic prospection[1]

1   Introduction

Archaeological structures in the ground cause small anomalies in the earth's magnetic field due to different magnetic susceptibilities compared to the surrounding ground. These anomalies are measured by high precision magnetometers (Neubauer 1990, 1991). The measured data are preprocessed and displayed as images and manually interpreted by experts (Scollar 1990). The archaeological interpretation of magnetic anomalies is very difficult for several reasons:

1. it is a 2-dimensional projection of a 3-dimensional world;
2. the anomalies of nearby structures may be superimposed;
3. there is always a large amount of noise in the measurement caused by the susceptibility variance of the top soil, by geological structures and by other sources.

Although an expert can estimate whether there is an anomaly of an archaeological structure or not and the probable kind of structure, he or she can estimate only rough dimensions (depth, size, ...) of these structures.

We introduce a method to estimate the position, shape and size of buried archaeological structures by reconstructing a 3-dimensional magnetic model of the subsurface. Our method inverts the idea of simulating magnetic anomalies of archaeological structures of arbitrary shape by dipole sources. A magnetic model of the subsurface is built with homogeneous dipole sources of equal size in a regular grid with different magnetic susceptibilities for different materials (soil, stones, bricks, etc.). The distribution of the dipole sources is automatically arranged so that the differences between the magnetic anomalies of the model and the measured data are minimized.

While the computational costs for the calculation of the anomalies of a subsurface-model are negligible for today's computers, the inverse problem, the determination of the parameters of the subsurface-model is, also with known magnetic properties, a non-deterministic problem with great computational costs. We use the forward modelling method for calculating the anomalies of the modelled archaeological structure and determine the parameters of the model according to an optimization criterion. A special optimization algorithm which is fast enough to find good solutions with the computational power of conventional workstations within a few hours is used.

The reconstruction of filled ditches of the neolithic ring ditch system Puch 1 in Lower Austria is used to demonstrate this method (Trnka 1991). The preprocessed magnetic anomalies of Puch 1 are shown in figure 1. The differences between the total intensities of the earth's magnetic field in 0.5 m and 2.0 m are measured by a cesiumgradiometer in a 0.5 m regular grid. The measured area is 120 m × 120 m, the image therefore has 241 × 241 measuring values. This measurement was carried out by ARCHEO PROSPECTIONS® (Melichar/Neubauer 1993).

2   Method

Figure 2 gives a general view of our method and the data flow through it. After collecting the data in the field they are preprocessed to remove errors.

The reconstruction starts with a classification of the preprocessed data. The classification computes the probability for each data value that does not originate from the expected archaeological structure.

Then, by using the data and the classification the expected archaeological structures are reconstructed. No assumptions about the position and shape of the expected archaeological structure are made, except that the result has to be *smooth*. Therefore this first reconstruction is called *free*.

The free reconstruction is used to determine the nearly exact horizontal positions and a rough estimation of the depth of the expected structures. The detected structures and a modelling of the shape of the expected structures are used to reconstruct the exact position, depth and shape of the expected structures. As the shape of the expected structures and the positions are restricted, the second reconstruction is called *constrained*.

Both reconstruction steps use the same optimization algorithm but the optimization criteria are different. The constrained reconstruction uses a finer spatial resolution.

3   Subsurface model

The subsurface is magnetically modelled by homogeneous dipol sources of equal size in a 3-dimensional regular grid.

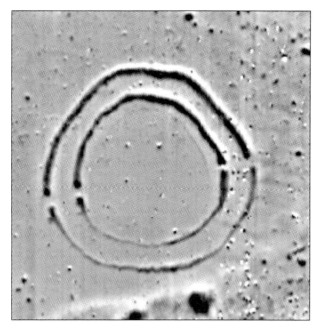

Figure 1. Preprocessed magnetic anomalies of Puch 1. [-4,8]nT → [white, black].

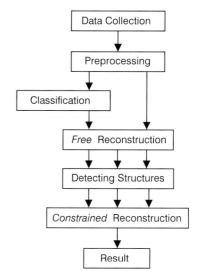

Figure 2. Method of reconstruction.

This method was proposed by I. Scollar to simulate anomalies of archaeological origin (Scollar 1969). The advantage of this method is that it is easy to calculate the anomaly of structures of any shape and any susceptibility distribution with any accuracy. The disadvantage, the computational costs for very accurate simulations, becomes less important due to the rapid progress of the power of computers.

Figure 3a, as an example, shows the profile of the modelling of a filled ditch. Each dipole source represents a cube whose sides are 0.5 m long according to the measuring grid of the prospection which was also 0.5 m. Susceptibility measurements of neolithic ditches in Austria lead to a model with four different layers and four different susceptibilities k:

1) top soil (k_t),
2) top soil above and near the ditch (k_d),
3) sub soil (k_s),
4) filling of the ditch (k_f).

The model can be simplified by subtracting horizontal layers which produce a constant magnetic anomaly. Therefore the top soil and the sub soil are removed. The result is a model of the filled ditch with the susceptibility-contrasts (top-contrast k_{tc}, sub-contrast k_{sc}) in an non-magnetic surrounding (fig. 3b).

$$k_{tc} = k_d - k_t \qquad k_{sc} = k_f - k_s$$

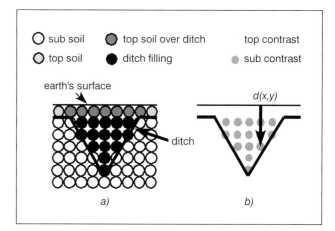

Figure 3. a. Profile of a ditch subsurface model with dipole sources; b. Susceptibility-contrast model of a ditch.

This simplification speeds up the computation of the anomalies because only the parts of the subsurface with a ditch are modelled.

Although there is remnant magnetization in the soil, only induced magnetism is considered for the model. It is assumed that the field vector of the ditch anomaly has the same direction as the field vector of the earth magnetic field (Oehler 1987). The remnant magnetization of the ditch is modelled by a higher susceptibility for the induced magnetization.

The magnetic anomaly (A_M) of a ditch is calculated by

$$A_M(x_s,y_s) = \sum_{x_d} \sum_{x_d} \sum_{z_d=0}^{d(x_s,y_s)} Fk(x_d,y_d,z_d)\ VM(x_s,y_s,x_d,y_d,z_d)$$

The subscript s stands for the positions of the sensor(s) and the subscript d for the positions of dipole sources. F is the total intensity of the earth's magnetic field. V is the volume and k the susceptibility-contrast of the dipole source. d is the depth of the ditch at the place (x_s, y_s). The influence of each dipole source on the measuring device is described by M.

For a gradient measuring device with one sensor in 0.5 m and one in 2.0 m M is calculated by (Linnington 1972):

$$M(x_s, y_s, x_d, y_d, z_d) =$$
$$D(x_s - x_d, y_s - y_d, 0.5 - z_d) - D(x_s - x_d, y_s - y_d, 2.0 - z_d)$$

$$D(x, y, z) = \frac{x^2(3\cos^2 I - 1) + z^2(3\sin^2 I - 1) - y^2 - 6xz\sin I\cos I}{(x^2 + y^2 + z^2)^{\frac{5}{2}}}$$

D is the anomaly produced by a single dipole source and I is the inclination of the earth's magnetic field. The declination of the earth's magnetic field is neglected.

This model is used for the *free* reconstruction where a first rough estimation of the ditches is calculated by a 0.5 m resolution in the depth. For the *constrained* reconstruction the dipole sources are divided into 5 slices to enhance the resolution to 0.1 m.

4   Reconstruction problem

The reconstruction problem is to find the distribution of the dipole sources of the subsurface model to minimize the difference between the model-anomalies and the measured data. All other parameters, the susceptibilies of the dipole sources, the inclination and the total intensity of the earth's magnetic field, are assumed to be known and constant.

To reconstruct ditches according to our susceptibility-contrast model, the depth d of the filling of the ditch at each measuring point (x_s, y_s) determines the position and shape of the ditch (fig. 3b). It is thus possible to estimate the shape of the ditch by estimating the depth-points d.

Our reconstruction problem is to estimate $d(x_s, y_s)$ for all measuring values by minimizing the square of the difference (E_D) between the model-anomalies (A_M) and the measuring data (A_D):

$$E_D = \sum_x \sum_y (A_D(x,y) - A_C - A_M(x,y))^2$$

A_C is the constant anomaly of the measuring device produced by the removed horizontal layers and all other influences on the sondes. A_C is equal to the mean value of all measuring values.

Two problems appear when using this minimization criterion:

1. The least-square-criterion is not a robust criterion. Big anomalies not caused by a ditch or noise lead to unrealistically deep ditches.

2. The intensity of the anomaly of a dipole source decreases with the third power of the distance of the dipole sources to the measuring device. Thus, deep structures like deep parts of a ditch have very little influence.

Two extensions of the minimization term E_D to solve these two problems are described in the following.

4.1   ROBUSTNESS

A weighting of the least-squares term is used to make the criterion robust. The weights $w(x,y)$ are a preclassification of the anomalies and represent the correctness of each data value. The weights have values between 1 and 0. 1 stands for a correct and 0 for an incorrect data value. By multiplying the data fitting (E_D) by these weights, anomalies which definitely do not originate from the expected source are neglected. E_D is extended to

$$E_D = \sum_x \sum_y w(x,y)(A_D(x,y) - A_C - A_M(x,y))^2$$

For anomalies of ditches, the possible maximum and minimum value (A_{min}, A_{max}) of an anomaly caused by a ditch and the difference between each data value and its four neighbours b are considered. The limits A_{min}, A_{max}, b_{min}, b_{max} are determined interactively for each prospected site.

$$b(x,y) = \log(\text{abs}(4A_D(x,y) - A_D(x-1,y) - A_D(x+1,y)$$
$$- A_D(x,y-1) - A_D(x,y+1)))$$
$$w(x,y) = \begin{cases} 0 & \text{if } b(x,y) > b_{max} \vee A_D(x,y) < A_{min} \vee A_D(x,y) > A_{max} \\ 1 & \text{if } b(x,y) < b_{min} \wedge A_D(x,y) > A_{min} \wedge A_D(x,y) < A_{max} \\ (b(x,y) - b_{min})/(b_{max} - b_{min}) & \text{otherwise} \end{cases}$$

Figure 4 shows the weights used to reconstruct the ditches of Puch. Black areas prevent a fitting of the data.

4.2   REGULARIZATION

To get plausible results the *smoothest* result is selected by regularizing the parameters which are optimized. A regularization term E_R is defined describing the relation of each parameter to its neighbours. E_R is multiplied by α to regulate the influence of the regularization. The new minimizing term E_G is calculated by:

$$E_G = E_D + \alpha E_R$$

The depth d of ditches cover a surface representing the border between the ditch filling and the sub soil. Due to the decreasing influence of a dipole source with the third power of the distance between the dipole source and the measuring sensor(s), ditches with too deep positions near too flat ones may occur. To avoid such unplausible ditches the depth d is regularized by smoothing the free reconstruction.

$$E_R = \sum_x \sum_y (2d(x,y) - d(x-1,y) - d(x+1,y))^2 +$$
$$(2d(x,y) - d(x,y-1) - d(x,y+1))^2$$

Figure 4. Classification w of Puch 1; [0, 1] → [black, white].

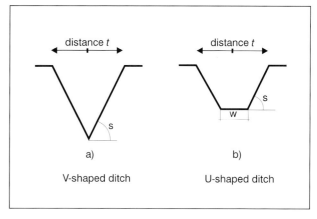

Figure 5. Ditch profile model.

The middle of the profile and the direction of the ditch are calculated in the detecting structures step (fig. 1). The detection of ditches is described below.

5   Optimization algorithm

For reconstructing ditches by using the susceptibility-contrast model, the depths d have only discrete values. Therefore the minimization problem is a combinatorial optimization problem. But this optimization problem has some further special conditions:

1. Many parameters have to be determined. The number of parameters is equal to the number of measuring values ($p = n \times m$).
2. The parameters have only a few discrete values. The number of different values (v) is ~10 for the free reconstruction and ~50 for the constraint reconstruction.
3. There are v^p different solutions. For the site Puch 1 with an area of 14,400 m^2 there are $10^{58,081}$ different solutions for the free reconstruction. (It is not possible to evaluate all of them!)
4. The parameters have a limited spatial relation due to the decreases of the magnitude of the magnetic field of a dipole source with the third power of the distance.

A partially iterative random search algorithm called *leaped annealing* is used to find a solution to this optimization problem (Eder-Hinterleitner 1994). Leaped annealing is similar to *simulated annealing* (Kirkpatrick *et al.* 1983; Romeo/Santigiovanni-Vincentelli 1991). Both have a term T, called temperature, which decreases with the progress of the algorithm and which determines the ability to leave a local minimum. The higher the temperature the easier it is to leave a local minimum. Whereas this is done in simulated annealing by accepting worse solutions temporarily, in leaped annealing it is done by changing the

4.3   MODELLING

For the constrained reconstruction the expected structure is modelled. A new regularization term E_R describes how close the reconstructed and the modelled structures are. A rough estimation of the position and size of the expected structures is necessary to have good starting solutions for the annaeling process.

The ditch profile model assumes that the direction and the middle of the ditch are known and that the ditch is symmetric. The normal distance t of each position (x, y) to the middle of the ditch is computed. By using t, the relative difference between each depth d and its four neighbours can be calculated locally. This local information is necessary for optimizing in subimages (see below).

For a V-shaped ditch (fig. 5a) only the slope s, for a U-shaped ditch (fig. 5b) also the width w of the bottom of the ditch has to be defined. No assumptions about the true depth d are made. The ditches are modelled from the bottom to the top. This model takes into account that filled ditches are eroded from the top to the bottom. The new regularization term E_R for a V-shaped ditch (for areas above a ditch) is:

$$E_R = \sum_x \sum_y \sum_{i=1}^{4} diff_i^2(x, y)$$

$$diff_1(x, y) = d(x-1, y) - s(t(x, y) - t(x-1, y)) - d(x, y)$$
$$diff_2(x, y) = d(x+1, y) - s(t(x, y) - t(x+1, y)) - d(x, y)$$
$$diff_3(x, y) = d(x, y-1) - s(t(x, y) - t(x, y-1)) - d(x, y)$$
$$diff_4(x, y) = d(x, y+1) - s(t(x, y) - t(x, y+1)) - d(x, y)$$

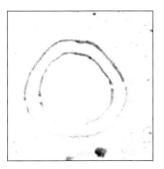

Figure 6. Free reconstruction of Puch 1; d: [0, 2] m → [white, black].

Figure 7. Ditches at depth d = -0.5 m.

Figure 8. Middle line of the detected ditches.

Figure 9. Distance t to the middle of the ditch; [0, 5] m → [black, white].

possible distance of the new solution to the old one. While the solution has to move up and down along the optimization-function in simulated annealing, it jumps from one random place to another and it never has to accept a worse solution in leaped annealing. At the beginning of the leaped annealing algorithm every possible state in the search space can be reached from every other state in one step.

The annealing process is not applied to the whole image at once but to subimages of 2 by 2 pixels in size due to the limited spatial relations of the dipole sources to each other. These subimages are optimized separately but in parallel to consider the mutual influence. The splitting into subimages reduces the solution space and is necessary to reach every possible state from every other state in one step. The algorithm converges as fast as possible when only about 10 percent of the subimages are changed during each iteration. With leaped annealing only 10^4 of $10^{58,081}$ possible solutions have to be evaluated to get a *good* result.

The algorithm is used for both the free and the constrained reconstruction.

6   Reconstructing ditches

The method is demonstrated by the reconstruction of the neolithic ring ditch system Puch 1. The result of the magnetic prospection survey is visualized in figure 1, the classification in figure 4. The magnetic parameters for the reconstruction are:

$F = 48000$ nT $I = 65°$ $V = 0.125$ m^2
$k_{tc} = 70 \ 10^{-5}$ $k_{sc} = 100 \ 10^{-5}$

The result of the free reconstruction is visualized in figure 6. It can be clearly seen that the upper half of the ditch is well preserved while the lower half is mostly destroyed. The regularization leads to a smooth ditch, yet, the ditch is too wide at the top and not deep enough in the middle. The varying shape of the ditch is caused by the

inhomogeneous susceptibilies of the ditch filling. Although the ditch is too wide, it is well located. Many pits are also reconstructed.

6.1   DETECTING DITCHES

To localize the ditches the result of the free reconstruction is first convolved with a 5×5 mean filter for smoothing. Then a threshold (fig. 7) at $d = -0.5$m is taken. The black areas are an estimation of the shape of the ditch after removing the A-horizon.

The middle of the ditch (fig. 8) is calculated by thinning the threshold image and removing short lines. Figure 9 visualizes the normal distance t of pixels which are above the ditch using the middle line (fig. 8) and the thresholded image (fig. 7). To overcome the disadvantage of the discretization in a 0.5 m grid the normal distances t are calculated with subpixel precision. The normal distances to a regression line calculated by using the next five pixels on the middle line are computed.

6.2   CONSTRAINED RECONSTRUCTION

The constrained reconstruction uses the modelling of the profile with a discretization of the depth d of 0.1 m. A V-shaped ditch with a slope $s=45°$ is modelled. The 3-dimensional visualization (fig. 10) gives a realistic impression of the remains of the ditches. In the best preserved areas the ditches are 4.5 m wide and 2 m deep. The two entrances are between 3 m and 5 m wide. The extensive destruction of both ditches towards the front was caused by soil removal when the site was graded. The soils removed fill the large pits at the very front of the reconstruction.

The many small pits look like flat basins due to the smoothing of the depth d. A modelling of the expected shape of the pits would lead to more realistic results.

The remains of the palisade, which can be seen partly in the anomalies, are not reconstructed due to the large horizontal grid of 0.5 m.

The whole reconstruction procedure, the determination of 58,081 parameters, of Puch 1 requires 2 hours of processing time on a Sun SPARCstation 20.

7 Conclusion

We present a method for the reconstruction of a 3-dimensional magnetic subsurface model with dipole sources. The reconstruction problem is formulated as a minimization problem. The difference between the model anomalies and the measured data as well as a regularization or modelling term are minimized by determining the distribution of the dipole sources using an iterative random search annealing algorithm. Although the optimization problem has a very large solution space, a practicable method by dividing the problem into many small subproblems is achieved. Dividing into subproblems offers the possibility of using massive parallel computers to speed up the annealing process by the number of available processors.

The method has two reconstruction steps to combine the following characteristics:

1. no assumptions about the location of archaeological structures are necessary,
2. pre-information about the expected archaeological structure can be integrated into the reconstruction process.

The first step determines rough positions and depths of the expected structures by using a rough subsurface model. The second one uses a finer resolution and a modelling of the expected structures to estimate the exact positions, depths and shapes of the archaeological structures.

The ring ditch system Puch 1 is modelled, reconstructed and visualized to demonstrate the method.

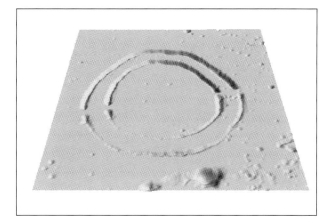

Figure 10. 3-dimensional visualization of reconstructed ditches of Puch 1.

This procedure can be easily applied to other archaeological structures, like pits, walls, etc. New regularization and modelling terms have to be developed, but the modelling with dipole sources and leaped annealing for solving the resulting optimization problem can also be used.

Acknowledgement

The authors would like to thank Amy Krois-Lindner, Axel Pinz and Christian Cenker for reading earlier drafts of this paper and Brigitta Galian for many useful hints.

note

1 This work was supported by the Austrian Science Foundation under grant P9242-HIS.

references

Eder-Hinterleitner, A.	1994	Ein Robustes Rekonstruktionsverfahren zur Bestimmung der Form von Gräben für die archäologische magnetische Prospektion. In: W.G. Kropatsch/H. Bischof (eds), *Tagungsband Mustererkennung 1994*, Informatik Xpress 5, 532-539.
Kirkpatrick, S. C.D. Gelatt P. Vecchi	1983	Optimization by simulated annealing, *Science* 220 (4598), 671-680.
Linnington, R.E.	1972	A summary of simple theory applicable to magnetic prospection in archaeology, *Prospezioni archeologiche* 7, 9-27.

Melichar, P.
  W. Neubauer
      1993 Magnetische Prospektion von Kreisgrabenanlagen in Niederösterreich, *Mitteilungen der Österreichischen Gesellschaft für Ur- und Frühgeschichte* 43, 61-68.

Neubauer, W.
      1990 Geophysikalische Prospektion in der Archäologie, *Mitteilungen der Anthropologischen Gesellschaft in Wien* 120, 1-60.

      1991 Magnetische Prospektion von Kreisgrabenanlagen. In: G. Trnka, Studien zu mittelneolithischen Kreisgrabenanlagen, *Verlag der Österreichischen Akademie der Wissenschaften*, 331-338.

Oehler, A.
      1987 *Zweidimensionale Modellrechnung zu magnetischen Prospektionsmessungen in der Archäologie.* Master thesis, Inst. f. Allgemeine und Angewandte Geophysik, Ludwigs-Maximilians-University, Munich, Germany.

Romeo, F.
  A. Santigiovanni-Vincentelli
      1991 A theoretical framework for simulated annealing, *Algorithmica* 6, 302-345.

Scollar, I.
      1969 A program for the simulation of magnetic anomalies of archeological origin in a computer, *Prospezioni archeologiche* 4, 59-83.

      1990 *Archeological prospecting and remote sensing.* Cambridge: Cambridge University Press, Topics In Remote Sensing.

Trnka, G.
      1991 *Studien zu mittelneolithischen Kreisgrabenanlagen.* Verlag der Österreichischen Akademie der Wissenschaften.

A. Eder-Hinterleitner
Dept. f. Pattern Recognition a. Image Processing
Technical University of Vienna
Treitlstr. 3/1832
1040 Vienna
Austria
e-mail: ahi@prip.tuwien.ac.at

W. Neubauer
Institute for Prehistory
University Vienna
F. Kleing. 1,
1190 Vienna
Austria
e-mail: Wolfgang.Neubauer@univie.ac.at

P. Melichar
Central Inst. f. Meteorology and Geodynamics
Hohe Warte 38
1190 Vienna
Austria

Phil Perkins

An image processing technique for the suppression of traces of modern agricultural activity in aerial photographs

1 The problem

Agricultural activity can make buried archaeological sites visible from the air. Ploughing creates soil marks and sowing creates crop marks. However, mechanised agriculture also creates other patterns in the soil or in crops. Ploughing leaves regular furrows and mechanised sowing leaves fine alignments of plants in the field and fertilisation or pesticide treatments can leave regular tractor tracks across fields. Traces of this agricultural activity are also visible from the air and may mask or confuse archaeological crop marks or soil marks. Archaeologists have employed image processing to aerial photographs for many reasons (Booth *et al*. 1991) and it offers some hope of enhancing this particular form of 'noise'.

A first approach in such cases where there is unwanted fine detail, such as furrows, is to convolve the image using an averaging filter. This removes fine detail in the image leaving coarse detail visible. However, the filter is indiscriminate and has the effect of blurring everything in the image equally. Certainly it removes traces of sowing and tractor tracks but it also corrupts the crop marks which are clearly visible in the data which have been removed from the image in the filtering process (fig. 1).

What is required is a filter which can discriminate between the regular traces of agriculture and the less regular traces of archaeological structures. Edge suppression filters offer some hope but in practice the edges of the archaeological features are also suppressed, reducing their legibility.

2 A solution

A solution to this problem is possible if we consider the image in the frequency domain as a sum of phase shifted sine waves. Determining which sine waves to use is the major concern of Fourier Analysis. Information about the amplitude and phase shift of the sine waves can be encoded as a Fourier transform, and since it is discrete sampled data we can use the Fast Fourier Transform. The image may now be filtered in the frequency domain as we might in the

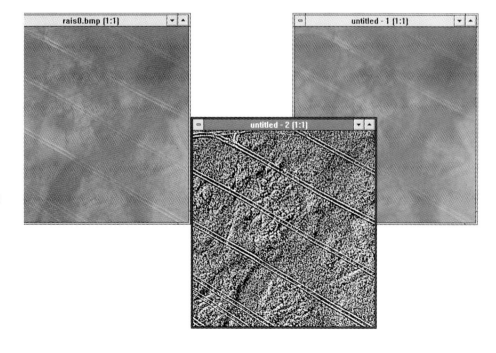

Figure 1. Left: the original photo. Right: blurred image after applying a 3 × 3 averaging filter. Centre: an equalised image of the difference between the before and after images. Many of the traces of the tractor tracks and alignments of plants have been removed and so are visible in the difference between the two images, however the crop mark itself is also visible and so has been corrupted.

Figure 2. Frequency filtering applied to a data set simulating a ploughed field. Top left: simulated data. Top right: Fast Fourier Transform of simulated data. Bottom left: Fast Fourier Transform filtered by hand. Bottom right: Inverse Fast Fourier Transform of filtered simulated data.

spatial domain. Truncation of the high frequencies is equivalent to blurring the image in the spatial domain, that is the high frequencies are filtered out (the technique is fully described in theory in the context of antialiasing in Foley *et al.* 1990: 623-46). Filtering in the frequency domain allows the possibility to selectively filter the transforms of the coarseness or fineness of regular patterning along with the orientation of features in the spatial (unfiltered) domain.

2.1   SIMULATED DATA
In order to test the effects of frequency filtering and explore its impact on defined signals, a simulated data set consisting of a 256 × 256 pixel field of black and white diagonal lines representing furrows at 45° was created (fig. 2 top left). When transformed to the frequency domain with a Fast Fourier Transform the image appears as three bright dots

aligned at 45° (fig. 2 top right). Filtering this image by hand these outlying peaks of high frequency are removed (fig. 2 bottom left). The Inverse Fast Fourier Transform applied to transform this filtered image back to the spatial domain results is a uniformly mid-grey field — the furrows have been effectively removed by filtering out their frequencies (fig. 2 bottom right). The filtering is extremely effective on such a simple image. However, add a simulated round barrow to the simulated field (fig. 3 top left) and the Fast Fourier Transform of the image appears much more complex (fig. 3 top right). Filtering out the frequencies known from the previous experiment to remove the traces of the furrows only (fig. 3 bottom left) and applying the Inverse Fast Fourier Transform (fig. 3 bottom right) effectively removes the traces of the furrows. The simulated round barrow, which was originally uniformly grey, rather than furrowed, has taken on zebra stripes due to the fact

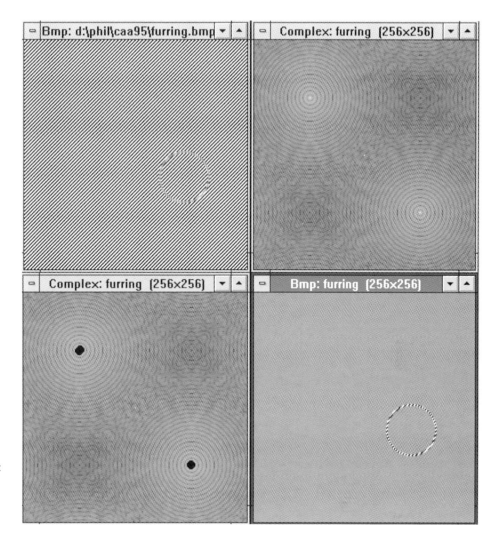

Figure 3. Frequency filtering applied to a data set simulating a ploughed field with a circular soil mark. Top left: simulated data. Top right: Fast Fourier Transform of simulated data. Bottom left: Fast Fourier Transform filtered by hand. Bottom right: Inverse Fast Fourier Transform of filtered simulated data.

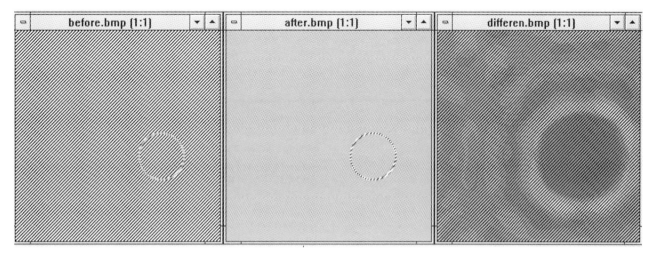

Figure 4. The simulated data of a ploughed field with a circular soil mark is shown before filtering (left) and after filtering (centre). The equalised difference between the two (right) shows, in an exaggerated way, the nature of the part of the signal that has been filtered out.

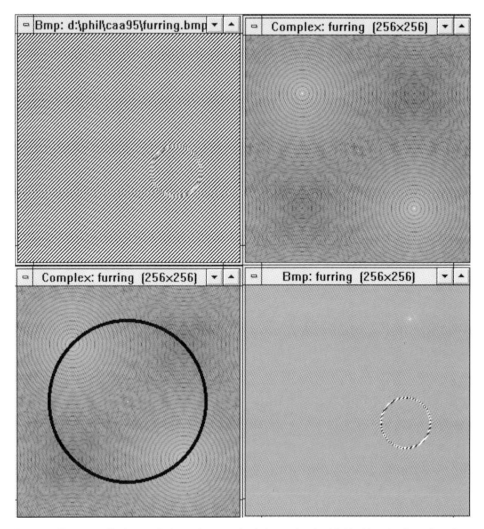

Figure 5. Frequency filtering applied to a data set simulating a ploughed field with a circular soil mark. Top left: simulated data. Top right: Fast Fourier Transform of simulated data. Bottom left: Fast Fourier Transform filtered with a band stop filter. Bottom right: Inverse Fast Fourier Transform of filtered simulated data.

that the values representing the furrows have been subtracted from it too. Around the ring there is some 'rippling' in the uniform grey of the field indicating that the technique is not perfect when more complex images are filtered. This is visualised in figure 4 where the simulated data is shown before (left) and after (centre) filtering and the equalised difference between the two (right) shows, in an exaggerated way, the nature of the part of the signal that has been filtered out.

Other filters instead of a heuristic hand filtering may also be applied to transformed images. For example a band stop filter, i.e. stopping the frequency which coincides with the peaks in frequency representing the furrows is applied in

figure 5. The results are similar but the 'rippling' around the ring has a different form. The Fast Fourier Transform of a simulated complex crop mark (fig. 6 top left and right) can be seen to be more complex and less structured than the simple simulation. The filtering is still effective but the 'rippling' effects become more apparent closer to the simulated soil mark (fig. 6 bottom left and right).

Using real world data, figure 7 illustrates a variety of filtering strategies applied to the same photograph. The first column on the left shows at the top the image before filtering and below the Fast Fourier Transform of the image. The second column shows at the top a heuristic filter removing only low frequencies, in the centre is the

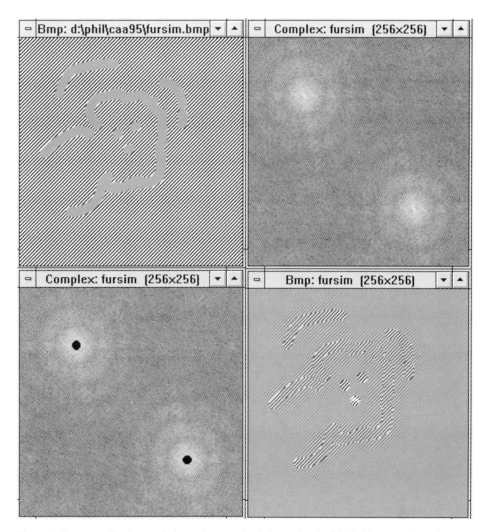

Figure 6. Frequency filtering applied to a data set simulating a ploughed field with a complex soil mark. Top left: simulated data. Top right: Fast Fourier Transform of simulated data. Bottom left: Fast Fourier Transform filtered by hand. Bottom right: Inverse Fast Fourier Transform of filtered simulated data.

filtered image and at the bottom an equalised image of the difference between the image before and after the filtering. Similarly the third column removes middle frequencies and the fourth only high frequencies. The fifth column on the right removes all frequencies with a particular frequency. Different filtering strategies may be adopted according to the nature of the noise to be removed from the image.

The Fourier Transform can only be applied to single band data, e.g., greyscale images only. To filter 'true' colour images it is first necessary to split the image into individual channels, in this case at Gussage All Saints red, green, blue. Each channel is then filtered separately and then the three filtered images may be recombined from the

channels to produce a 'true' colour filtered image (fig. 8). Although differing parts of each band are filtered out when used carefully the technique does not impair the colour balance of the image.

3   Conclusions

This technique of filtering images of aerial photographs in the frequency domain has been found to be effective in the removal of systematic 'noise' in the images. It has been used in experiments to remove traces of ploughing thereby enhancing soil marks, traces seeding in young and mature crops, and tractor or machine tracks. It has been tested on images of regular olive groves but with limited success.

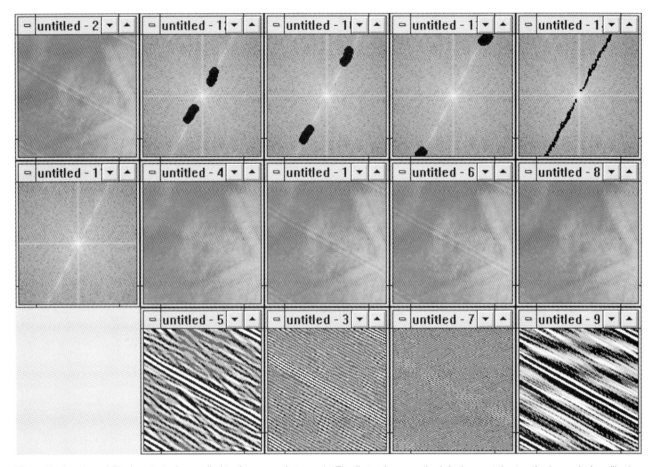

Figure 7. A variety of filtering strategies applied to the same photograph. The first column on the left shows at the top the image before filtering and below the Fast Fourier Transform of the image. The second column shows at the top a heuristic filter removing only low frequencies, in the centre is the filtered image and at the bottom an equalised image of the difference between the image before and after the filtering. Similarly the third column removes middle frequencies and the fourth only high frequencies. The fifth column on the right removes all frequencies with a particular frequency.

Such filtering has its limitations: the mathematics requires the image to be a perfect square, and large squares are computationally intensive. Most significant is that the filtering will only be effective on certain images. The 'noise' in the image, e.g. ploughing, needs to be reasonably regular in its linearity, spacing and orientation for good results to be obtained. The filtering will work on any square image, but if there is no regular 'interference' in the image, the Fourier Transform of the image becomes relatively even and offending frequencies become difficult to identify and filter out.

The technique has only been tested on aerial photographs to date but other forms of remote sensing, particularly those prone to banding due to systematic instrumentational mis-alignment or those that also detect agricultural phenomena might also benefit from filtering in the frequency domain.

Technical note

Large images were processed on a Sun Sparc IPX running IP an image processing suite which uses VIPS an image processing library written in C and developed as part of the VASARI Project at Birkbeck College. Smaller images were processed using a combination of Aldus PhotoStyler and ProFFT V. 1 a project developed by Marius Kjeldahl and four other students learning C++ at the Norwegian Institute of Technology, Trondheim, running on a variety of Viglen PC's.

Acknowledgments

Thanks are due to Blaise Vyner who provided many of the aerial photographs used to experiment with the technique and to Kirk Martinez who introduced me to the frequency domain.

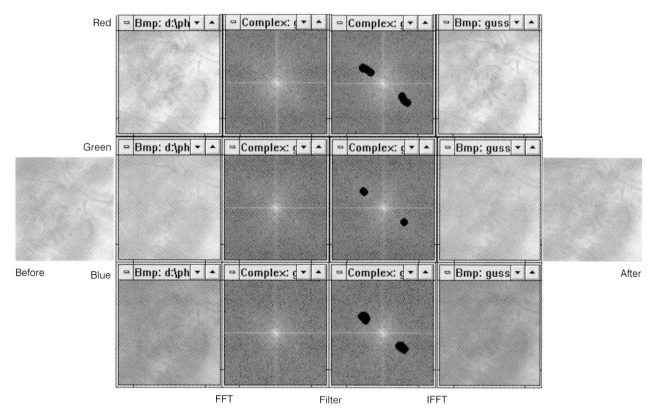

Figure 8. To filter 'true' colour images split the image into individual channels. Each channel is then filtered separately and then the three filtered images may be recombined from the channels to produce a 'true' colour filtered image. This image is of the Iron Age enclosure at Gussage All Saints (Original © Crown Copyright).

references

Booth, W.
  S.S. Ipson
  J.G.B. Haigh

1992   An inexpensive PC-based imaging system for applications in archaeology. In: G. Lock/
        J. Moffett (eds), *Computer Applications and Quantitative Methods in Archaeology 1991*,
        197-204, BAR International Series 577, Oxford: Tempus Reparatum

Foley, J.
  A. van Dam
  S. Seiner
  J. Hughes (eds)

1990   *Computer Graphics: Principles and Practice*, (2nd ed). Reading, Massachusetts: Addison
        Wesley.

Phil Perkins
Department of Classical Studies
The Open University
Walton Hall
Milton Keynes
MK7 6BT
United Kingdom
e-mail: P.Perkins@open.ac.uk

Statistics and Classification

Clive Orton   **Markov models for museums**

1   Introduction

This paper is a sequel to studies of the use of sampling methods in the assessment of the condition of museum collections, carried out at the Museum of London (Keene/Orton 1992) and the British Museum (Leese/Bradley 1995). These studies looked mainly at the problem of obtaining a 'snapshot' of the condition of a collection at a point in time; this paper looks at the related problem of monitoring changes in condition over time.

The methods described below arose from a request from the Horniman Museum in south London for advice on the statistical aspects of monitoring the condition of the Museum's collections, following a 'census' of their condition (Walker/Bacon 1987). The design work was mainly done in 1991, but for various reasons (including the subsidence of the Ethnographic Gallery) has not yet been fully implemented. As the Museum is now fully engaged in preparations for its Centenary in 2001, it seems useful to publish 'the story so far' without waiting for full implementation.

2   Background

The Museum has three separate collections: ethnography, natural history, and musical instruments. In each collection, objects are stored by location code (e.g. type of object) and within that, by broad provenance. In the course of the census, information had been recorded on the condition of every object, on a four-point scale of priority: G (good), F (fair), U (urgent), and I (immediate), reflecting the need for remedial treatment. These correspond roughly to the four conservation priorities of the Museum of London survey (Keene/Orton 1992: 163) — Little, Low, High and Urgent — but the precise definitions may differ. Objects were generally recorded individually, i.e. one to each line of the census form, but the records for some types were 'bulked', e.g. recorded as 'F(X5), G(X20)' (meaning five objects in fair condition and twenty in good condition) on one line. It was believed that, for most types, the objects included in a 'bulk' record could be recognised individually in any subsequent survey. Exceptions are the eggs and fossils groups of the natural history collection; a different approach is needed for such groups (see below).

3   Aim

The aim was to design a system of sample surveys which would enable the condition of the collections to be monitored annually. Particular attention was to be paid to:

i.   locating problem areas in stores ('hot spots'),
ii.   identifying problem materials, with implications for specialist help,
iii. assessing long-term trends, e.g. suitability of particular stores,
iv.   assessing staffing implications.

Points (i) to (iii) are inter-related, in that 'hot spots' are likely to occur where the environment is wrong for the type of material stored there, while 'problem materials' are usually only problems in terms of long-term preservation if they are in the wrong environment. The long-term suitability of particular stores will depend on material types and their needs. In museums which do not store objects by function and type, these points will be less interconnected.

It is not practical to carry out a census every year, nor is one needed in order to meet these aims. The need is for sample survey methods which will enable (a) the numbers of objects currently in each of the four priorities, and (b) the rate of movement of objects from one priority to another, to be estimated for each type of object.

4   Model

Objects must at any point in time be in one, and only one, of the four priorities. They may at any time move from a priority to a higher priority (i.e. their condition may worsen), but they cannot (without intervention) move to a lower priority. We cannot observe this process directly: all we can observe is the condition of selected objects at fixed intervals of time (in this example, the interval is one year). This situation can be modelled as a Markov chain (Cox/Miller 1965: 84), in which the probability of objects moving from one priority to another is expressed as a matrix of 'transition probabilities' p_{ij} from state i to state j over the fixed interval. The 'states' of the statistical theory correspond to the priorities described above.

For any chosen group, we say that the number of objects in the census, held at time 0, is $N(0)$, of which $N_i(0)$ ($i = 1, ..., 4$) are in the i th priority (G, F, U, I). The number $N_j(t)$ in the j th priority at time t is given by

$$N_j(t) = \sum_i N_i(t\text{-}1)p_{ij}, \quad i = 1, ..., 4; \; j = 1, ..., 4; \; t = 1, 2, ...,$$

or in matrix notation $N'(t) = N'(t\text{-}1)P$.

The transition matrix P is initially given the form

$$P = \begin{matrix} p_{11} & p_{12} & p_{13} & p_{14} \\ 0 & p_{22} & p_{23} & p_{24} \\ 0 & 0 & p_{33} & p_{34} \\ 0 & 0 & 0 & p_{44} \end{matrix}$$

where $\sum_j p_{ij} = 1$ for $i = 1, ..., 4$.

This model is a simplification, and in real life further factors would have to be taken into account:

1. gain of objects: at any time, new objects may be added to the collections,

2. loss of objects: at any time, objects may be removed from the collection, either by disposal, by temporary absence (e.g. for display, or for loan to another museum), or because they have decayed irretrievably. Depending on the exact meaning given to the priority 'immediate', one might say that any object in priority I in year t will have decayed irretrievably by the year $t + 1$ (or perhaps $t + 2$?). This could be modelled by introducing a fifth priority D (= dead)), with a transition probability p_{45} depending on the definitions (e.g. $p_{45} = 1$),

3. remedial action to individual objects: surveys of collection condition are set in a context of programmes of conservation work designed to maintain or improve the overall condition of a collection. Thus the 'below diagonal' elements of the transition matrix P will not in practice be zeros. However, there are benefits in using survey data to monitor condition 'without treatment', and to write in transition probabilities reflecting actual or planned treatment programmes.

4. remedial action to stores: as one aim of monitoring is to improve overall storage conditions, it would be surprising and disappointing if the transition probabilities did not change over time, with the aim being to increase the 'diagonal' elements and decrease the 'above diagonal' ones. This means that the transition probabilities should be re-estimated at each survey, to see whether improvement has in fact taken place.

The fourth point might seem to invalidate the use of the Markov chain model, since that model assumes that the transition probabilities are independent of time (Cox/Miller 1965: 84). However, the model can be usefully employed to predict the future condition of a collection on assumptions of (for example) no intervention, or intervention at a set level of conservation of objects, and to assess the likely impact of different programmes of intervention.

The predictive abilities of a Markov chain model arise from its independence from time. Since $N'(t) = N'(t\text{-}1)P$, the matrix P can be estimated by comparing $N(0)$ (the census) with $n(1)$ (results from the first survey). This can be used to predict, or more correctly project, $N(t)$ as $N'(0)\hat{P}^t$, although it must be realised that, as t increases, errors in the estimate $\hat{P}$ will accumulate through successive N s, which will therefore become less and less reliable. Although they are not to be believed, such projections have considerable descriptive, political and management value. They can provide a dynamic description of condition: not just the present state, but also incorporating rates of change. For example, one could use the formula to project the date by which a certain proportion (e.g. 50%) of a collection will be in priority 4 (immediate), and hence (for example) the likely half-life of the collection. Such a figure could be used to highlight a need for additional resources, and the effect on such a date of the application of extra resources could be calculated. Projections made on the basis of successive surveys could show whether the collection is 'gaining' or 'losing' ground, according to whether the expected life (or half-life) is increasing or decreasing.

It has been pointed out that in standard Risk Assessment models the risk is assessed as:

Risk = Threats + Vulnerabitities + Asset value.

In the museum context, the 'asset value' of an object is made up of its historic value, its uniqueness, and its relevance to the institution. The overall condition should in principle be weighted to take account of this, since a collection in which a few valuable objects were deteriorating rapidly, while the rest were relatively stable, would be in worse condition than the raw data would imply. This has not been attempted in this survey; it would be straightforward to take account of variations is asset value between types, but much more difficult for variation within types.

5 Sample design and implementation
5.1 SAMPLING: THEORY
It seems reasonable to make each group or location code (see above) correspond to a stratum in the statistical sense, and to use stratified random sampling methods. Results can then be obtained separately for each group (type of object) and aggregated to give an overall picture of the collection.

For any one stratum, we suppose that the population at the time of the survey is N, and that a sample of size n is selected. For the objects in this sample, we know both their priority at the time of the census and their priority at the time of the survey. The number in the i th priority at the census we call n_i, the number in the j th priority at the survey we call n_j, and the number in the i th priority at the census and in the j th at the survey we call n_{ij}.

Then we can estimate the transition probabilities $\{p_{ij}\}$ by

$$\hat{p}_{ij} = n_{ij} / n_i$$

and the numbers N_j in each priority by

$$\hat{N}_j = \sum_i N_i \, \hat{p}_{ij},$$

adjusting if necessary to allow for acquisitions and disposals.

It can be shown (see below) that this approach to the estimation of the N_j, known as *ratio estimation*, will give better estimates than the simpler approach $\hat{N}_j = N \, (n_j / n)$, at least for the sorts of values of $\{p_{ij}\}$ that are likely to be encountered.

Results can be aggregated across groups to give figures for the entire collection.

This approach is very straightforward, but it assumes that the census is followed by a single survey. Our aim is to carry out a series of surveys at regular intervals, thus leading us to the theory of *repeated sampling*. Sampling on two or more occasions is discussed in detail by Cochran (1963: 341-352), who lists three aspects that one may wish to estimate:

1. the change in N from one occasion to the next,
2. the average value of N over all occasions,
3. the value of N for the most recent occasion.

Our interests are likely to lie in 1 and/or 3, but not in 2.

He gives the optimum sampling strategy for each case (*ibid.*: 342) as:

for 1, it is best to retain the same sample throughout,
for 2, it is best to obtain a new sample on each occasion,
for 3, equal precision is obtained by keeping the same sample or by replacing all of it. Replacing part of the sample may give better results than either of these.

He then goes on (*ibid.*: 345-352) to discuss sampling on more than two occasions, showing that if we are only interested in need 3, it is best to replace 50% of the sample on each occasion (*ibid.*: 347), but if we are also interested in need 1, we should increase the proportion retained to, for example, 75% (*ibid.*: 349). This increase 'produces only small increases in the variance of the current estimates and gives substantially larger reductions in the variances of the estimates of change' (*ibid.*). He suggests retaining 2/3, 3/4 or 4/5 of the sample from one survey to the next if one is interested in needs 1 *and* 3.

In the event, a retention rate of 2/3 was recommended to the Museum, i.e. one-third of the sample would be replaced at each survey, so that the selected objects would be surveyed on three occasions each (except for those 'dropping out' after the first or second survey).

I had not appreciated at that time (1991) the complexities that this would bring about in the estimation of transition probabilities after the first survey. Since the priority of each object in the current survey is known from both the census and the current survey, transition probabilities from the census to the current survey can be estimated without difficulty. But since one-third of the sample in the current survey did not participate in the previous survey, estimating transition probabilities from one survey to the next is more difficult.

The approach suggested at the time was to divide the sample into a 'matched' part (observed in the current and the previous survey) and an 'unmatched' part (observed for the first time since the census in the current survey), denoted by suffices u and m respectively. Transition probabilities between the k th and l th surveys are denoted by $\boldsymbol{P}(k, l)$, and the census is called survey 0. I suggested forming one estimate from the matched part:

$$_m\hat{\boldsymbol{N}}'(t) = \hat{\boldsymbol{N}}'(t\text{-}1) \, \hat{\boldsymbol{P}}(t\text{-}1, t)$$

and one from the unmatched part:

$$_u\hat{\boldsymbol{N}}'(t) = \boldsymbol{N}'(0) \, \hat{\boldsymbol{P}}(0, t)$$

These could be combined by weighting them according to the inverses of their variances (a standard variance-minimising technique). Revised estimates of $\boldsymbol{P}$ could then be obtained from the combined estimates of $N(t)$.

The estimation of the transition probabilities from such data has been approached more thoroughly by Klotz and Sharples (1994). In a remarkably parallel study (the development of coronary disease in cardiac transplantation patients), they show that maximum-likelihood estimators of the transition probabilities can be obtained, but only by iterative methods (Newton-Raphson approximation).

A more practical problem is that the transition probabilities may well change from one survey to the next. Indeed, we hope they will change (for the better), as this indicates improvements in the management of the condition of the collection. Therefore, only the matched sample should be used in estimating current transition probabilities, since including the unmatched sample may bias the outcome. From this it follows that the matched sample should be as large as possible, say 4/5 of the total sample, rather than 2/3 as recommended above. I would be reluctant to recommend retaining the entire sample for each successive survey, unless there were plans to hold a census at regular intervals (e.g. 5- or 10-yearly).

As mentioned above, it was decided to use stratified sampling with the groups as strata. This raises the question of 'optimum allocation': should the same proportion of each stratum be chosen for the survey, or could better results be obtained by choosing different proportions?

The question of optimum allocation when sampling for proportions has been discussed by Cochran (1963: 106-109). Since transition probabilities relate to proportions of objects in a priority that change to another priority, this is a useful approach. He concludes that there is little difference in precision between optimum and proportional allocation unless the proportions are (a) very small (e.g. ≤5%) and (b) vary widely from one stratum to another (e.g. from 0.1% to 5%), and that 'the simplicity and the self-weighting feature of proportional allocation more than compensates for the slight loss in precision' (*ibid.*: 109). Elsewhere he comments that 'The simplicity and self-weighting feature of proportional allocation are probably worth a 10-to-20% increase in variance' (*ibid.*: 102).

The calculation of optimum allocation would be very difficult in our situation, as we are sampling for several proportions (not just one) which are weighted in a complicated way. Also, there is no *a priori* evidence of large systematic differences between strata (although they may be revealed as work progresses). The simple approach of proportional allocation was therefore recommended.

The recommendation might have been different for a museum with a predominance of ceramic and/or stone objects in its collections. Many such objects, unless in a weakened state on arrival, are unlikely to suffer deterioration other than from mechanical damage or a general storeroom disaster. They could therefore be sampled less intensively than more vulnerable objects, either by using a smaller sampling fraction or perhaps by sampling less frequently.

5.2   SAMPLING – PRACTICAL ISSUES

Theoretical considerations are only part of the story. The design of a sampling scheme must also take account of the fact that it will be undertaken by museum staff, or possibly temporary staff on short-term contract, who cannot be expected to have any statistical expertise. This means that any scheme should be as simple as possible, and appear straightforward and reasonable to the user. It should also be designed so that the analysis is straightforward. These points reinforce the decision to use the same sampling fraction in all strata (proportional allocation).

They also point towards a scheme of systematic sampling in each stratum, as was used in the Museum of London survey, with simple instructions for the replacement of a proportion of the sample at each survey.

The design was presented to the Museum as a 'rotating panel', selected systematically. The selected objects were to be numbered 1, 2, 3, 1, …, as they were selected, so that after the first year all the '1s' would be replaced, the next year all the '2s', and so on. Replacement would be by the next object at the same location; if the last object were to be replaced, it would be by the first. This approach would maintain the systematic nature of the same and make its implementation simple.

5.3   BULK SAMPLING

The strata which have been identified as having 'bulk' records (see above) have to be treated differently, both for selection and estimation. The practical problem is that it is not reasonable to expect a surveyor to remember which of a tray of (say) 200 bird eggs were in which condition at the census. The suggested solution was to treat the 'unit' (i.e. whatever grouping of objects had been entered on one line of the census form) as the unit of sampling, instead of the individual object. Systematic sampling would be used to 'select' an object, but the entire unit to which it belonged would then be sampled for the sample. This is the technique known as sampling 'with probability proportional to size' (i.e. of the unit), abbreviated to pps (*ibid.*: 308).

6   Estimation

The formulae used for estimating numbers currently in each priority, and the transition probabilities, were given above. However, they should not be presented to museum staff in this form. Ideally, specialist software covering sample design, selection, data input and analysis, should be provided, analogous to the Rothamsted General Survey Program (Anon 1989). Neither the time nor the resources were available for this task, so a spreadsheet was designed for calculating numbers in each priority, their standard deviations, and the transition probabilities. A second spreadsheet was needed to perform the calculations for the bulk samples, because they require rather different calculations.

The use of these spreadsheets has not been tested; for reasons given above I would now place more emphasis on the short-term transition probabilities and in detecting trends in them.

7   Conclusions

Statistical sampling techniques have potentially an even greater role in monitoring changes in the condition of museum collections than they do in establishing the conditions at a point in time, because the scale of resources that can be devoted to a 'one-off' census is not likely to be available on a regular (e.g. annual) basis. Modelling the

varying conditions of a collection can help in the design of
regular surveys, as well as suggesting novel statistics
which may be of use for management or political purposes.
Statistical nicety needs to be tempered with practicability
to achieve a design which is reasonably efficient and which
can be implemented by staff whose expertise lies
elsewhere.

Acknowledgements
I am grateful to Louise Bacon of the Horniman Museum
for introducing me to this problem, for discussing practical
and theoretical issues with me, and for making data
available. Elaine Sansom of UCL Institute of Archaeology
made some constructive comments on a first draft of this
paper.

references

Anon.   1989   *The Rothamsted General Survey Program (RSGP)*. Rothamsted, Herts: Lawes Agricultural
                               Trust.

Cochran, W.G.   1963   *Sampling Techniques*. 2nd edition. New York: John Wiley.

Cox, D.R.   1965   *The Theory of Stochastic Processes*. London: Methuen.
  H.D. Miller

Keene, S.   1992   Measuring the condition of museum collections. In: G. Lock/J. Moffett (eds), *Computer
  C. Orton   Applications and Quantitative Methods in Archaeology 1991*, 163-166, BAR International
                               Series 577, Oxford: Tempus Reparatum.

Leese, M.N.   1995   Conservation condition surveys at the British Museum. In: J. Huggett/N. Ryan, (eds),
  S.M. Bradley   *Computer Applications and Quantitative Methods in Archaeology 1994*, 81-86, BAR
                               International Series 600, Oxford: Tempus Reparatum.

Klotz, J.H.   1994   Estimation for a markov heart transplant model, *Journal of the Royal Statistical Society D*
  L.D. Sharples   43 (3), 431-438.

Walker, K.   1987   *A Condition Survey of Specimens in the Horniman Museum*, 337-341. London: Summer
  L. Bacon   Schools Press.

Clive Orton
UCL Institute of Archaeology
31-34 Gordon Square
London WC1H 0PY
United Kingdom
e-mail: tcfa002@ucl.ac.uk

Juan A. Barceló

Heuristic classification and fuzzy sets. New tools for archaeological typologies

1 Introduction: from sherds to pots

Although Classification Theory has a long history in archaeology, sherd fitting has always formed an unsolved problem. Determining form from part of a vessel is limited by the fact that potters made vessels for different purposes starting with a few basic shapes. Since potters work by combining standard elements — base, bodies, rims, handles and so on — it is not always possible to infer the complete form from the fragments present in a deposit, because rims and bases of similar size and shape might actually have come from vessels of differing size and shape (cf. Montanari/Mignoni 1994; Orton *et al.* 1993). If one is trying to study pottery forms using only sherd material, then the definite absence of certain features may become as important a point to record as their presence. The usual assumption that all attributes have equal importance is wrong in that case. Therefore, we cannot describe different shapes distinguishing the individual aspects that determine relevant attributes for each aspect of the complex, because not all attributes are present in the sherd; 'relevance' cannot be computed when a part of the required information is missing.

2 The 'brittleness' problem

To classify a pot as a member of a type can be seen as a formal proof of the expression: 'pot *a* is member of Type *A*'

As logical proof we use the mechanism called logical implication. Suppose we have 5 attributes to determine the shape of Type *A* vessels. The logical implication needed to fit any sherd to the shape is:

IF   object *i* has
               attribute 1
     AND   attribute 2
     AND   attribute 3
     AND   attribute 4
     AND   attribute 5
THEN
       object *i* has shape Type *A*.

Let us call this rule 'proof *P*'. Archaeological descriptions (attributes) are elements of *P* because they are used in the proof. An element of proof, such as *attribute 5* (for example, ORIENTATION OF PROFILE) may have any number of instances (for example: ORIENTATION OF PROFILE = 30°, 45°, 90°, 180°, etc.). However, an element must have only one instance in each proof. When we are dealing with a fragment, and information about that element of proof is lacking, we assign a MISSING instance to that attribute.

Suppose only 2 attributes have been measured in the sherd. Following formal *modus ponens* this production rule cannot be fired; object *i* cannot be assigned to shape Type *A*. If we consider items one through five to be of equal importance, and we have to delete attribute 3 to 5 (because only attributes 1 and 2 are present in the sherd), the typology would malfunction and sherds are not classified because they do not present enough descriptive information.

This problem can be defined as the *brittleness problem*, that is, the inability of standard typologies to give a 'partial answer' in a graceful way (Sypniewski 1994). The cause of brittleness in typologies and classificatory systems is the use of an inadequate assumption about data. If we assume all necessary truths to express the idea of logical necessity are equally important to a proof, we are saying, in effect, that unless we can demonstrate all necessary truths we cannot prove what we are trying to prove. This is the problem of brittleness.

To solve the problem we can consider that *any* element of *P* can be used in the proof. We do not require all attributes but only the *necessary* elements of *P* to be present in the sherd. No reason exists why we cannot use the accidental elements of *P* in the proof, but they cannot substitute for one or more missing necessary attributes. This scenario provides a first glimpse into the definition of *importance*: Some elements of *P*, while legitimate members of *P* do not contribute to the actual proof (they are missing in the sherd). If we remove all members of *P* that are accidents or are unnecessary for *P*, we are left with P^{1}, which is composed of the necessary elements of *P*; all of them contribute to the proof. The theory of importance (Sypniewski 1994: 26) says that not all members of P^{1} necessarily contribute to the proof process in the same way or to the same extent. The extent of that contribution is demonstrated by the importance weight of every attribute or element (E_i). Any E_i that has a larger importance weight than an E_j is more important to a particular P than E_j. An element of proof that is irrelevant has an importance weight of 0.0; the same value has an attribute with missing value.

It is important to realise that no item of data has an intrinsic importance weight. All weights are relative to some P. Also note that a particular situation may provide elements whose combined importance weights exceed 1.0. In those cases more data are available than is strictly necessary for a proof.

The degree to which an attribute contributes to prove a typological assignment is determined empirically. When we gather the data or knowledge we need for our classification, we will, as a by-product, gather information about the elements of a proof. If we introduce this material into a matrix, we will see that some bits of information fill one cell of the matrix and some bits fill more than one cell. The number of cells filled with a particular piece of data or knowledge is a rough gauge of the importance of that particular piece of data or knowledge. As a general rule, *the more often a particular piece of data or knowledge appears in our hypothetical grid or matrix, the less important it is* (Sypniewski 1994: 29). We can say that if two proofs differ only by one item of data or knowledge, then this piece of knowledge is the most important item for that proof.

Consequently, a strong importance weight is equivalent to a branch point in a decision tree.

3 Fuzzy Logic: a way to solve the problem of 'brittleness'

Starting from the idea that every sherd is a certain proportion of the whole pot it once formed part of, we can (in theory) assign a weight or importance to attributes, and compute them to obtain a class assignation. In this chapter we will study how to describe importance weights through fuzzy numbers, and how to translate classification functions as membership function to fuzzy sets (Bezdek/Pal 1992; Cox 1993; Dubois *et al.* 1994; Klir/Folger 1988; Kosko 1992; Zadeh 1965).

Fuzzy logic deals with uncertainty. It holds that all things are matters of degree. It measures the degree to which an event occurs, not whether it occurs. Mathematically fuzziness means multivaluedness or multivalence and stems from the Heisenberg position-momentum uncertainty principle in quantum mechanics. Multivalued fuzziness corresponds to degrees of indeterminacy or ambiguity, partial occurrence of events or relations. In 1965 Lofti Zadeh introduced the concept of *fuzzy set*, as a way to represent the logical nature of categories. Fuzzy sets are constituted by elements, however those elements are not crisp instances of the categories but elements that belong only *to a certain degree*. The essence of fuzzy logic is then the notion of fuzzy membership as a continuous value

measuring the elementhood or degree to which element x belongs to set A.

We can translate logical implications (proof of classificatory assignments) using fuzzy production rules, where the output of the rules is a fuzzy set, whose members are the elements of the proof. Each element, as a member of a fuzzy set, has a fuzzy membership value or importance weight. For instance,

IF   object i 's PROFILE is concave   (0.875)
        object i 's RIM has shape B (0.358)
        object i 's MAX. DIAMETER is on
        top of the pot   (0.47)
THEN
        object i has shape *Type A*

The values in the rule's antecedent are *fuzzy*, because they belong to a fuzzy set. This value is not the confidence we have in that information, but the importance this element of a proof has in type A's logical implication. To evaluate these rules, fuzzy logic software computes the degree to which each rule's situation applies. The rule is active to the degree that its IF part is true; this in turn determines the degree to which each THEN part applies. Since multiple rules can be active simultaneously, all of the active rules are combined to create the final result. At each cycle, the full set of logical implications is scanned to see which fires. A rule or logical implication will fire when its condition made up of a (fuzzy) logical combination of its antecedents, results in a non zero value. Each rule therefore samples its inputs and calculates the truth value of its condition from the individual importance weight of each input. In this way, the fuzzy membership function of each element acts as a kind of restriction or constraint on the classification process.

Let us imagine that P, a proof for a classificatory assignment, is a set. Then P = {attribute 1, attribute 2, attribute 3, attribute 4, attribute 5}, where each attribute or descriptive feature are the elements of proof needed to prove P (for example, to prove *Type A*). We can assume that P is a fuzzy set, and consequently, each element has a membership value. Given the fact that P is fuzzy, the membership value for each element is a continuous number between 0 and 1, meaning the importance weight of that attribute in the logical implication described by P. In this case, fuzziness is only a general methodology to compute the sum of partial implications. I do not think that archaeological types have to be intrinsically *fuzzy*, but the sherd fitting process will only be computed if type is described in a fuzzy way: if we do not know how an instance relates with its type, the relationship remains fuzzy. Inferences made using incidental associations ('always' in archaeological classification) are inherently uncertain. And some associations are 'less' uncertain than others.

Fuzzy logic permits ambiguous instances to be included in a fuzzy set through a membership value. The degree of membership is given by the membership function, which has a value between 0 and 1. The interpretations is that 0 means no membership (or that the instance is certainly not in the set) and 1 denotes complete membership (or that the instance is certainly in the set), and a value in between denotes a partial or uncertain membership. Fuzzy logic thus overcomes a major weakness of crisp sets: they do not have an arbitrarily established boundary separating members from non members.

Fuzzy systems directly encode structured knowledge but in a numerical framework, where each rule stands for an input-output transformation, where inputs are the antecedent of fuzzy rules, and outputs are their consequent. In our case, inputs are the descriptive features we can measure on sherds, and outputs are an assignation of the sherd to an artefact or class of artefacts. Most fuzzy systems represent inputs and outputs as membership functions whose interactions are the bases for rules. The fuzzy input and desired output ranges are based on fuzzy set values and used to create a matrix called *fuzzy associative memory*. When actual input values enter the system, the entire memory fires at once, producing multiple outputs. Each input's membership in the fuzzy input sets must be calculated — this is called the truth value or importance weight. The information from all inputs is then applied to the rule base, which results, for each system output, in several fuzzy outputs. Since system inputs have multiple fuzzy values and each can be involved in the triggering of multiple rules, since each rule can have several fuzzy input values for its antecedents and each rule also can produce several outputs, and since each output itself has multiple fuzzy values, this process becomes quite complex.

A *Fuzzy Cognitive Map* (FCM) is a special type of *fuzzy associative memory* where the variable concepts are represented by nodes, which can also be called *conceptual states*, and the interactions by the edges, or *causal events*. Consequently, FCMs model the world as a collection of classes and causal relations between classes. Each node is a fuzzy set (fig. 1). In our case, logical implication between different elements of a proof is represented by fuzzy causal flows. The fuzzy cognitive map tries to represent the way a scientist thinks, because the nodes (concepts) affect each other, either directly or indirectly and either positively or negatively (Kosko 1986, 1992; McNeill/Thro 1994; Taber 1991).

The logical structure of an FCM allows each state (or node) to have any value between 1 and -1:

- +1   meaning that the originating or causing state results in a complete increase in the target or affected state;

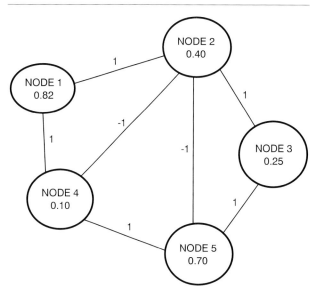

Figure 1. A Fuzzy Cognitive Map.

- -1   meaning that the causing state results in a complete decrease in the affected state;
- 0   meaning that the causing state does not change the affected state.

The number is the degree of causation and ranges from a negative one through zero to a positive one. Zero means no causal effect. Negative importance weights are used to say that some proof element instantiation tends to disprove or reduce the likelihood of a proof. Disproofs can be active or passive. To be an active disproof, the instantiation of some element of proof E_i must have an importance weight that is a negative number. Therefore, the system will subtract effectively the value of its importance weight from the current proof value V. A passive disproof, on the other hand, is simply a proof element that is not available (MISSING), and because it has not been observed, it is never added to V.

Disproofs can be calculated using a formula for fuzzy entropy:

$$\frac{\text{degree of overlap between every pair of outputs}}{\text{degree of underlap between every pair of outputs}}$$

Overlap is the result of logical intersection between types, whereas the *underlap* can be defined as the union between them (Kosko 1992; McNeill/Thro 1994).

As in a neural network, each state or node is 'squashed' through an activation function. In other words, each state value is a modification from the previous value during each forward step of the dynamic map. Each state's value is the result of taking all the event weights pointing into the state, multiplying each by the causing state's value, and adding up all the results of these multiplications. The results are then squashed so that the result is between 0 and 1 (0 and 100%). This multiply- and sum-process is a linear operation; that is, the new activation value for a fuzzy set (output node) is a weighted sum of all membership values for that set. If the unit's input is less than some threshold level (0.00 in our case), then the new activation value is equal to that unit's minimum activation range (also 0.00). Otherwise, if the inputs are positive (greater than the threshold 0.00), then the new activation value is set equal to the inputs.

FCM nodes act as binary neurones in a neural net. They sum, weight and threshold the causal energy that flows into them through the fuzzy causal edges. The states in an FCM are *state machines*, that is, they receive some input from somewhere (other units in the network), use it, change and 'export' a value. Given the fact that these states are linked in a graph, each one receiving unique inputs from other states, changing as a result, and affecting some other states. Time is a component of this architecture, because dynamic action continues as long as one state is able to effect a change in another one. This function (or *gain*) determines the high and low values of a cycle and can affect the map's operation. The higher the gain is, the more exaggerated the cycle.

Before activation all elements for all the possible proofs in the system are zero because none of them is active. You begin with a static diagram of the system. It shows the assumptions of the model. Then you set up an initial condition and perform iterated vector-matrix multiplication until a limit cycle is found. The limit cycle shows how the system behaves. In other words, vector matrix multiplication changes the state to something else. What we get as a result is a classification assignment.

4   PYGMALION: using Fuzzy Logic to classify Phoenician pottery

PYGMALION is the code name for a joint project, currently under way at the Universitat Pompeu Fabra Dept. of Humanities and the Universitat Autònoma de Barcelona Dept. of Prehistory. The goal is to create a computer system able to classify Phoenician pottery (800-550 BC), and to derive chronologies, production characteristics and exchange networks from descriptive features of archaeological material. PYGMALION release 0.1 is a prototype version to study the logical properties of the full-scale Expert System (PYGMALION release 1.0). This prototype is a Fuzzy Cognitive Map acting as a pattern recognition machine for pottery sherds.

The process of recognising a pattern is the classification of a sample into one or more predefined categories. If the pattern is successfully associated with a previously known type, the pattern is said to be recognised. At the end, the system should provide a confidence estimate in the classification; for example, the system is 75% confident that this sherd is part of a Type *A* pot and 25% confident that it is a type *B*. This confidence estimate is a measure of the degree to which the pattern-recognition system believes that the pattern data belongs to the specified class. To carry out this task, PYGMALION is implemented as a graph with evaluated nodes and evaluated arcs that represent relational structures among types. The aim is to decide whether the reality represented by a sherd qualitative description matches prior knowledge about the whole pot incorporated into the graphical model.

4.1   DESCRIBING SHAPE

Defining the shape of an object can prove to be very difficult. Pottery shape is influenced by a large number of factors. The decisions made by the potter, the tools and materials available and his/her skill in manipulating them all contribute to the finished product. While many practical shape description methods exist, there is no generally accepted methodology of shape description. The principal disadvantage of most pottery shape description systems is that they cannot be applied to the sherd material which forms the majority of the pottery recovered from archaeological sites (see amongst others Kampffmeyer *et al.* 1988; Orton *et al.* 1993; Rice 1987).

We have designed a new 'qualitative' descriptive framework, based on modern theory of robot vision (Biederman 1987; Saund 1992; Sonka *et al.* 1993).

Representation of visual shape can be formulated to employ knowledge about the geometric structures common with specific shape domains. We seek representations making explicit *many* geometric properties and spatial relationships at many levels of abstraction. Therefore, the problem of visual shape representation is to determine what information about objects' shapes should be made explicit in order to classify sherds as parts of whole pots. Knowledge about the pottery making process can be built into a shape representation in the form of a descriptive vocabulary making explicit the important spatial events and geometrical relationships comprising an object's shape.

The decomposition approach is based on the idea that shape recognition is a hierarchical process. Shape *primitives* are defined at the lower level, primitives being the simplest elements which form the region. Then, an object's shape will be analysed largely in terms of the spatial arrangement of labelled chunks or fragments of shape. A decomposition of the contour, for instance, uses its structural properties, and a syntactic graph description is the result. This graph is constructed at the higher level–nodes result from primitives, arc describes the mutual primitive relations. Particular shape fragments are labelled by individual *shape tokens* instantiated in the appropriate type. Each token is tagged with the characteristics (location, orientation and size) of the archaeological item it denotes. That is to say, a shape is described simply in terms of *primitive-edge* tokens placed along the bounding contour at the finest scale.

We are working with a contour-based object description method which uses as input information the properties of object boundaries. The contour or border of an object is the set of pixels within the region that have one or more neighbours outside that object. In other words, the contour or profile is the set of points at the limit of the object. We are dealing with partial segmentation looking for non-disjoint subregions in the contour. That is, the existing border is divided into separate regions that are homogeneous with respect to a chosen property. *Curvature* is that property. As profiles are a continuous series of pixels, curvature can be defined as the rate of change of slope. The curvature scalar descriptor (or boundary straightness) finds the ratio between the total number of boundary pixels (length) and the number of boundary pixels where the boundary direction changes significantly. The smaller the number of direction changes, the straighter the boundary. Contour primitives are delimited by the gradient of the image function that is computed as the difference between pixels in some neighbourhood. The evaluation algorithm (not fully implemented in PYGMALION 0.1) is based on the detection of angles between line segments positioned by boundary pixels in both directions (fig. 2).

Consequently, we are representing a boundary using segments with specified properties. If the segment type is known for all segments, the boundary can be described as a chain of segment types. The problem lies in determining the location of boundary vertices. Boundary vertices can be detected as boundary points with a significant change of boundary direction using the curvature (boundary straightness) criterion.

Once segmented, contour parts can be described qualitatively. Our approach is based upon the psychological theory by I. Biederman (Biederman 1987). He proposes to use only four qualitative features in describing objects. We have translated his ideas into the following components:

- CONTOUR: straight or curved
- CURVATURE: convex or concave
- COMPLEXITY: number of contour primitives
- ORIENTATION: in a 8-neighbourhood area.

The prior knowledge we have about the contour of a pot allows us to know the starting point (INIT) and the ending point (BASEX) of the border (fig. 3). The process is then a decomposition of the external *and* the internal profile in its

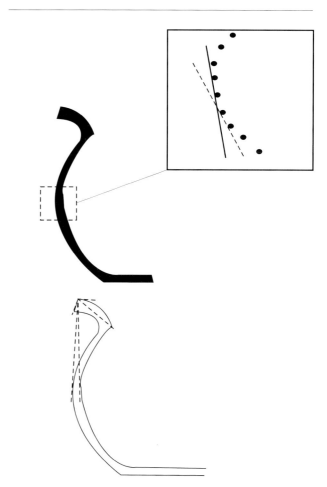

Figure 2. Describing the curvature of a contour.

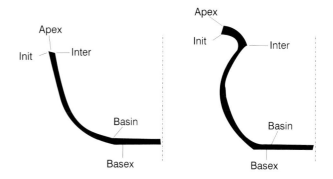

Figure 3. Main points for dividing contour into segment.

primitive curves. We begin describing the *body* of all whole pots we know by looking at the right and the left profile and determining symmetry or asymmetry. The *exterior profile* and *interior profile* are described by detecting the

number of 'curvatures'; they can be continuous or
discontinuous. *Exterior and interior discontinuity* is defined
by counting the number of profile primitives after detecting
more than one 'curvature'. We consider also the *shape of
exterior and interior profile* (straight, concave or convex) if
there is only one curve; or the *exterior and interior profile
primitives shape* if discontinuity is present. The *location*
(the place where curvatures have been measured) of all
profile primitives is also a very useful attribute: between
rim and body, at the centre of the body, at the centre of the
rim, etc. The *maximum diameter location* (in the upper part
of the pot, at the centre, at the rim etc.) helps to distinguish
some types; and the same is true for some different
descriptions of *orientation: external profile orientation,
internal profile orientation, rim orientation*. Finally, *rim
shape* (geometric form from APEX to INTER) is evaluated.
All orientations are calculated according to an 8-neighbour-
hood window (fig. 4).

4.2   BUILDING A *FUZZY COGNITIVE MAP*
Any object, even with non-regular shape, can be
represented by a collection of its topological components.
Topological data structures describe the pot as a set of
elements and their relations. These relations are represented
using a Fuzzy Cognitive Map, containing the object
structure. The elementary properties of syntactically
described objects are called primitives; these primitives
represent parts of contours with a specific shape. After each
primitive has been assigned a symbol, relations between
primitives in the object are described, and a relational
structure results. However, given the indeterminacy of
PYGMALION inputs (incomplete pots) we have decided
not to use arcs representing binary relations such as
adjacent to, to the left of, above, etc., but a fuzzy cognitive
map where arcs represent the importance weight of
primitives (nodes).

The actual version of our program is a continuous-state
model, because every node may have any value between 0
and 1. A negative weight (between -1 and 0) means the
element is a disproof for some particular type. This value is
less than the unit's threshold, consequently, the goal of
negative weights is only to deactivate units previously
activated.

PYGMALION 0.1 contains 54 units or nodes. 36 of these
are input nodes and represent qualitative information
introduced by the user; 18 nodes represent the answer of
the system, or the outputs of the classification (fig. 5).
Input nodes are connected among themselves using negative
weights. That is to say, there are relationships between
elements of different fuzzy sets. There is only a single
membership link between every element (attribute) and the
fuzzy set (type) it belongs to. Negative links also connect

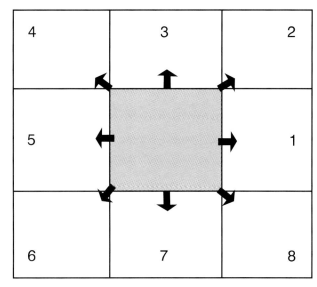

Figure 4. A schema to fix orientations of contour segments.

fuzzy set units (output nodes) among them, because
some sherds cannot be part of two very different shapes.
Negative links among output units represent the degree of
overlapping *allowed* by the classificatory system. For
instance, there is no degree of overlapping between a
carinated bowl and an amphora; however the degree of
overlapping between two different kinds of plates can be
very high. In the prototype presented here, all output units
are linked by the same negative weight: the maximum
activation level for a unit (1.00) divided between the
number of competing units.

Causal energy flows synchronously between elements
and sets (fig. 6). That means that there is no control of
rigid timing signals. Instead, each element (node) in
PYGMALION sends fuzzy membership values and
importance weights as it is ready (as there is input
information for it). As long as the element and the type are
set up to send and recognise the right combination, the
membership message will get through. In general, the signal
being sent from one node to another is equal to the
activation value of the first node multiplied by the weight
from the first to the second. The FCM performs these
computations every time the network is *cycled*. When we
cycle the network, we give each input node some information from an archaeological description. Given the fact
that we are processing sherds, not all inputs are activated.
The aim is to obtain a degree of activation on the output
nodes, even though input activation is incomplete. Negative
links and asynchronous updating help in this process. The
program stops when all activations have been distributed
around the network.

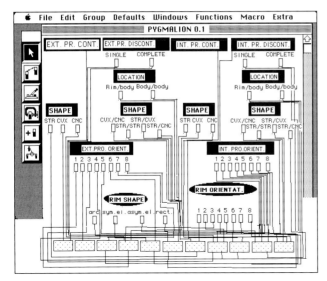

Figure 5. An ideal representation of PYGMALION Cognitive Graph.

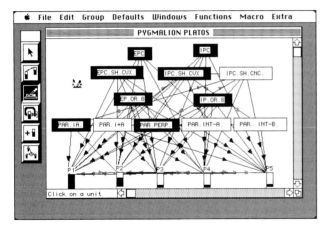

Figure 6. A subset of PYGMALION 0.1 Fuzzy Cognitive Map.

4.3   DETERMINING IMPORTANCE WEIGHTS

The importance weights assigned to a particular item or data or knowledge are, in a sense, always relative. These numbers have to be *fuzzy* because not all elements of a proof will have a fixed importance weight. Therefore, the importance weight of all nodes in the FCM must be determined in relation to the elements of other proof sets. For instance it is more important to know the shape of a rim when distinguishing between a bowl and a plate than if we were distinguishing between a bowl and an amphora.

The importance weight of any item of data or knowledge has been calculated from empirical evidence and its environment. By environment, we mean the number and nature of the proofs possible in the specific domain of

discourse in which the data are being used. To determine the weight of an item of data, we must determine whether it does not depend on any other item of data. However, in any collection of data patterns, some individual data items will appear in more than one data pattern. This enables us to say that one data pattern is similar or dissimilar to another depending on how many individual data they have in common. The more they share, the more similar they are and vice versa.

Then, their importance weight can by calculated by the ratio of their non-occurrence in all fuzzy sets.

- if an element *attribute* x_i of the proof set *Type A* completely proves *Type A* without condition, then *attribute* x_i has an importance weight of 1.0; otherwise *attribute* x_i has an importance weight less than 1.0 under all circumstances.
- for every *attribute* x_i that is shared by all conflicting proof sets *Type N* , *attribute* x_i has an importance weight of 0.0; otherwise *attribute* x_i has an importance weight greater than 0.0 under all circumstances.

Weights have floating-point values such as 0.5, 0.2, 0.9 according to their importance weights in a proof. Those values have been calculated dividing the number of types with that feature between all types in the classification. We are doing some experiments with more complex measures of 'importance', such as *entropy*. Table 1 shows a subset of importance weights between the elements of the proof (descriptive features) and axioms to be proved (Types). The first row shows the effect of attribute 1 on all types. The second row shows the effect of the second attribute on the types. The matrix is square, since we have a place for the effect of each attribute on all types.

Table 2 shows negative weights or disproofs among elements. They have been calculated from the degree of overlapping among fuzzy sets. For instance, a continuous convex shaped internal contour appears sometimes in pots with coincident parametric points; however, it is impossible to see a continuous convex shaped internal contour with the INTER parametric point below the INIT parametric point. Coincidences have been tabulated as a 0.00, and discrepancies as a -1.

The Fuzzy Cognitive map topology can be described using a set of specific variables (see figs 7a, b).

4.4   USING THE FUZZY COGNITIVE MAP TO IDENTIFY INCOMPLETE POTS

PYGMALION 0.1 is being used to validate a typology for Phoenician open forms. We have worked with a data set of nearly 200 whole pots from Phoenician sites in the southern Iberian Peninsula (mostly Toscanos, Trayamar, Almuñecar, Cerro del Villar). Validation is carried out by comparing the

Table 1. Fuzzy membership values between elements and fuzzy sets.
Abbreviations: E.- external; I.- Internal; P.- Profile; C.- Continuous; SH.- Shape; STR.- Straight; CVX.- Convex; CNC.- Concave; ORIENT.- Orientation; PAR.- Parametric Points. IA.- Inter = Apex. I+A.- Inter ≠ Apex. PERP.- perpendicular to Init; INT-A.- Inter above Init; INT-B.- Inter below Init.

	P1	P2	P3	P4	P5
EPC	.2	.2	.2	.2	.2
IPC	.2	.2	.2	.2	.2
EPC.SH.CVX	.2	.2	.2	.2	.2
IPC.SH.CVX	.5	.5	0	0	0
IPC.SH.CNC	0	0	.3	.3	.3
EP.OR.8	.2	.2	.2	.2	.2
IP.OR.8	2	.2	.2	.2	.2
PAR. IA	.5	.5	0	0	0
par. I+A	0	0	.3	.3	.3
PAR. PERP.	1	0	0	0	0
PAR. INIT-A	0	0	1	1	0
PAR. INIT-B	0	0	0	0	1

Table 2. Negative Weights among elements (descriptive features).
Abbreviations: E.- external; I.- Internal; P.- Profile; C.- Continuous; SH.- Shape; STR.- Straight; CVX.- Convex; CNC.- Concave; ORIENT.- Orientation; PAR.- Parametric Points. IA.- Inter = Apex. I+A.- Inter ≠ Apex. PERP.- perpendicular to Init; INT-A.- Inter above Init; INT-B.- Inter below Init.

	IPC.SH.CVX	IPC.SH.CNC	PAR.IA.	PAR.I+A	PAR.PERP.	PAR.INT-A	PAR.INT-B
IPC.SH.CVX	0	-1	0	-1	0	-1	-1
IPC.SH.CNC	-1	0	-1	0	-1	0	0
PAR. IA	0	-1	0	-1	0	-1	-1
PAR. I+A	-1	0	-1	0	-1	0	0
PAR.PERP.	0	-1	0	-1	0	-1	-1
PAR.INT-A	-1	0	-1	0	-1	0	-1
PAR.INT-B	-1	0	-1	0	-1	-1	0

classificatory assignments made by the program to assignments made by experienced archaeologists.

Once we confirm the quality of the *answers* proposed by our *automatic archaeologist*, we will begin introducing descriptions for incomplete pots. PYGMALION 0.1 then computes partial membership functions and proposes a fuzzy assignment. Of course, *natural archaeologists* have to use these assignments and decide what has more sense, that a sherd be 55% of Form 3 or 45% of Form 13.

5 The concept of heuristic classification

When using fuzzy logic tools to build classification systems, we have proceeded through identifiable phases of data abstraction, heuristic mapping onto a hierarchy of pre-enumerated solutions, and refinement within this hierarchy. We have obtained a classification, but with the important twist of relating concepts in different classification hierarchies by non-hierarchical, uncertain inferences. This combination of reasoning has been called *heuristic*

classification (Clancey 1985). The heuristic classification model builds on the idea that categorisation is not based on purely essential features, but rather is primarily based on *heuristic*, non-hierarchical, *but direct* associations between concepts.

Heuristic classification is a method of computation, not a kind of problem-to-be solved. In other words, it is a way to solve an archaeological problem (sherd fitting to form) and not a new philosophy about archaeological classification. We must not confuse what gets selected at the end of the FCM — what constitutes a solution — with the method for computing the solution. A common misconception is that there is a kind of problem called a 'classification problem'. Heuristic classification as defined by W. Clancey (1985) is a *description of how a particular problem is solved by a particular problem-solver*. If the problem solver has a priori knowledge of solutions and can relate them to the problem description by data abstraction, heuristic association, and refinement, then the problem can be solved by classification.

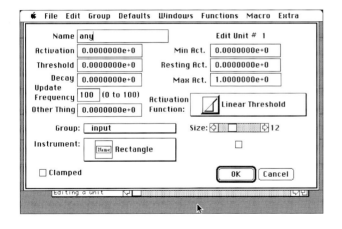

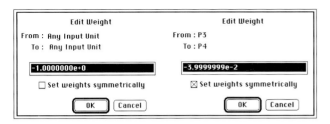

Figure 7. a. An FCM node's topology. b. Two different FCM weights' topology.

Often problems of classification are not amenable to solution by heuristic classifications because possible final states cannot be practically enumerated, exhaustively learned or for some reason a previously used solution is just not acceptable; solutions must be constructed rather than selected. However, even when solutions are constructed, classification might play a role.

In this paper we have described what an expert system does by describing it in terms of inference-structure diagrams (Fuzzy Cognitive Maps). This demonstrates that it is highly advantageous to describe systems in terms of their configuration, *structurally*, providing dimensions for comparison. A structural map of systems reveals similar relations among components, even though the components and/or their attributes may differ.

Acknowledgements

I would like to thank M.E. Aubet, P. Báscones, E. Curià, A. Delgado, A. Fernandez, M. Párraga and A. Ruiz for their work on the Guadalhorce Project, and for suggestions and encouragement. Although the work on a General Tipometry for Phoenician Pottery is a collective effort by all members of the Guadalhorce Project, none is responsible for any mistake I may have committed in this paper.

This research has been supported by the Ministerio Español de Educación y Ciencia (DGYCIT, PB93-0397).

references

Bezdek, J.C.
S.K. Pal   1992   *Fuzzy systems for Pattern Recognition.* Piscataway (NJ): IEE Press.

Biederman, I.   1987   Recognition by component: A Theory of Human Image Understanding, *Psychological Review* 94 (2), 115-147.

Clancey, W.J.   1985   Heuristic Classification, *Artificial Intelligence* 27, 289-350.

Cox, E.   1993   *The Fuzzy Systems Handbook. A practitioner's guide to building, using and maintaining fuzzy systems.* Cambridge (MA): Academic Press.

Dubois, D.
H. Prade
D. Smets   1994   Partial truth is not uncertainty. Fuzzy logic versus possibilistic logic, *IEE Expert. Intelligent Systems and their applications* 9 (4), 15-19.

Kampffmeyer, U. P. Zamperoni W.R. Teegen I. Graça	1988	*Untersuchungen zur rechnergestutzen Klassifikation der Form von Keramik.* Frankfurt: Peter Lang Verlag.
Klir, G.J. T.A. Folger	1988	*Fuzzy Sets, Uncertainty and Information.* Englewood Cliffs (NJ): Prentice Hall.
Kosko, B.	1986	Fuzzy Cognitive Maps, *International Journal of Man-Machine Studies* 24, 65-75.
	1992	*Neural Networks and Fuzzy Systems. A dynamical Systems Approach to Machine Intelligence.* Englewood Cliffs (NJ): Prentice Hall.
McNeill, F.M. E. Thro	1994	*Fuzzy Logic. A practical approach.* Boston: Academic Press.
Montanari, A. S. Mignoni	1994	Notes on the bias of dissimilarity indices for incomplete datasets. The case of archaeological classification, *Questió. Quaderns d'Estadística i Investigació Operativa* 18 (1), 39-49.
Orton, C. P. Tyers E.A. Vince	1993	*Pottery in Archaeology.* Cambridge: Cambridge University Press.
Rice, P.	1987	*Pottery Analysis. A source book.* Chicago: The University of Chicago Press.
Saund, E.	1992	Putting knowledge into a visual shape representation, *Artificial Intelligence* 54, 71-119.
Sonka, M. V. Hlavac R. Boyle	1993	*Image Processing, Analysis and Machine Vision.* London: Chapman and Hall.
Sypniewski, B.P.	1994	The importance of being data, *AI-Expert* 9 (11), 23-31.
Taber, R.	1991	Knowledge processing with Fuzzy Cognitive Maps, *Expert Systems with Applications* 2 (1), 83-87.
Zadeh, L.A.	1965	Fuzzy Sets, *Information and Control* 8, 338-353.

Juan A. Barceló
Area de Prehistoria
Facultat de Lletres
Universitat Autonoma de Barcelona
08193 Bellaterra
Spain
e-mail: ilphd@blues.uab.es

Kris Lockyear

Dmax based cluster analysis and the supply of coinage to Iron Age Dacia

1   Introduction

The analysis of Roman Republican coin hoards presents a number of statistical opportunities and problems. For example, the well-dated nature of the material provides an excellent test for seriation techniques. Conversely, the inherent time gradient will dominate a correspondence analysis (CA). Figures 1 and 2 present the sample and variable maps from a CA of 241 coin hoards, each of which has more than 30 well recorded denarii, dating from 147-2 BC (Lockyear 1996: section 8.2.3).[1] As can be seen, the 'horseshoe effect' dominates the results (Lockyear 1996: section 8.2.2). Although some interesting points can be made from these maps, the dominant gradient is time — other information is masked. Mixing hoards from different periods in one analysis does not 'aid interpretation', *contra* Creighton (1992: 32-35).[2]

One possible solution is to examine small subsets of the data, each with a restricted range of dates. The hoards presented in figures 1-2 were subdivided into 22 groups, each of which was analysed using CA (Lockyear 1996: section 8.3). This revealed many interesting aspects of variation in these hoards, often linked to the region from which the hoards were found, and some general observations are given below.

However, one particular question arose which suggested that some form of cross-period comparison would be useful. This paper will outline this question, and then will discuss the solution devised by the author in detail. Finally, the results and archaeological conclusions will be briefly presented. Full details can be found in Lockyear (1996); details of the data and the archaeological results and conclusions will be published elsewhere. Additional information including figures, tables and the data are available via the World Wide Web (http://caa.soton.ac.uk/caa/CAA95/LockyearA/) or from the author.

2   The problem

As Crawford notes:

'One of the most remarkable phenomena within the pattern of monetary circulation in antiquity is the presence of large numbers of Roman Republican denarii, for the most part struck between about 131 and 31 [BC], on the soil of present-day Romania, roughly ancient Dacia.'

Crawford 1985: 226

What makes this phenomenon remarkable is that Dacia was not incorporated into the Roman Empire until the Trajanic Wars (AD 101-102, 105-106). The situation is further complicated by the evidence for the copying of denarii by the Geto-Dacians (Chiţescu 1971b, 1980, 1981; Glodariu *et al.* 1992; Lupu 1967) although the scale of the copying is disputed (cf. Chiţescu 1981; Crawford 1980). The date at which the denarii arrived in Romania has also been a topic of some debate. Mitrea (1958) has argued that there are three phases of the 'penetration' of denarii: the end of the second century BC, 90-80 BC and 49-30 BC. Many other scholars have basically agreed, although some have argued for 'more than a sporadic penetration of denarii into Romania by the year 100 BC (Chiţescu 1971a). Some Romanian scholars have disagreed. Preda (1971: 74) argues for a date after 80 BC; Babeş (1975) argues for a mid-1st century date based on the excavated finds from Cîrlomaneşti. Crawford (1977, 1985: 226-235) argues for a date from the mid or late 60s, and quite rightly notes that the periods claimed by Mitrea, and others, for the arrival of large numbers of denarii into Romania correspond to periods of high levels of official coin production. In her final work, Chiţescu maintained that these new alternatives were wrong and that the 'penetration' of denarii must have started by 100 BC (Chiţescu 1981). Poenaru Bordea and Cojocărescu (1984) argue that the majority of denarii arrived between *c.* 75 BC and *c.* 65 BC.

Before any interpretation of *why* these coins were there, and why they were copied, these basic questions need to be addressed. As part of a wider project, the author has been constructing a database of Roman Republican coin hoards. At the time of writing this database contained detailed information of 420 hoards, some 87,240 coins. Of these, 126 hoards were found in Romania. By analysing these hoards in the context of others from the rest of Europe, some important observations could be made.

– Although 13 of the 126 hoards from Romania date before 79 BC, the biggest hoard from Iclănzel has only 18 well identified denarii (ICL[3]; Chirilă/Grigorescu 1982). The small size of these hoards makes it likely that there is a large discrepancy between their closing dates and the true date of their deposition. Lockyear (1993:

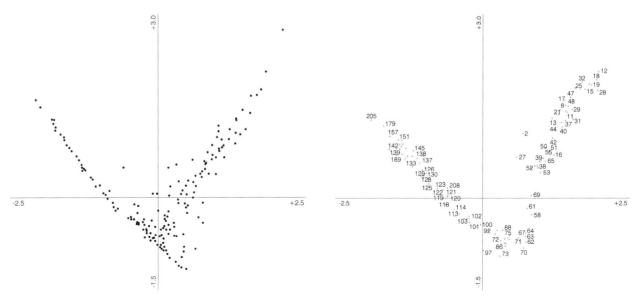

Figure 1. Sample map from CA of 241 Roman Republican coin hoards dating from 147-2 BC each with 30 or more well identified denarii. Data points are hoards. First (horizontal) and second axes of inertia.

Figure 2. Species map from CA of 241 Roman Republican coin hoards dating from 147-2 BC each with 30 or more well identified denarii. Data points are years of issue. First (horizontal) and second axes of inertia.

373-375) discusses the problem of hoard size and dating in detail.

– Romanian hoards with closing dates in the 70s BC are very similar in structure[4] to Italian hoards of the same date. For example, cf. Zătreni (ZAT; Chiţescu 1981: No. 215) with San Mango sul Calore (MAN; Pozzi 1960-1961: 162-172).

– By the 50s BC Romanian hoards are archaic[5] in structure when compared to contemporary hoards from Italy. For example, cf. Dunăreni (DUN; Popilian 1970) with Mesagne (MES; Hersh/Walker 1984).

– In the 40s and 30s BC the pattern is more complicated with Romanian hoards being quite variable, but always more archaic than contemporary Italian hoards.

We can conclude that denarii did not arrive in this region in significant quantities, if at all, prior to 80 BC. The structure of hoards from the 70s suggests that significant supplies started at that time. The differences between Italian and Romanian hoards in the following decades suggest that the supply of coinage to Romania was not constant and did not reflect supply to Italy.

At this stage it seemed that further information concerning the supply of coinage to Romania could be gained by comparing hoards across date ranges. Various methods were considered. Comparisons were made by running CA on all hoards and then using the colour plotting

facilities of WinBASP.[6] Although it was possible to see the sorts of comparisons needed in this fashion, it was difficult to produce some form of grouping in the continuum displayed. The methods used by Creighton (1992: section 2.5, 78-103) were rejected as they lack any sound statistical foundation. The problem appeared to be one which could be addressed by cluster analysis providing that the resulting clusters are viewed as subdivisions of a continuum of variation, not as clear, unequivocal groups.

3 Dmax based cluster analysis

Cluster analysis is a range of techniques with the basic aim of subdividing a set of objects or assemblages into subsets. There is no 'best' method of achieving this — see Orton (1980), Shennan (1988) and Baxter (1994) for the use of the technique in archaeology. In this particular case, the aim was to produce a moderately large number of subsets in order that we could examine the grouping of hoards and see if this provided us with any further insights, especially as regards the supply of coinage to Romania.

Some form of hierarchical agglomerative cluster analysis seemed appropriate. In this form of analysis, the analyst firstly has to choose a similarity or dissimilarity coefficient. Most standard texts list three common measures, Euclidian, squared Euclidian and city-block distance (e.g. Shennan 1988, 198-202). Many others exist for different data types. For example, SPSS allows for the use of χ^2 or Φ^2 as measures for count data (Norušis 1993: Chapter 5 especially 128, 133).

In this case, the variables used to describe the hoards are of an ordinal data type — the coins grouped by date of issue. For example, the Cosa hoard (COS; Buttrey 1980) has 2004 coins and closes in 74 BC. It has 9 coins of 211 BC, 3 of 209, 1 of 207, 4 of 206 and so on until… 32 of 74 BC. The author therefore wanted a measure which would:

a. not be over-influenced by rare issues especially if those rare issues were defining a hoard's closing date;
b. make full use of the ordinal nature of the data.

None of the software available to the author provided such a measure.

The author has had occasion to compare hoards using the Kolmogorov-Smirnov statistic, a significance test suitable for ordinal data (Shennan 1988: 55-61). This test involves calculating $Dmax_{obs}$, defined as the maximum difference between two cumulative proportion curves, and then comparing it to a critical figure for the significance level desired. Mass comparisons using this method (e.g. Lockyear 1989: section 2.2) were unsatisfactory for a number of reasons. For example, the large number of comparisons used in that study would lead to some results being significant by chance — the problem of multiplicity (Mosteller/Tukey 1977: 28f.). More importantly, we already know that the hoards are drawn from a global coinage pool with major regional variations and therefore should expect differences.

$Dmax_{obs}$ can, however, be viewed as a type of dissimilarity coefficient suitable for ordinal data, just as χ^2 can be used for nominal data. Dmax could, therefore, be used in cluster analysis, or some form of multidimensional scaling, as a dissimilarity coefficient. At the time of the analysis, the author did not know of the use of Dmax in this fashion.[7] No theoretical objections were raised by statisticians consulted[8] and it was decided to try the method and see if the results 'made sense' in the context of what was already known about these hoards.

Two hundred and seventeen hoards were selected from the database, closing between 147-29 BC, all with 30 or more securely identified denarii. The 23,436 dissimilarity coefficients were calculated using a dBASE program, and then converted into a triangular matrix. The only software available to the author which would allow the input of a user calculated dissimilarity matrix was MV-ARCH (Wright 1989). The matrix was therefore input to the HIERARCH module of that package for clustering. Output was produced on a plotter using the HIERPLOT module.

Seven types of clustering algorithm are available in MV-ARCH. Single-link cluster analysis (Shennan 1988: 213-214) tends to produce dendrograms with a strong chained effect (Baxter 1994: 158), especially when the technique is applied to data which does not have strong grouping. With this data set the chaining was such that the results were not usable. Ward's method (Shennan 1988: 217-220) produces strong clusters even from random data (Baxter 1994: 161-162) and again, the results from this data set were difficult to use.[9] Theoretically, Ward's method should only be used with squared Euclidian distance (Baxter 1994: 156). Wright (1989) strongly recommends the use of between-group average linkage despite the objections of Jardine et al. (1967). This method did indeed produce usable results (fig. 3) and it is these which will be discussed below. Calculation of some diagnostic statistics such as the cophenetic correlation coefficient (Shennan 1988: 230-232) would have been useful but these are not offered in the MV-ARCH package, and derivation from the dendrogram is not a viable proposition given the size of the matrix. Other validation techniques are not necessarily appropriate given that we are already aware that we are subdividing a continuum, although one method suggested by Aldenderfer (1982), comparison to other multivariate methods, had already been applied in the form of the CAs discussed above.

The final question of how many clusters to examine is not easy to answer in any problem. In this case, as noted above, we are slicing up a continuum, not identifying clear groups, and thus any decision is somewhat arbitrary, and the application of techniques such as Mojena's stopping rule (Aldenderfer 1982: 64-65) would be inappropriate. It was decided to cut the dendrogram at two levels, at 20%[10] and 30% dissimilarity.

4 Discussion of the results

4.1 ARCHAEOLOGICAL RESULTS

The groups derived from the dendrogram given in figure 3 are presented in tables 1, 2, and 3. In the following discussion groups derived at a 20% dissimilarity are called 'groups', groups derived at a 30% dissimilarity are called 'supergroups'. A detailed list of the hoards used, and their group membership, is given in Lockyear (1996: table 10.1) and on the CAA WWW server.

An initial examination of the clusters revealed patterns which were in accord with the results of the CAs discussed above. For example, group *a* (table 1) contained three hoards, all of which closed in 32 BC, and all of which contained substantial numbers of legionary denarii (*Roman Republican Coinage* [RRC], Crawford 1974: No. 544).[11] A CA of all hoards dating to 32 BC showed that these three hoards were extremely similar (Lockyear 1996: section 8.3.19).

Group *b*, however, contained 40 hoards and had a range of closing dates from 82-32 BC. A more detailed

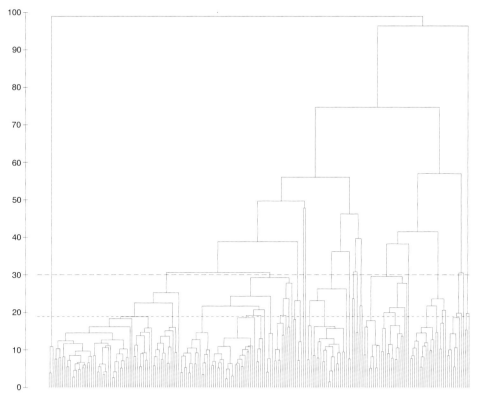

Figure 3. Dendrogram from average link cluster analysis of 217 Roman Republican coin hoards using Dmax as a dissimilarity coefficient. Short-dash line shows the cut to create the "groups" discussed in the text, long-dash line the "supergroups".

examination showed that of these hoards, ten came from Italy and Sicily. Of these ten, one closed in 82 BC, the remaining nine closed in the 70s BC. Twenty-one hoards in group *b* came from Romania, nine from other countries including Spain, Portugal, France, Greece, Elba and the former Yugoslavia. The non-Romanian hoards all closed in the 70s BC; the Romanian hoards close anywhere between the 70s and 32 BC with fifteen hoards from the 50s-40s BC.

In contrast, most hoards from the 40s occur in groups *f* or *g-i*. In the former group, 14 out of 16 hoards are from Italy, and 8 of those close in the 40s BC. Groups *g-i* contain 12 Romanian hoards, 9 of which close in the 40s BC.

Group *j* only contains four hoards all of which close in the 50s, three of which come from Italy, and again this is in accord with the results of the CAs (Lockyear 1996: sections 8.3.11-8.3.12). Hoards of the 50s are generally rare due to the low numbers of coins struck in that decade. Despite this, there are nine hoards from Romania closing in that decade but seven of these have been assigned to group *b*, and one each to groups *d* and *g*.

A detailed examination of the rest of the groups continued to reveal consistent patterns (Lockyear 1996: chap. 10) and therefore the groups made archaeological sense, especially when the hoards contained within them were examined by country of origin (table 2). Comparison

of these results with the results of the 22 detailed CAs also showed a high level of agreement.

The broader pattern can be made clearer by examining the supergroups (table 3). Two supergroups are of interest, B and Γ. Supergroup B contains 64 hoards of which 16 come from Italy, and 31 from Romania; the Italian hoards close 82-71 BC whereas the Romanian hoards close 79-32 BC with a median of 56 BC. Group Γ contains 57 hoards of which 29 come from Italy and 17 come from Romania. The range of closing dates was surprisingly large for the Italian hoards: 80-29 BC, although the median was 46 BC. Consulting the agglomeration schedule it was found that groups *f-i* and *k-n* merged at a level of 29%. Splitting supergroup Γ into two along these lines resulted in supergroup $Γ_1$ containing 47 hoards, and supergroup $Γ_2$ containing 10 hoards. Supergroup $Γ_1$ contained 46 hoards of which 22 came from Italy with a range of 58-29 BC and a median of 46 BC. It also contained 14 Romanian hoards with a range of 54-29 BC and a median of 42. Supergroup $Γ_2$ has seven Italian hoards closing 80-72 BC and three Romanian hoards closing in 74, 62 and 49 BC. The only Romanian hoard not in supergroups B or Γ was Işalniţa (ISA; Mitrea/Nicolaescu-Plopşor 1953) which occurs in supergroup N with Italian hoards of 101-82 BC, despite closing in 41 BC.

Table 1. Summary of cluster analysis results at a dissimilarity of 18.9%. Columns three and four give the next cluster to which the listed cluster joins and at what dissimilarity level. The final two columns give the range of 'end dates', and the median. Hoards CST and GRE omitted.

cluster	number of members	next cluster	level	'end dates' range	median
a	3	b-ρ	95.229	32-32	32
b	40	c	18.992	82-32	71
c	10	b	18.992	81-63	76
d	13	b-c	22.474	82-32	74
e	1	b-d	25.041	-	74
f	16	g-i	21.676	48-29	42
g	22	h	19.338	55-39	46
h	4	g	19.338	47-29	44
i	1	g-h	20.736	-	29
j	4	f-i	24.180	58-55	57
k	6	l	19.338	74-49	73
l	1	k	19.338	-	74
m	2	k-l	23.590	80-79	79h
n	1	k-m	27.501	-	79
o	2	p	23.063	87-81	84
p	3	o	23.063	87-82	86
q	1	r	46.556	-	46
r	1	q	46.556	-	74
s	3	t	23.055	40-29	29
t	17	s	23.055	46-29	41
u	1	s-t	26.034	-	46
v	2	s-u	35.522	49-48	48h
w	1	x	23.550	-	41
x	1	w	23.550	-	41
y	2	w-x	30.365	32-29	30h
z	1	α	21.736	-	43
α	1	z	21.736	-	45
β	9	γ-ζ	29.218	118-86	109
γ	3	δ	20.073	104-85	101
δ	9	γ	20.073	112-83	102
ε	1	γ-δ	21.310	-	104
ζ	1	γ-ε	27.495	-	115
η	1	β-ζ	37.474	-	113
θ	13	ι	21.723	100-82	92
ι	2	θ	21.723	46-41	43h
κ	3	λ	20.640	101-92	100
λ	1	κ	20.640	-	92
μ	7	ν	19.929	125-112	121
ν	1	μ	19.929	-	130
ξ	1	μ-ν	30.108	-	136
π	2	ρ	19.885	147-141	144
ρ	1	π	19.885	-	146

From both the groups and the supergroups we can make a number of broad generalisations.

1. Within the groups/supergroups, Italian hoards are of broadly similar dates. Each decade has at least one group associated with it. This reflects the dynamic nature of the Italian coinage pool with new coins entering the system, coins being lost from the system, and a reasonable speed of circulation to distribute coinage around the system.

Table 2. Cluster analysis – date ranges and median 'end date' for groups by region. Ordered by median 'end date' for Italian (including Sicilian and Sardinian) hoards. Hoards CST and GRE omitted.

group	Italy total	Italy range	Italy median	Romania total	Romania range	Romania median	Iberian peninsula total	Iberian peninsula range	Iberian peninsula median	total total	total range	total median
ρ	1	-	146	-	-	-	-	-	-	1	-	146
π	2	147-141	144	-	-	-	-	-	-	2	147-141	144
ξ	1	-	136	-	-	-	-	-	-	1	-	136
ν	1	-	130	-	-	-	-	-	-	1	-	130
μ	5	125-112	121	-	-	-	-	-	-	7	125-112	121
β	6	118-86	115	-	-	-	3	109-101	104	9	118-86	109
δ	3	102-83	100	-	-	-	6	112-101	106h	9	112-83	102
κ	3	101-92	100	-	-	-	-	-	-	3	101-92	100
γ	2	101-85	93	-	-	-	1	-	104	3	104-85	101
λ	1	-	92	-	-	-	-	-	-	1	-	92
θ	11	100-82	92	-	-	-	2	100-100	100	13	100-82	92
p	2	87-82	85h	-	-	-	-	-	-	3	87-82	86
o	2	87-81	84	-	-	-	-	-	-	2	87-81	84
d	1	-	82	9	79-32	74	2	74-74	74	13	82-32	74
m	2	80-79	80h	-	-	-	-	-	-	2	80-79	80h
c	5	81-74	79	1	-	63	2	74-74	74	10	81-63	76
n	1	-	79	-	-	-	-	-	-	1	-	79
b	10	82-71	74	21	77-32	54	4	78-71	74	40	82-32	71
l	1	-	74	-	-	-	-	-	-	1	-	74
k	3	74-72	74	3	74-49	62	-	-	-	6	74-49	73
r	1	-	74	-	-	-	-	-	-	1	-	74
j	3	58-55	56	-	-	-	-	-	-	4	58-55	57
g	7	55-42	51	11	54-39	42	2	51-46	49h	22	55-39	46
v	1	-	48	-	-	-	-	-	-	2	49-48	49h
α	1	-	45	-	-	-	-	-	-	1	-	45
z	1	-	43	-	-	-	-	-	-	1	-	43
t	8	46-38	42h	-	-	-	2	46-44	45	17	46-29	41
f	12	48-29	42	2	42-29	36h	1	-	42	16	48-29	42
s	1	-	40	-	-	-	1	-	29	3	40-29	29
a	1	-	32	-	-	-	-	-	-	3	32-32	32
y	2	32-29	31h	-	-	-	-	-	-	2	32-29	31h
e	-	-	-	-	-	-	1	-	74	1	-	74
h	-	-	-	1	-	47	1	-	46	4	47-29	44
i	-	-	-	-	-	-	-	-	-	1	-	29
q	-	-	-	-	-	-	-	-	-	1	-	46
u	-	-	-	-	-	-	1	-	46	1	-	46
w	-	-	-	-	-	-	-	-	-	1	-	41
x	-	-	-	-	-	-	-	-	-	1	-	41
ε	-	-	-	-	-	-	1	-	104	1	-	104
ζ	-	-	-	-	-	-	1	-	115	1	-	115
η	-	-	-	-	-	-	1	-	113	1	-	113
ι	-	-	-	1	-	41	-	-	-	2	46-41	44h

2. Romanian hoards can be divided into two broad classifications:

    – Class One hoards are mainly similar to Italian hoards of the 70s BC (supergroups B, Γ₂, N);

    – Class Two hoards (supergroup Γ₁) are generally similar to Italian hoards of the 50s-30s BC, although of the Italian hoards that close in this time period, those which occur in supergroup Γ_1 are more archaic than Italian hoards of the same date which occur in supergroups H, Θ and Ω.

3. At a more detailed level, Class Two Romanian hoards tend to occur in groups together, e.g. group *g*, whereas

Table 3. Cluster analysis supergroups - date ranges and median 'end date' for supergroups by region. Hoards CST and GRE omitted. †Only one hoard, from Sardinia (BER), closes in 82 BC; without this hoard the group range is 101-88.

supergroup	group	Italy total	Italy range	Italy median	Romania total	Romania range	Romania median	Iberian total	Iberian range	Iberian median	total total	total range	total median
A	a	1	-	32	-	-	-	-	-	-	3	32-32	32
B	b-e	16	82-71	74h	31	79-32	56	9	78-71	74	64	82-32	74
Γ	f-n	29	80-29	49	17	74-29	46	4	51-42	46	57	80-29	46
Γ₁	f-i	22	58-29	46	14	54-29	42	4	51-42	46	47	58-29	46
Γ₂	k-n	7	80-72		3	74-49	62	-	-	-	10	80-49	74
Δ	o-p	4	87-81	84h	-	-	-	-	-	-	5	87-81	86
E	q	-	-	-	-	-	-	-	-	-	1	-	46
Z	r	1	-	74	-	-	-	-	-	-	1	-	74
H	s-u	9	46-38	41	-	-	-	4	46-29	45	21	46-29	41
Θ	v	1	-	48	-	-	-	-	-	-	2	49-48	48h
I	w-x	-	-	-	-	-	-	-	-	-	2	41-41	41
K	y	2	32-29	30h	-	-	-	-	-	-	2	32-29	30h
Ω	z-α	2	45-43	44	-	-	-	-	-	-	2	45-43	44
Λ	β-ζ	11	118-83	101	-	-	-	12	115-101	104h	23	118-83	104
M	η	-	-	-	-	-	-	1	-	113	1	-	113
N	θ-λ	15	101-82†	92	1	-	41	2	100-100	100	19	101-41	92
Ξ	μ-ν	6	130-112	123	-	-	-	-	-	-	8	130-112	123
Π	ξ	1	-	136	-	-	-	-	-	-	1	-	136
Y	π-ρ	3	147-141	146	-	-	-	-	-	-	3	147-141	146

Italian hoards in the same supergroups mainly occur in separate groups, e.g. group *f*. This suggests variation at a detailed level.

My interpretation of this pattern is as follows. The main influx of coinage to Romania from Italy is in the late 70s and early 60s BC. Thereafter, the supply of coinage is at a much lower level and Romanian hoards become archaic in structure. The similarity between Romanian hoards in these periods is due to the similarity of the coinage pool from whence the coins were withdrawn. Hoards closing in the 70s BC have a high probability of actually being concealed in the 60s and 50s BC as there were few coins struck in those decades, and even fewer imported to Romania. During the 40s BC a second influx of coinage enters the area. This second influx is not simply a result of the increased levels of coin production at this time. This influx results in some hoards looking similar at a general level to contemporary hoards in Italy, but at a detailed level having some differences leading to an archaic structure. Other contemporary hoards, however, continue to have a structure similar to hoards from Italy from the 70s. This suggests that the circulation of coinage in Romania was slow and erratic.

This pattern also gives us a context for the copying of coins in Romania. If the original influx of denarii into Romania resulted in those coins obtaining a specific and important role in some aspect of Dacian society, the lack of supply from the late 60s to the mid-40s may have stimulated the production of the copies. Indeed, this author has yet to detect copies in the early coin hoards examined whereas copies have been detected in later hoards such as Poroschia (PRS; Chiţescu 1980) which closes in 39 BC (Lockyear 1996; Lockyear *et al.* forthcoming).

What is more difficult is to suggest a context for these periods of import. Romanian scholars generally suggest that trade was the major reason (e.g. Mitrea 1945). Crawford (1977, 1985) suggests that the slave trade, in conjunction with Spartacus' revolt and the suppression of piracy, was the primary cause although this suggestion has met with some hostility from Romanian scholars (Chiţescu 1981; Poenaru Bordea/Cojocărescu 1984). The latter influx is only partly due to the large numbers of coins minted at that date — an observation given more weight by the fact that the huge legionary issue is, comparatively, not very common in Romanian hoards. The Akornion inscription, from Dionysopolis on the Black Sea Coast (Dittenberger 1917: No. 762; Sherk 1984: No. 78), records a meeting between Akornion acting as emissary for Burebista (the 'first and greatest of the Kings in Thrace', lines 22-23 of the inscription), and Pompey, at some point during the Civil Wars. Although Burebista is an ill-known figure, and unfortunately communist propaganda used him extensively, clouding further what is actually known, he does seem to

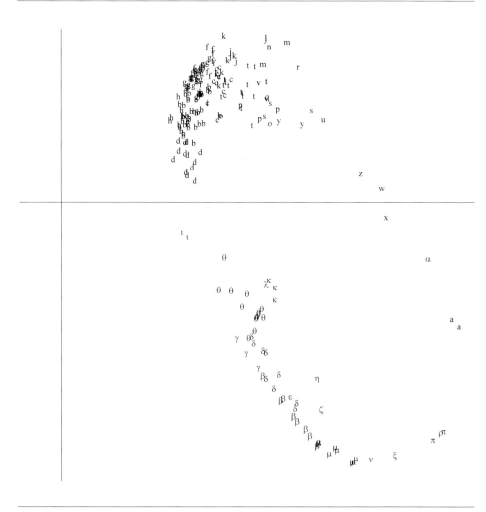

Figure 4. Map from Principal Co-ordinates Analysis of the same 217 hoards analysed using cluster analysis. This analysis has also used Dmax as a dissimilarity coefficient. Data points are hoards; the point symbol is the group membership from the cluster analysis (table 1); first (horizontal) and second axes.

have been in a powerful position in Dacia for a short period.[12] The Akornion inscription shows that he had some influence in the Black Sea region, whereas Strabo (*Geography* 7.3.11, 7.5.2) records a campaign beyond the river 'Parisus' (Παρίσου, probably the Tisza in modern Hungary). It *may be* that Pompey paid Burebista to keep out of the civil wars. Much of this is, and will have to remain, at least for the moment, unsatisfactory speculation, and still leaves many archaeological questions unanswered. For a more detailed discussion see Lockyear (1996; forthcoming).

4.2   STATISTICAL RESULTS

Although it is dangerous to suggest the validity of a statistical method solely on the basis of the archaeological credibility of its results, this cluster analysis using $Dmax_{obs}$ as a dissimilarity coefficient has produced results which make sense in archaeological terms. Comparison to the 22 CAs showed consistency between the two types of analysis.

A check on the results was undertaken by using the same matrix of dissimilarities and performing a principal co-ordinates analysis, also known as classic metric multi-dimensional scaling. This was performed using the DIRPCORD module of the MV-ARCH package (Wright 1989). Figures 4 and 5 are the first and second, and the second and third axes from this analysis; the data points are the groups from the cluster analysis. As is expected, the results do not entirely match those of the cluster analysis but there is large degree of similarity which lends confidence to the results as a whole.

The measure also appears to be robust. Included in the analyses were three hoards which were thought to contain extraneous coins or to have other data problems. The Castelnovo hoard (CST; Crawford personal records) appeared odd in the CA of hoards from 46 BC (Lockyear 1996: section 8.3.14) and contained only three coins dated after 71 BC, which is highly unusual for Italian hoards of

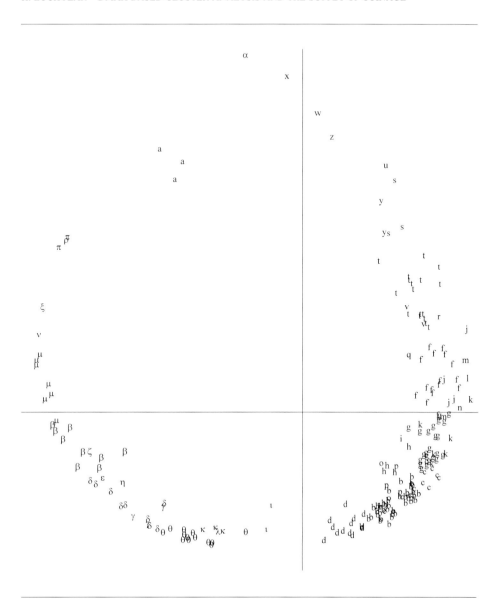

Figure 5. As for figure 4 – second (horizontal) and third axes.

46 BC. This hoard was placed in group *b* with other Italian hoards of the 70s BC, and would be dated to 71 BC if the three aforementioned coins are omitted. The Torre de Juan Abad hoard (JUA; Vidal Bardán 1982) contains two coins of 82-79 BC which were thought by Vidal Bardán to be extraneous; without them the hoard dates to 105 BC. With or without these two coins, this hoard is placed in group *δ* which consists of other hoards of that date. Finally, the San Gregorio di Sassola hoard (GRE; Cesano 1903) appeared to close in 44 BC but was placed in group *g* with 7 other Italian hoards, and 15 hoards from elsewhere. Six of the Italian hoards date from 55-49 BC, one from 42 BC. A re-examination of the database showed that a couple of coin types had been wrongly entered by myself and the correct

closing date for San Gregorio is in fact 58 BC. Conversely, there is no obvious explanation for the Piedmonte d'Alife hoard (PIE; Crawford 1969: No. 406, data from Crawford's personal records) having such an archaic profile that it is grouped with hoards from 58-49 BC.

Leese has used Dmax as a similarity coefficient in two papers (Leese 1983; Middleton *et al.* 1985). In the former paper she compares the size distributions of inclusions in pottery thin sections using Dmax as a dissimilarity coefficient; the results reflecting sherd groups originally defined by other criteria. In the latter paper she compares different methods of counting grains from ceramic thin sections using Dmax, called Kolmogorov-Smirnov distances (K_{ij}), input to non-metric multidimensional scaling. Again, significant grouping is displayed on the resultant plot (Middleton *et al.* 1985: fig. 6).

Leese (1983: 52) suggests that the area between the two curves, rather than Dmax, could be used. This is the procedure used by Creighton (1992). Using the area between the curves would be space dilating, analogous to using squared Euclidian distances instead of Euclidian distance. In Leese's paper she has control over the number of grains in each sample and is able to ensure an adequate sample size. In the analysis of hoards, the number of coins in a hoard is beyond the analyst's control although a lower size bound has to be set. Small hoards will have a jagged cumulative proportion line and thus will create a large area between the lines; larger hoards will have smoother lines and the distortion will be less. Although this problem of sample size will affect both the area measure and Dmax, the former method will exaggerate the problem. Creighton sets his lower bound at five coins which creates severe problems with his analysis. My results, using a lower bound of 30 well identified denarii and Dmax, are not affected by variations in hoard size.

Dmax has also been used in other situations. Geman *et al.* (1990) use the measure in texture based image segmentation. They compare the distribution of gray scales between blocks of pixels using this measure.

5   Conclusions

Dmax has been successfully used as a dissimilarity coefficient suitable for ordinal data in cluster analysis or multidimensional scaling although a theoretical appraisal of its properties (cf. Sibson 1972) is still needed.

The cluster analysis performed has significantly added to our understanding of the supply of Roman Republican denarii to ancient Dacia, roughly modern Romania, although the archaeological and historical explanation of the pattern revealed will continue to be the subject of some debate. However, the solution of the basic aspects of the 'Romanian problem' means that the debate now has firmer foundations and can focus on the more interesting aspects of Dacian society, and its use of these coins.

Acknowledgements

I would like to thank Michael Crawford for allowing access to his personal records, and to Andrew Burnett, Roger Bland and the staff of the Department of Coins and Medals for arranging easy access to those records and their library. Thanks are also due to Clive Orton for his help with the original research, Bob Laxton for his comments at the conference, and Richard Wright for his help and comments. I would also like to thank Morven Leese for bringing my attention to her papers, and Thomas Hofman for bringing my attention to the paper by Geman *et al.* (1990). I would

also like to thank the Department of Archaeology, University of Southampton, especially Timothy Sly, for allowing me access to their hardware and software. Finally, I would like to thank all my friends and colleagues in Romania, especially Adrian Popescu, Gh. Poenaru Bordea and Virgil Mihăilescu-Bîrliba and their families, for making my research in Romania both possible and pleasant. Any errors remain, as always, the responsibility of the author.

notes

1 The analysis was undertaken using CANOCO (Ter Braak 1987-1992) and the plots produced using CANODRAW (Smilauer 1992). The analysis was performed using symmetric scaling and no transformation of the original variables was performed. The first axis has an eigenvalue of 0.460 explaining 18.5% of the variation in the data set; the second axis has an eigenvalue of 0.305 explaining 12.3% of the data set. Given the size of this data set, these figures are quite acceptable.

2 In his analysis, Creighton is performing Principal Components Analysis, not cluster analysis as stated. Also, for unstated reasons, he uses percentages rather than the original counts and thus needlessly introduces the problem of compositional data (Aitchison 1986).

3 Hoards mentioned in the text are followed by a three-letter code in SMALL CAPITALS; these codes are the unique identifiers from the author's *Coin Hoards from the Roman Republic* (CHRR) database and allow cross-reference to that database, the material deposited on the WWW, and previous publications (e.g. Lockyear 1993). The CHRR database will be made publically available (Crawford and Lockyear forthcoming).

4 The 'structure' of a coin hoard in this paper refers to the pattern of representation of coins in a hoard, grouped by their date of manufacture. Creighton uses the term 'age profile' (Creighton 1992). The term derives from the statistical literature where the aim of some multivariate techniques is described as looking for 'latent structure' (Wright 1989).

5 The terms 'archaic' and 'modern' were coined by Creighton (1992). In this paper, a hoard with an archaic structure has relatively more old coinage than other contemporary hoards; a modern hoard has relatively more new coins than other contemporary hoards; an average hoard is a hoard which has a structure between the two extremes.

6 The Windows version of the *Bonn Archaeological Statistics Package*.

7 Subsequent to the analysis and the presentation of this paper, Morven Leese kindly drew my attention to her papers (Leese 1983; Middleton/Freestone/Leese 1985) which used Dmax as a dissimilarity coefficient. Note however, that Leese uses the term *Kolmogorov-Smirnov distance* to denote Dmax as used here, and *Dmax* to denote the maximum diameter of inclusions in pottery fabrics.

8 Consultation included a posting to the statistics mailing list ALLSTAT.

9 The dendrograms from both these analyses are available on the CAA web server.

10 The initial examination of the results was performed using the dendrogram only. When the detailed results were compiled the agglomeration schedule was consulted, and it was found that the 'cut' had been made at 18.9%. As the level of the cut was arbitrary, it was decided to continue with these groups.

11 This coinage, produced to pay the troops prior to the battle of Actium, is dated by Crawford to 32-31 BC. In all cases where a cointype has a range of dates, the earliest date is used. Hence, these three hoards close in 32 BC, but are almost certainly not concealed until 31 BC or very soon after.

12 Little is written in English about Burebista. Crişan (1978) gives an account, in English, of what is known, although much of the book is speculative.

references

Aitchison, J.A.	1986	*The Statistical Analysis of Compositional Data*. London: Chapman and Hall.
Aldenderfer, M.S.	1982	Methods of cluster validation in archaeology, *World Archaeology* 14 (1), 61-72.
Babeş, M.	1975	Problèmes de la chronologie de la culture Geto-Dace à la lumière des fouilles de Cîrlomăneşti, *Dacia* New Series 19, 125-139.
Baxter, M.J.	1994	*Exploratory Multivariate Analysis in Archaeology*. Edinburgh: Edinburgh University Press.
Braak, C.J.F. ter	1987-1992	Canoco; a Fortran program for Canonical Community Ordination. Ithaca, New York: Microcomputer Power.
Buttrey, T.V.	1980	The Cosa hoard, *Memoirs of the American Academy at Rome* 34, 79-153.
Cesano, L.	1903	S. Gregorio di Sassola – Ripostiglio di monete familiari rivenuto nel territorio comunale, *Notizie degli Scavi*, 604-620.
Chirilă, E. M.Fl. Grigorescu	1982	Tezaurul monetar de la Iclănzel, *Acta Musei Porolissiensis* 6, 141-144.
Chiţescu, M.	1971a	Cîteva tezaure monetare romane republicane din Moldova, *Carpica* 4, 159-166.
	1971b	Copii şi imitaţii de denari romani republicani în Dacia, *Memoria Antiquitatis* 3, 209-258.
	1980	Tezaurul de la Poroschia (jud. Teleorman) şi unele probleme privind monedele geto-dacice de tip roman republican, *Studii şi Cercetări de Numismatică* 7, 53-70.
	1981	*Numismatic Aspects of the History of the Dacian State*. BAR International Series 112. Oxford: British Archaeological Reports.
Crawford, M.H.	1969	*Roman Republican Coin Hoards*. London, Royal Numismatic Society Special Publication No. 4.
	1974	*Roman Republican Coinage*. Cambridge: Cambridge University Press.
	1977	Republican denarii in Romania: the supression of piracy and the slave trade, *Journal of Roman Studies* 67, 117-124.
	1980	Imitation of Roman Republican Denarii in Dacia, *Studii şi Cercetări de Numismatică* 7, 51-52.
	1985	*Coinage and Money under the Roman Republic*. London: Methuen and Co. Ltd.
Crawford, M.H. K. Lockyear	forth-coming	*Coin Hoards of the Roman Republic*. Forthcoming combined paper and electronic publication.
Creighton, J.D.	1992	*The Circulation of Money in Roman Britain from the First to the Third Century AD*. Unpublished PhD thesis, Durham University.
Crişan, I.H.	1978	*Burebista and his time*. Bucureşti: Editura Academiei Republicii Socialiste România.

Dittenberger, W.	1917	*Sylloge Inscriptionum Graecarum,* volume 2. Leipzig. Photomechanical reprint 1960, Hildesheim: Georg Orms.
Geman, D. S. Geman C. Graffigne P. Dong	1990	Boundary dectection by constrained optimization, *Institute of Electrical and Electronic Engineers: Transactions on Pattern Analysis and Machine Intelligence* 12 (7), 609-628.
Glodariu, I. E. Iaroslavschi A. Rusu	1992	Die Münzstätte von Sarmizegetusa Regia, *Ephemeris Napocensis* 2, 57-68.
Hersh, C. A. Walker	1984	The Mesagne Hoard, *American Numismatic Society Monographs and Notes* 29, 103-134, pls. 16-19.
Jardine, C.J. N. Jardine R. Sibson	1967	The structure and construction of taxonomic hierarchies, *Mathematical Biosciences* 1 (2), 173-179.
Leese, M.N.	1983	The statistical treatment of grain size data from pottery, In: A. Aspinall/S.E. Warren (eds), *Proceedings of the 22nd Symposium on Archaeometry, Bradford,* 47-55. Bradford.
Lockyear, K.	1989	*A Statistical Investigation of Roman Republican Coin Hoards.* Unpublished M.Sc. dissertation submitted to the Department of Archaeology, University of Southampton.
	1993	Coin hoard formation revisited.... In: J. Andresen/T. Madsen/I. Scollar (eds), *Computing the Past. Computer Applications and Quantitative Methods in Archaeology CAA92,* 367-376. Aarhus: Aarhus University Press.
	1996	*Multivariate Money. A statistical analysis of Roman Republican coin hoards with special reference to material from Romania.* PhD thesis submitted to University College London.
	forth-coming	State, symbol or swindle? The problem of Roman Republican *denarii* in Romania.
Lockyear, K. M.J. Ponting Gh. Poenaru Bordea	forth-coming	Metallurgical analysis of Roman Republican *denarii* from Romania. To be submitted to *Dacia.*
Lupu, N.	1967	Aspekte des Münzumlaufs im vorrömischen Dakien, *Jahrbuch für Numismatik und Geldgeschichte* 17, 101-121.
Middleton, A.P. I.C. Freestone M.N. Leese	1985	Textural analysis of ceramic thin sections: evaluation of grain sampling procedures, *Archaeometry* 27 (1), 64-74.
Mitrea, B.	1945	Penetrazione commerciale e circolazione monetaria nella Dacia prima della conquista, *Ephemeris Dacoromana* 10, 1-154.
	1958	Legături comerciale ale Geto-Dacilor din Muntenia cu Republica Romană, reflectate în descoperiri monetare, *Studii şi Cercetări de Numismatică* 2, 123-238.
Mitrea, B. C.S. Nicolaescu-Plopşor	1953	Monete din timpul republicii romane descoperite la Işalniţa (Dolj), *Materiale Arheologice* 1, 543-587.
Mosteller, F. J.W. Tukey	1977	*Data Analysis and Regression.* Reading, Massachusetts: Addison-Wesley.

| Norušis, M.J. | 1993 | *SPSS for Windows, Professional Statistics Release 6.* Chicago: SPSS. |

Orton, C.R. | 1980 | *Mathematics in Archaeology.* London: Collins.

Poenaru Bordea, Gh.
　M. Cojocărescu | 1984 | Contribuţii la circulaţia monetară din centrul Transilvaniei în secolul I î.e.n.: tezaurul monetar descoperit la Icland (com. Ernei, jud. Mureş), *Studii şi Cercetări de Numismatică* 8, 53-75.

Popilian, G. | 1970 | Tezaurul de monede romane republicane descoperit la Dunăreni (jud. Dolj), *Historica* 1, 53-66.

Pozzi, E. | 1960-1 | Ripostigli Repubblicani Romani nel Museo Archeologico Nazionale di Napoli, *Annali dell'Instituto Italiano di Numismatica* 7-8, 153-245.

Preda, C. | 1971 | Monedele getice de tip Vîrteju-Bucureşti, *Studii şi Cercetări de Numismatică* 5, 51-79.

Shennan, S.J. | 1988 | *Quantifying Archaeology.* Edinburgh: Edinburgh University Press.

Sherk, R.K. | 1984 | *Rome and the Greek East to the death of Augustus.* Translated documents of Greece and Rome volume 4. Cambridge: Cambridge University Press.

Sibson, R. | 1972 | Order invariant methods for data analysis, *Journal of the Royal Statistical Society Series B* 34, 311-338. With discussion, 338-349.

Smilauer, P. | 1992 | *Canodraw. A companion program to Canoco for publication-quality graphical output.* Ithaca, New York: Microcomputer Power.

Vidal Bardán, J.M. | 1982 | Tesorillo de denarios romano-republicanos de Torre Juan Abad (Ciudad Real) en el Museo Arqueológico Nacional, *Acta Numismàtica* 12, 79-95.

Wright, R. | 1989 | *Doing Multivariate Archaeology and Prehistory.* Sidney: Department of Anthropology, University of Sydney.

Kris Lockyear
88 Kent Road
St. Denys
Southampton SO17 2LH
United Kingdom
e-mail: K.Lockyear@soton.ac.uk

Christian C. Beardah
Mike J. Baxter

MATLAB Routines for Kernel Density Estimation and the Graphical Representation of Archaeological Data

1 Introduction

Histograms are widely used for data presentation in archaeology, but have many potential limitations. They are appropriate for variables where the measurement scale is continuous (e.g., length, height). The scale is divided into a set of contiguous intervals; the frequency count of observations in each interval is obtained; and the count is represented graphically by a bar whose *area* is proportional to the frequency. Although not essential, it is usual for intervals to be defined to be of equal width, in which case the height of a bar is also proportional to the frequency. We shall refer to this common interval width as the *bin-width*.

The choice of bin-width is essentially an arbitrary one. A second arbitrary choice is the starting position of the first interval to contain any data, and we refer to this position as the *origin*. It is well known (e.g., Whallon: 1987) that the appearance of a histogram can depend on both the choice of origin and bin-width. In particular, the archaeological interpretation of a histogram depends on the appearance which can be markedly affected by these two arbitrary choices.

A common use of histograms in archaeology is for comparative purposes; for example, comparing the distribution of the ratio of length to breadth of flint flakes from different contexts. Arguably, histograms are usually inefficient for this kind of purpose, and better methods such as the use of box-and-whisker plots exist (Cleveland 1993). Generalisation of the histogram to display the joint distribution of two variables is sometimes desirable, but is unwieldy and requires lots of data.

Kernel Density Estimates (KDEs), which at their simplest can be thought of as smoothed histograms, avoid many of these problems. They have been little used in archaeology, notwithstanding Orton's (1988) implicit reference to their potential. One reason is undoubtedly that the methodology has not been readily available in the packages used by archaeologists. A possible second reason is that archaeologists may find the mathematics underlying the methodology forbidding.

In this paper, after describing briefly the methodology, routines for implementing KDEs in the MATLAB package,

that have been developed by the first author, are described. We illustrate the utility of these routines using several archaeological examples.

2 The Mathematics of KDEs

2.1 UNIVARIATE KDEs

Unless otherwise stated the sources for the material in this and the next section are either Wand and Jones (1995) or Silverman (1986).

Given n points $X_1, X_2, ..., X_n$ a KDE can be thought of as being obtained by placing a 'bump' at each point and then summing the height of each bump at each point on the X-axis. The shape of the bump is defined by a mathematical function — the kernel, $K(x)$ — that integrates to 1. The spread of the bump is determined by a window- or band-width, h, that is analogous to the bin-width of a histogram. $K(x)$ is usually a symmetric probability density function (pdf).

Mathematically, this gives the KDE as

$$\hat{f}(x) = \frac{1}{nh} \sum_{i=1}^{n} K(\frac{x - X_i}{h})$$

Compared to the histogram the shape of $\hat{f}(x)$ does not depend upon the choice of origin, but is affected by the bandwidth h. Large values of h over-smooth, while small values under-smooth the data. Choice of both h and $K(x)$ is discussed later. Generalisations to higher dimensions, d, are relatively direct. For descriptive use only the case $d=2$ is likely to be of widespread interest, and is considered in the next section.

2.2 MULTIVARIATE KDEs

The representation of the KDE as a sum of 'bumps' is easily extended to the higher dimensional case. We shall restrict our attention to the case of bivariate data points of the form (X_i, Y_i). The kernel now becomes a function of two variables, $K(x,y)$, which again integrates to 1 and is usually radially symmetric. (For example, the bivariate normal pdf.) The mathematical representation of the KDE, $\hat{f}(x,y)$, depends, in general, on a 2 by 2 symmetric positive definite matrix, **H**. In this paper we shall only consider the case where **H** is diagonal, i.e.

$$H = \begin{bmatrix} h_1^2 & 0 \\ 0 & h_2^2 \end{bmatrix}$$

With this simplification the representation of the bivariate KDE, $\hat{f}(x,y)$, is given by

$$\hat{f}(x,y) = \frac{1}{nh_1h_2} \sum_{i=1}^{n} K\left(\frac{x\text{-}X_i}{h_1}, \frac{y\text{-}Y_i}{h_2}\right)$$

where h_1 and h_2 are the window-widths in the X and Y directions.

The smoothing parameters h_1 and h_2 control the amount of smoothing in the two co-ordinate directions. If $h_1 = h_2$ then we can think of the 'bumps' of the kernel function as being spherically symmetric (with circular contours). On the other hand, if $h_1 \neq h_2$ then the 'bumps' have elliptical contours with the ellipsoidal axes parallel to the two co-ordinate axes. A further generalisation (not considered here) introduces an off-diagonal value h_3 to the symmetric matrix **H** and allows the ellipsoidal axes to have arbitrary orientation. Whilst taking $h_1 = h_2$ clearly makes understanding and implementation rather more straightforward, the fact that this involves the same amount of smoothing in each co-ordinate direction is regarded as a serious shortcoming (Wand/Jones 1995: 105). In the routines described below the user has the option to interactively vary the smoothing parameters, using one, two or three values of h as discussed above. The default number of smoothing parameters is two.

3   MATLAB Implementation

Here we describe, by way of examples, routines for performing exploratory data analysis using KDEs. These routines have been implemented in MATLAB, a scientific computing environment which has developed a strong user base in Further and Higher Education institutions, particularly in Departments of Mathematics and Engineering. Many such departments have copies of the package available for general use. MATLAB is particularly useful in applications involving numerical matrices and graphical presentation. Multivariate data is most naturally represented as a matrix of values, where columns indicate different components. This matrix representation of data, when coupled with MATLAB's matrix manipulation and programming capabilities, provides a powerful, accessible platform for mathematical and statistical programming and algorithm development.

Powerful graphics facilities are available within the standard package and the Graphical User Interface (GUI) is programmable also. This feature means that software can be designed to be user-friendly, with an assumption of little knowledge on the user's part. Windows, menus, sliders, buttons etc. can be used to create an interface familiar to anyone who has worked within a Windows environment, and quickly learned by those who have not. We have taken advantage of these features to develop a suite of routines allowing the user to interactively vary the kernel function, the smoothing parameter(s) and various aspects of the graphical depiction of the resulting KDEs, including contouring in the bivariate case. The use of mathematical packages such as MATLAB to create such Windows based software is a new and hitherto underexploited option for users with specific applications in mind. While a significant amount of effort must be invested in the production of such routines, we believe that the portable and re-usable nature of the software justifies this effort.

All of the figures in the remainder of section 3 were generated either using these routines exclusively, or in combination with basic MATLAB commands for plotting multiple images (fig. 1).

3.1   EXAMPLE: THE UNIVARIATE CASE

In practice the choice of kernel function makes little difference to the appearance of the KDE. Figure 1 shows four KDEs generated using the same value of h, yet with different kernel functions. The names of the kernels are given in the graphs and their mathematical definitions in Silverman (1986). These data represent the rim diameters of 60 Bronze Age cups from Italy (Source: Baxter 1994: 233-234), based upon Lukesh and Howe (1978)).

Each of the kernels used in figure 1 has *bounded support*, meaning that the kernel function is non-zero only for the range $x \in [-1,1]$. In practice this makes the 'bumps' that form the KDE spread out rather less than the more commonly used normal kernel, which has *infinite support*. Compare the KDEs of figure 1 with those of figure 2(c), also obtained using $h = 2.5$ but using the normal kernel. It is clear that the KDE obtained using the normal kernel oversmooths relative to those KDEs produced with finite support kernel functions (for the same value of h).

In contrast to variation of the kernel function, the degree of smoothing (controlled by h) is of crucial importance in density estimation. If h is too large we 'oversmooth', erasing detail. If h is too small we 'undersmooth', and fail to filter out spurious detail. Several methods of automatically choosing an *optimal* (in some sense) value of h exist, though a subjective choice is often equally valid.

Some simplistic methods of automatically choosing h depend upon an assumption of normality in the data. If this assumption is not valid 'oversmoothing' often results. This explains the oversmoothing apparent in figure 2(c), which was obtained using the rim diameter data; a near 'optimal' value of h and the normal kernel. It is clear from figure 1 that this data is far from normal in structure. For the reasons outlined above, it is important to have the facility to

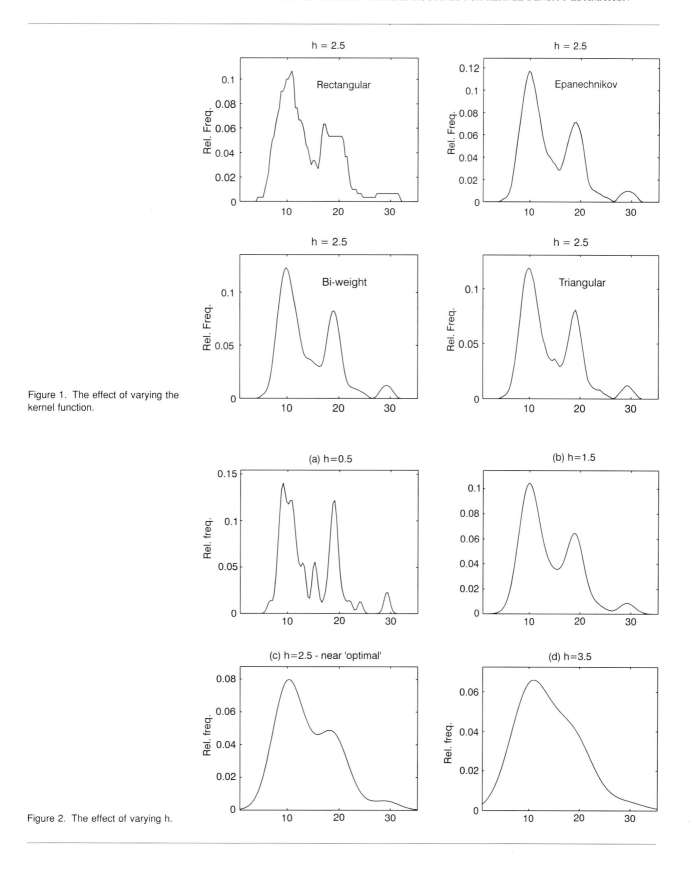

Figure 1. The effect of varying the kernel function.

Figure 2. The effect of varying h.

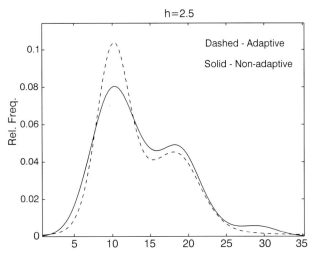

Figure 3. Adaptive Kernel Density Estimation.

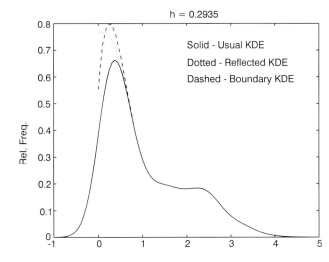

Figure 4. Bounded and Unbounded KDEs.

interactively vary the smoothing parameter h. Where an 'optimal' value is automatically used by a routine, it is sensible to reduce this value and recompute the KDE. The boundary between over- and undersmoothing is quite large in our experience, and a visual inspection of KDEs obtained using various values of h should quickly lead to a satisfactory value of h being found. In this respect it is helpful to be able to overlay several KDEs on the same axes, or to use subplots as in figures 1 and 2. Each of these methods is supported.

3.2 ADAPTIVE METHODS

The basic idea of *adaptive* methods is identical to that described above, i.e. we construct a KDE by placing kernel functions at the observed data points. The difference is that here we allow the smoothing parameter, h, to vary from one data point to the next. More specifically, we use a larger value of h for observations in regions of low density, in particular for observations in the tails of the distribution. The intention is to reduce the effect of outliers on the KDE.

This procedure requires that we can first identify data points which lie in regions of low density. This can be achieved by initially computing a *pilot estimate* of the KDE by the standard methods of section 2. An adaptive KDE can then be constructed based upon this information. See Silverman (1986: 100-110) for a detailed discussion. Figure 3 shows both adaptive and non-adaptive KDEs for the cup diameter data and the normal kernel.

3.3 BOUNDED DATA

If the data represents some measured quantity, for example the rim diameter data considered above, then it makes little

sense to use a density estimate which is positive for negative values of x. However, if the data set includes data points near zero, it is inevitable that the kernel or 'bump' associated with such data points will stray into the region where x is negative. This is especially true of the normal kernel function, since it has infinite support.

A natural, simplistic way of dealing with this situation is to reflect the part of the KDE to the left of zero in the line $x = 0$. Figure 4 shows three KDEs. The solid curve was produced using the normal kernel and an 'optimal' value of h as described in section 2 above. This density estimate has the undesirable property that it overlaps the line $x = 0$. In contrast, the KDE represented by the dotted curve in figure 4 was produced by reflecting the appropriate portion of the solid curve in the line $x = 0$. The data in this case represents the Na_2O content of a sample of 361 fragments of French medieval glass. Clearly this quantity cannot be negative.

More advanced methods of dealing with so-called 'bounded' data exist. In particular, there are classes of 'boundary' kernel functions which take into account the proximity of the boundary and ensure that it is not crossed. These boundary kernels have the unusual property that $K(x)$ may be negative for some x. In addition to the simple reflection method, we have implemented a boundary kernel method as described in Jones (1993). In figure 4 the broken line represents such a KDE.

3.4 THE BIVARIATE CASE

Just as in the univariate case the choice of kernel function makes little difference to the appearance of the final KDE, though for completeness we have provided a

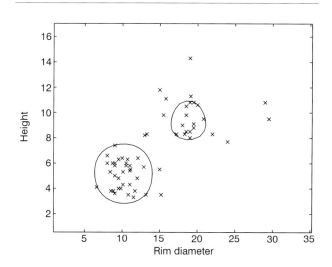

Figure 5. A 75% contour for the Bronze Age cup data.

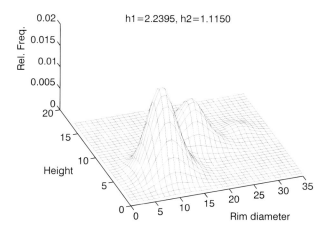

Figure 6. The KDE used to generate the contour of figure 5.

choice of four commonly used bivariate kernel functions. On the other hand, the choice of smoothing parameters again *does* have a significant effect. Our routines automatically choose values for h_1 and h_2 based upon the univariate method of selection for each of the two components considered separately. However, interactive subjective choices by the user are also supported.

An important use of bivariate KDEs is in contouring. Since a KDE is a *function*, we can apply standard contouring methods based upon the height of the function. In addition, we have found some useful applications of a new contouring method reported in Bowman and Foster (1993) (see Baxter/Beardah 1995; Baxter *et al.* 1994 for more details). This method consists of forming a KDE, then ranking the data points by descending density as estimated by the KDE. The contour enclosing $p\%$ of the data is then formed by drawing a contour line corresponding to the value of the kernel estimate of a data point $p\%$ through the ordered list. Since this technique involves calculation of the KDE at each of the data points it can be computationally expensive for large data sets. Figure 5 shows a 75% contour overlaid upon a scatter plot of data representing the rim diameter and overall height of 60 Bronze Age cups from Italy. The contour encloses the 'most dense' 75% of the data set. Figure 6 shows the bivariate KDE (obtained using the bivariate normal kernel and 'optimal' values for h_1 and h_2) which was used to generate the contour shown in figure 5.

Our routines allow interactive variation of the smoothing parameters h_1 and h_2 as well as the type of kernel function. In addition, the resulting KDEs and percentage contour plots can be viewed from any angle by means of sliders.

Acknowledgements
We conclude by acknowledging the contribution of Miss K. Bibby to this work and by inviting interested parties to obtain the software by contacting the first named author.

references

Baxter, M.J.   1994   *Exploratory Multivariate Analysis in Archaeology.* Edinburgh: Edinburgh University
                                        Press.

Baxter, M.J.   1994   A Statistical Re-Analysis of Some French Medieval Glass Compositional Data With an
    C.C. Beardah   Application. *Department of Mathematics Research report* 7/94. Nottingham Trent
    I.C. Freestone   University.

Baxter, M.J.   1995   Graphical Presentation of Results from Principal Components Analysis. In: J. Huggett/
    C.C. Beardah   N. Ryan (eds), *Computer Applications and Quantitive Methods in Archaeology 1994,*
                                        63-67, BAR International Series 600, Oxford: Tempus Reparatum.

Bowman, A.   1993   Density Based Exploration of Bivariate Data, *Statistics and Computing* 3, 171-177.
    P. Foster

Cleveland, W.S.   1993   *Visualising Data.* New Jersey: Hobart Press.

Jones, M.C.   1993   Simple Boundary Correction for Kernel Density Estimation, *Statistics and Computing* 3,
                                        135-146.

Lukesh, S.S.   1978   Protoapennine vs. Subapennine: Mathematical Distinction Between Two Ceramic Phases,
    S. Howe   *Journal of Field Archaeology* 5, 339-347.

Orton, C.R.   1988   Review of Quantitative Research in Archaeology, M.S. Aldenderfer (ed.), *Antiquity* 62,
                                        597-598.

Scott, D.W.   1992   *Multivariate Density Estimation.* New York: Wiley.

Silverman, B.   1986   *Density Estimation for Statistics and Data Analysis.* London: Chapman and Hall.

Wand, M.P.   1995   *Kernel Smoothing.* London: Chapman and Hall.
    M.C. Jones

Whallon, R.   1987   Simple Statistics. In: M.S. Aldenderfer (ed.), *Quantitative Research in Archaeology:*
                                        Progress and Prospects, 135-150, London: Sage.

Christian C. Beardah and Mike J. Baxter
Department of Mathematics, Statistics and Operational Research
The Nottingham Trent University
Nottingham NG11 8NS
United Kingdom
e-mail: ccb@maths.ntu.ac.uk
        mat3beardcc@newvax.ntu.ac.uk

John W.M. Peterson

A computer model of Roman landscape in South Limburg

1 Introduction

Edelman and Eeuwens (1959) proposed that the landscape of south Limburg (fig. 1) reveals the effects of a Roman centuriated land survey. This idea attracted some support (Lambert 1971: 48), but it is not generally accepted.[1] Despite this, we should keep an open mind. The hypothesis is difficult to dismiss on theoretical grounds, and it is supported by empirical results which show anomalies in the distribution of Roman sites, similar to those observed in other areas of centuriation.

The centuriation grid (fig. 2) can be located accurately by calculation (Peterson 1993: 43-47). The module is 711.61 m and the orientation is N 42.064° E. One point is located at the Limbricht St-Salviuskerk (186680, 336320) which, according to Edelman and Eeuwens (1959: 53), stands 'precies aan een hoekpunt' (precisely at a corner).

Their evidence for the centuriation is of five sorts: firstly a large number of existing boundaries have a consistent orientation; secondly major boundaries or roads are spaced at multiples of 2400 Roman feet (hence they could represent remnants of major divisions, or *limites*, of the grid); thirdly several medieval churches are positioned on these hypothetical *limites*; fourthly the orientation of some of these churches accords with the proposed grid, and fifthly Roman villas are positioned in a non-random way near the *limites*.

Some of their views can be supported by inspection. Maps show that existing roads, paths and boundaries coincide with the hypothetical *limites* of the centuriation, and on the ground it is clear that several of these features do not conform locally to natural topography.

Quantitative approaches may also be used, and are likely to provide a more secure basis for judgement. An earlier study was that of J.A. Brongers, B.M. Hilwig-Sjöstedt and E. Milikowski, who conducted a numerical analysis of the distribution of the orientation of boundaries. They concluded that the dominant orientations, which vary from place to place, are better related to the morphology of different parts of the landscape than to any overall general Roman influence on the parcelling in the whole region. However, they do not say that there is no centuriation, but that the information cannot be extracted solely from an analysis of modern parcel boundaries (Brongers, pers. comm.).

2 Quantitative study of site distribution

Since this earlier quantitative study was inconclusive, and since, in any case, undateable boundaries may not be seen as a good source of evidence, another approach is adopted here. This measures the claimed association between the grid and Roman sites of all types, including villas, using a database already independently assembled by Martijn van Leusen (1993: 105), using information from the Netherlands State Archaeological Service (ROB). In 1992 it held about 1300 records, of which 491 referred to Roman sites, including villas. This is a large data set which had not been collected together to suit Edelman and Eeuwens' hypothesis. It may therefore be used to test their claim. Given that many Roman (and later) sites are expected to be associated with the *limites*[2], we can examine the distribution of distances of sites from the grid lines, when compared to the distribution of distances which would be expected if the points are scattered uniform randomly with respect to the grid. It seems reasonable to assume that, for a large grid, this latter distribution would arise. The sites may be non-randomly related to natural features, but there is, in many places, very little relationship between these features and the grid (fig. 5).

The Kolmogorov-Smirnov single sample test may be used. The test statistic, D+, is the largest positive difference between the number of points observed at a given distance from the lines of the grid, and the number of points which would be expected on the basis of the null hypothesis (Lapin 1973: 422). In this case it is the maximum value of

$$\left| \frac{i}{n} - (1 - (1 - x_i)^2) \right|$$

where x_i is the distance of the ith point in order of distance from the grid lines (Peterson 1993: 69).

Tables of critical values of D+ show with what confidence we can reject the null hypothesis. One such table, giving values for sample sizes up to 100 was first presented by Miller (1956). For larger samples the critical value, D^+_α for a given probability, α, can be calculated

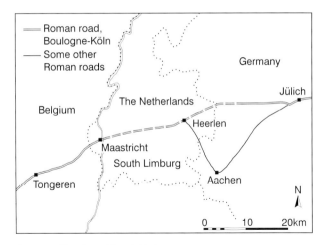

Figure 1. Situation of South Limburg.

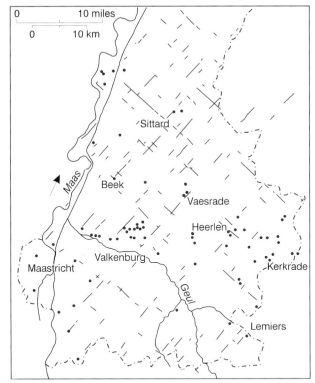

× Remnants of decumani and cardines
• Remains of Roman buildings, mainly villas

Figure 2. South Limburg Roman grid (after Edelman and Eeuwens (1959)).

using a version of the asymptotic formula given by Miller, which was originally due to Smirnov:

$$D^+_\alpha = \frac{\sqrt{\dfrac{-\log_e \alpha}{2}}}{\sqrt{n}}$$

We can calculate values of the numerator of this expression for commonly used significance levels (table 1).

Each numerator value divided by the square root of the sample size gives the critical value of D^+. So, for example, if we have 400 observations (square root = 20) the critical value for the .005 significant level is .082. If the D value for the observations achieves this then we can say that the observed distribution would have occurred with less than 0.5% probability on the basis of the null hypothesis.[3]

3   Treatment of the data and initial results

The 491 Roman records were most kindly supplied by Martijn van Leusen, who was not aware of the parameters which had been calculated for the hypothetical grid (and who has no responsibility for my conclusions). They were transmitted as a text e-mail message and read directly into a Microsoft works database (fig. 3).

Prior to performing the tests no attempt was made to modify the data in any way. It was clear that some coordinates referred to the same site, which might for example have both signs of habitation (bewoning) and graves (graf). It was supposed that an objective way of treating the data would be to ignore these cases, on the assumption they were not likely to bias the result of the tests in any particular direction. Several sets of data were tested (table 2) These calculations were performed originally by purpose-written programs on a DEC VAX

minicomputer, and again more recently by a Microsoft Excel spreadsheet. Very similar results were obtained in both cases.

In this table, the column headed 'Near %' gives the percentage of the sites in each category which lie in the half of the area nearest to the *limites*. For this category the value of distance is less than 0.29289.

'Significance Level' indicates which critical value of D is exceeded for the particular number of records. There is clearly some approximate inverse correspondence between this and the measure of bias.

The first line of the table shows that if we take all the data, making no attempt to alter or analyse it in any way, we can say that (as a formal result) there is less than a 0.25% chance that the 491 values are drawn from a set of points distributed at random with respect to the hypothetical survey grid. In other words, it appears that the odds are more than 400:1 against the hypothesis of random distribution.[4] The relatively high significance of this D value must be attributed to the large size of the population, since the degree of bias towards the grid lines is low.

The D values for properly defined subset populations were also considered, since, according to David Clarke

Table 1. Numerator values for calculating significance levels of D+.

Probability of rejection (α)	.1	.05	.025	.01	.005	.0025	.001	.0005
Numerator Value ($D^+_\alpha \times \sqrt{n}$)	1.07	1.22	1.36	1.52	1.63	1.73	1.86	1.95

Table 2. Some Kolmogorov-Smirnov test results for Limburg data.

	Type	No.	D	Near %	Signifance level
1	All types of record	491	.0825	56.4	0.0025
2	All types (definite and not IA)	419	.0846	56.8	0.0025
3	Definite dwellings (not IA)	85	.1793	62.4	0.005
4	All dwellings	107	.1223	57.0	0.05
5	All villas	153	.1198	56.9	0.025
6	Definite villas	135	.1045	54.8	0.1
7	Temples	2	.8007	100	0.05

 File Edit Window Organize Format Report Macro					
Limburg DB (DB)					
Volgnr	**X**	**Y**	**Tag**	**Type**	**Period**	**Note**

Volgnr	X	Y	Tag	Type	Period	Note
1313	203090.00	323810.00	62EN049	GRAFF	ROM	1E
430	204420.00	325520.00	60GZ004	BEWONING	ROM	1E, WEG
429	204350.00	325500.00	60GZ004	BEWONING	ROM	1E, WEG
1299	202350.00	322200.00	62EN029	AW	ROM VME LME	1-13E
85	181150.00	331600.00	60CN017	VILLA	ROM	1-2E
760	196450.00	322160.00	62BN021	BEWONING	ROM	1-2E
737	196250.00	321825.00	62BN004	BEWONING	ROM	1-2E
505	179100.00	313600.00	61FZ063	GRAF	ROM	1-2E
507	177900.00	317840.00	61FZ064	GRAF	ROM	1-2E
1125	184801.00	308860.00	62CN010	AW	ROM	1-2E
820	191700.00	321630.00	62BN091	VILLA	ROM	1-3E
692	180750.00	316640.00	62AZ013	VILLA	ROM	1-3E 150X150M
749	196630.00	321910.00	62BN013	BEWONING	ROM	1-4E
1312	202275.00	323410.00	62EN048	GRAFF	ROM	210X200M
621	181400.00	321450.00	62AN036	VILLA	ROM	2E
769	197250.00	323580.00	62BN032	VILLA	ROM	2E
754	196260.00	322210.00	62BN016	GRAF	ROM	2E

Figure 3. Initial part of database of Roman archaeological records for South Limburg.

(1978: 150), 'One important corollary of the aggregate or composite nature of archaeological entities is that such populations exhibit their own specific 'behavioural' characteristics which are more complex than the simple sum of the characteristics of the components and more predictable than that of the individual components. One of the main tasks therefore, is to detect and trace these persistent regularity patterns in archaeological data and to use these predictable regularities as tests for real data. If the real data displays the regularity predicted then it should fulfil some already established conditions. If the real data departs from the predicted pattern then some conditions are not fulfilled and the nature of the discrepancy may suggest the divergent conditions responsible for the anomaly.'

Clarke seems to be suggesting that we can split up the data and observe the discrepancies to see if they suggest divergent conditions. Only one variable is being measured in this case (the distance of sites from *limites*), but we can consider predefined subset populations (those have already been defined by attribute values in the database). This does nothing to invalidate the result obtained from the population as a whole, and may provide us with additional useful information.

One subset of the data is obtained if we exclude sites with previous Iron Age use, together with sites not certainly identified or not certainly Roman. For this set (table 2, line 2) the bias towards the grid lines increases slightly, but otherwise we gain little new information.

Another way of selecting subsets is by the type of site. Settlement sites are called 'bewoning' (dwelling) or 'villa'. Definite Roman dwelling sites with no Iron Age occupation on the same site (see line 3) have a very definite bias towards the *limites*. Their distribution is approximately 20 times more unlikely than that of dwelling sites in general (see line 4). This seems to confirm our expectation that, in general, sites with signs of Iron Age habitation will not be significantly associated with the grid, and that their inclusion in the set of Roman dwelling sites will reduce its apparent degree of association.

For villas (table 2, lines 5 and 6) we see the opposite. The more certainly they are villas, the less anomalous is their distribution. This apparently paradoxical result may not be totally due to a reduction in the sample size. It has been suggested (Peterson 1993: 75) that some genuine villas, as opposed to Roman dwellings of lower status, would be deliberately placed away from *limites*.

These results are shown in graphical form (fig. 4). The continuous lines show the levels of significance for D+.

Finally, table 2 also gives a D value for the two temples in the area. The significance of this is high because, to the accuracy of 10 m with which grid location is determined, the temples both lie on *limites*. This was predicted, following the example of other centuriations and written evidence on the practice of the Roman land surveyors.

4 Studies of a sample area

Willems (1987) considers in greater detail the area of Heerlen (Coriouallum), near the centre of South Limburg, in which there are 118 database records, including data on 52 settlement sites. There are relatively few possible traces of *limites* in existing landscape features, but the D value for records of all types, which is significant at the 5% level, gives us no reason to think that the area is different from South Limburg as a whole. This independently selected sample thus seems suitable for tests of two alternative hypotheses on the origin of the landscape.

Willems' view (1987: 50), in reference to his map of Roman site distribution in the area (fig. 5), is that 'Waar het landschap door beken wordt doorsneden is ook heel fraai te zien dat op elk plateau daartussen steeds een villa

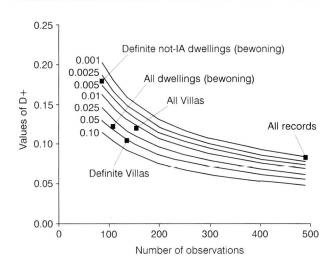

Figure 4. D values for all records for different types of settlement.

ligt. Er was dan ook geen sprake van een kunstmatige landindeling — (*centuriatie*) maar men paste zich aan het landschap aan.' (Where the landscape is cut through by streams it is very satisfying to see that on each intervening plateau there is the site of one villa. There is thus no question of an artificial land allotment (*centuriation*). Rather, the sites are related to the [natural] landscape.)

Willems' hypothesis is, therefore, that natural topography, and nothing else, has determined settlement locations. If this is really so, then it seems to be influencing settlement distribution in a way normally associated with centuriation, as the Kolmogorov-Smirnov statistic indicates. Assuming for a moment that the villas really are located on the plateaux between streams, could the spacing and orientation of these plateaux be in some way peculiar? Perhaps they are regularly spaced at about 710 m, and by some strange chance the grid (which was determined by distant and independent features) happens to coincide with their crests. This seems unlikely. We already have evidence of a number of differently oriented, naturally induced, parcel boundaries in different parts of South Limburg, which implies that the natural topography does not have significant uniform orientation or regularity. In fact, on this map there is little evidence of the grid coinciding with natural topography. Only in the northwest corner is this so; but there we see *limites* coinciding with the valleys of streams, not with plateaux.

Could these difficulties be caused by the assumption that Willems' claim is true? Does a close look at the map confirm that the villas really are on the plateaux? The answer is 'only in some cases', for we can see villa sites (A-E) which appear to be on the boundary between 'beekdal'

1   stream valley (beekdal)
2-4 loess
5   peat
6   quarry
7   grave (field)
8   road
9   villa
10   non-villa settlement
11   industry

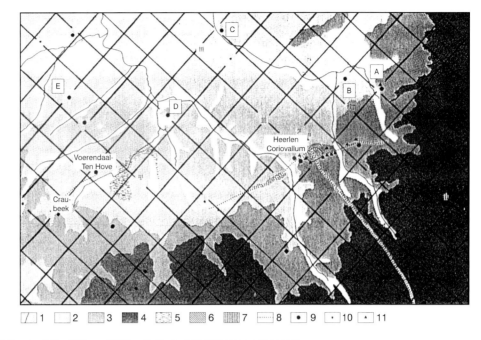

Figure 5. Roman sites in the area of Heerlen (after Willems 1987), with theoretical *limites* superimposed).

(stream valley) and loess. The villa at point E is a case in point, despite the fact that it also lies on the plateau between two other streams. Thus Willems' statement about villa siting in relation to the natural landscape results from a particular interpretation of the data. He did not draw the centuriation on his map. He was thus not in a position to see the coincidences of settlements and *limites* to the west and north of Heerlen, and in particular those counter-examples to his theory of environmental influence which might be better explained by the presence of the centuriation.

However, it is not just a question of interpretation. Judgements also vary according to the evidence which is presented, as we can see if we compare the settlement sites (villas and dwellings) on the database with those Willems shows on his map. Willems' map of sites can be matched to a reduced copy of the Topographische Dienst 1:25,000 topographic map, which includes the Dutch survey grid. When duplicates had been eliminated from the data base, it was possible to identify those database sites most closely corresponding to Willems' map features. Hence we can identify the discrepancies in the data, including settlements on the database which he does not show, and settlements shown by him which are not on the database (see table 3).

D values can also be calculated (fig. 6). It is curious to see how the database records (the author's data source) give the highest D value (P< 0.01), and the map points (Willems' source) the lowest. In fact, the distribution of the

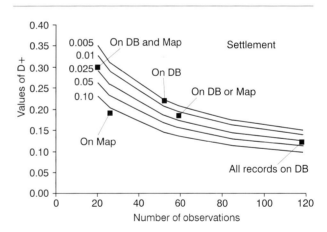

Figure 6. Comparison of D values for settlement in the Heerlen area on Database (DB) and on Willems' (1987) map.

latter with respect to the centuriation could not be regarded as significantly different from random. Nevertheless, there are 20 records, those in both sets, about which there is agreement. An independent arbitrator who selected these would find that they have a significantly high D value. The idea that they are randomly distributed with respect to the grid can be rejected at odds of 40:1.

So, if we select from Willems' sites only those which are independently confirmed, we find that they do not speak against the idea that the centuriation exists.

Table 3. Comparison of Willems map and Database data.

| Volgnr | Tag | Coordinates | | | Type | | Notes |
		X	Y	dist.	(DB)	(Map)	
767	62BN030	19010	32090	61	BEWONING	N G V	N G V = non villa settlement
846	62BN111	19048	32435	64	BEWONING	N G V	
840	62BN108	19085	32069	47	BEWONING	N G V	
746	62BN011	19108	32315	7	VILLA	VILLA	Nearest of four Volgnr
824	62BN094	19120	32450	54	VILLA	VILLA	Nearest of two Volgnr
864	62BN127	19140	32310	248	VILLA	-	
843	62BN109	19145	32262	89	VILLA	VILLA	
818	62BN091	19166	32163	18	VILLA	VILLA	Voerendaal, nearest of two Volgnr
810	62BN081	19206	32044	311	VILLA	VILLA	
860	62BN123	19207	32165	164	?BEWONING	-	
771	62BN035	19215	32130	108	VILLA	-	?Error, in area of "veen" (bog)
819	62BN091	19215	32165	110	VILLA	-	
770	62BN034	19240	32070	64	BEWONING	-	
		19260	31910			N G V	
869	62BN131	19278	31965	41	BEWONING	N G V	
868	62BN130	19335	32278	109	VILLA	VILLA	
836	62BN104	19412	32095	22	?VILLA	N G V	
835	62BN103	19452	32460	110	VILLA	VILLA	
870	62BN132	19458	31926	216	?BEWONING	N G V	
855	62BN119	19470	32400	24	?BEWONING	N G V	
907	62BN163	19501	32017	4	?BEWONING	-	
831	62BN099	19593	31990	78	VILLA	VILLA	
772	62BN037	19595	32030	10	VILLA	-	
733	62BN001	19597	31995	74	BEWONING	-	
		19610	32190			VILLA	?A generic point
737	62BN004	19625	32183	76	BEWONING	VILLA	
778	62BN043	19628	32178	93	BEWONING	-	
777	62BN042	19630	32160	75	BEWONING	-	
779	62BN044	19640	32180	2	BEWONING	-	
764	62BN025	19640	32240	175	BEWONING	-	
780	62BN045	19642	32190	90	BEWONING	-	
792	62BN056	19645	32186	80	BEWONING	-	
760	62BN021	19645	32216	303	BEWONING	-	
739	62BN006	19650	32185	94	BEWONING	-	
743	62BN010	19652	32180	46	BEWONING	-	
789	62BN052	19657	32197	122	BEWONING	-	
784	62BN048	19660	32180	14	BEWONING	-	
776	62BN041	19660	32185	20	VILLA	-	
793	62BN057	19660	32190	53	BEWONING	-	
816	62BN088	19660	32205	154	BEWONING	-	
761	62BN022	19660	32207	167	BEWONING	-	
749	62BN013	19663	32191	38	BEWONING	-	
753	62BN015	19670	32180	88	BEWONING	-	
785	62BN049	19670	32195	12	BEWONING	-	
775	62BN040	19690	32215	2	BEWONING	-	
847	62BN112	19698	32208	108	BEWONING	-	
769	62BN032	19725	32358	15	VILLA	VILLA	
		19760	32210			VILLA	
806	62BN073	19780	32215	41	BEWONING	-	
		18790	32150			N G V	?Badly plotted Volgnr 806
		19810	32330			VILLA	
833	62BN101	19839	32026	192	VILLA	-	
808	62BN076	19845	32020	188	VILLA	VILLA	
925	62BZ015	19900	31865	117	BEWONING	VILLA	
748	62BN012	19906	31955	114	BEWONING	-	
		19940	32080			N G V	
814	62BN085	19980	32133	142	VILLA	-	
834	62BN102	19990	32126	21	VILLA	VILLA	

5   The trustworthiness of the Kolmogorov-Smirnov test results

The statistics of Roman site distribution in general, and especially the distribution of settlement in the area of Heerlen, seem to provide evidence against the well-established belief that the centuriation of Limburg does not exist. We must therefore examine them carefully for possible flaws. For this purpose a number of simulations were run, generating a further 812 Kolmogorov-Smirnov D values.

First, duplicate grid references were eliminated, giving 456 (rather than 491) data items. For this set the probability of observing the D value at random was 1:280, rather than 1:802. This reduction in significance suggests that an 'objective' approach to the data, as used originally, may give a misleading result. Clearly, the significance of a particular D value will be increased
by maintaining the same cumulative distribution of observations, while increasing their number. For this reason the settlement data for the Heerlen area were processed to remove duplicates. Another surprise was that a shift of origin of the grid — from that originally used to another point calculated using the grid parameters — produced a noticeable change in the probability of the D value. For the 491 original data items it changed from 1:802 to 1:594. For 456 unique sites it changed from 1:280 to 1:222. These changes are probably caused by the precision of calculating grid intersection coordinates, which is only to 10 m.

Following a suggestion by Irwin Scollar, it was tested whether the same grid, with the same origin points, might fit the data just as well at other angles. All possible angles (42.064° ±45°, at intervals of 1°) were tried, using both data sets for the original origin and the reduced set for the shifted origin. This produced 267 D values for other angles. Of these, seven were less probable than 1:89 — that is about twice as many as expected — and two were less probable than the values observed at 42.064°. A further simulation was run with 456 randomly generated grid references in a 4 km by 4 km square. Again there were 3 trial runs, each covering 90°. The results showed 40 D values with a probability of less than 1:5 — roughly the expected value. However, there were five D values which were less probable than 1:90. This is again more than expected, but further work would be needed to see if the difference is significant.

The conclusion for the tests on the whole data set is that the significance may be exaggerated by a factor of two, but the reason for this is currently unknown. The practical implication is that the p values for the significance levels given above (table 2) should be doubled. Despite this, inferences drawn from the figures are unchanged.

Similar simulations were conducted on the Heerlen data. For 3 runs of 90° each, there were 52 D values with a probability of less than 1:5 and 31 with a probability of less than 1:10 — very near the expected values. However, excluding the values for 42.064°, there were five values with a probability less than 1:89. Hence, looked at from random angles, these site coordinates have the characteristics of random data, but the lowest probabilities obtained in 'real' trials may be not totally reliable. Nevertheless, the test results (fig. 6) are still useful, even if the significance level p values are doubled.

6   Proposals for further work

To test Edelman and Eeuwens' hypothesis further, even more data would be useful. This might be obtained from areas of the centuriation lying outside the modern day borders of the Netherlands, which would have to be located on other national maps. Dutch maps use the national rectangular coordinate system (as does the ROB database), but they also include in the margin the lines of the UTM zone 31 kilometre grid. From this the parameters of the centuriation may be recalculated. Hence coordinates for the grid intersections may be calculated and plotted for Belgium, which uses UTM grids.

Similarly the centuriation grid may be extended to Germany, using slightly different methods. The geographic coordinates of two intersection points of the centuriation could perhaps be calculated from their UTM zone 31 coordinates, and then used to calculate the equivalent Gauss-Krüger (GK) coordinates for German maps, by means of Scollar's (1989) computer programmes. Alternatively, it is easier in practice to plot intersection points, already plotted on overlapping Dutch and Belgian maps, at the same positions on the German maps. Coordinates can then be read directly, and the angle of the centuriation calculated in terms of north in the local GK grid.

Preliminary results show that near Aachen (fig. 1) some existing topographic features and the former main road from Aachen to Jülich have the same orientation as the hypothetical grid. This is also true of three of the four villas (Gaitzsch 1987) which were excavated in the Hambacher Forst, east of Jülich, between that place and Köln. Wolfgang Gaitzsch in another article (1986: 427) concludes that 'Die regelmäßigen Eingrenzung der Wohn- und Wirtschaftsbereiche ist der Ausdruck einer planmäßigen Limitation des Nutzlandes der CCAA' (the regular boundary layout of living and working space is the expression of a planned *limitatio* [i.e. Roman land survey] of the productive land of CCAA [Köln]). Further data on site location in this area could be used to test the compatibility of Edelman and Eeuwens' with Gaitzsch's hypothesis.

7 Conclusions on the objections to the centuriation hypothesis

There are two principal theoretical objections to the centuriation hypothesis. The first is that a large centuriation such as that of South Limburg could not exist and that it could not extend so far. This view is mistaken. A larger and much less visible system existed in an equally marginal situation in the empire, in southern Tunisia (Trousset 1978). Not only was it very large, but it ignored tribal boundaries, which were established in the area of the existing survey. So, we may, with Monique Clavel-Lévêque (1993:19), be sceptical that a centuriation could cross a Roman provincial boundary which in this case is thought to lie at about Aachen (King 1990: 212), but such a thing is possible. As Tate (1992) has suggested in the case of Roman surveys in Syria, 'Juxtaposés ou superposés, ces réseaux ne dépendent pas des *limites* entre provinces, cités ou finages de villages. Ils occupent des aires si vastes qu'ils ne peuvent avoir été construits que par ordre d'une autorité supérieure, ...'. So, according to him also, surveys ignored provincial boundaries. There is thus no theoretical objection to the extension of the South Limburg centuriation across the border, even if we knew precisely where it was.

The second objection is the one Willems raises. In short, if natural features explain settlement location, then an alternative explanation is false. This is mistaken in practice, because close examination of the map of sites — in conjunction with the database — does not confirm that they are really located according to some simple environmental constraint. It is also mistaken in principle. Even if a convincing demonstration had been made that settlement in the area of Heerlen is strongly influenced by natural topography, the centuriation could not be ruled out. Surely, we must allow the world to be a complex reality in which many factors act at the same time to influence human actions, a world in which human beings, by use of their intellect within a cultural framework, manage to satisfy different types of constraint simultaneously.

Much of 'hard' science seems to be founded on a mistrust of complexity, on a feeling that simple answers are most likely to be true and on the acceptance of William of Occam's principle that explanations need not be expanded beyond what is necessary. This is not appropriate to the study of landscapes which have been worked and reworked by man. They need a more open approach, such as that advocated by Lawson and Staehali (1990), which fits the author's experience of Roman systems of land management (Peterson 1993: 255). If investigation methods were framed in this spirit, we would be more suspicious of attempts to give such simple answers and we would more easily avoid the self-destructive over-application of Occam's razor.

notes

1 It is surprising that sceptics include Oswald Dilke (1971: 140), who discussed other equally controversial systems in favourable terms.

2 This association is hardly in doubt. It may be for symbolic reasons, as in the case of Roman temples marking the survey lines. It may also be economic, since *limites* existing as means of communication, i.e. roads or canals, provide low cost access. There are very clear examples, such as sites in the northern *Ager Cosanus* dated to the 2nd century BC, which have been found 'only on the major axes of the centuriation' (Attolini *et al.* 1990: 145). Again, according to Caillemer and Chevallier (1954: 458), 'Des routes, des voies ferrées, des pistes d'aérodrome, des *limites* de commune s'orientent de même pour éviter de couper les cultures dont les contours correspondent toujours à la répartition antique du sol; il arrive souvent que des grandes fermes modernes soient situées à l'emplacement de ruines romaines, dans l'angle de centuries.' It should, however, be noted that these are extreme cases in which all or most sites are on or near *limites*. Other cases are less clear. They may require statistical techniques in order to measure the association.

3 If we were interested in both positive and negative values of D, we would calculate the critical values, D_α using the very similar asymptotic formula (Rohlf/Sokal 1969: 249):

$$D_\alpha = \frac{\sqrt{\dfrac{-\log_e 1/2\alpha}{2}}}{\sqrt{n}}$$

However, in this case it seemd most appropiate to follow Lapin in considering only positive values, since this is the deviation from randomness which has meaning in the context of our theory. Lapin's published critical D values for a sample of 100 (taken from Miller), are then close to values calculated using Smirnov's formula.

4 According to the calculations described above, the chance of such a high D being seen at random is about one in 800.

references

Attolini, I.
  F. Cambi
  M. Castagna
  M. Celuzza
  E. Fentress
  P. Perkins
  E. Regoli
	1990	Political geography and productive geography between the valleys of the Albegna and the Fiora in northern Etruria. In: G. Barker/J. Lloyd (eds), *Roman Landscapes: Field Survey in the Mediterranean*, 142-151, Rome: British School at Rome.

Caillemer, A. R. Chevallier	1954	Les centuriations de l'Africa Vetus: Sous l'œil d'Asmodée..., *Annales ESC* 9, 433-460.
Clarke, D.L.	1978	*Analytical Archaeology*. 2nd ed. London: Methuen.
Clavel-Lévêque, M.	1993	La cadastració en l'espai imperial. Memòria i raó, *L'avenç* 167, 18-23.
Dilke, O.A.W.	1971	*The Roman Land Surveyors*. Newton Abbot: David & Charles.
Edelman, C.H. B.E.P. Eeuwens	1959	Sporen van een Romeinse landindeling in Zuid-Limburg, *Berichten Rijksdienst Oudheid-kundig Bodemonderzoek* 9: 49-56.
Gaitzsch, W.	1986	Grundformen römischer Landsiedlungen im Westen der CCAA, *Bonner Jahbücher* 186: 397-427.
	1987	Het patroon van de landelijke bewoning in het Rijnland. In: P. Stuart/M.E.Th. de Grooth (eds), *Langs de Weg*, 55-61, Heerlen: Thermenmuseum.
King, A.	1990	*Roman Gaul and Germany*. London: British Museum Publications.
Lambert, A.M.	1971	*The Making of the Dutch Landscape*. London: Seminar Press.
Lapin, L.L.	1973	*Statistics for Modern Business Decisions*. New York: Harcourt Brace Jovanovich.
Lawson, V.A. L.A. Staehali	1990	Realism and the Practice of Geography, *Professional Geographer* 42.1, 13-20.
Miller, L.H.	1956	Table of Percentage Points of Kolmogorov Statistics, *Journal of the American Statistical Association* 51, 111-121.
Peterson, J.W.M.	1993	*Computer-aided investigation of ancient cadastres*. PhD Thesis. University of East Anglia.
Rohlf, F.J. R.R. Sokal	1969	*Statistical Tables*. San Francisco: Freeman.
Scollar, I.	1989	Geodetic and cartographic problems in archaeological databases. In S.P.Q. Rahtz/ J. Richards (eds), *Computer Applications and Quantitative Methods in Archaeology 1989*, 251-273, BAR International Series 548, Oxford: British Archaeological Reports.
Tate, G.	1992	*Les campagnes de la Syrie du Nord du IIe-VIIe siècle*, vol 1. Paris: Geuthner.
Trousset, P.	1978	Les bornes de Bled Segui: nouveaux aperçus sur la centuriation romaine du Sud Tunisien, *Antiquités Africaines* 12, 125-177.

van Leusen, P.M.   1993   Cartographic modelling in a cell-based GIS. In: J. Andresen/T. Madsen/I. Scollar (eds), *Computing the Past, Computer Applications and Quantitative Methods in Archaeology, CAA92*, 105-123, Aarhus: Aarhus University Press.

Willems, W.J.H.   1987   De grote villa van Voerendaal. In: P. Stuart/M.E.Th. de Grooth (eds), *Langs de Weg*, 46-50, Heerlen: Thermenmuseum.

John W.M. Peterson
School of Information Systems
University of East Anglia
Norwich NR4 7TJ
United Kingdom
e-mail: jwmp@sys.uea.ac.uk

Sabine Reinhold

Time versus Ritual – Typological Structures and Mortuary Practices in Late Bronze/Early Iron Age Cemeteries of North-East Caucasia ('Koban Culture')

1   Introduction

In North Caucasian archaeology the Late Bronze Age and Early Iron Age, covering the period of the 14th to 4th century BC is one of the most prominent periods of archaeological research. The cultures of this era are predominantly known for their outstanding metallurgy which is shown in the quantity of weapons and adornment of the burials. As early as the 19th century AD the enormous wealth of these burials led to 'archaeological' activities, looting rather than excavating being the predominant method of this time. This resulted in the huge collections of Caucasian bronzes in European museums (Virchow 1881). Only in the 30s of the present century did real scientific research begin with excavations and chronological studies (Kozenkova 1990; Krupnov 1960).

Despite the exceptional number of graves and the long-lasting tradition of Soviet and foreign research, some problems remain regarding the historical interpretation of this material. Archaeological research has particularly been dominated by chronological and spatial discussions (Kossack 1983; Kozenkova 1990; Krupnov 1960, 1962). Differences in spatial distribution of items and in burial customs have been used for marking different 'cultures' or subgroups within such 'cultures' (Krupnov 1962). Interpreted against the historical background (Herodotus, Book IV), they have been seen in the light of ethnic movements such as the Scythic expansion during the 8th century. Other questions, e.g. on social organisation and the mode of production and exchange have never been the focus of research although they have been discussed before (Iessen 1941; Černych 1992: 275-295).

Reconstructing the way of social communication of the Late Bronze Age/Early Iron Age tribes, as expressed in the wealth of the burial goods, the mode of building such tombs and the exchange of prestige items, may be one way of answering such questions. Spatial distribution of graves, different degrees of wealth and energy expenditure for the funeral of the individual person as well as differences in grave good types, quality and number usually constitute the set of criteria which is used by archaeologists to examine the way of social communication during the funeral act,

reflecting the main principles of social structuration of the burying community (Bietti-Sestrieri 1992; Saxe 1970; for critique of such analogies see Härke 1993; Pader 1982; Steuer 1982). The Seržen'-Jurt cemetery which is one of the largest and best published graveyards of the north Caucasian Koban culture forms an excellent case to study such patterns. Statistical methods can be used to identify structures as statistical patterns in the archaeological record. Multivariate analyses could be an instrument giving multicausal explanation for such patterns (Bietti-Sestrieri 1992; Müller 1994).

2   The cemetery of Seržen'-Jurt (Čečeno-Ingušetia) as an example for analysing ritual behaviour in the late Bronze/Early Iron Age of NE-Caucasia

The cemetery of Seržen'-Jurt is situated at the edge of the northeastern Caucasian mountains where a small river leaves the hilly zones of these mountains (fig. 1). It is closely connected with a nearby settlement which covers about 0.5 ha. The settlement with approximately 10 houses could have existed for 550 years — as indicated by several radiocarbon dates covering the period from 1350 to 800 BC (Kozenkova 1992: 67). The graveyard can be dated to the Late Bronze Age, the end of its use to the beginning of the Early Iron Age. This is some time before the end of the 9th century BC. Obviously burials had taken place for about 300 years (Kozenkova 1992: 73).

The cemetery extends over an area of 2000 sq m. It was excavated during the late sixties and early seventies and published by V. Kozenkova (1992). It contains about 100 graves, inhumations in rectangular tombs with flexed bodies, orientated mostly towards the NE. The burial equipment is quite large and usually consists of bronze or iron items — adornment, weapons, a few tools — and large quantities of ceramic vessels. Eleven graves are additionally equipped with horse offerings, similar to those which have been reported from antiquity (Herodotus, Book IV: 70) to the beginning of the 20th century by ethnographic researchers (Nioradze 1931). Spatial structurations of the cemetery can be assumed to be in six separate groups of graves, two of which are quite large (fig. 2).

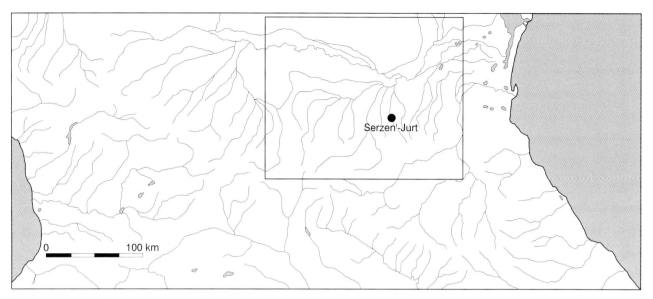

Figure 1. Location of Seržen'-Jurt.

Although no anthropological investigation of the skeletal remains has been carried out, the difference of gender seems quite clear from the material equipment of the inhumations. From the size of the skeletal remains it also has been possible to determine several burials of children or juveniles (Kozenkova 1992: 11-14). Following this distinction a representative part of the Seržen'-Jurt population is supposed to be buried here. However, attention must be drawn to the relations of the settlement and graveyard. If the assumption is correct that 10 households, i.e. families, had occupied the settlement for over 500 years, the 100 graves of the cemetery could not represent the whole of the ancient population. As there are no other burial places known from the surrounding area with the exception of some burials in pits within the settlement itself, it can be supposed that special criteria, e.g. social status or religious motives, are responsible for the deposition of only some individuals in the burial ground.

2.1   SERIATION AND CORRESPONDENCE ANALYSIS OF
        STYLISTIC TYPES AS A PROPOSED CHRONOLOGICAL
        BACKGROUND
The deposited objects in the graves can be divided into three functional classes. These classes concern the personal adornment in its function as funerary costume, weapons and tools as technical equipment, ceramic sets and jewellery as goods from 'everyday life' (Reinhold 1995).

The statistical basis for analysing the grave goods from the Seržen'-Jurt cemetery are 1280 objects which can be assigned to 140 stylistic types. The classification of the objects follows the method described by Hodson (1990) for the classification of the Hallstatt cemetery. For seriation and correspondence analysis the Bonn Archaeological Statistic Program (BASP) has been used (Herzog/Scollar 1987). In addition, the significance of the results has been checked by using the statistical tests of the SPSS package.

Following the model described by Djinjan (1985) the parabolic structure of the correspondence analysis has been used to suppose normally distributed data which could be correlated with a continuous process of production and/or deposition of items (Bakker 1994). Non-parabolic geometric structures could point to non-linear processes of production/ deposition (Djinjan 1985), e.g. special ritual needs for a proper burial which corresponds to the culturally determined ideology of the burying community.

Non-linear structures as mentioned above are the visible results of typological seriation of the funeral goods. The correspondence analysis shows the typological proximity of the inventories (fig. 3). It is dominated by two types of ceramic vessels which occur in large quantities in 62% of the graves in combination and in another 12% of the burials as single pottery forms. Excluding these types the structure is dominated by the distance of the few Early Iron Age inventories and the fission of the armed and non-armed Late Bronze Age burials (fig. 4). The distinction of gender represented in armed males and non-armed females and males is obviously shown at this level, apart from the general differentiation of the Late Bronze and Early Iron Age.

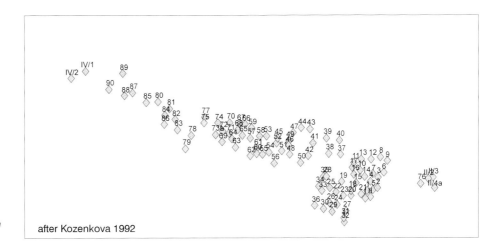

Figure 2. Spatial distribution of the Seržen'-Jurt cemetry.

after Kozenkova 1992

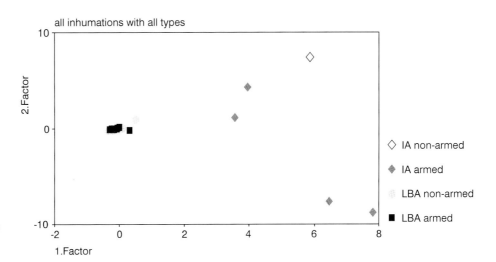

Figure 3. Correspondence analysis Seržen'-Jurt. All inhumations with all types.

all inhumations with all types

◇ IA non-armed
◆ IA armed
⬦ LBA non-armed
■ LBA armed

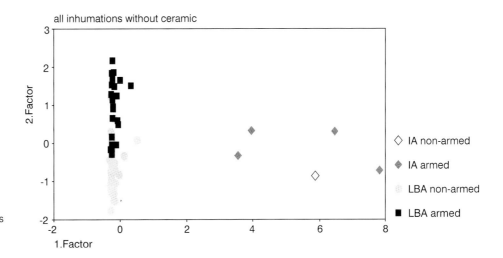

Figure 4. Correspondence analysis Seržen'-Jurt. All inhumations without ceramics.

all inhumations without ceramic

◇ IA non-armed
◆ IA armed
⬦ LBA non-armed
■ LBA armed

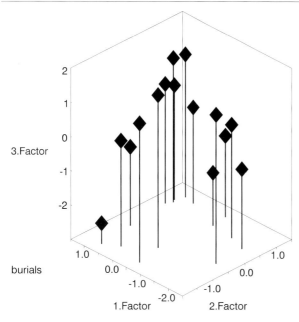

Figure 5. Seržen'-Jurt. LBA armed inhumations without common types.

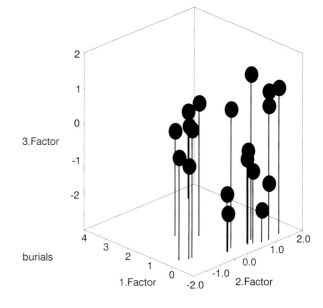

Figure 6. Seržen'-Jurt. LBA non-armed inhumations without common types.

In separate seriations both armed and non-armed Late Bronze Age data are still dominated by types occurring in more than 25% of the inventories. Just by reducing the database once more a parabolic structure is obtained which can be interpreted as a sign of continuous, normally distributed production/deposition (figs 5, 6).

Summarising this evidence it can be pointed out that the complete database of the Late Bronze Age burials is dominated by very frequent types occurring in nearly all graves which compel to reduce the database by 95% of the ceramic vessels and by 53% of the metal items to receive a statistical result which can be interpreted in terms of a chronological order. However 21% of the grave goods are single types and therefore excluded. At this point of the analyses it becomes clear that several components underlie the assemblages of the inventories of which chronology is just one.

2.2 FUNCTIONAL CLASSES AS STRUCTURATION CRITERIA

The second level of classification focuses on the functional classes. By using hierarchical cluster analysis, the differentiation between armed and non-armed males again becomes quite clear. In addition several other significant correlations are visible which can be identified by using a simple table of clusters of different costume groups or clusters of weapons. Six main costume groups can be identified, composed of bracelets and head-dresses (fig. 7).

Five of these are correlated with the non-armed, obviously female group of inventories and one group is correlated with armed individuals but occurs also without arms. They are supposed to represent male individuals. Compared with the typological database the main components of these costume groups are identical to the excluded types in the seriation set.

In addition to the costume groups seven combinations of arms can be identified. They consist of different types of weapons — lance, axe or daggers — in combinations of three, two or one types. The complete set of arms correlates also with the horse burials and marks the outstanding male burials. When these groups are mapped into the typological correspondence analysis the sets with two or more arms cluster in one part. The less wealthy sets, i.e. the ones with just one weapon cluster in another (fig. 8). An explanation of this division is provided by chronology but also by social differences in the status of the buried men.

2.3 SOCIAL DIFFERENTIATION BY WEALTH

Classification of wealth is generally influenced by subjective criteria such as the number of items, presence of exotic goods, gold or other (for a critique see Eggert 1991). To get a more objective indication of the individual wealth of the single burials compared with the other graves, it will be necessary to construct an independent value by statistical means (Jorgenson 1990; Müller 1994). As basic data for this calculation were used the number of items, the plurality

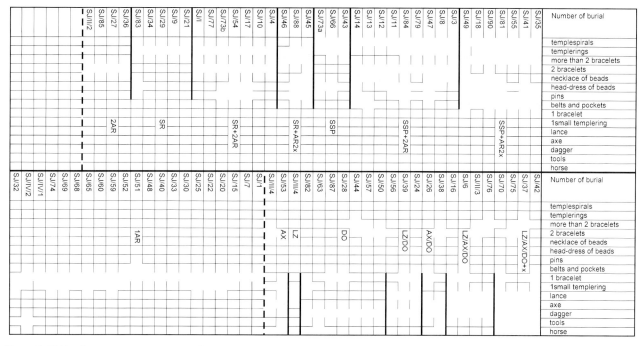

Figure 7. Table of graves versus grave goods.

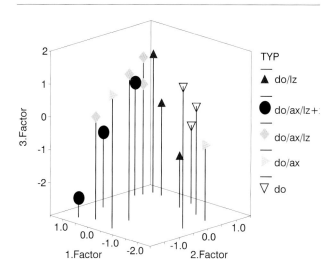

Figure 8. Seržen'-Jurt. LBA armed inhumations with different equipment.

of functional classes, the weight of metal, the plurality of material used, the scarcity of material and the expenditure of energy required for the building of the tomb (quantity of excavation calculated with 0,3 m³/person/h (Müller 1991)). All values were calculated in percentages.

Separating the different clusters of gender, several remarks can be made in relation to the functional groups mentioned. The differences between rich and poor graves do not coincide with the differences of gender. The average wealth of both genders is nearly the same (but note that individual types have not been weighted). Differentiation takes place within the gender group and can be related to the different functional clusters, costume groups for females and combinations of arms for males.

A second aspect applies to the kinds of grave goods. Male individuals obviously had been equipped with more ceramic vessels than females. The female graves contain more bronzes on average, in number as well as in weight, especially of the individuals with large temple finery (fig. 9). Moreover the distances between outstanding and poor graves is even larger within the male group of graves. The lowest social index is closely connected with the unarmed males, i.e. the group with just one bracelet. The same applies to the female group with temple rings and two bracelets and those with temple spirals and two bracelets. Both cluster with the next higher levels of wealth (fig. 9). The wealthiest graves are those of the well-equipped males and the females with large temple spirals and sets of bracelets. It is noteworthy that the best armed males with horse burials do not belong to the richest group of graves.

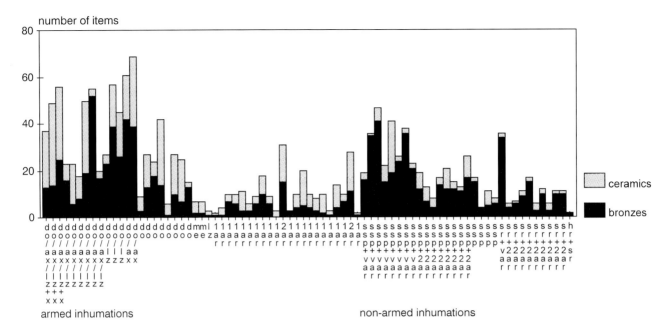

Figure 9. Seržen'-Jurt. Armed inhumations and non-armed inhumations.

3   Conclusion

The interpretation of the inventories at Seržen'-Jurt in terms of a social communication process seems to be quite clear. Without anthropological investigation one cannot be sure of gender and age of the deceased but the general differentiation into armed male and non-armed female individuals is supported by other cemetery material of the Koban area which were examined anthropologically
(see e.g. Krupnov 1960: 404-420). The interpretation of the costume and weapon groups determined e.g. by age is more difficult. If one regards the temple spirals and the number of bracelets or the number of arms as a sign of age, the determination of the Seržen'-Jurt society by gender and age classes would be a logical conclusion. The different stages of wealth and the other socially determined groups follow a normal distribution by number as well as by distribution in the cemetery. With one exception, all grave groups contain more or less the same number of individuals in costume or armament groups. The exception is the smallest unit of the cemetery with just four graves (fig. 2). Three of these are very wealthy male burials with horses. Except for this outstanding group the rest of the burials, though well equipped, are

nearly on the same level of energy expenditure for their burial.

The longlasting use of several types of costumes, the uniformity of the costumes and their avoidance of individuality corresponds with the use of costumes in recent societies (Hirschberg 1988: 425). Costumes are also reported to be one of the most prominent signs of social differentiation and age groups (Müller 1994; Pader 1982; for a sociological background see Bourdieu 1976; Elias 1976).

Most notable is that the types used to signify social categories — bracelets, ceramics and other — and the composition of the inventories by socially determined patterns dominate over the chronological development of the whole Late Bronze Age sequence. Things did not change very much for more than 250-300 years and when they did change it was significant (Reinhold 1995). The traditional customs handling deceased people counteract the changes in production over this time span. The ritual behaviour which was obviously based on a fixed frame of ritual acts including the burial in traditional costumes, with traditional armament and fixed sets of ceramic vessels, must be taken into account in the interpretation of Late Bronze Age sites in this area in general.

bibliography

Černych, E.N.   1992   *Ancient metallurgy in the USSR*. Cambridge: Cambridge University Press.

Bakker, J.A.   1994   Bemerkungen zu Datierungsmethoden: 14C-Methode, Dendrochronologie, Seriation und
                                       Typologie. In: *Beiträge zur frühneolithischen Trichterbecherkultur im westlichen Ostsee-
                                       gebiet*. 1. Internat. Trichterbechersymposium in Schleswig, Marz 1985. 1. Untersuchungen
                                       und Materialien zur Steinzeit in Schleswig-Holstein, 51-69.

Bietti-Sestrieri, A.M.   1992   *The Iron Age community of Osteria dell'Osa. A study of socio-political development in
                                       central Tyrrenian Italy.* Cambridge: Cambridge University Press.

Bourdieu, P.   1976   *Entwurf einer Theorie der Praxis*. Frankfurt a. Main: Suhrkamp.

Djinjan, F.   1985   Seriation and toposeriation by correspondence analysis. In: A. Voorrips/S.H. Loving
                                       (eds), To Pattern the Past, *PACT* 11, 119-135.

Eggert, M.K.H.   1991   Prestigegüter und Sozialstruktur in der Späthallstattzeit: Eine kulturanthropologische
                                       Perspektive, *Saeculum* 42, 1-28.

Elias, N.   1976   Über den Prozeß der Zivilisation. Soziogenetische und psychogenetische Untersuchungen.
                                       Bd. I, *Wandlung des Verhaltens in den weltlichen Oberschichten des Abendlandes*. Bd.II.
                                       18. Aufl. (1. Aufl 1976), Frankfurt a. Main: Suhrkamp.

Härke, H.   1993   Intentionale und Funktionale Daten. Ein Beitrag zur Theorie und Methodik der Gröber-
                                       archäologie, *Arch. Korrbl.* 23 (3), 141-146.

Herzog, I.   1987   Ein 'Werkzeugkasten' für Seriation und Clusteranalyse, *Arch. Korrbl.* 17, 273-279.
   I. Scollar

Hirschberg, W. (ed.)   1988   *Neues Wörterbuch der Völkerkunde*. Berlin: D. Reimer Verlag.

Hodson, F.   1990   *Hallstatt. The Ramsauer graves. Quantification and analysis*. Bonn: Habelt.

Iessen, A.A.   1951   Prikubanskij očag metallurgii i metalloobrabotki v konece medno-bronzogo veka. In:
                                       E.I. Krupnov (ed.), *Materialyi i issledovanija po archeologii Severnogo Kavkaza*. MIA
                                       23. Moskau, Leningrad: Izdatel'stvo Akademii Nauk.

Ihm, P.   1983   Korrespondenzanalyse und Seriation, *Arch. Inform.* 6 (1), 8-21.

Jorgenson, L.   1990   *Baekegard and Glasergard. Two cemeteries from the Late Iron Age on Bornholm.*
                                       Kopenhagen: Akademisk Forlag Universitetsforlag i Kobenhaven.

Kossack, G.   1983   Tli 85. Bemerkungen zum Beginn des skythenzeitlichen Formenkreises im Kaukasus,
                                       Beitr. Allg. Vergl. Arch. 5, 89-186.

Kozenkova, V.I.   1977   Kobanskaja kul'tura. Vostočnyi variant, *Arch. SSSR. Svod V* 2, 5. Moskau: Izdatel'stvo
                                       Nauk.

                             1990   Chronologija Kobanskoj kul'turoj: dostiženja, opyt utočenija, nerešennye problemy, *Sov.
                                       Arch. 1990* (3), 64-92.

                             1992   *Seržen'-Jurt. Ein Friedhof der späten Bronze- und frühen Eisenzeit im Nordostkaukasus.*
                                       Mat. zur Allg. Vergl. Arch. Bd. 48. Mainz: Phillip von Zabern.

Krupnov, E.I.   1960   *Drevnjaja istorija Severnogo Kavkaz*. Moskau: Izdatel'stvo Akademii Nauk.

                       1962   *A propos de la chronologie de l'age du fer au Caucase*. VI Congr. Int. Science. Préhis-
                                toriques et Protohistoriques, Moskau. Sek. Va, 3-13. Moskau: Izdatel'stvo Akademii
                                Nauk.

Müller, J.   1991   Arbeitsleistung und gesellschaftliche Leistung bei Megalithgräbern. Das Fallbeispiel
                                Orkney. *Acta Prähist. et Arch.* 22, 9-35.

                       1994   Zur sozialen Gliederung der Nachbestattungs-gemeinschaft vom Magdalenenberg bei
                                Villingen. *Prähist. Zeitschr.* 2, 175-221.

Nioradze, G.   1931   *Begräbnis und Totenkultus bei den Chewssuren*. Stuttgart: Strecker und Schröder.

Pader, E.J.   1982   *Symbolism, social relations and the interpretation of mortuary remains*. BAR Inter-
                                national Series 130. Oxford: British Archaeological Reports.

Reinhold, S.   1995   *Chronologische und sozialgeschichtliche Untersuchungen an ausgewählten Gräberfeldern
                                der späten Bronze- und frühen Eisenzeit im Nordostkaukasus ('Koban-Kultur')*. MA thesis
                                FU Berlin.

Saxe, A.A.   1970   *Social Dimensions of Mortuary Practices*. PhD dissertation. University of Michigan.

Steuer, H.   1982   *Frühgeschichtliche Sozialstrukturen in Mitteleuropa. Eine Analyse der Auswertungs-
                                methoden des archäologischen Quellenmaterials*. Göttingen: Vandenhoek and Ruprecht.

Virchow, R.   1881   *Das Gräberfeld von Koban im Lande der Osseten, Kaukasus. Eine vergleichend-
                                archäologische Studie*. Berlin: Asher and Co.

Sabine Reinhold
Seminar für Ur- und Frühgeschichte
Freie Universität Berlin
Altensteinstr. 15
14195 Berlin
Germany

L. García Sanjuán
J. Rodríguez López

Predicting the ritual? A suggested solution in archaeological forecasting through qualitative response models[1]

Hamlet	*A man may fish with the worm that hath eat of a king, and eat of the fish that hath fed of that worm...*
King	*What dost thou mean by this?*
Hamlet	*Nothing, but to show you how a king may go a progress through the guts of a beggar.*

1   Introduction

The analysis of mortuary practices is critical in the archaeological interpretation of the structure of social relations of production of prehistoric communities. Patterns of association between the different dimensions of the funerary ritual (grave goods, sex and age categories of the deceased, burial structure and burial position) are one of the pillars of a good part of current interpretation of the evolution of social structures in European Prehistory.

Quantitative methods have largely contributed to the interpretation of the funerary record in terms of social structure; significance tests, cluster analysis and multivariate techniques are commonly used in order to test the existence of different funerary categories and infer their social correlates. This paper intends to discuss further the question of how quantitative techniques can improve the archaeological knowledge of past social structures through the analysis of the funerary record. The *statistical models* discussed here fall into the group of Qualititative Response Models (henceforth called QRMs), which have mainly been studied by biometricians and econometricians but apparently have received little attention from archaeologists. The *archaeological problem* that provides the empirical background for testing the model is the funerary record of the southwestern Iberian Peninsula Bronze Age (*c.* 1700-1100 BC). The development of social complexity in the Early and Middle phases of Bronze Age in SW Iberia remains poorly understood; in this context, it seems clear that, in comparison with recent trends prevailing in the study of the synchronic southeastern (Argaric) Bronze Age, little or no debate has taken place in the past on the theoretical and methodological basis of the empirical evidence.

2   The problem

Common patterns shared by a set of necropoleis located in southern Portugal (Algarve and Alentejo) and western

Andalucia, suggest that from *c.* 1700 BC onwards, a transition takes place from a communal-based structure of social relations of production to a ranked social structure where individual roles and leadership are more clearly defined in the mortuary ritual.

On the one hand, in some necropoleis the pre-eminence of specific individuals is underlined by means of the construction of a stone ring and *tumulus* structure around and over the burial. Thus, three basic categories of tombs are visible in the SW Bronze Age in terms of architectural features, namely central burials with a complete stone ring and *tumulus* (type A), peripheral burials with a tangent stone ring and *tumulus* (type B), and peripheral burials with no stone ring and *tumulus* (type C). In necropoleis such as Atalaia (Schubart 1975), Provença (Farinha/Tavares 1974) or Alfarrobeira (Varela 1994) all three types are found, while in the vast majority of necropoleis so far explored, only burials of type C have been identified (Amo 1975; Schubart 1975).

On the other hand, from *c.* 1700 BC on, prestige items such as bronze halberds, swords, daggers and ornaments given as grave goods, as well as engraved stones depicting metal weapons (appearing only in some tombs of southern Portugal), suggest the growing military character of social leadership. The military character of grave goods during this period, however, seems sharply limited if compared to the intensity and extent of weapon-oriented grave goods in other areas of Iberia or Europe. The fact that the amount of metal prestige items found in the funerary contexts of SW Iberia is very low, is perfectly coincident with evidence drawn from settlements suggesting that copper mining and metalworking in the southwest pyritic belt was rather limited between *c.* 1700 and 1100 BC (see for example Blanco/Rothemberg 1981; Hurtado/García 1994; Monge Soares *et al.* 1994)

Therefore, if compared with the Middle and Late Copper Ages, the initial stages of the Bronze Age in SW Iberia seem to involve an increase in internal ranking, different evidence suggests, however, that this increase in social inequality should not be regarded as a transition to a stratified model of society.[2] First, the statistical distribution of prestige items across the burial categories does not assume a stratified pattern; second, unlike in Argaric societies, infant burials are not provided with prestige items, which suggests that social roles are still acquired and not ascribed by birth (García 1992, 1994); third, the fact that many tombs with engraved *stelae* depicting weapons were not supplied with *real* weapons suggests that the leadership is more founded on an ideological than on a material basis — weapons as symbols rather than as a means of coercion supporting a stratified pattern of access to subsistence resources (Barceló 1991).

Hence, if the presence or absence of metal prestige items (weapons and ornaments) in burials is a key indicator in the inference of social status in archaeology, the obvious relevant question arising would be the following: to what extent would it be possible to *predict* the presence or absence of metal items in the tombs *in terms of probability*, having previously achieved some prior knowledge about the trends underlying a given set of data? In other words, under what conditions (i.e. patterns of association between variables) is the probability higher of a metal artefact being found in a specific empirical context?

A previous general approach based on quantitative methods conventionally used in archaeology (Aldenderfer 1987; Carr 1989; Shennan 1988) suggested the existence of some interesting patterns affecting metal artefacts distribution within the funerary record of the SW Iberian Bronze Age.[3] After a cluster analysis based on the Group Average method, three categories (rich, semi-rich and poor necropoleis) were delimited according to the mean values observed for the frequency of different artefact types — not only bronze items — in necropoleis (fig. 1A). Also, a number of categories was defined on the basis of the mean frequency of a series of architectural attributes (fig. 1B). No classes were defined *within* the necropoleis in terms of artefact distributions, not even where there were different architectural types present (scarcity seems to be shared by almost all members of the communities as far as the funerary ritual was concerned).

The three basic levels of artefactual wealth defined were then used as a basis to test the association between funerary patterns and environmental factors such as soil type or land agricultural capability. A correspondence analysis suggested that a general positive association existed between the potential agricultural capability and the cemeteries where metal artefacts are more frequent (fig. 2). This might suggest that the use of costly metal status symbols depended on the general capacity for surplus production within the community — see two spatial (geographical) views of the bronze items frequencies in figure 3. Yet, a much more interesting — predictive — approach to this problem can be achieved by means of the QRMs described below.

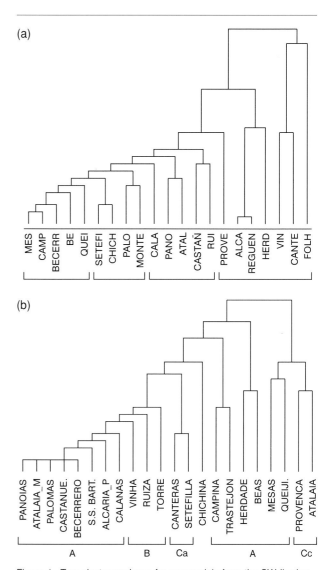

Figure 1. Two cluster analyses for necropoleis from the SW Iberian Bronze Age.

3 The model (the suggested solution)

3.1 WHY QRM?

Prior to the development of a rather tedious algebra, a justification should be given about why QRMs have been chosen to examine the archaeological phenomenon described above. This might be achieved by proceeding along two lines of reasoning: one theoretical, since the referents pointed out by the theory must be taken into account; and another technical, since this type of model is regarded here as a potentially valuable tool to be applied in archaeological analysis.

Regarding the theoretical aspect, a brief description of how these models became useful in other Social Sciences can be of help. The use of QRMs was extended in the

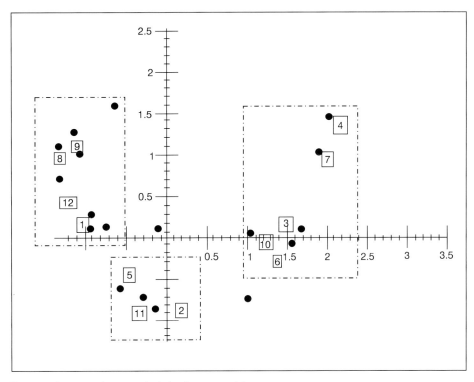

Figure 2. Correspondence analysis for the necropoleis.

sixties by biometricians, who faced the problem of making predictions about some events where the observed values had a discrete form, (i.e., presence/absence of an attribute or, yes = true, no = false). One model, which became very popular in Biology, was that where QRMs were used to predict the effectiveness of an insecticide: a QRM could explain in terms of probabilities whether an insect would remain alive (that is, yes = true = 1), or would die after having been exposed to a given dosage of insecticide (independent/causal variable). Bypassing the evident lethal aspects of the model this example suffices to compare the applicability of these models in Natural and Social Sciences. In an excellent survey, Amemiya (1981) suggested that the QRMs could be used to explain the behaviour of a utility-profit maximizing rational economic agent. For instance, when one has to model the problem faced by a householder of whether to buy or not to buy a car, and to explain this decision with the level of income, taxes, availability of other transport means, … the final choice relies upon a utility maximizing consumer, conditioned by a budgetary and a time restriction. An insect does not enjoy the possibility of choosing to be or not to be. That may be one of the basic differences of the meaning of these models in the Natural and Social Sciences: the nature of the dynamics of the variables involved in a theory.

Amemiya's survey also provides a sample of articles that could surprise a reader not familiar with these issues, since applications are quoted from labour markets, unionized workers, and consumption of non-durables, to criminology, efficiency of educational programs, etc.[4]

Finally, with reference to the technical aspect (*why* and *how* these models could be applied in archaeology) previously mentioned, QRMs provide an elegant tool for solving an elementary problem in archaeological multivariate analysis:

a. It is known that many of the data sets used in archaeological analysis are coded in a discrete form; for instance, if the value of the *aggregate production* cannot be measured through the archaeological record — as Econometrics is supposed to be able to do for modern and present records — the only feasible approach to the construction of a *Bronze Age econometric model* would be a discrete form index (proxy variables) compressing variables referring to different levels of production (for example, metal prestige items).

b. The former aspect would not be a technical-statistical problem at all whenever variables are used as causal regressors in the multivariate analysis. However, if predictions are intended to be over a discrete form

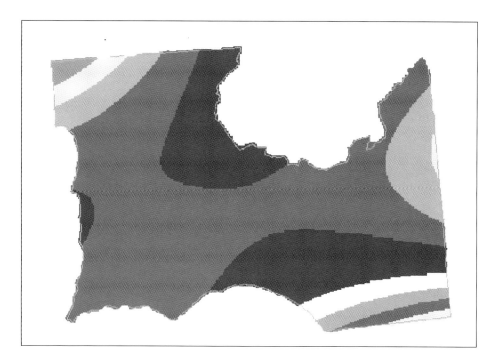

Figure 3A. Surface trend map.

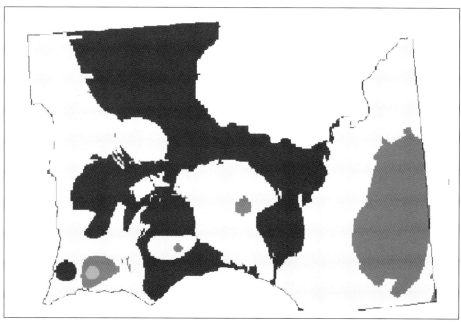

Figure 3B. Interpolation map.

variable, the traditional least square estimation fails to give an answer. For example, a variable reflecting a structure of true or false, (and then, 1 or 0, respectively), cannot be used as dependent variable in a linear model estimated by least squares as will become clear below.

In our opinion, QRMs can easily overcome this problem, improving the efficiency of data analysis and, therefore, hypothesis testing. Thus, an attempt is made to obtain a prediction about a discrete dependent variable (M1-M2) by using a QRM against the dataset mentioned above.

3.2   MATHEMATICAL SET-UP OF THE MODEL

Let us think of a discrete variable m (say $m = presence\ of$ *metal elements in a burial*), showing a dichotomous form 0 or 1, ($m \in \{0,\ 1\}$), that is a boolean structure, this means that m adopts value 0 when a certain property is absent (metal element not found in the archaeological record), and, consequently, value 1 when the property is present. Furthermore, this variable is stochastically distributed according to a discrete Bernouilli model with probability p, that is:

$$m \sim B(p)_{m=0,1} = p^m(1-p)^{1-m}$$
$$E(m) = p = P(m=1) \qquad (1)$$
$$Var(m) = p\,(1-p)$$

where $E(.)$ denotes the expected operator, $P(.)$ stands for probability, and $Var(.)$ is the variance. Since a Bernouilli model is regular, one can use the statistic $\Sigma x_i \,/\, n,\ (i=1,...,n)$, that is the sample arithmetic mean, as an efficient estimator for p.

Assume now that we have to relate this variable to a set of k independent variables, X. Suppose further that we have been asked whether this variable will adopt value 1 under certain conditions X_i, that is, forecasting whether the property will be present. A first answer could be given using a simple linear (probability) model of the form:

$$m = \alpha + \beta'X + u \qquad (2)$$
$$E(u) = 0 \Rightarrow E(m) = P(m=1) = \hat{\alpha} + \hat{\beta}'X$$

where u is the error term. Hence, one can use the classical least square method to estimate the set of k+1 unknown parameters involved in the equation (2), and then use the model to set a prediction. Note that now the predicted values of m will not necessarily be 0 or 1, but rather will be in the interval (0, 1). Next, we would interpret these predicted values in terms of probability.

However, this method involves serious limitations since it produces several problems, namely:

1. *A heteroscedasticity problem*, since it can be proved that the error term variance is equal to

$$Var(u) = p(1-p) = E(m_i)\,[1-E(m_i)] =$$
$$[\hat{\alpha} + \hat{\beta}'X]\,[1 - \hat{\alpha} - \hat{\beta}'X] = Var(m)$$

and, hence, the ordinary least squares estimators from equation (2) are inefficient. A weighted least square procedure is then needed. Goldberger (1964) proposes to estimate $m=\alpha+\beta'X + u$ by least squares, then compute a weight of the form

$$\hat{w}_i = \sqrt{\hat{m}_i(1-\hat{m}_i)}$$

and finally regress $[m_i/w_i]$ on $[x_i/w_i]$. However, as has been noted by other authors such as Maddala (1989), the product $m_i(1-m_i)$ in the root, can be negative, and hence the operativeness of this weighted procedure is invalidated .

2. *Predictions may still fall outside the [0, 1] interval*, and, consequently, the outcome cannot be interpreted in terms of probability:

$$\hat{m} = \hat{\alpha} + \hat{\beta} = E(m|z = \alpha + \beta'X) = P(m = 1|z = \hat{\alpha} + \hat{\beta}'X)$$

3. *The distribution of the error term is not normal*, (Maddala 198: 16-18), implying that the classical hypothesis tests, where construction relies on the assumption of normality of the error term, are no longer valid, unless we also assume that the explicative variables have a multivariate normal distribution. This suggests that the problem should be modelled using a non linear instead of a linear model.

What is the solution? In the remaining part of this section some basic ideas were borrowed from the literature on QRMs in order to provide an answer. In section IV a case is examined where the dependent variable, m, is a dummy variable taking the value 1 when a metal element has been found inside an individual burial, and 0 otherwise. A set of variables serves to explain the presence/absence of such elements: a discrete index for agricultural capability of the land where the necropolis is located, the volume of the tomb, and some dummy discrete variables (namely, a dummy for ceramic typology, and other dummies indicating the presence/absence of other funerary items near the burial). Thus, prediction about m is interpreted as the propensity of a burial to contain a metal element (hence the *metal detector*). Two models, PROBIT and LOGIT, are an appealing suggestion to the problems not solved by the linear probability model aforementioned. The basic difference between PROBIT and LOGIT relies on the assumption made about the stochastic distribution of the error term u in equation (2) as will be seen below.

Let $m*$ be some continuous but *latent* variable. We have just said that this variable is to be interpreted as the 'propensity of a burial to be accompanied by a metal item'. But, instead, we observe a discrete dummy variable m according to

$$m = \begin{pmatrix} 1 & if\ m* > \psi \\ 0 & if\ m* < \psi \end{pmatrix}$$

where ψ is a certain threshold, above which one can say that there is a metal element, $m=1$. This concept of a threshold is relevant when interpreting the results as probabilities. Imagine, for instance, that the variable whose realizations we are observing is the score record of a class of students, and we have classified this into two categories: *passed*, whenever the student has been scored *at least with a five over ten*, and *failed* otherwise. In the first case the variable would be valued as 1, and 0 for the second one. In this example the threshold ψ would be equal to 5. Nevertheless, and without loss of generality, let us assume that $\psi = 0$. The model becomes as

$$m* = \alpha + \beta'X + u$$

And the probability of a metal element is

$$P(m=1) = P(m^* > \psi = 0) = P(\alpha + \beta'X + u > \psi = 0)$$
$$= P[u > \psi - (\alpha + \beta'X)]$$ (3)
$$= 1 - F[(\psi - (\alpha + \beta'X)] = 1 - F[-(\alpha + \beta'X)]$$

where $F(.)$ is the cumulative distribution of the error term u.

Once it is assumed that this cumulative distribution is symmetrical, specification (3) becomes clearer since we can write that $F(-Z) = -F(Z)$ and therefore it can be written that $P(m=1) = 1-F(-(\alpha + \beta'X))= F(\alpha + \beta'X)$. Recall that, through specification (1), the variable m_i , presence of metal elements, follows a Bernouilli model with probability p, $m_i\sim B(p)$. It is important to note that the present model is intended to be based on the fact that the realizations m_i are independent from burial to burial, otherwise the mathematical set up would be much more complicated. Thus, let us assume that the different realizations m_i's are independent of each other. Consequently, the likelihood function can be written as

$$\mathcal{L} = \prod_{m_i=1} P(m_i=1) \prod_{m_i=0} Pm_i=0) = \prod_{m_i=1} P(m_i=1) \prod_{m_i=0} [1 - P(m_i=1)]$$

Finally, the difference between PROBIT and LOGIT models relies upon a different cumulative distribution of the error term u. If the cumulative distribution is normal, taking the form:

$$F(\alpha + \beta X) = P(m=1 \mid \alpha + \beta X) = \int_{-\infty}^{m^* = \alpha + \beta X} \frac{1}{\sqrt{2\pi}} e^{-\frac{u^2}{2}} du$$

this is just the PROBIT, or normit, specification. While the LOGIT model is set when the error term distribution follows the next logistic distribution, that is:

$$P(m=1 \mid \alpha + \beta X) = F(\alpha + \beta X) = \frac{e^{\alpha + \beta X}}{1 + e^{\alpha + \beta X}}$$

Note that both distributions are bounded by 0 and 1. The normal distribution has a variance equal to 1 (see that it has been normalized, so $\sigma^2=1$), and the logistic distribution variance is equal to $\pi^2/3 = 3.2898$. Using these properties, one can approximate the estimated regressors of both distributions by multiplying the β's estimates obtained from the PROBIT distribution by $\pi/\sqrt{3} = 1.8138$. Amemiya (1981) proposes to multiply it by 1.6, since he finds that, by trial and error, this value provides a better fit to the data.

Due to the proposals of the present paper, we will not further discuss the point of how to choose one or the other model, since the exercise we are to develop next does not involve such a problem. As a reference, we will quote the work of Chambers and Cox (1967) where a hypothesis test is proposed for distinguishing the correct model.

4 The test (the metal detector)
4.1 VARIABLES AND DATA

A sample of 144 tombs from 19 SW Iberian Bronze Age necropoleis has been selected for this study (fig. 4A, the original data are available via the CAA World Wide Web server (http://caa.soton.ac.uk/caa/CAA95/Garcia/)). All tombs that were considered seriously altered by the excavators have been excluded altogether, so that all the information processed in the following analyses has been recorded from unaltered contexts. The total amount of artefacts found in these 144 tombs is: 23 metal artefacts, 74 pots, 5 lithic artefacts and 3 necklace beads (fig. 4B)

The dependent variable (presence/absence of metal artefacts) has been divided into two main groups: ornaments (rings, armrings or diadems) and weapons (halberds, daggers or swords), that is to say highly ideological prestige items (M1), on the one hand, and arrow points and pointed tools, less ideological items (M2), on the other hand.

Four main axes of variability are taken into account as potentially explicative of the presence/absence of metal items (dependent variable), namely size and structure of the burial, category of the deceased, other (non-metal) grave goods and soil attributes. These four axes of variability contain 10 variables that are regarded as independent across the study:

Two variables are regarded as representative of the general size and structure of the burial:

- Volume (VO). Continuous variable measured in cubic metres (length × width × depth)
- Ring/*tumulus* (AT). Discrete binary variable: 1 (presence) 0 (absence)

It is assumed here that both the volume of the funerary chamber and the presence/absence of a ring and tumulus provide an indication of the investment of labour made in the construction of the burial.

Another two variables account for the biological status of the deceased:

- Sex. Discrete binary variable: 1 (male) 0 (female)
- Age. Discrete binary variable: 1 (adult) 0 (infant)

Other grave goods are included in order to examine whether the presence of metal items is dependent or not on the presence of other artefactual categories:

- Pottery class 1 (CE1). Discrete binary variable: 1 (presence) 0 (absence)
- Pottery class 2 (CE2). Discrete binary variable: 1 (presence) 0 (absence)
- Lithic artefacts (LT). Discrete binary variable: 1 (presence) 0 (absence)
- Necklace beads (CU). Discrete binary variable: 1 (presence) 0 (absence)

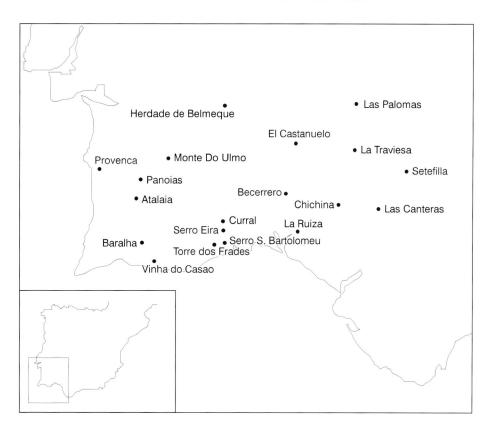

Figure 4A. 19 SW Iberian Bronze
Age necropoleis.

Finally, two variables have been used to examine the
relationship between the presence/absence of metal items
and environmental factors, under the assumption that the
production of an agricultural surplus would stimulate the
production and/or consumption of metal prestige items
among social elites. The soil attributes were measured
according to D. Rosa and J.M. Moreira (1987) for Western
Andalucia and by A.M. Soares (1984) for southern
Portugal. Land agricultural capability (CA) is a discrete
ordinal variable that provides an indication of the potential
productivity of the soil in terms of a number of geographic
parameters (see D. Rosa and J.M. Moreira (1987) and
A.M. Soares (1984) for a description). Four categories are
considered: class 0 for no agricultural capability, class 1
for moderate or poor agricultural capability — severe
limitations —, class 2 for good agricultural capability —
some limitations — and class 4 for excellent agricultural
capability — no limitations — (fig. 5A). For some tests
however, these four categories have been simplified into
two (A for classes 0 and 1 and B for classes 2 and 3) in
order to compress the variability as much as possible. The
lithology (LI) is coded as discrete nominal variable with
four classes: class 1 for shales, graywackes and sandstones,
roughly matching the SW pyritic belt, class 2 for sands,

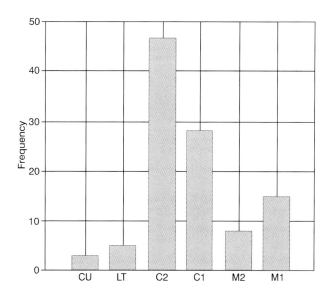

Figure 4B. Different artefact classes for the 19 SW Iberian Bronze
Age necropoleis.

rounded pebbles, poorly consolidated sandstones and clays,
class 3 for argillaceous marls and class 4 for sandy argilles,
sand and conglomerates (fig. 5B).

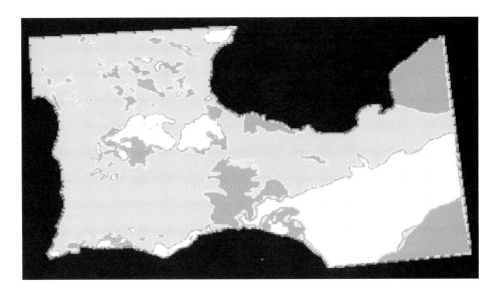

Figure 5A. SW Iberian peninsula land agricultural capability.

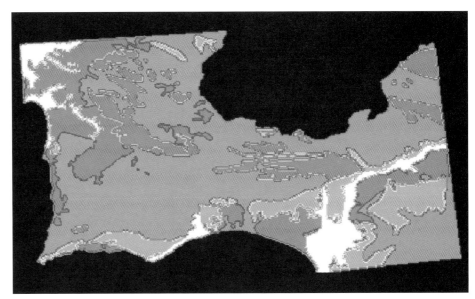

Fig. 5B. SW Iberian peninsula lithology.

4.2   TESTING

In this section, a test of the models described above is made against the data described in section 4.1. The ultimate purposes of this test are, firstly, to provide an indication of what variables explain better the presence or absence of metal in the burials (variables M1 and M2), and secondly, to give a numerical prediction of the probability of a metal artefact being found under certain conditions. As already discussed, since the dependent variable is discrete taking only two values, 1 or 0, predictions can only be given, and can only be interpreted, in terms of probabilities. Hence, if the observations are 1 or 0, and if the forecast values for the limited dependent variable falls in the interval (0,1), the traditional measures for the goodness of fit, likewise the R^2,

will no longer be useful in explaining the validity of an estimated model. That is the reason why the R^2 will be too low compared with traditionally obtained R^2s for the linear least square regression. Further discussion on the goodness of fit and its alternative measures can be found in Maddala (1983, 1989).

Table 1 expresses the results of a PROBIT regression of M1 over the set of variables (AT, CE1, CE2, LT, CU, AGR). Three estimations have been run in order to set the proper structure of the model, the (***) symbol denoting that the corresponding variable has been deleted for that particular estimation (the removal criterium has been given by the *t-ratio* content together with the coefficient associated with each variable). A first interesting result emerging from these tests is that the most significant variable among the estimations is land agricultural capability (expressed in the dummy variable AGR), which is coincident with the pattern emerging from the correspondence analysis mentioned above. The *sign* of some of the parameters is also of interest: for instance, the parameter associated with CE1, the ceramic category 1, is always negative for both model 1 and 2 (deleted for model 3 due to its low significance level expressed by the t-value). On the contrary, CE2 is always positive and significant, showing a strong positive correlation with the limited dependent variable. This could be interpreted in the sense that ceramic category 2 is associated with a higher social *status*, therefore setting a grave good pattern with metal prestige items. Variables LT and AT do not seem to help much in predicting the ritual in model 1 (t-values around 0) and they have subsequently been removed from models 2 and 3, (both in this first PROBIT and the next, as in the rest of the tables presented below).

Similar results hold for the first LOGIT estimates (table 2). Again, the most significant variable is land agricultural capability, and the same variables are deleted in the three estimated models. The sign of the parameters do not contradict the results of the PROBIT estimation.

One interesting thing to note in both table 1 and table 2 is that variable CU displays a good significance in explaining the presence/absence of metal elements. Nevertheless, when the variables AT and LT have been removed, the t-ratio for CU falls below the acceptable range (1.6 as a rule of thumb). Why? This is a problem of multicollinearity among the variables, since they are probably highly correlated. This is a perverse effect that makes it very difficult to separate the partial effect of each variable from the explained one.

Finally, note that PROBIT and LOGIT estimates can be compared by multiplying the first one by 1.813, (*verbi gratiæ*, the parameter associated with AGR in model 1 PROBIT is 1.331, multiplied by 1.813 gives 2.414, which is very similar to the LOGIT estimate of 2.289).

The fact that all the variables that have been included in these models are of discrete form, could be regarded as a source of criticism from a purely statistical point of view. Due to this limited form, the number of possible outcomes is limited to 2^K, where k is the number of variables included in the regression. Thus, for the first model where k is equal to 6, the number of possible cases that an archaeologist can face is limited to 64 (16 and 4, for models 2 and 3, respectively). This produces the problem that the prediction is again a limited discrete prediction. Furthermore, and due to the multicollinearity problem aforementioned, whenever there is a strong statistical association among the variables included in the model, the number of possible outcomes, is less than could be expected (for instance, at first glance the

data matrix indicates a relationship between variables LT and CU).

The next step will be to include the only continuous variable considered in the present paper to predict the presence/absence of metal items, namely, the log of the volume of the tomb. The results for PROBIT and LOGIT are presented in tables 3 and 4. Very similar conclusions are obtained from these new estimations. See, for instance, the low significance level of the coefficient for CU whenever variables AT and LT have been removed. It seems possible to conclude that the set of variables AT, LT, C1 and CU fail to *predict the ritual*, that is to say, fail to *predict the presence of metal prestige items*. In terms of social organisation this is a quite an interesting point, as the presence of funerary monuments (stone rings and *tumuli*) does not correlate with the presence or absence of weapons and ornaments.

Yet, a contradictory result arises since the coefficient for AGR displays the poorest significance level of the set of variables included in the last model (the t-ratio is not significant in any of the three models). In fact, the only significant variable in this case is the grave's volume (VOL). This could be explained both by the fact that VOL is the only continuous variable included in the *metal detector model*, and by a multicollinearity problem involved in the distinct partial correlations between the set of the explanatory variables. The same conclusions apply to the LOGIT estimations.

However, two more sets of partial estimations have been run in order to check the validity of the results described sofar. This has been done by estimating a new model for M1 over CA, (note that the index for land agricultural capability is now measured as an ordinal variable 0-1-2-3, and not as the dummy AGR), and another model for M1 over VOL (tables 5, 6).

The coefficients R^2s are just too low to consider any of the models as definite, the main conclusion to be drawn being that the partial t-ratio for variables CA and VOL are sufficiently significant to consider both variables as explicative for M1. Despite this low R^2, a simple forecasting exercise is carried out (as a *metal detector*), to show how this coefficient should be interpreted. To do this, the PROBIT model presented in table 5 has been chosen. Here, the only explicative variable for the presence of metal items is the discrete index for agricultural capability. Table 7 presents the probabilistic computations for the four categories:

The last two columns are very similar except for CA=1 due to the sampling, that is, the models in table 5 have been constructed from a sample of 143, of which 112 correspond to category *CA = 0*, 14 to CA = 1, 7 to CA = 2, and 10 to CA = 3. On the other hand, the limited dependent variable M1 has a value 1, presence, 8 times in the category CA = 0, none for CA = 1, 2 for CA = 2, and finally there are 4 in

Table 1. PROBIT model for M1.

	MODEL 1		MODEL 2		MODEL 3	
	Coefficient	t-Value	Coefficient	t-Value	Coefficient	t-Value
constant	-1.779	-4.942	-1.813	-6.913	-1.844	-7.371
ring/*tumulus*	-0.136	-0.347	***	***	***	***
pottery class 1	-0.195	-0.439	-0.146	-0.334	***	***
pottery class 2	0.710	2.087	0.651	2.002	0.696	2.184
lithic artefacts	-5.892	0.120	***	***	***	***
necklace beads	1.561	1.574	0.447	0.568	***	***
dummy variable	1.331	3.010	1.199	3.254	1.213	3.314

Table 2. LOGIT model for M1.

	MODEL 1		MODEL 2		MODEL 3	
	Coefficient	t-Value	Coefficient	t-Value	Coefficient	t-Value
constant	-3.075	-4.349	-3.185	-5.904	3.243	6.346
ring/*tumulus*	-0.448	-0.558	***	***	***	***
pottery class 1	-0.311	-0.358	-0.215	-0.255	***	***
pottery class 2	1.293	1.957	1.166	1.850	1.243	2.026
lithic artefacts	-13.582	-0.084	***	***	***	***
necklace bead	2.876	1.789	0.746	0.485	***	***
dummy variable	2.289	2.896	2.122	3.213	2.154	3.298

Table 3. PROBIT model for M1.

	MODEL 1		MODEL 2		MODEL 3	
	Coefficient	t-Value	Coefficient	t-Value	Coefficient	t-Value
constant	-0.716	-1.224	-0.724	-1.496	-0.862	-1.929
ring/*tumulus*	-0.188	-0.429	***	***	***	***
volume	0.873	2.588	0.922	2.769	0.864	2.722
pottery class 1	-0.445	-0.792	-0.389	-0.701	***	***
pottery class 2	0.634	1.573	0.561	1.486	0.616	1.674
lithic artefacts	-5.336	-0.106	***	***	***	***
necklace bead	1.816	1.788	0.953	1.154	0.982	1.188
dummy variable	0.571	0.994	0.421	0.850	0.390	0.790

Table 4. LOGIT model for M1.

	MODEL 1		MODEL 2		MODEL 3	
	Coefficient	t-Value	Coefficient	t-Value	Coefficient	t-Value
constant	-1.283	-1.155	-1.290	-1.394	-1.501	-1.777
ring/*tumulus*	-0.491	-0.569	***	***	***	***
volume	1.560	2.473	1.67	2.704	1.591	2.691
pottery class 1	-0.587	-0.578	-0.514	-0.508	***	***
pottery class 2	1.198	1.521	1.011	1.339	1.114	1.524
lithic artefacts	-12.633	-0.075	***	***	***	***
necklace bead	3.372	2.016	1.822	1.246	1.865	1.276
dummy variable	0.913	0.865	0.634	0.686	0.590	0.636

Table 5. PROBIT model and LOGIT model.

| | Probit model | | Logit model | |
	Coefficient	t-Value	Coefficient	t-Value
constant	-1.5306	-8.616	-2.7062	-7.288
Land agricultural capability	0.3909	2.867	0.72841	3.012
$R^2 =$		0.0777		

Table 6. PROBIT model and LOGIT model.

| | Probit model | | Logit model | |
	Coefficient	t-Value	Coefficient	t-Value
constant	-0.3555	-1.171	-0.5810	-1.148
volume	0.9921	3.586	1.8357	3.676
$R^2 =$		0.1320		

the category CA = 3. Thus, there are a total of 14 cases where M1 has taken value 1. The sample used to construct these models has been drawn from a bigger sample of 374, and the selection criteria were to choose those tombs where we could know, at least, the volume, the presence/absence of the ceramic typology, and, of course, those which had not been expoliated. 24 tombs of the 374 were of type CA = 1, and 5 of them contained a metal item. Note that none of these 5 have been included in the reduced sample of 143. However, let us have a look at what is going to happen when we remove the observations for CA = 1, and we estimate a PROBIT model:

$$M1^* = -1.4623 + 0.41287CA$$
$$(-8.248) \quad (3.057)$$

The normal probability values in table 8 have approached the observed values of the last column in table 7. Thus, this estimated probability can be considered as the marginal propensity of a determinate area to contain burials with metal elements. But, what about a prediction for CA = 1? It is easy to see that the latent variable adopts a value of M1* = -1.4623 + 0.41287 = -1.04943, and the table for the cumulative normal distribution indicates that this happens with a probability of 0.1492 (= $P(M1=1$ *conditioned to CA = 1)$). Therefore, if 24 tombs out of 374 fall in the category of *CA = 1*, the metal detector predicts the existence of about 4 metal items (that is, 0.1492 × 24 = 3.58 ≃ 4), the real number of observations being 5. The proximity between the predicted and the observed values is therefore clear (the metal detector works!).

Of course, this is only a simple example where there is only one explicative discrete variable, showing only four possible states, and, hence, implying that, again, the predictions of a discrete binomial variable are discrete as well as the observations.

Finally, note that our insistence on the significate of the R^2 coefficient stems from the fact that it cannot be interpreted in the same sense as in the traditional least square regression, since the meaning and source of the residuals are quite different. Some authors refer to this as the *R² syndrome*.

5   Conclusions

From a methodological point of view, an attempt has been made in this paper to increase the predictive capacity of archaeological reasoning through econometric experience. A case study has been chosen where some previous indications existed about the pattern of association and dependence among the relevant variables (*i.e.* that previous knowledge has served as a basis for hypothesis testing). This predictive view has been constructed on discrete variables with only two states {0,1}. Furthermore, the PROBIT and LOGIT models have allowed us to construct an innovative (predictive) view of the pattern of relationships among the variables in terms of the t-statistic (*i.e.* estimated value divided by the standard error).

On an empirical level, the presence of bronze prestige items in Bronze Age tombs is closely related to the variables VO, CE2 and CA, that is to say, to the size of the burial chamber, a set of carinated pots and the general agricultural potential of the soil where the community was settled. Alternatively, the presence of bronze items is not dependent on the variables AT, CE1, LT, CU and LI, that is to say, presence of ring/tumulus structures, a set of non-carinated pots, lithic artefacts, necklace beads and lithology class of the soil (associated with availability of mineral resources). For the sake of simplicity, and in order to keep the lenght of this article within reasonable limits, only those tests considered more relevant have been included and discussed.

Table 7. Probabilistic computations for four categories.

	$m^* = \alpha + \beta\,CA$	Normal Probability	Observed %
Land agricultural capability = 0	-1.5306	0.0629	0.0714
Land agricultural capability = 1	-1.1396	0.1272	0
Land agricultural capability = 2	-0.7486	0.2271	0.2857
Land agricultural capability = 3	-0.3576	0.3603	0.4

Table 8. Probabilistic computations for three categories.

	$m^* = \alpha + \beta\,CA$	Normal Probability
Land agricultural capability = 0	-1.4623	0.0718
Land agricultural capability = 2	-0.6366	0.2622
Land agricultural capability = 3	-0.2237	0.4115

Remark

The data in this paper were processed with the MV-ARCH (Wright 1989), Idrisi (Eastman 1990) and LIMDEP (Greene 1990) systems.

notes

1 For the original data, please refer to the CAA World Wide Web server on http://caa.soton.ac.uk/caa/CAA95/Garcia/.

2 Recent literature on the European Bronze Age displays rather diverse and contradictory applications of terms such as *stratified society*, *class society* and *state*. The term *stratified society* is used here in opposition to *ranked society,* according to the definition given by M. Fried (1967). However, and unlike Fried, we conceptualise the *stratified society* as an equivalent to *class society* and therefore to the *state* itself (Hindess/Hirst 1975).

3 Study carried out within a wider dataset of 31 necropoleis and 321 tombs (Garcia 1992) from which the sample used in this paper has been drawn.

4 It could be objected that the above mentioned survey is rather old, and that recent developments in econometrics have followed different trends. But we still are in favour of QRM since many of the areas mentioned by Amemiya in 1981 are receiving nowadays important contributions. See also Nelson (1987) for an introductory treatment on QRMs.

references

Aldenderfer, M.S. (ed.)   1987   *Quantitative Research in Archaeology.* Progress and Prospects. London: Sage Publications.

Amemiya, T.   1981   Qualitative Response Models: A Survey, *Journal of Economic Literature* 19, 1483-1536.

Amo, M.   1975   Enterramientos en cista en la provincia de Huelva. In: M. Almagro Basch (ed.), *Huelva, Prehistoria y Antiguedad*, 109-182, Madrid: Editorial Nacional.

Barcelo, J.A.   1991   *Arqueología, Lógica y Estadística. Un análisis de las estelas de la Edad del Bronce en la Península Ibérica.* Barcelona: Publicaciones de la UAB.

Blanco, A. B. Rothemberg   1981   *Exploración arqueometalúrgica de Huelva.* Barcelona: Labor.

Carr, C. (ed.)   1989   *For Concordance in Archaeological Analysis. Bridging Data Structure, Quantitative Technique and Theory.* Prospects Heights: Waveland Press.

Chambers, E.A. D.R. Cox   1967   Discrimination between Alternative Binary Response Models, *Biometrika* 54 (3-4), 573-578.

Eastman, J.R.   1990   *Idrisi. A Grid-Based Geographic Analysis System.* Worcester.

Farinha, M. C. Tavares   1974   A necropole da Idade do Bronze da Provença (Sines). Campanha de excavaçoes de 1972, *Arqueologia e Historia* 5. Lisboa: Associaçao Arqueologos Portugueses.

Fried, M.   1967   *The evolution of political society: an essay in political anthropology.* New York: Random House.

García, L.   1992   *La variabilidad de los enterramientos individuales en el Suroeste de la Península Ibérica (1500-1100 a.C.): una aproximación estadística.* Sevilla: Unpublished Ph.D. dissertation.

   1994   Registro funerario y relaciones sociales en el SO (1500-1100 a.n.e.): indicadores estadísticos preliminares. In: J. Campos/J.A. Pérez/F. Gómez (eds), *Arqueología en el entorno del Bajo Guadiana. Actas del Encuentro Internacional de Arqueología del Suroeste (Huelva, Marzo 1993)*, 209-239, Huelva: Universidad de Huelva.

Golberger, A.S.   1964   *Econometric Theory.* New York: John Wiley (ed.).

Greene, w. H.   1990   *LIMDEP version 5.1.* New York: Econometric software.

Hindess, B. P. Hirst   1975   *Pre-Capitalist Modes of Production.* London: Routledge and Keegan.

Hurtado, V. L. García   1994   Areas funcionales en el poblado de la Edad del Bronce de El Trastejón (Zufre, Huelva). In: J. Campos/J.A. Pérez/F. Gómez (eds), *Arqueología en el entorno del Bajo Guadiana. Actas del Encuentro Internacional de Arqueología del Suroeste (Huelva, Marzo 1993)*, 240-273, Huelva: Universidad de Huelva.

Maddala, G.S.   1983   *Limited-Dependent and Qualitative Variables in Econometrics.* Cambridge: Cambridge University Press.

   1989   *Introduction to Econometrics.* New York: Maxwell Macmillan Editors.

Monge Soares, A.M.   1994   Vestigios da prática de metalurgia em povoados calcolíticos da bacia do Guadiana, entre
  M. Araujo   o Ardila e O Chança. In: J. Campos/J.A. Pérez/F. Gómez (eds), *Arqueología en el*
  J.M. Peixoto Cabral   *entorno del Bajo Guadiana. Actas del Encuentro Internacional de Arqueología del*
                            Suroeste (Huelva, Marzo 1993), 165-201, Huelva: Universidad de Huelva.

Rosa, D.   1987   *Evaluación Ecológica de los Recursos de Andalucía.* Sevilla: Agencia Medio Ambiente.
  J.M. Moreira

Schubart, H.   1975   *Die Kultur der Bronzezeit in Sudwesten der Iberischen Halbinsel.* Berlin: Walter de
                            Gruyter & Co.

Shennan, S.J.   1988   *Quantifying Archaeology.* Edinburgh: Edinburgh University Press.

Soares, A.M.   1984   *Carta Ecologica. Noticia explicativa do Atlas do Ambiente de Portugal.* Lisboa:
                            Comissao Nacional do Ambiente.

Varela, M.   1994   *A Necropole de Alfarrobeira (S. Bartolomeu de Messines) e a Idade do Bronze no*
                            Concelho de Silves. Xelb 2. Silves: Camara Municipal de Silves.

Wright, R.   1989   *Doing Multivariate Archaeology and Prehistory. Handling Large Datasets with MV-
                            ARCH.* Sydney: University of Sydney.

L. García Sanjuán
Department of Prehistory and Archaeology
University of Sevilla
María de Padilla s/n. 41004
Sevilla
Spain
e-mail: lgarcia@sevax1.cica.es

J. Rodríguez López
Department of Economics and History of Economic Institutions, University of Huelva
Plaza de la Merced s/n. 21002
Huelva
Spain

Johannes Müller

The use of correspondence analysis for different kinds of data categories: Domestic and ritual Globular Amphorae sites in Central Germany

1 Methodological assumptions

Usually in prehistoric archaeology the application of seriation methods aims at the detection of continuous, normally distributed changes within the material remains of the past. Primarily reciprocal averaging and correspondence analysis are used to separate chronological phases, spatial differences and functional developments (e.g. Baxter 1994; Ihm 1978; Madsen 1988). The analyst presumes the classical situation of a unimodally distributed innovation pattern: at the start of a development new types or influences are represented only by a small number of artefacts out of the total. In the middle of the type's history an increasing production rate is visible. In a third and last phase the 'old fashioned' tools or decoration types are once again represented by small numbers, and finally no indication of the type remains.

I would like to name this simple approach a 'battleship' paradigm (compare Ford 1962). It combines the idea of a standardisation of human behaviour with a functional approach to the detriment of the influence of many different depositional processes.

Nevertheless, this paradigm had a huge impact on the use of correspondence analysis in archaeology. Because the first and second eigenvectors form a parabolic curve in the case of normally distributed data ('a horseshoe'), many analysts are acquainted with the manipulation of their data input: we are producing 'horseshoes' and discounting types and values which destroy the clear symmetric structure of our thinking and our results.

However, we have to admit the following mismatches:

1. The innovation of new techniques, new symbolic expressions or new ritual approaches to life produces a wide variety of expression in material culture. There might be a normally distributed representation over time, but there might also be an abrupt appearance of many artefacts at the beginning, a few in the middle and again many at the end of a development. Ethnoarchaeological case studies describe so many different distribution patterns of artefact types during time that do not have anything in common with unimodal models (Hodder 1982; Pétrequin/Pétrequin 1993). We might term this the 'effect of multimodal appearance'.

2. For example the acceptance of changes might be different in prehistoric communities, which produced the material remains of our case studies. Hence, the results are a nonlinear representation of conservative and non-conservative activity areas of our spatial record. Thus the 'spatial effect of activity areas' disarticulates the archaeologically available data.

3. Especially non-industrial societies handle artefacts in different ways, dependent on spheres of intercommunication. In the sphere of production artefacts have different distribution patterns from the ritual sphere of burial. Household organisation has a different distribution than the communal order. As a result, the handling of artefacts is non-normally distributed due to the 'effect of social spheres'.

4. To concentrate on funeral sites, the distribution of artefacts in single graves might be different, or analogous to contemporacy burial customs of the same community. The burial items might be a representation of the goods which were available during the lifespan of the dead person. Or they might be especially produced for the day of the funeral ritual and represent the production options of daily work, or they might be the personal gifts of members of the funeral party to the deceased. The multiple possibilities for variations in funeral rituals, which are practised today by small non-industrial communities, are just as probable for prehistoric societies. Again, a non-normal distribution of artefacts is the result of this 'effect of burial variability'.

5. Last but not least, depositional processes are responsible for non-normal distributions. For example the fill of Linearbandkeramik pits might represent the original assemblage that was deposited as rubbish by the community in a period of less than fifty years. As no earlier ceramic-producing community lived on LBK-sites, the fill usually lacked non-LBK ceramics. But on sites where domestic activities took place for centuries, the fill of pits is full of pre-pit remains. The assemblages cannot represent normally distributed patterns but only skewed curves. We call this the 'effect of passive rubbish'.

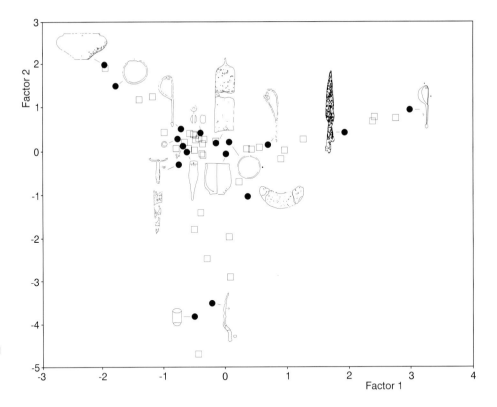

Figure 1. Scatterplot of the 1st and 2nd CA-eigenvectors for Hallstatt male burials of the Magdalenenberg, Southwest Germany.

6. Another effect, which probably destroys a 'horseshoe' in the mathematical representation, is the problem of interregional contacts. Interregional seriation was ironically called the 'Doppler effect in archaeology' by Deetz and Dethlefsen (1965) or the 'Horizon distortion effect' by Bakker (1994). 'This effect is caused by the fact that the propagation of style features over large regions takes time, and takes often different speed... While assuming that similarly styled, locally made pottery has everywhere the same date the researcher grossly distorts the chronological perspective' (Bakker 1994: 66).

As a result, artefact assemblages must not be seen as the residuals of a single closed system, where a closed archaeological system is defined as an archaeological deposit that can be precisely described in terms of units of time, location and type of deposit. Artefact assemblages represent open systems, which are significantly influenced by different channels of information on prehistoric societies and are affected by different depositional and post-depositional processes.

Obviously, the patterning of prehistoric material is not necessarily 'unimodal'. The majority of artefact deposits are not normally distributed in time and space. Therefore, we cannot test for and should not manipulate our data to form a 'horseshoe'. But at the same time they are not necessarily randomly distributed.

The interpretation of eigenvectors should therefore be done without any manipulation of the data, following an idea of Djindjian, which he expressed in 1985: the residuals from any predicted normal distribution pattern constitute a large quantity of information about prehistoric societies: every kind of figure, which appears in scatterplots of eigenvectors, may indicate unique approaches to prehistoric processes, e.g. divergence, double evolution, breaks etc. (Djindjian 1985).

An example of such a non-random distribution and functional variability, which is observable in the CA-eigenvectors, is displayed for the male graves of the Magdalenenberg, West Germany (Müller 1994: fig. 26). The scatterplot shows a threefold pattern (fig. 1): Factor 1 separates the burial items on different arms and fibulae, which on the one hand describe graves without weapons but which include ceramics, and on the other burials with daggers and lances. Factor 2 separates the graves with fibulae from graves without fibulae, but instead with iron needles and miners hammers. As the pattern contradicts chronology, it is probable that sociological differences between richly and poorly equipped male graves as well as different male roles are reflected.

With such an approach in mind, the author would like to analyse Globular Amphorae sites of Central Germany and tackle the results of correspondence analyses.

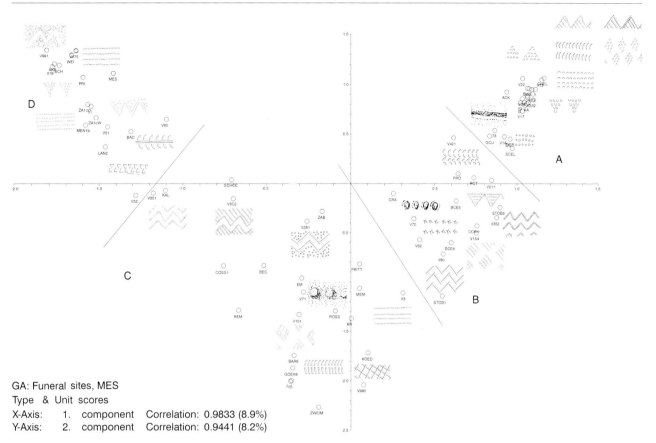

GA: Funeral sites, MES
Type & Unit scores
X-Axis: 1.   component   Correlation: 0.9833 (8.9%)
Y-Axis: 2.   component   Correlation: 0.9441 (8.2%)

Figure 2. Scatterplot of the 1st and 2nd CA-eigenvectors for Globular Amphorae burial sites. The decoration motifs describe four assemblage groups A-D.

2   Central German Globular Amphorae

During the Neolithic, Central Germany displays regional traditions of social differences, which are discernible in settlement hierarchy as well as in grave construction. Within such a framework wider influences play an important role (Beier/Einicke1994). Until now, the representation of such widespread phenomena as Corded Ware pots or Globular Amphorae has not been investigated in detail with respect to the contemporaneous local and regional substrata. In this paper I would like to discuss results of CAs, which are prepared for Globular Amphorae (GA) sites.

Apart from Bernburg-Walternienburg, the earliest phase of Corded Ware and the latest Alttiefstich and Salzmünde Globular Amphorae are present in different kinds of funeral and domestic sites between 3200 and 2600 cal BC. While Globular Amphorae represent a general phenomenon of Late Neolithic societies, which spans from the Ukraine to the western Baltic sea, clear differences are observable from region to region (Nortmann 1985). Until now a chronological differentiation of GA has not been demonstrated by research. Interaction with Bernburg has been discussed, but

not explained (Beier 1988: 40-46). Yet, important inter- and intraregional differences are on record.

Correspondence analysis was chosen to investigate the similarities and dissimilarities, firstly between the decoration pattern of the assemblages of single and multiple burial sites, including cattle graves; secondly, between the assemblages of domestic structures, mainly pits; thirdly, between both domestic and funeral sites in a combined seriation. It was hoped to discover a relation between ritual and domestic sites. With respect to the basic assumptions, non-continuous results were expected along with normal distributed artefact patterns.

3   The recording system for decoration

Until now, Globular Amphorae pots of Central Germany have been analysed only by classification systems that underline the connection between pot shape and decoration and interrelate decoration patterns in a hierarchical order (Beier 1988; Meyer 1993). In this study I prefer a classification system that decodes the ornamentation as independent, equally weighted design elements. These elements appear on every shape and — ideally — in every position on the pot. 93 design motifs were classified, and their presence stored in a data bank for each assemblage.

4 CA of the Globular Amphorae funeral sites

For the purpose of the analysis, only closed or nearly closed assemblages are used. From 177 sites with 204 funerals only 66 single, multiple or cattle graves fulfil the condition that they are not disturbed by later intrusions and/or are properly reported. The correspondence analyses describe a 'horseshoe structure' for the first and second eigenvectors (fig. 2). By the exclusion of vertical line ornaments, the first component has a correlation of 0.98, the second of 0.94. Four clusters of decoration elements and corresponding assemblages are detectable in the graph: assemblage group A with a high degree of curved and angular dots; B with angular bands and diamonds of corded lines; C with incised diamonds and D with punctate decoration, e.g. triangles.

What do the clusters indicate? Stratigraphies and mixed assemblages of GA sites with older and younger Bernburg or Corded Ware prove the chronological character of the observed sequence with A being the oldest and D the youngest association. Based on C14 dates this development starts around 3200 cal BC and ends around 2600 cal BC (Müller in prep.).

Beside the chronological effect, other differences are visible, if we plot special aspects of artefact distribution into the graphical display. For example the third eigenvector shows different loadings, especially concerning cluster D (fig 3). The burial association helps us to describe lower loadings of Factor 3 as a representation of multiple burials, whereas higher loadings are mainly of single burials. Furthermore, some chronological order of the funeral rites is visible: cattle graves only appear during the phases A, B and C, while double and multiple burials are only known from C and D. Similar developments are visible with items or indicators of ritual behaviour: the range of the number of associated vessels is the highest in A, the lowest in D (fig. 4). In A-C parts of cattle are deposited in human graves, in C-D only caprovids. The range of the number of adzes in A is higher than in D. Otherwise, no differences are visible with respect to sex or age. All results mentioned have been tested with the χ^2 and Fisher's F test.

In summary, the sequence reflects the socio-chronological development of the Globular Amphorae society or of the practice of Globular Amphorae funerals within a regional social framework: the process starts with elaborated differences of grave furniture and the rite of cattle graves. It changes around 2800 cal BC to the practice of rather less 'expensive' sheep/goat associations, a reduction of the differences between grave items and an emerging practice of double and multiple burials. Perhaps the change to Corded Ware graves that started around 2800 cal BC in

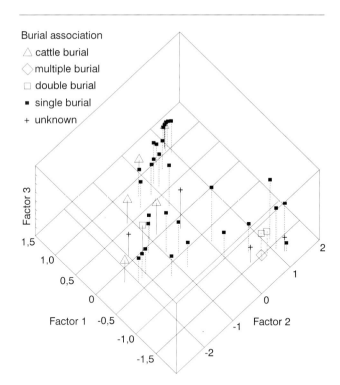

Figure 3. Plot of three CA-eigenvectors for Globular Amphorae burial sites. Different burial associations are indicated.

Central Germany represents a new ritual system of status expression during the funeral rite for important members of the communities.

5 GA ceramics in domestic structures

There are only a few settlements where GA forms the only ceramic tradition. Normally, GA ceramics are found on Bernburg sites (Beier 1988). In all, only 40 pit structures have been evaluated as 'geschlossene Funde' (closed finds). Although only 30 sites are useful for the analyses, a clear sequence appears within the ordered matrix of the first eigenvector. The scatterplot of the first and second eigenvectors (not illustrated) does not display a horseshoe, but a 'cloud' along the first axes. Still three clusters of pottery design are visible: SA with incised diamonds, partly with curved and angular dots, SB with partly curved and angular stabs and plastic decoration and SC with angular bands. Again, the association of mixed assemblages and the stratigraphic order at Görschen (Beier 1988: 132) point towards a chronological interpretation.

6 GA: Domestic and funeral sites

The common seriation of both domestic and funeral sites with GA has a twofold problem: on the one hand the two types of sites possess different depositional histories that result in different qualities of chronological closeness. On

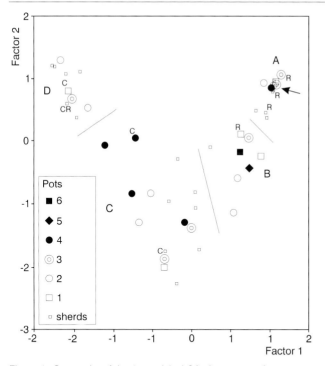

Figure 4. Scatterplot of the 1st and 2nd CA-eigenvectors for Globular Amphorae burial sites. The number of pots per grave, bones of caprovides (C) and cattle (R) and the burial with the highest number of adzes (arrow) are indicated.

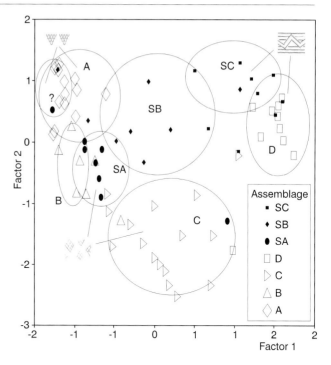

Figure 5. Scatterplot of the 1st and 2nd CA-eigenvectors for Globular Amphorae burial (open symbols) and domestic (filled symbols) sites. The assemblage groups and some characteristic decoration motifs are shown.

the other hand the change within the social life of things, here perhaps the change of symbolic expressions used on pottery may lead towards a different value of things.

In spite of this there exists the chance to investigate the mode of symbolic change within the society or at least a part of the society.

The result is displayed in figure 5. Again we find the horseshoe structure of funeral sites with their sequence of decoration clusters and the stretched structure of the domestic assemblages with their sequence of domestic clusters. It seems interesting that the sequences overlap and are correlated, because parts of the domestic dots form a part of the parabolic structure.

We observe the following sequence:

1. The funeral A group and two domestic sites represent the beginning of the common sequence with motifs of curved and angular dots.
2. The domestic SA group with incised diamonds follows along with the funeral B group on the parabolic structure, followed by the funeral C group with incised diamonds.
3. As a parallel the domestic B group is contemporary with the funeral C group. It is of interest that the assemblages with angular and curved stabs are distributed with

negative values, while those without these attributes have positive values.
4. The funeral D group and the domestic C group form the final part of the sequence on the right hand side.

There is no question concerning the chronological order which appears here. Obviously, the interrelation of symbolic expressions is different in domestic and funeral sites. While 'Bogen/Winkelstich' is no longer used in funeral rites, it is still present on some domestic sites. In contrast, incised diamond motifs first appear on domestic sites and are later introduced (and restricted) to the funeral sites.

7   Conclusion

Having equipped ourselves with a time scale, we can turn to the question: what happened? Obviously, the changing role of ceramic decoration is visible in the distinction between domestic and funeral pottery. The denotation of the symbolic expression of the ceramic decoration changes. Perhaps this is related to the changes of ritual behaviour within the GA sequence and the appearance of Corded ware.

With respect to methodology, correspondence analyses of different site categories can be applied for the modelling of such changes.

references

Bakker, J.A.	1994	Bemerkungen zur Datierungsmethode: 14C-Methode, Dendrochronologie, Seriation und Typologie. In: J. Hoika (ed.), *Beiträge zur frühneolithischen Trichterbecherkultur im westlichen Ostseegebiet, Schleswig*, 85-132.
Baxter, M.J.	1994	*Exploratory multivariate analysis in archaeology*. Edinburgh: Edinburgh University Press.
Beier, H-J.	1988	Die Kugelamphorenkultur im Mittelelbe-Saale-Gebiet und in der Altmark, *Veröffent-lichungen des Landesmuseums für Vorgeschichte Halle* 41, Berlin.
Beier, H.-J. R. Einicke (eds)	1994	*Das Neolithikum im Mittelelbe-Saale-Gebiet und in der Altmark*, Beiträge zur Ur- und Frühgeschichte Mitteleuropas 4. Wilkau-Hasslau.
Deetz, J. E. Dethlefsen	1965	The Doppler effect and archaeology, a consideration of the spatial aspects of seriation, *Southwestern Journal of Anthropology* 21, 196-202.
Djindjian, F.	1985	Seriation and toposeriation by correspondence analysis. In: A. Voorrips/S.H. Loving (eds), To Pattern the Past, *PACT* 11, 119-135.
Ford, J.A.	1962	*A Quantitative Method for Deriving Cultural Chronology*. Washington D.C.
Hodder, I.	1982	*The Present Past*. London: B.T. Batsford LTD.
Ihm, P.	1978	*Statistik in der Archäologie*. Archeophysica. Bonn.
Madsen, T. (ed.)	1988	*Multivariate analysis in Scandinavian archaeology*. Jutland Archaeological Society Publications XXI, Moesgard.
Meyer, M.	1993	*Pevestorf 19. Ein mehrperiodiger Fundplatz im Landkreis Lüchow-Dannenberg*. Oldenburg.
Müller, J.	1994	Zur sozialen Gliederung der Nachbestattungsgemeinschaft vom Magdalenenberg bei Villingen, *Prähistorische Zeitschrift* 69, 194-240.
	in prep.	*Zur Soziochronologie des Mittelelbe-Saalegebietes im Spätneolithikum und der Frühbronzezeit.*
Nortmann, H.	1985	Die Ornamentik der Kugelamphorenkultur, *Prähistorische Zeitschrift* 60, 16-46.
Pétrequin, P. A.-M. Pétrequin	1993	*Écologie d'un outil: la hache de pierre en Irian Jaya (Indonésie)*. Monographie du CRA 12, Paris.

Johannes Müller
Seminar für Ur- und Frühgeschichte
Altensteinstr. 15
14195 Berlin
Germany
e-mail: free@fub46.zedat.fu-Berlin.de

J. Steele
T.J. Sluckin
D.R. Denholm
C.S. Gamble

Simulating hunter-gatherer colonization of the Americas

1   Introduction

Simulation modelling of the Palaeoindian expansion into the Americas was pioneered by Paul Martin, who proposed an 'overkill' model in 1967. Taking demographic parameters from a compilation of data by Joseph Birdsell (1957), he calculated that humans reproducing at a rate of about 3.5% per annum, with directional migration southwards at an average rate of 16 kilometres per year, would have reached Tierra del Fuego 1,000 years after entering the land south of the ice sheets. His model had a dense 'front' of pioneers overexploiting the megafauna in their path, and moving on to leave a faunally depauperate environment occupied by humans at merely one tenth of that initial population density (Martin 1973). With James Mosimann, he developed this 'overkill' model in a later paper in 1975, in which it was demonstrated that hunters with unchecked population growth and moderate or heavy kill rates, or alternatively a focus on preferred mammoth and mastodon prey, could push their prey species into extinction throughout North America in a period of 300-500 years (Mosimann/Martin 1975). Calculations of the velocity of expansion of the front were also made in this paper, and reinforced the finding that rapid growth (2.5 to 3.5% per annum) was a necessary condition of very rapid expansion, although a slow growth model was summarized in which pioneers reached the Gulf of Mexico 1,157 years after entry at Edmonton, with an intrinsic growth rate of only 0.65%.

In our own work, we have been concerned to evaluate the effect of spatial habitat variation, and of the distribution of geographical barriers to dispersal, on the rate and routes of expansion of pioneer Palaeoindian populations. Such effects have generally been omitted in previous models, which have used averaged habitat values applied to the whole continental land area; but their importance has nonetheless been noted. Mosimann and Martin (1975: 306) observed that 'while we acknowledge their importance in an ideal model, we do not attempt to [...] incorporate the inevitable local differences in carrying capacity at the time of invasion.' Whittington and Dyke (1984: 462), who developed the Mosimann and Martin model, also observed that 'a better approximation of reality than uniform population densities would be a model that allows for interactions between

megafaunal and human populations whose densities were based on the distribution of various resources. Since this would be a radical departure from Mosimann and Martin's simulation, a reformulation of the model was not undertaken.' Finally, Belovsky (1988: 353) also set the parameters for his own simulation of Palaeoindian expansion so that 'rather than tracing the growth of the human population from vegetation type to vegetation type across the two continents, an average primary productivity was used.'

2   The simulation model

In modelling the effects of barriers and habitat variation on the rate of expansion of pioneer human populations, we have departed radically from the simulation paradigms of these workers. We have discretized both time and space for our simulations, using a two-dimensional lattice in which each cell has cell-specific fixed values for the habitat terms, and an updated cell-specific value for the human population size. The update algorithm is a discretized approximation of a continuous differential equation describing the process of demographic expansion. For our initial phase of work, we have been using a discrete approximation of R.A. Fisher's classic equation for the 'wave of advance' of advantageous genes (Fisher 1937), which has already been generalized to the case of animal range expansion and is widely used for this purpose in biogeography. Fisher's model is also the basis for Ammerman and Cavalli-Sforza's work on the expansion of Neolithic colonists in Europe.

The Fisher equation is:

$$\frac{dn}{dt} = f(n;K) + D\nabla^2 n \tag{1}$$

where $n(\mathbf{r},t)$ denotes the local human population density (number per unit area) at time t and position $\mathbf{r} = (x,y)$. The diffusion constant D (in km^2 yr^{-1}) and the carrying capacity $\mathbf{K}$ are functions of position. The function

$$f(n) = \alpha n \left(1 - \frac{n}{k}\right)$$

describes the rate of population increase, and is the logistic function widely used in theoretical ecology (Murray 1990); the quantity α denotes the annual population growth rate.

We approximate time differentials at particular sites by finite differences (Press *et al.* 1986):

$$\frac{dn(\mathbf{r},t)}{dt} \approx \frac{n(\mathbf{r},t+\Delta_t) - n(\mathbf{r},t)}{\Delta_t} \qquad (2)$$

Typically we use $\Delta_t = 1$ year.

Space differentials are similarly approximated by finite differences:

$$D\nabla^2(\mathbf{r}_0) = h^{-2}\sum_\alpha w_\alpha D_\alpha[n(\mathbf{r}_\alpha)-n(\mathbf{r})], \qquad (3)$$

where for a given position $\mathbf{r}_0$ the sum is taken over nearest neighbour sites $\mathbf{r}_\alpha$ on the lattice, and where the lattice size is h. There are two types of neighbour sites: those along the lattice axes and those along the diagonals. The sum is weighted appropriately with parameters w_α; this parameter is typically 2/3 for sites α along the lattice axes and 1/6 along the diagonals. The effective diffusion parameter D_α', appropriate to motion between the sites $\mathbf{r}_0$ and $\mathbf{r}_\alpha$, is given by

$$D_\alpha' = \sqrt{D(\mathbf{r}_\alpha)D(\mathbf{r}_0)}.$$

In practice in any given simulation, only two values of D are used: $D = D_0$ and $D = 0$, the latter representing the fact that the particular cell is inaccessible.

The crucial input parameters for the model are then the carrying capacity K, the so-called Malthusian parameter α and the diffusion constant D. D represents the degree of mobility of an individual (e.g., Ammerman/Cavalli-Sforza 1984). In general individuals will move from their birth place a distance λ during their lifetime τ. The square of this distance will in general be proportional to the time available; the constant of proportionality is the diffusion constant D:

$$D = \frac{\lambda^2}{4\tau} \qquad (4)$$

The differential equation (1) in the case of constant D and K, and for populations which can only move in one rather than two dimensions, predicts that there will be a population wave of advance, with the frontier travelling with velocity (Ablowitz/Zepetella 1979):

$$v = 2.04\sqrt{D\alpha} \qquad (5)$$

Our discretized model gives accurate results so long as the natural length scale in this equation

$$\xi = \sqrt{\frac{D}{\alpha}} > h$$

Otherwise the simulated velocity is faster than that predicted analytically. For simulations with h ~ 50 km with 0.005 yr$^{-1}<\alpha<.05$ yr^{-1}, and with D>10km^2 yr^{-1}, our discretized lattice yields consistently accurate results (fig. 1).

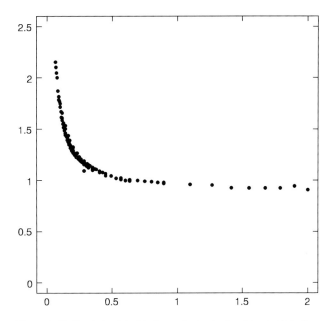

Figure 1. Ratio of simulated to theoretical velocity of expansion of the front, plotted against the 'natural length scale' (the independent variable). The latter is given by dividing $\sqrt{(D/\alpha)}$ by the cell dimension (in these simulations, 50 km).

We note also a methodological point; in principle (even if in practice this will be difficult!) we may have independent estimations of D, α, K and v. We predict that v will be independent of K and dependent on D and α according to equatation (5). If these predictions are not borne out — if, for example, the values of D and α required to be consistent with archaeologically sensible values of v are not themselves plausible — we are bound to use more sophisticated models of population movement, for which the Fisher equation, at least in its naive form, would no longer be helpful.

3 The use of geographic information in the lattice model

For the first set of experiments, we have used a projected representation of the surface of North America and its surrounding oceans, rasterized from an interpolated surface generated in IDRISI from the original vector format point file as a grid of cells coded for their accessibility to a diffusing population. Sea and other impassable areas are '0', colonizable land is '1'. Population can either diffuse into the cell, or not. The projection transformation (Transverse Mercator, meridian 90° W., scale factor = 1) was selected to avoid distortion of area and orientation, and the interpolated vector file was used to generate raster output with a cell size of approximately 50 km by 50 km. To make it easier to understand the real time output to

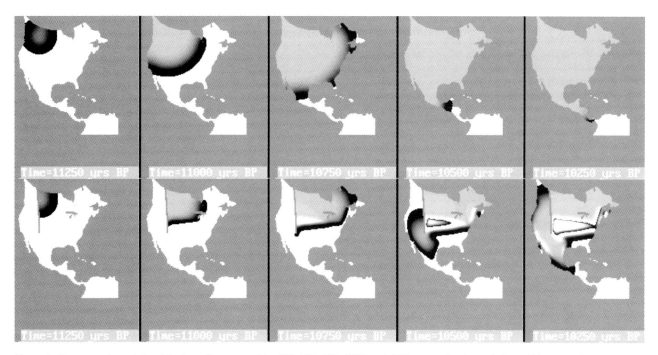

Figure 2. Screen capture shots of the travelling wave at t = 250, 500, 750, 1000 and 1250 years. Seed population at Edmonton. Carrying capacities: 0.04 p.p.km^2 (background), 0.2 p.p.km^2 (coasts and plains). Population growth rate = 0.03 p.a. (background), 0.01 p.a. (coasts and plains). Dispersal rate = 400 km^2 p.a. (background), 100 km^2 (coasts and plains).

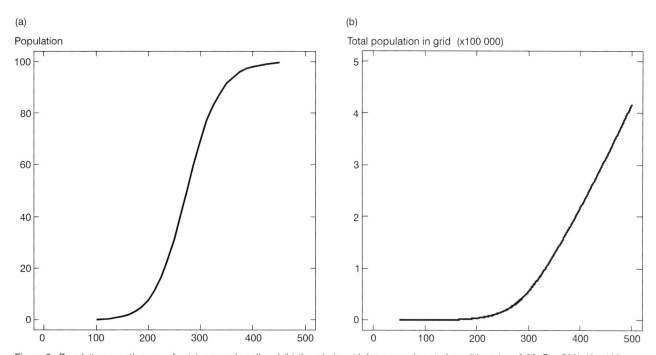

Figure 3. Population growth curves for (a) a sample cell and (b) the whole grid, for a sample set of conditions (α = 0.03, D = 500). K = 100 persons per cell.

screen while the simulation is running, barrier cells are coloured blue — since they are mostly sea — while cells where people can go are coloured green (since they are nearly all areas of land surface with significant primary plant production). Population densities on the colonized portion of the accessible surface are grey-scaled, making it easy to follow the expansion of the front as it is updated and written to screen in real time during the simulation (fig. 2). Figures 3 (a) and (b) show the curves for increasing population in a single cell and in the whole colonizable portion of the grid, against time, for an example set of values for the demographic parameters. It is evident from these that while the population in each of the cells follows a logistic growth curve, the growth curve for the total population is exponential. This is what we would expect from the original model.

The simulations shown in figure 2 also demonstrate the effects of varying the barrier locations and the demographic parameters as cell-specific attributes. The first series represent demographic expansion over a homogeneous plane, while the second series has barriers at the Rockies and the Great Lakes, and two categories of habitat with covariation in the carrying capacity (κ), mobility (D) and growth rate (α) terms. The varying times taken to first colonization of points on the surface if they are located beyond such hypothetical barriers, or in habitats with differing carrying capacities or disease ecologies, will clearly be detectable in archaeological radiocarbon dating of earliest cultural remains at such locations. Thus the simulation model is capable of generating archaeologically testable predictions about the effect on demographic expansion of spatial heterogeneity in barriers and in vegetation zones.

4 Future development of the model and its applications

These initial results are now being extended in a second phase of development of the model, in which ice sheet locations and vegetation mosaics at successive periods in the earliest Holocene of the Americas will be reconstructed by a palaeoecologist and used to predict spatial variation in Palaeoindian carrying capacities, and more extensive sets of simulations will be run to generate alternative predictions about possible effects of such spatial variation on colonization rates and routes.

Young and Bettinger (1995), in a study which independently developed the same demographic diffusion equation to model late Pleistocene human demic expansions, suggest that the high values of α and D needed to generate the observed velocity of Palaeoindian expansion into the New World under the conditions of Fisher's model are nonetheless biologically plausible. They suggest values for α of 0.03 and for D of 1000 km^2/yr (which would mean the travelling front would reach Tierra del Fuego in about 1,500 years). We believe that such values for the diffusion constant are, in fact, biologically implausible for almost all hunter-gatherer social systems for which recent ethnographic parallels exist. It is essential to remember that the diffusion term denotes mobility which is random with respect to direction: it is not a term denoting 'directional migration'. The value for D chosen by Young and Bettinger (1995) implies a lifetime mean dispersal distance for all individuals of about 300 km from the place of birth, or of about 600 km for the dispersing sex where diffusion is due to dispersal from the natal group by all members of one dispersing sex. It is difficult to see how such a high level of lifetime mobility, random with respect to direction, could be adaptive in a landscape that was also sustaining such a high net population growth rate. We therefore suspect that the rate of colonization of the Americas was driven by some further dynamic, such as directional migration by 'over-exploiters' up a gradient of herbivore prey densities in a very fragile ecosystem, and we are currently exploring new models which can be implemented in the existing discrete time and space simulation paradigm.

Acknowledgement
We are very grateful to Nolan Virgo for his work on the simulation program during the summer of 1994.

references

Ablowitz, M.
A. Zeppetella

1979   Explicit solutions of Fisher's equation for a special wave speed, *Bulletin of Mathematical Biology* 41, 835-840.

Ammerman, A.J.
L.L. Cavalli-Sforza

1984   *The Neolithic Transition and the Genetics of Populations in Europe.* Princeton: Princeton University Press.

Belovsky, G.E.

1988   An optimal foraging-based model of hunter-gatherer population dynamics, *Journal of Anthropological Archaeology* 7, 329-372.

Birdsell, J.

1957   Some population problems involving Pleistocene man, *Cold Harbor Springs Symposium on Quantitative Biology* 22, 47-69.

Fisher, R.A.

1937   The wave of advance of advantageous genes, *Annals of Eugenics* 7, 355-369.

Martin, P.S.

1973   The discovery of America, *Science* 179, 969-974.

Mosimann, J.E.
P.S. Martin

1975   Simulating overkill by Paleoindians, *American Scientist* 63, 304-313.

Murray, J.D.

1990   *Theoretical Biology.* Berlin: Springer-Verlag.

Press, W.H.
B.P. Flannery
S.A. Teukolsky
W.T. Veterling

1986   *Numerical Recipes: The Art of Scientific Computing.* Cambridge: Cambridge University Press.

Whittington, S.L.
B. Dyke

1984   Simulating overkill: experiments with the Mosimann and Martin model. In: P.S. Martin/ R.G. Klein (eds), *Quaternary Extinctions*, 451-465, Tucson: University of Arizona Press.

Young, D.A.
R.L. Bettinger

1995   Simulating the global human expansion in the Late Pleistocene, *Journal of Archaeological Science* 22, 89-92.

J. Steele
Department of Archaeology
e-mail: T.J.M.Steele@soton.ac.uk

T.J. Sluckin
Department of Mathematics

D.R. Denholm
Department of Physics,

C.S. Gamble
Department of Archaeology
University of Southampton
Highfield
Southampton SO17 1BJ
United Kingdom

Paul M. Gibson

An Archaeofaunal Ageing Comparative Study into the Performance of Human Analysis Versus Hybrid Neural Network Analysis

1   Introduction

This paper briefly reports on the completion of the first phase of a project that began in 1991 to develop a prototype computer system that could perform archaeofaunal ageing from a set of sheep mandibles. The computer system uses artificial intelligence models known as neural networks to analyse images of mandibles to assess their degree of wear and relative age (Gibson 1992a, 1992b, 1993).

In order to assess the performance of the computer system in relation to its human counterpart a comparative study that involved the analysis of a sample set of sheep mandibles by archaeologists, non-archaeologists and the computer system was undertaken. A overview of the results is presented here.

2   Overview of the comparative study

Age at death data of common domestic ungulates can be used to formulate an interpretation of the economy and exploitation of the livestock on a site. A number of approaches to age estimation are based on the analysis of teeth attrition. The age of an animal can be estimated by grouping its teeth into a set of wear stages based on the amount of attrition. In general, older animals have a greater degree of wear.

There are two commonly used methods of age estimation using attrition, namely Payne (1973) and Grant (1982). Payne has studied the wear stages of Anatolian sheep and goats and as a result has devised a methodology for age estimation. A more widespread study, that includes the common ungulates of pig, sheep/goat and cattle, has been undertaken by Grant.

Both methodologies concentrate on the third premolar (m3 or dP4), the fourth premolar (P4) and the three permanent molars (M1, M2, and M3). An archaeological sample can be aged by comparing the wear pattern of each tooth with the wear stages, in the form of ideograms, outlined by either methodology. This analysis results in a *tooth wear stage value* for each tooth. These values are then used to produce a *mandible wear stage value* that represents the relative age of the sample. Statistical analysis is then carried out to group all mandibles on the site into relative age stages which can be interpreted by examining the

kill-off patterns to suggest the method of animal husbandry (Payne 1973).

It is the above process of analysing the mandibles to determine age at death that has been implemented on a PC using both traditional artificial intelligence techniques and hybrid neural network models (see Gibson 1992a, 1992b, 1993). Neural networks are computing paradigms that attempt to model the cognitive phenomena of the human brain so that complex problems can be solved. In doing so, they exhibit a number of intuitive characteristics such as learning, generalisation and abstraction (see Wasserman 1989 for an explanation).

In order to establish the performance of the system a number of willing participants have been asked to attribute age to a set of mandibles using both Grant and Payne methodologies. These results have then been compared with each other and against the computer application. The aim has been to study how different the results are between each participant and between the computer system and the participants in order to determine the degree of subjectivity and accuracy. The analysis has been divided into two parts, namely

- Human *vs.* Human Comparison
  Establishes the inter-observer performance
- Human *vs.* Computer Comparison
  Establishes the computer's performance in relation to the humans' performance

Measuring the performance of humans provides a guide to establishing the reliability of the computer system. In the course of identifying the performance of human analysis a number of interesting points have been highlighted regarding the methodologies involved and the human's use of the methodologies.

The participants were a cross section of people with varying degrees of archaeological experience. The set of people also had a spread of experience in terms of the two archaeofaunal ageing methodologies. A number of the group are acknowledged experts in the use of the archaeofaunal techniques under study. In contrast, a number of the group had never before used these techniques to age animal remains. In all eleven participants undertook the study.

The sheep mandibles used for the comparative study were taken from two sources. The first set was supplied by the Environmental Archaeology Unit (EAU) at the University of York with the assistance of Dr Keith Dobney. The second set was kindly lent by Prof. Don Brothwell from his own collection.

The aim of the selection of mandibles was to provide as wide a range of wear stages, and teeth morphologies as possible without overburdening the participants. Consequently, a sample set of 22 mandibles was selected that had a combination of missing teeth, unerupted teeth, teeth in early stages of wear and teeth in moderate stages of wear. A group of mandibles was selected that appeared to be in the same state of wear. Finally, some teeth had been subject to disease.

3 The human *vs.* human comparison

In order to carry out the comparative study a questionnaire was designed to record the results of the participants' analysis and to determine facts about the participant that would be useful in the analysis, such as archaeological experience, number of years using each methodology and the preferred method. The participants were asked to age each mandible in any order using both methodologies and record the results on the questionnaire sheet. For teeth that the participant could not record they were asked to use a **?** for unsure wear stages, **X** for present but unrecordable and a - for missing teeth.

A computer database system using DATAEASE was devised to record the results of the analysis. The source of the data entered into the database was used to produce a data file that could be analysed by another computer program, written in QBASIC, that presented the results in a manner that helped to answer the underlying objectives of the study.

4 Devising a method for analysing the results

Before analysing the data the main objectives of the analysis had to be made clear. To determine the performance of the human participants a number of questions needed to be addressed as part of the analysis, for example,

– Are some mandibles easier than others to age?
– Which are the most difficult mandibles and why?
– Which is the most difficult tooth in the set and in general and why?
– Which is the wear stage that causes the most disagreement and why?
– Are the experienced participants of the methodology more consistent in their interpretation than those with less experience?
– What are the factors that determine ease of observation?

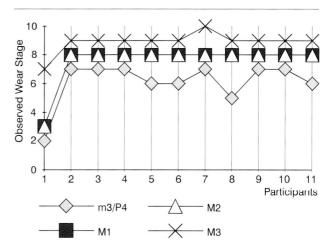

Figure 1. The Participant's Observed Wear Stage Values for Sample 2, where true wear stage values for m3 is 7, M1 is 8, M2 is 8 and M3 is 9.

– Is there any relationship between the analysis of left and right mandibles to ease of observation and general agreement?
– Which of the methodologies provides the most consistent results and why?

To answer the above questions it was necessary to establish a means of objectively analysing all the results from the participants. Keeping the objective of inter-observer comparison in mind, it was obvious that a true wear stage value for each measurement had to be used as a basis for comparison. In other words, for each of the results recorded there must be a real value by which to compare the actual observed wear stages. This *'true' wear stage value* can be calculated using the mode of the participants results where *'true'* effectively means 'expected in this study'. By taking the absolute value of the difference between the true wear stage and the observed wear stage it was possible to determine the amount of discrepancies between observers. Figure 1 shows a subset of the actual results using the Payne methodology illustrating discrepancies between observers.

Using the calculated discrepancy it was possible to determine the percentage agreement of tooth wear stages and mandible wear stages across participants. In addition, it was possible to rank the performance of the participants. This formed the basis for determining the reliability of the methodologies.

5 Analysing the data

At first glance the ranked results would appear to indicate a range of difficulties in the analysis of teeth and mandibles. On the whole both methodologies seem to perform quite well in some areas and badly in others. It is hard to objectively state what causes such difficulties. Are they related to structure, colour, orientation of the mandible; degree of experience of the participant, speed of recording, lighting in the room at the time of analysis or to the sequence in which the mandible was examined? These questions may demand exact answers but only speculative reasons can be given through examination of the teeth and mandibles.

Firstly, there seems to be no real problem in identifying the teeth types since there were no values in the teeth columns that were invalid. Also, there is no evidence to suggest a correlation between the percentage agreement and a left or right mandible. In addition, the teeth that resulted in the most agreement were those that were missing or unerupted. All these facts suggest that the human is good at recognising simple shapes and manipulating them in order to achieve the requirements of the analysis. This may seem an obvious statement to make but such tasks are very complicated to implement using a computer. Therefore, a machine must match this performance if it is to be of any practical use.

The presence of calculus on the tooth does not appear to affect observations provided it does not obscure any important tooth structures that would differentiate wear stages. Humans have the ability to ignore such 'noise' in the analysis of surface patterns and structures, something that a computer finds more of a problem. The only time that it may affect results is when the calculus appears at a transition point from one wear stage to another.

A general observation for the overall percentage agreement graphs is that there is less accuracy in the earlier wear stages. Perhaps this is because

1. there are more features to match,
2. less distinction between wear stages since there are more wear stages in the early years, or
3. the enamel/dentine distinction is often harder to determine.

In contrast, there appears to be more accuracy in the later wear stages. Well-worn stages seem to be easier to identify perhaps because the features on the surface of the tooth are simple. The smaller distinctions between wear stages are more difficult to pick up. When the break is only partially worn a discrepancy can occur. It appears that both methodologies suffer from this problem.

In general when the tooth does not fit a single wear stage then the percentage agreement drops. The smaller the transition between wear stages, the greater the disagreement. Therefore, visual clues based on distinct structures that are evident in the ideograms are an important element in identifying wear stages. The clarity of the enamel/

dentine border is also important in the identification of wear stages.

It appears that any disfigurement of the occlusal surface of the tooth caused by a disease may affect the estimation of a wear stage depending on the degree of deformation. For example, one of the sample's M3 teeth was slightly deformed and the structure of the cusps was not as represented in the ideograms. This made establishing a wear stage rather difficult and was reflected in the percentage agreement for both methods.

To establish the overall estimate of the agreement for mandibles the average of agreements for the teeth of each mandible was considered for both methodologies. On the whole both the Payne and Grant faired similarly, with Grant gaining better agreement than Payne on some occasions and vice versa. However, the overall average agreement for Payne was 70.4% and for Grant 69.1%. Figure 2 shows a comparison of percentage agreement between Payne and Grant approaches.

To determine whether experience had any bearing on the analysis the participants were ranked for the results of mandibles, and each tooth. Again, it can be stated that experience has no real influence on the establishment of age. This conclusion is gained by examining the experience of individuals and noting where they rank in the group for each tooth. The top five were not always the most experienced.

Although this study has aimed to cover all aspects that may lead to misinterpretation of results it obviously has not been able to address all of them. There has been no consideration to the sequence in which mandibles were analysed to see if this had any influence on the results. The influence of broken and partial teeth has not been fully addressed, although they were considered in part. A larger group of participants would perhaps provide a more general and global view. Also, the effects of speed were not analysed.

This study has shown that there is not always 100% agreement in the results of observers. In addition, it has suggested why there may be discrepancies in the data. However, the main purpose of the study has been to provide a set of data that can be compared to the computer system to measure its performance.

6   The human *vs.* computer comparison

The key to the success of a neural network based system is the reliability of the data that is presented to it during the training stage of the system's development. The testing of the system is an integral part of its development and requires data that contains representative examples of all general cases that the neural network would be expected to cope with during its active operational running. Therefore, the system was trained using a series of images of

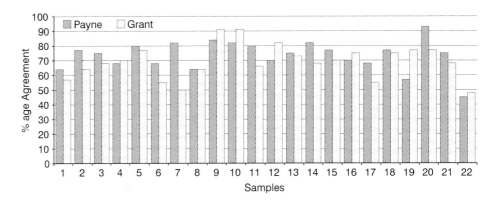

Figure 2. Comparison of percentage agreement of Payne and Grant.

mandibles with various degrees of wear. Once the system had been trained the mandibles given to the participants were presented to the computer and the results compared.

The system was measured against the participants and found to have an overall performance of 65.2% agreement. Of those results that did not match the system was only one or two wear stages out from the participants agreement. Like the human participants the system appeared to have difficulty in assessing early wear stages whilst having greater success with later stages. Again, this could be linked to the smaller transitions in some of the early wear stages. The performance of the system when faced with disfigurement of the occlusal surface was equal to that of the participants. It appeared to produce acceptable answers on the basis of what it saw and what it had learnt.

By comparing the system's performance to the overall percentage agreement of the Payne and Grant methods the result above is encouraging. However, we must be cautious not to overestimate the success of the system. It is important to note that in preparing the images for analysis, effort was made to ensure that the mandibles were presented in such a way that the system would not get confused. The success of the system relies heavily on the quality of the image. Giving the system images that had mandibles in a bad orientation or obscured by calculus deposits deteriorated the acceptability of the results. The human overcomes this problem by moving the mandible into the best position for analysis; something which is difficult to implement using a computer.

It has been seen that the system does not perform well when it is trained using a small number of examples, typically ten. By increasing the number of training examples the system shows greater tolerance to situations that it has not seen before. In one session the system was approaching a rate of 70% success in comparison to the results expected with a training data set consisting of

50 images. However, too many training examples saturate the system and its performance drops. Therefore, it is questionable whether the system will perform much better than currently measured without restructuring its basic architecture.

7   Conclusion and future

The human *vs*. human comparative study has illustrated that there is a degree of subjectivity in the analysis of age estimation using both methodologies. It has identified some areas where the subjectivity originates. Furthermore, it has shown that although the comparative study was carried out rigorously there are areas that the study has not been able to address. Although, the study has taken a *small* number of participants it has still been useful as a means of comparing the computer system.

The human *vs*. computer comparative study shows that given the correct conditions the system can perform acceptably in relation to the human participant. However, the human participants are still better adapted to under-taking this type of subjective analysis.

The next stage of the project is well on the way to implementing a system capable of interpreting kill-off patterns of sheep in order to ascertain their exploitation. Again, it will be necessary to undertake a comparative study to determine the performance of the computer system in terms of its human counterpart.

Acknowledgements
The author would like to thank all the participants who took part in the comparative study. In addition, the loan of the mandibles by Dr Keith Dobney and Prof. Don Brothwell is appreciated. The support by Dr Julian Richards, University of York and Dr Terry O'Connor is gratefully acknowledged. Finally, the author is thankful for his parents' support and help.

references

Gibson, P.M.

1992a   The potentials of hybrid neural network models for archaeofaunal ageing and interpretation. In: J. Andresen/T. Madsen/I. Scollar (eds), *Computing the Past; Computer applications and quantitative methods in archaeology CAA92*, 263-271, Aarhus: Aarhus University Press.

1992b   An application using hybrid neural network models to perform archaeofaunal ageing, *Archaeological Computing Newsletter* 32, 1-6.

1993   The application of hybrid neural network models to estimate age of domestic ungulates, *International Journal of Osteoarchaeology* 3, 45-48.

Grant, A.

1982   The use of tooth wear as a guide to the age of domestic ungulates. In: B. Wilson/ C. Grigson/S. Payne (eds), *Ageing and Sexing Animal Bones from Archaeological Sites*, 91-108, BAR British Series 109, Oxford: British Archaeological Reports.

Payne, S.

1973   Kill-off patterns in sheep and goats: the mandibles from Asvan Kale, *Anatolian Studies* 23, 281-303.

Wasserman, P.D.

1989   *Neural computing, theory and practice.* New York: Van Nostrand Reinhold.

Paul M. Gibson
Department of Archaeology
University of York
Micklegate House
Micklegate
York YO1 1JZ
United Kingdom
e-mail: GBYORK04.GIBSONPM@WCSMVS.INFONET.COM

Peter Durham
Paul Lewis
Stephen J. Shennan

Image Processing Strategies for Artefact Classification

1 Introduction

It need hardly be stated that the identification of objects (usually artefacts) is a fundamental requirement for the practice of archaeology. In particular, when the identification takes the form of assignment of the artefact to a classification (pre-existing or not) the information associated with the artefact is greatly increased. In the case of assignment to a pre-existing classification, the task may be called recognition, but the procedure(s) are the same. Classification, which may be defined as the division of a set of artefacts into subsets containing objects that are more like each other than other members of the set (Doran/ Hodson 1975: 159), is very closely related to identification/ recognition.

Identification has traditionally been carried out by experts in the field. The task requires a large amount of training and experience, because although in many cases specific features are diagnostic of a particular class of artefacts, the identification often rests on a visual judgement by the worker. Of course every method has its pros and cons, but for our purposes the most important disadvantage of the traditional approach stems from the limitations of the human brain when it comes to large data sets. Humans find it difficult to think of more than 3 or 4 things simultane- ously, let alone several hundred (or even tens of thousands as is often the case with pottery). Large data sets also take time for the human to consider, introducing the possibility that fatigue may affect the results. A third factor is the lack of repeatability of this method. As the results depend on human judgements, there is no guarantee that a different person will produce the same result, or that the same person will produce the same result at a different date. We have been looking at ways of producing an automatic aid to classification that will alleviate these problems.

Much work has been done on computer-based classification in archaeology (e.g. Doran/Hodson 1975; Gero/Mazzullo 1984; Main 1988; Wilcock/Shennan 1975). However these methods have not been as successful as might have been hoped when applied to practical situations.

Our work has concentrated on using the shape information contained in images of the artefacts. Shape is an important factor in identification. Visual identification as we have implemented it, requires a 2 stage strategy (see fig. 1). The first stage is to use an image processing algorithm to extract shape information from the image. This information may then be used individually to identify the object, or when this information is extracted for a set of objects, to classify that set. It should be noted that the image processing algorithms can be used on any shapes, not just whole objects. Thus, although the case study in this paper is concerned with the identification of the profile shapes of whole artefacts (pots), the methodologies used can equally well be applied to other categories of shapes, such as partial/broken artefacts, or surface decoration motifs.

Figure 1. The 2 stages of visual identification and classification.

In the remainder of this paper, we describe and compare the abilities of several different strategies that have potential for classifying a set of artefacts on the basis of their profile shapes. These strategies are different combinations of alternative algorithms for each of the two stages of the procedure, both for extracting the shape information, and for identifying the object statistically on the basis of this information.

2 SMART

The first part of the work was to create a visual lookup front-end for a database. Such a system could be used by the excavator in the field to help identify newly-excavated objects. A prototype of this interface was implemented as the System for Matching ARTefacts (SMART see fig. 2; Durham et al. 1995). This uses a pattern matching algorithm known as the generalised Hough transform (GHT) to compare the unknown image to a set of known library images. The GHT calculates a value for the similarity between two images. The similarity of the

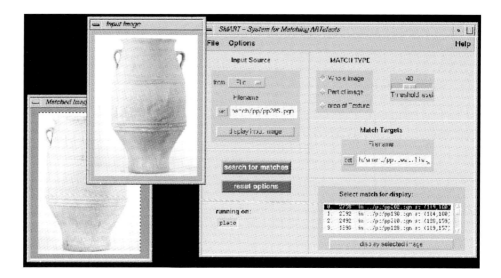

Figure 2. The SMART interface.

unknown image to each of the library images is calculated, and a ranked list of the library images is displayed. It should be noted that the system does not assign the unknown image to a specific class, but indicates which library images have shapes most similar to the unknown.

In the SMART identification method, the calculation of the similarity values is the first of the 2 stages mentioned above, the ranking of the list is the second. To extend the method to classification, only one set of images is used. Every image in the list is compared to each of the others, and the table of similarity values so produced is used to classify the artefacts (Durham *et al.* 1994).

The GHT gives good results but is very slow, especially when classifying large sets of objects. This is because it calculates a relationship between two images which needs to be done for each possible pair in the set (in the classification case this calculation is Order $\mathbf{n}^2$). It would be much quicker if the shape information calculated were a property of the individual images rather than a comparative measure between images. This would only require the calculations to be made $\mathbf{n}$ times, and would have the added bonus that the information could be calculated in advance, as it is a property of the individual image itself and will be independent of the other images. Thus the incorporation of a new artefact would only require a single set of calculations to be made.

Many such measures exist, but the one we have concentrated on is shape moments. These are statistical characteristics of the shape, based on the arrangement of its parts. Many different moments can be calculated, and the more that are used, the more detailed the description of the shape will be. An infinite set of moments will completely describe the shape (cf. Fourier harmonics). In practice it is

sufficient to use a subset of lower-order moments to give a fingerprint for each shape with the desired level of detail.

A commonly used set of moments is the set of invariant moments (Sonka *et al.* 1993: 228ff). When considered together these moments provide a description of the shape that is translation-, scale-, and rotation-invariant (that is, the result will be the same irrespective of where the shape is, what size it is and which way up it is in the image). These moments have been used successfully to identify aeroplanes, etc. (Cash/Hatamian 1987; Mertzios/Tsirikolias 1993). However early experimentation revealed that the invariant moments were inappropriate for symmetrical shapes, such as pot profiles as they consist of combinations of a few low order moments most of which are zero for symmetrical shapes. A simpler form of moments, known as normalised central (NC) moments do not suffer from this problem as they may be calculated to any order. However, they do not possess the property of rotation-invariance, but this is not a problem if care is taken to ensure that all the shapes have the same orientation.

In our 2-stage scheme for visual identification, the GHT or the moments are used to do the first stage: to extract the shape information. Several techniques can be used to perform the identification based on this information. The GHT produces a single number for each comparison, so a simple ranked list can be used here as related above. A set of moment values can be thought of as a set of features of the shape, and the object can be identified by the use of classical statistics such as the well-known k-nearest neighbour method (looking at its nearest neighbours in the feature space defined by the moments, the neighbours being known examples). Alternatively, the moments can be used as the inputs to a back-propagation neural network, which is

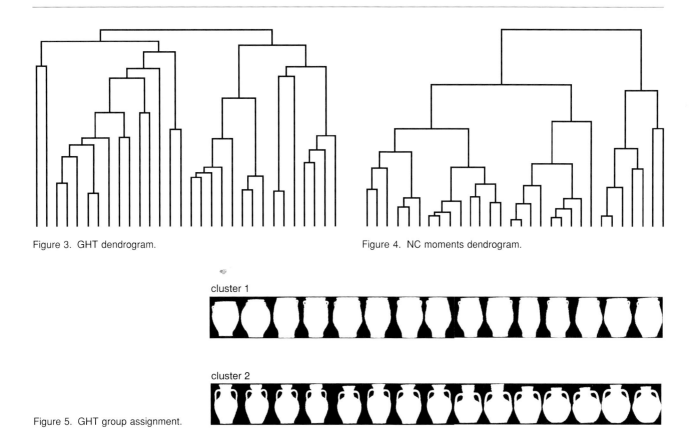

Figure 3. GHT dendrogram.

Figure 4. NC moments dendrogram.

Figure 5. GHT group assignment.

cluster 1

cluster 2

trained to identify shapes using known examples. Both of the methods have been implemented, and their performances were compared to the GHT method.

3   Testing

To compare the methods a set of 30 pots were used. The pots are modern, from Crete, and have been classified by a human (S.J. Shennan) into two groups. These groups are obvious to even the untrained eye, the pithoi being jars with very small handles, and the amphorae having large handles. Although the methods are quite capable of using the raw images, the images were pre-processed to give a solid shape. This was easily accomplished by extracting the edge map of the image, then joining the gaps in the profile, filling in the interior of the shape and removing noise from the background, using an image painting package. Thus the images used were ideal shape representations, and the quality of the images would not affect the results. The first 7 NC moments were calculated for each image and the neural net which was used had 7 input nodes, 2 output nodes and 4 nodes in the hidden layer. The 3 methods were compared using the leave-one-out method, where each

member of the set is identified on the basis of the others, and the percentage of correct identifications is recorded.

4   Results

The relative performances of the 3 methods were as follows:

GHT	100%
NC moments - k-nearest neighbours	97%
NC moments - neural net	63%

It can be seen that the NC moments were slightly less successful than the GHT when used with the k-nearest neighbours method. The neural net results were rather poor, but this work is still at a very preliminary stage and it is expected that further work on this will produce better results by using a different net topology and experimenting with different parameters in the back propagation algorithm.

The reasons for the different performances of the GHT and the NC moments becomes apparent if the shapes are classified on the basis of these methods. As mentioned above, the shape information derived in the first part of the

group 1

group 2

group 3

group 4

Figure 6. NC moments group assignment.

identification procedure can also be used to classify the objects. To do this the second stage is to use Principal Component analysis and Hierarchical Agglomerative cluster analysis (Shennan 1990: chs 12, 13) to group the objects into clusters based on the shape information. The Principal Components extracted from the shape information variables

are used for a Group Average Cluster Analysis. (More details of this procedure can be found in Durham *et al*. 1994). The relationships between the pots are shown in the accompanying dendrograms (figs 3, 5).

The GHT successfully divides the shapes into two groups, which correspond exactly with the pithoi and amphorae (figs 3, 4). The level of resolution of the GHT is demonstrated by the fact that the two shapes on the extreme left of the dendrogram are in the pithoi group, but are markedly separated from the other pithoi. From inspection of the pithoi cluster in figure 4 it can be seen that these two pots on the left are noticeably different from the rest, while still being obviously pithoi.

On the other hand, the shape information from the NC moments does not produce such a clear classification (figs 5, 6). The pots are divided into 4 groups. Two of these correspond to pithoi and two to amphorae. However, one of the amphorae groups (group 3, the third from the left) is classified as being more similar to the pithoi than to the other amphorae. In addition, one of the pithoi has been classified in this group. This is because the set of moments used does not give a sufficiently detailed description of the shape to make the necessary distinction. The moments can only distinguish that group 3 are tall and thin, groups 1 and 2 tall and fat and group 4 are short and fat, but cannot distinguish more subtle differences. The use of more, higher-order moments should alleviate this problem.

5   Conclusions

We have shown that automatic identification and classification of artefact shapes is feasible, if rather slow, using the GHT. Our preliminary results suggest that other methods exist that have a performance approaching that of the GHT, and will be much quicker to use. These results promise to produce a practical tool for automatic classification of artefact shapes in the foreseeable future.

references

Cash, G.L.   1987   Optical character recognition by the method of moments, *Computer Vision, Graphics, and*
   M. Hatamian   *Image Processing* 39, 291-310.

Doran, J.E.   1975   *Mathematics and Computing in Archaeology*. Edinburgh: Edinburgh University Press.
   F.R. Hodson

Durham, P.   1994   Classification of archaeological artefacts using shape. In: *Dept. of Electronics &*
   P.H. Lewis   *Computer Science: 1994 Research Journal*, University of Southampton.
   S.J. Shennan   <URL:http://www.ecs.soton.ac.uk/research/rj/im/lewis/phl.html>

| | 1995 | Artefact matching and retrieval using the Generalised Hough Transform. In: J. Wilcock/ K. Lockyear (eds), *Computer Applications and Quantitative Methods in Archaeology 1993*, 25-30, BAR International Series 598, Oxford: Tempus Reparatum. |

Gero, J.
   J. Mazzullo
1984   Analysis of artifact shape using Fourier series in closed form, *Journal of Field Archaeology* 11, 315-322.

Main, P.L.
1988   Accessing outline shape information efficiently within a large database II: database compaction techniques. In: C.L.N. Ruggles/S.P.Q. Rahtz (eds), *Computer Applications and Quantitative Methods in Archaeology 1987*, 243-251, BAR International Series 393, Oxford: British Archaeological Reports.

Mertzios, B.G.
   K. Tsirikolias
1993   Statistical shape discrimination and clustering using an efficient set of moments, *Pattern Recognition Letters* 14, 517-522.

Shennan, S.J.
1990   *Quantifying Archaeology*, 2nd edn. Edinburgh: Edinburgh University Press.

Sonka, M.
   V. Hlavac
   R. Boyle
1993   *Image Processing, Analysis and Machine Vision*. London: Chapman & Hall.

Wilcock, J.D.
   S.J. Shennan
1975   The computer analysis of pottery shapes with applications to bell beaker pottery. In: S. Laflin (ed.), *Computer Applications in Archaeology 1975*, 98-106, Birmingham: University of Birmingham Computer Centre.

Peter Durham
Multimedia Group
Department of Electronics & Computer Science
University of Southampton
e-mail: pd@ecs.soton.ac.uk

Paul Lewis
Department of Electronics & Computer Science
University of Southampton
e-mail: phl@ecs.soton.ac.uk

Stephen J. Shennan
Department of Archaeology
University of Southampton
Highfield
Southampton SO17 1BJ
United Kingdom
e-mail: sjs1@soton.ac.uk

Gijsbert R. Boekschoten
Dick Stapert

A new tool for spatial analysis: 'Rings & Sectors plus Density Analysis and Trace lines'

1   Introduction

Intrasite spatial analysis of Stone Age sites has often involved the use of quite complex mathematical or statistical procedures (e.g. Blankholm 1991). The present authors felt that the output of such techniques is often unsatisfactory and difficult to interpret. Therefore, they wished to develop more transparent ways of dealing with horizontal distributions of artefacts. Out of this desire, the computer program 'Rings & Sectors' (R&S) was created; it is designed as a simple tool for intrasite spatial analysis.

R&S comprises four techniques: ring and sector analysis, trace lines, and density analysis. Furthermore, it offers many options for creating distribution maps. The program has been designed in such a way that non-specialists in the computer world can easily work with it without having to go through time-consuming learning processes. This has been achieved by applying two basic principles. The first is that it is a what-you-see-is-what-you-get program; the maps, graphs, etc. on the printer output are exactly as on your screen (except for some minor details). The second principle is that we have tried to keep the screen as clear as possible by removing all superfluous information and by applying a top-down order wherever possible, so that the user automatically encounters all possibilities of the program.

2   Ring Analysis and Trace lines

The Ring & Sector Method was especially developed for Stone Age sites with a central hearth, more or less in the middle of an artefact scatter. In principle, however, it can be applied to any site with a suitable central point (Stapert 1992). The idea behind the Ring & Sector Method is that the hearth was a focal point in the daily life of a small group of people. It attracted many activities, and also played an important role in social life. Therefore, using rings and sectors around the hearth centre seems to be a 'natural' way of charting spatial patterns in such situations (fig. 1).

An attractive aspect is that the method is closely related to Binford's 'hearth model', based on ethnoarchaeological research (Binford 1983). Binford described a characteristic pattern of 'drop and toss zones' around outdoor hearths.

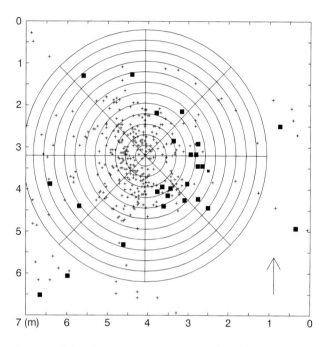

Figure 1. Distribution map of the tools (crosses) and the cores (squares) at the Magdalenian site of Pincevent, unit T112. The core symbols have been filled. A ring and sector system radiates from the centre of the hearth; in this case 8 sectors, and 12 rings of 25 cm width were employed.

The drop zone was located in the site-half where the people sat and worked most of the time, windward of the hearth in order to avoid the smoke. It can be shown that in the case of Late Palaeolithic sites with outdoor hearths, the drop zone was generally located in the tool-richest site-half.

In a ring analysis, the frequencies of artefacts are counted per distance class. One of the most important applications of the Ring & Sector Method relates to the question whether a hearth was located inside a dwelling or in the open. The ring distributions of tools from the analysed sites are found to be of two different types: unimodal and multimodal. Unimodal ring distributions point to hearths in the open (fig. 2). Artefacts that were tossed away were not stopped by tent or hut walls, with the result that ring frequencies gradually decrease away from the hearth.

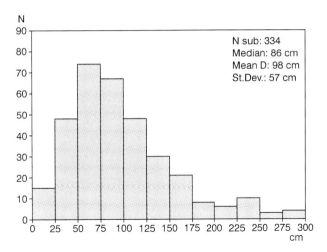

Figure 2. Ring diagram of the tools at Pincevent. The ring width can be changed to any size, so that the best resolution for any site can be found. Here rings of 25 cm have been used. The result is a unimodal graph which points to a hearth in the open air.

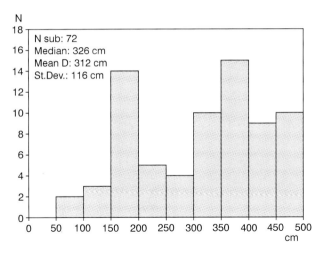

Figure 3. Ring diagram of the backed bladelets in the NW quarter of the Magdalenian site Gönnersdorf II. Bimodal or multimodal ring distributions indicate a hearth inside a dwelling. The first peak is the drop zone, where the people were sitting and working; the second peak is caused by the barrier effect of the tent wall. By executing a ring analysis for a series of sectors, a reliable reconstruction of the tent wall can be obtained (see also Boekschoten/Stapert 1993: fig. 10).

Multimodal ring diagrams are thought to be typical for artefact distributions created inside dwellings. Figure 3 shows the ring diagram for the backed bladelets in the NW quarter, up to 5 metres from the hearth centre, at the Magdalenian site of Gönnersdorf Concentration II. The first peak represents the drop zone near the hearth. The second peak is caused by the barrier effect of the tent wall. We concluded from a series of diagrams such as this that the tent had a diameter of about 7 metres (Boekschoten/Stapert 1993: fig. 10).

When a ring analysis is done for all 4 quarters, or even for 8 sectors, it will be possible to produce a reliable reconstruction of the tent wall. It should be noted that if a tent was not exactly circular, or when the hearth was located eccentrically, a ring analysis for all sectors taken together may produce an unintelligible diagram.

One of the advantages of the computer program Rings & Sectors is that one can establish the optimum level of resolution, by exploring the whole scale of measurements: from fine- to coarse-grained. In this way the best parameters for any site may be found. Our experience is that one should preferably choose a ring width between 20 and 50 cm, depending on the number of artefacts. Too narrow a ring will lead to fragmentation of the curve and obscure its character; too wide a ring may give a meaningless or even misleading picture.

An alternative way of analysing distance data is the trace line. The artefacts are ranked according to their distance from the hearth centre; in the bottom left corner the artefact closest to the hearth is plotted; in the top right corner the farthest one. This results in characteristic S-shaped curves for artefact scatters around fireplaces

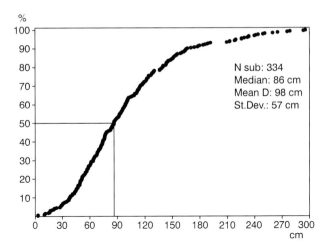

Figure 4. Trace line of the tools at Pincevent. The trace line is an alternative way of displaying distance data; the artefacts are ranked according to distance from the hearth. Characteristic S-shaped curves result for hearths in the open air. The advantage of trace lines over ring diagrams is that no class division is needed; they are therefore more precise. The median is indicated in the diagram.

in the open (fig. 4). The steep part of the S-curve coincides with the only peak in the corresponding unimodal ring diagram: the drop zone. At tent sites, 2 or 3 S-shaped curve-parts will follow each other in the trace line (fig. 5). The first 'S' reflects the drop zone. The second one is caused by the tent wall which will have been located just after the end of the steep part. The third S-shaped

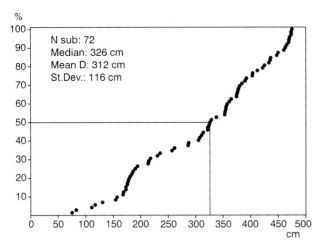

Figure 5. Trace line of the backed bladelets in the NW quarter of Gönnersdorf II. At tent sites, three S-shaped curve-parts follow each other. The first steep part, between 150 and 200 cm, represents the drop zone; the second, between 300 and 400 cm, is caused by the barrier effect of the tent wall; the third, between 450 and 500 cm, may indicate a door dump.

curve-part, if present, represents the door dump, outside the tent entrance. The advantage of trace lines over ring diagrams is that no class division is needed. It is therefore a more precise method for establishing the position of the tent wall.

3   Sector Analysis

Once it has been established whether the hearth was in the open or in a tent, a new series of questions may be approached. Figure 6 immediately makes it clear that in Pincevent (T112) the western site-half contains most of the tools. As stated above, in the case of outdoor hearths the tool-richest half is the half where people were sitting and working most of the time. We can therefore now reconstruct the prevailing wind direction during occupation: from the west. We call a diagram such as figure 6 a sector graph, which in fact is a combination of a bar graph and a pie chart. The centre of the circle represents the hearth, around which, in this case, 16 sectors are positioned. The frequencies of the artefacts are counted for each sector. The centre has the value zero; the circle represents the mean number per sector. Sectors with a frequency higher than average are given a black bar protruding outwards. Sectors below the mean have a bar protruding inwards. In this way a powerful visual presentation of the data is achieved.

One may wish to perform an analysis of the richest half only. The program is then able to calculate the position of this richest half. It will count the tools in 72 sectors of 5 degrees, and establish the richest site-half.

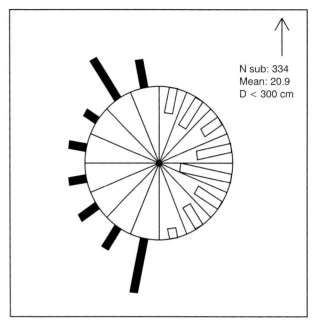

Figure 6. Sector graph of the tools at Pincevent. The centre of the circle represents the centre of the hearth. Sectors with frequencies higher than the average get black bars protruding outwards; sectors with frequencies lower than the average get a white bar protruding inwards. The circle represents the mean. It is immediately clear that in Pincevent the western half is the richest site-half.

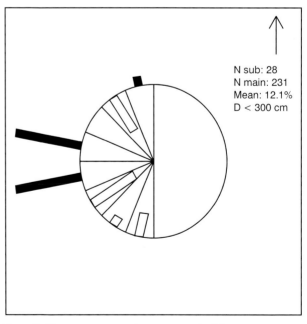

Figure 7. Pincevent, comparative sector graph of the scrapers, shown here as a percentage of the tools. The "mean" is the percentage of the scrapers in the richest site-half only.

The program Rings & Sectors offers the possibility of selecting two groups of artefacts for analysis; a 'main-selection' and a 'sub-selection'. The actual analysis is carried out on the sub-selection, which preferably should be part of the main-selection. One can compare the two sets of data, both in ring and sector analysis, and in density analysis. The frequencies of the sub-selection are then presented as percentages of the frequencies of the main-selection. This 'comparative option' may be very useful in bringing out locally occurring high proportions of, for example, tool types. Figure 7 shows the tool-richest half at Pincevent T112 (calculated by the program), with the scrapers presented as a percentage of all tools per sector. It is immediately clear that there are proportionally many scrapers in the two sectors in the middle, while they are underrepresented in most of the remaining sectors. In this case, the circle indicates the percentage of scrapers in the richest site-half (called 'mean' in the diagram).

For sector analysis, several optimizing techniques have been included in the program. Apart from the possibility to calculate the richest site-half (see fig. 7), the program also offers options to calculate the 'richest sector' and the 'highest contrast', by rotating the sectors. These calculations can be done both 'absolutely', on the basis of the sub-selection only, and 'comparatively', in which case the sub-selection is presented as a percentage of the main-selection.

With a given number of sectors, the richest sector option seeks the sector system in which (at least) one sector has the highest possible frequency (or percentage). The option 'highest contrast, absolute' seeks the sector system that maximizes the sum of the squared numbers of artefacts in the sectors: $\sum(n^2)$. The 'comparative' option maximizes the sum of the differences between the observed percentage and the overall percentage in all sectors (fig. 8).

4   Density Analysis

Density analysis is a generally applicable technique not requiring a central hearth. Over the excavated terrain a system of square cells is positioned, which can be of any size. Grids with cells of 50 × 50 or 100 × 100 cm are most common as such cells often form the basic excavation units. Inside these cells black circles are placed, the size of which reflects the relative frequency of artefacts in the cells. Figure 9 shows a density map of the tools at Pincevent (T112); a grid size of 50 cm was used.

Just as in the case of the Ring & Sector Method, the program offers the possibility to establish the optimal resolution for density analysis. In figure 10 the same data have been used as in figure 9, but here the density map is based on a grid size of 25 cm. This clearly gives much more detail.

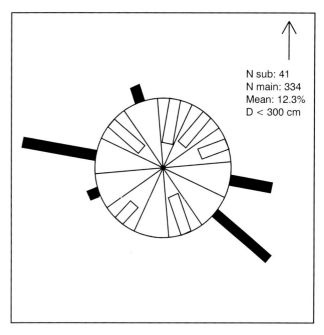

N sub: 41
N main: 334
Mean: 12.3%
D < 300 cm

Figure 8. Pincevent, sector graph of the scrapers as a percentage of all tools. The graph has been optimized by rotating the sector system, so that the highest possible contrast is obtained.

The program includes several options for the parameters of density maps, in order to make these maps more analytical. It is possible, for example, to use three different systems of class division (Cziesla 1990):

1. the linear class division, which simply divides the highest cell frequency by the number of classes (fig. 10);
2. the peripheral class division, which emphasizes the lower frequencies; class intervals grow according to a square power function (fig. 11);
3. the central class division, which emphasizes the higher frequencies; class intervals decrease according to a square root function (fig. 12). All detail is lost in the latter case, but it may be useful for stressing certain activity areas characterised by high local densities, such as flint-knapping locations or dumps.

Cziesla (1990) advocates the linear option for class division. The visual effect of density maps, however, depends on the surface areas of the circles and not on their radius. Therefore, the surface areas of the circles in the peripheral option are in fact linearly proportional to the cell values (or to be more precise: to the maximum values of each class). Consequently, the linear option results in a 'central' display of the data (and the central option is in fact super-central; see Stapert/Boekschoten in press).

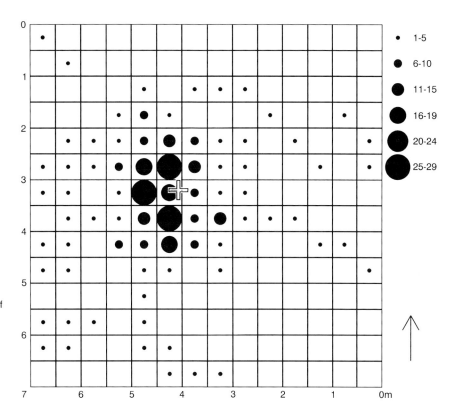

Figure 9. Pincevent, density map of the tools. The cross indicates the centre of the hearth. A grid size of 50 cm was used. Note that with a linear class division, a maximum cell value of 29, and 6 classes, there will be always one class with an interval of only 4, instead of 5.

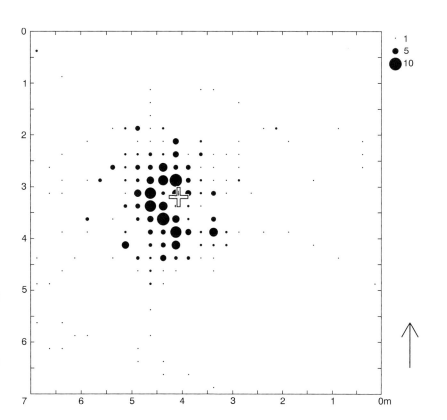

Figure 10. Pincevent, density map of the tools, based on a grid size of 25 cm. The program Rings & Sectors allows the use of any grid size for density maps, so that the optimum level of resolution may be established. Note that the grid lines were omitted in this picture. No classes were used in this case. Linear.

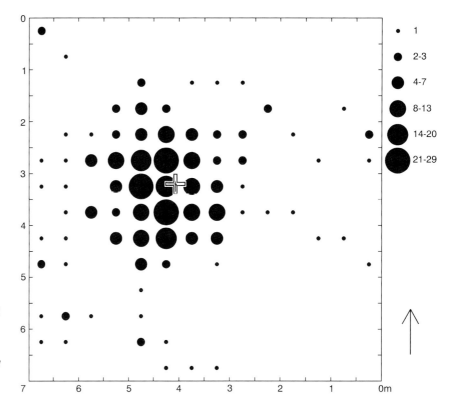

Figure 11. Pincevent, density map of the tools, based on a grid size of 50 cm. In this case a peripheral class division is used, resulting in relatively many classes for the lower frequencies and relatively few for the higher frequencies; this makes the map relatively "black".

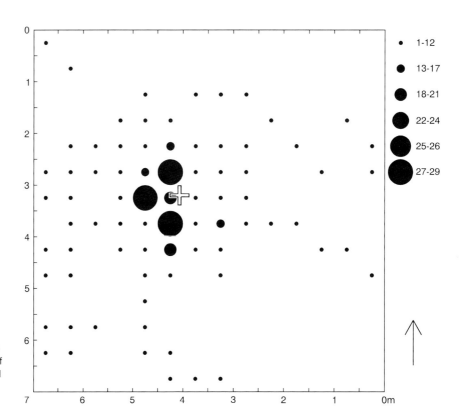

Figure 12. Pincevent, density map of the tools. In this case the size of the circles is defined by the central class division which emphasizes the higher frequencies.

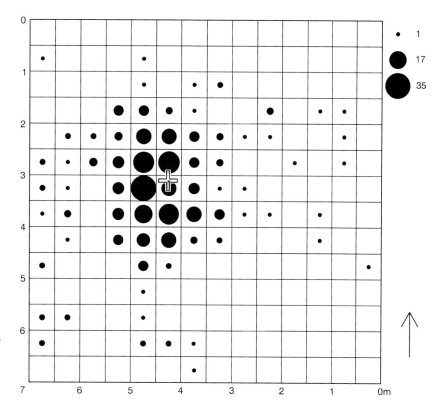

Figure 13. Pincevent, density map of the tools. In this picture, the richest cell option was used. The richest cell now contains 35 artefacts instead of 29 as in the standard position (see fig. 9). In this case no classes were used. To the right the minimum, median, and maximum cell values are shown. Peripheral.

In the computer package Rings & Sectors one can choose from 0 to 10 classes. In case one or more classes are used, the radius of the circles changes in a linear way, but the class intervals (contents) may vary, depending on how the class boundaries are calculated (linearly, peripherally or centrally). If, however, one chooses to use no classes, the diameters of the circles are calculated as a proportion of the highest cell value, for each frequency. Again, one can choose between the linear, peripheral and central options; in the latter cases the diameters of the circles are transformed by square root or square power functions, respectively. Figures 10, 13 and 14 are density maps without a class division.

In our opinion, the peripheral option without class division results in the clearest, and — more importantly — the most 'honest' pictures.

As in the case of sector analysis, the program offers several options for optimizing density maps. It is possible to move the grid freely over the excavated area; this of course only makes sense when artefact locations were measured individually. The most straightforward optimizing technique included in the program is the richest cell option: the grid is moved by the program so that the richest possible cell is found. This can be done either with absolute frequencies of the sub-selection, or comparatively (the sub-selection

expressed as a percentage of the main-selection: see below). Figure 13 presents the same data as in figure 11, but using the richest cell option (absolutely). The richest cell now contains 35 artefacts, instead of 29 as in the standard grid position; an increase of 21 %. This procedure results in 'standardizing' a density map, so that different sites can be compared in a more meaningful way. One could also say that in this way a density map is 'focused', so that the sharpest picture is obtained (in fig. 13, there is only one cell in the highest class, in figure 11 there are three). When using the 'highest contrast option', the program calculates the grid system for which the sum of squared cell frequencies is maximized.

The program offers several alternative ways to calculate class divisions. For example, one can suppress extreme values, as advocated by Cziesla (1990), or one can manually define class intervals in whichever way one desires.

A special utility is the frequency map (fig. 14), which is a numerical representation of the density map.

5   Proportion maps
One may wish to know not only the frequency distribution of the artefacts (of a specific group) over the cells, but also their proportion, relative to a greater population (for example, the percentage of scrapers, relative to the

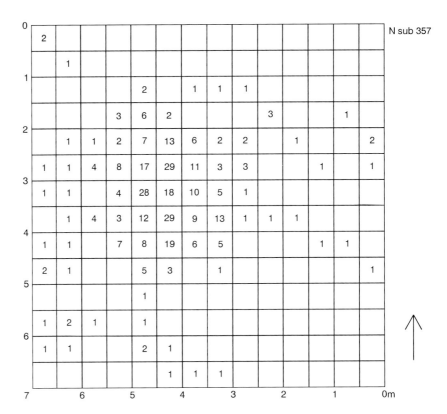

Figure 14. Pincevent, frequency map of the tools. The actual cell values which form the basis of density maps are shown.

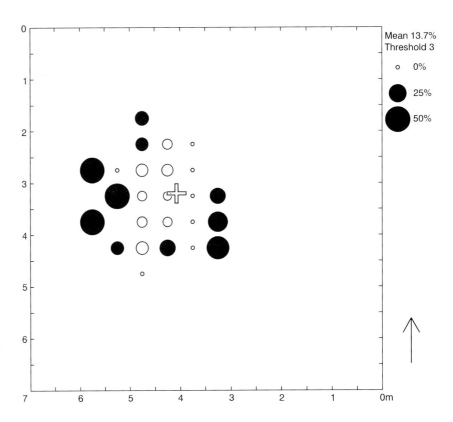

Figure 15. Pincevent, proportion map of the scrapers shown as a percentage of the tools. Black circles represent cells in which the percentage is higher than that over the whole site; open circles represent cells with a percentage lower than average. This map makes it clear that the scrapers occur particularly at some distance away from the hearth. In this case a threshold value of 3 was chosen; this means that only cells with 4 or more tools (in the main-selection) are shown. Again, the peripheral option without classes was used.

total number of tools). As noted before, the program allows 2 selections. These selections can be compared to each other in a so-called proportion map (fig. 15). In such maps, cells with black circles have a percentage that is higher than the proportion over the whole site. Open circles indicate cells containing less than the overall percentage (indicated to the right of the map: 'mean'). In this way, areas with higher or lower percentages than average are immediately visible.

A problem of proportion maps is that cells with low frequencies easily dominate the whole picture; all cells with only 1 artefact will result in either 0 or 100 percent. To avoid this problem, the program allows you to give a threshold value. Cells with a number of artefacts (in the 'main-selection') equal to or lower than this threshold value are not shown on the map. As can be seen in figure 15, only cells close to the hearth pass the threshold (and contain at least 4 tools).

The program is able to optimize proportion maps by moving the grid. For example, it can find the grid position with the highest possible proportion in one (or more) cells. It is also possible to calculate the grid in which the sum of the difference between the percentage over the whole site and the observed percentage in all cells is maximized. The result will be that cells with a low percentage of an artefact type and cells with a high percentage contribute more to the position of the grid than cells with a value around the mean.

6　　　　Cartography

Cartography is, of course, the most basic tool for the analysis of any spatial distribution. The program always starts with a distribution map as a basis for all subsequent analyses, so that one remains aware of the raw data that are being analysed.

There are several options for producing distribution maps. Three selections can be made:

a. The sub-selection, to which only one symbol (out of 19) can be attached; in this way any group of artefact types can be given the same symbol.
b. The main-selection; here one can assign symbols within a record field (artefact type, burnt/unburnt, broken/unbroken, etc.). Every category of artefacts within any field may have its own symbol. One can easily switch between several fields.
c. The fill selection, in which artefact types can be selected that must have filled symbols in the map. For example, all tools may be selected in the main-selection, with a different symbol for each tool type; in the fill selection one can then choose those artefacts that are burnt. Many other combinations are possible, so that clear and analytical maps of different types can be produced.

7　　　　Summary

The program Rings & Sectors supports four techniques for spatial analysis that are considered by the authors to be transparent: ring and sector analysis, trace lines, and density analysis. Furthermore, it offers many options for creating distribution maps. The program makes it possible to explore the whole scale of measurements from coarse- to fine-grained. In this way the optimal level of resolution for any site can be established, a prerequisite for meaningful quantitative approaches.

All results, whether maps, tables or diagrams, can be printed out on laser printers.

references

Binford, L.R.   1983   *In Pursuit of the Past. Decoding the Archaeological record.* London: Thames and Hudson.

Blankholm, H.P.   1991   *Intrasite spatial analysis in theory and practice.* Århus: Århus University Press.

Boekschoten, G.R   1993   Rings & Sectors: a computer package for spatial analysis; with examples from Oldeholt-
  D. Stapert   wolde and Gönnersdorf, *Helinium* 33 (1), 20-35.

Cziesla, F.   1990   *Siedlungsdynamik auf steinzeitlichen Fundplätzen. Methodische Aspekte zur Analyse
                                         latenter Strukturen.* Bonn: Holos.

Stapert, D.   1992   *Rings and sectors: intrasite spatial analysis of Stone Age sites.* PhD thesis, University of
                                         Groningen.

Stapert, D.   in press   Density analysis with many options; a new computer program, *Helinium.*
  G.R. Boekschoten

Gijsbert R. Boekschoten
Stoeldraaierstraat 15
9712 BT Groningen
The Netherlands

Dick Stapert
Department of Archaeology
Groningen University
Poststraat 6
9712 ER Groningen
The Netherlands
e-mail: stapert@let.rug.nl

Susan Holstrom Loving

Estimating the age of stone artifacts using probabilities

1   Introduction

This article describes an application of the Bayesian approach to estimate the age of lithic artifacts collected by surface surveys in West Central Italy (fig. 1). Although the application refers to very specific circumstances and cannot be directly transferred to a different situation or region, the general procedure may be useful as a way to systematically pull together disparate information to assign materials to classes.

2   The archaeological problem

The problem was to estimate the age of lithic artifacts collected on the surface of older land formations during archaeological surveys of the Agro Pontino (Voorrips *et al.* 1991), the Fondi Basin (Bietti *et al.* 1988), and the area around Cisterna (Attema 1993) in West Central Italy (fig. 2). Physical geographers from the University of Amsterdam, who mapped the soils in the area, established the relative ages and surface stability of various formations (Sevink *et al.* 1982: 1984). Subsequent research provided absolute dates for some of the older formations with stable surfaces (Hearty/Dai Pra 1986; De Wit *et al.* 1987), which is where Palaeolithic materials could be found coming up in the plough zone. On these stable surfaces one would not expect to find sites for excavation, but instead recover a portion of a fossil archaeological landscape in the form of a palimpsest of artifacts discarded over thousands and thousands of years.

Some of the stone artifacts collected could be assigned to tool types that are considered chronologically diagnostic in the region. These artifacts were used to date sets of aggregated fields, termed sites, in a very general way, i.e., Middle Palaeolithic, Early Upper Palaeolithic etc. This is a standard procedure for dealing with lithic scatters, at least in America (e.g. Bamforth 1986) and Northern Europe (e.g. Arts 1989). Information published about the coastal area north of the Agro Pontino, where surfaces are also rather stable, led us to believe that we, too, could identify changes in site distribution over time in this way. In working with the materials, however, it became apparent that this would not be possible.

As part of the survey project and fulfilment of requirements for his doctorate, Kamermans (1993)

Figure 1. Location of study area.

conducted a land evaluation study of the region using artifacts collected by the Agro Pontino survey. Basing himself on presence/absence of periods represented at sites, determined by the presence of chronologically diagnostic tools and cores in the region, as stated above, he found that all the apparent differences in land use throughout the Palaeolithic could be explained by intervening geological processes. Thus, he concluded that the region was regarded as a single unit, at least for resource exploitation, throughout the Palaeolithic.

In the course of my investigation of the Agro Pontino materials, I found that there seemed to be so many sites with more than one chronological component that it would be unlikely that we should discover any spatio-temporal differences using presence/absence of components at sites.

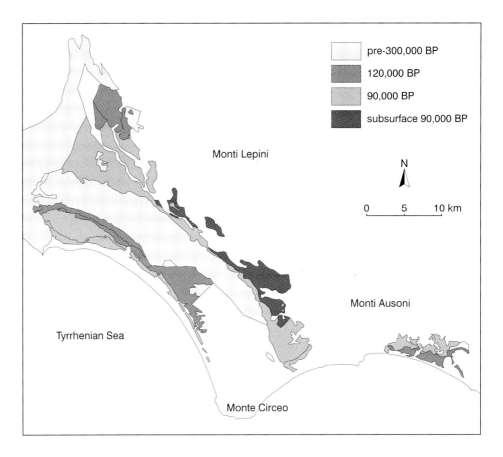

Figure 2. Distribution of older formations in the study area.

This aspect of the archaeological record of the Agro Pontino is brought into relief by comparing it with a more extensive sample along the Tyrrhenian coast. Mussi and Zampetti (1984-1987), two Italian researchers, had compiled the association of three Palaeolithic cultures — Mousterian, Aurignacian, and Epigravettian — represented in 49 sites along the coast from the Tevere to the Monte Circeo, including several on the Agro Pontino.

A set of chi-square tests on the co-occurrence or lack of it between these cultures shows that associations are due to chance (fig. 3), whereas the associations between the three cultures in sites on the Agro Pontino are all more than expected and the probability that this is due to chance is less than .05 in each case. Thus, the archaeology of the Agro Pontino appears to be quite different from the coastal area in general.

This situation meant that the evidence for differential use of the landscape within a cultural period and any changes through time would require an estimate of age at the level of the individual artifact rather than at the level of the site or location. To my knowledge, this had never been done with surface artifacts.

3 Expertise for estimating the age of artifacts

A recent article by Buck and Litton (1991) not only encouraged archaeologists to use Bayesian approaches, but provided a clear description about how to do so. Their idea that prior probabilities and additional data collected were forms of expertise was absolutely crucial. Bayes's theorem provides a way to pull together various kinds of expertise.

We did have or could collect various types of information, or forms of expertise, that might contribute to estimating artifact age.

3.1 AGE OF LAND SURFACES AND ARCHAEOLOGICAL CULTURES IN THE REGION

The first type of information was the age of land surfaces in the area (fig. 2). Absolute dates for the latest tuff deposits are .338 Myr BP, stage 9-10 (?) (Fornaseri 1985) and for the Latina level are .54 Myr BP, stage 15 (De Wit *et al.* 1987). Minturno level deposits, including the beach ridge and associated aeolian sands, the coastal and inland lagoons, and the travertines, were dated to the last inter-glacial, *c.* .12 Myr BP, stage 5e, and Borgo Ermada level deposits, the beach ridge and coastal and inland lagoons,

Table 1. Approximate ages of geological formations on the Agro Pontino and archaeological cultures in West Central Italy.

Years BP	Formation	Archaeological culture
9,000		*Mesolithico*
12,000	Late Glacial aeolian sands	- - - - - - - - - -
		Epigravettiano
20,000		- - - - - - - - - -
		Gravettiano
		Aurignaziano
		Uluzziano
35,000		- - - - - - - - - -
90,000	Borgo Ermada level	*Pontiniano*
120,000	Minturno level	- - - - - - - - - -
		Musteriano
		Acheuleano
350,000	Colli Albani tuff	
550,000	Latina level	

Open air and cave sites along the Tyrrhenian coast, West Central Italy (N = 49)

Aurignaziano

Musteriano		present	absent
	present	17 (17.6)	4 (3.4)
	absent	24 (23.4)	4 (4.6)

Chi-square = 0.19, df = 1
Approximate p = .65

Aurignaziano

Epigravettiano		present	absent
	present	13 (10.7)	12 (14.3)
	absent	8 (10.3)	16 (13.7)

Chi-square = 1.76, df = 1
p = .18

Surface scatters on older formations in the Agro Pontino and Fondi Basin (N = 208)

Aurignaziano

Musteriano		present	absent
	present	68 (52.6)	82 (97.4)
	absent	5 (20.4)	53 (37.6)

Chi-square = 24.7, df = 1
p < .05

Aurignaziano

Epigravettiano		present	absent
	present	59 (41.8)	60 (77.2)
	absent	14 (31.2)	75 (57.8)

Chi-square = 25.61, df = 1
p < .05

Figure 3. Comparison between sample on the coast of West Central Italy as compiled by Mussi and Zampetti (1984-1987) and sample from surfaces of older formations on the Agro Pontino and Fondi Basin.

were dated to about .09 Myr BP, stage 5b (Hearty/Dai Pra 1986).

Table 1 shows the temporal juxtaposition between the archaeological cultures and the age of land surfaces. Given the approximate ages of archaeological cultures, the Lower Palaeolithic *Acheuleano* and Middle Pleistocene Middle Palaeolithic *Musteriano* and *Pontiniano*, would be restricted to the tuff and Latina levels.

3.2   TYPOLOGY AND TECHNOLOGY OF LITHIC ARTIFACTS RECOVERED FROM EXCAVATIONS

The second source of information was the artifacts recovered from major excavations in the area reported in the literature (table 2). Altogether, the information conveyed by the excavators constitutes a kind of collective expertise for the area. The completeness and detail of the reports, however, vary considerably, and, of course, the typologies used to describe the materials also vary according to whether the assemblages are Lower or Middle Palaeolithic or Upper Palaeolithic. In the more complete reports diverse kinds of information are offered. In addition to counts of typed tools are counts of different types of cores, counts of different types of debitage (flakes, blades, bladelets, burin spalls, etc.), counts or indices of Levallois flakes, and in some cases, counts of Pontinian scrapers (Middle Palaeolithic side scrapers with Quina retouch), which is a kind of 'stylistic' category.

As an archaeologist wanting to tap this expertise for my particular problem, I asked, 'given the contents of excavated sites, what is the probability that a particular

artifact collected on the surface of the Agro Pontino comes from each of the 7 archaeological cultures?'.

The first step in the application was to construct probabilities for tool and core types etc., from the excavation reports available. This was done in three steps:

1. The Middle and Upper Palaeolithic type lists (Bietti 1976-1977; Bordes 1961) were combined to create a single type list that could incorporate the more common types. The artifact illustrated in figure 4 will be used as an example. It is typologically and technologically an end scraper on a flake. All Middle Palaeolithic end scrapers, Bordes types 30 and 31, most of which are made on flakes, were put into the same category as Upper Palaeolithic end scrapers on flakes, Bietti type 3.
2. Then, for each archaeological culture, counts of tool types were summed across the sample for that culture and percentages calculated.
3. Then, two probability tables were constructed, which were made conditional on the age of the land surface (table 3). The first table, to be used for artifacts found on tuff soils and the Latina level, was made by summing the percentages for each type across all seven

Table 2. Archaeological cultures represented in excavated sites in West Central Italy (compiled from: Bietti 1976-1977, 1984a, 1984b; Kuhn 1990; Piperno/Biddittu 1978; Segre-Naldini 1984; Taschini 1967, 1979; Tozzi 1970; Vitagliano/Piperno 1990-1991; Zampetti/Mussi 1988).

Archaeological culture	Site	Absolute dating, BP
Mesolithico	Riparo Blanc	8,565 ± 80
Epigravettiano	Peschio Ranano	9,730 ± 150
Epigravettiano	Riparo Salvini	12,400 ± 170
	Palidoro	15,900 ± 150
Aurignaziano	Grotta Barbara	
	Fosselone, level 21	
Pontiniano	Grotta Breuil	36.6 ± 2.7 (Kyr)
Must. denticulato	Fosselone, level 27	
Pontiniano	Grotta di San Agostino (levels 1 to 3)	54 ± 11 to 43 ± 9 (Kyr)
Pontiniano	Grotta Guattari (levels 1-5)	77.5 ± 9.5 to 54.2 ± 4.1 (Kyr)
Pontiniano	Grotta della Cava	
Pontiniano	Grotta dei Moscerini (levels 39-25)	96 ± 1 to 79 (Kyr)
Pontiniano	Monte delle Gioie	
Pontiniano	Sedia del Diavola	
Musteriano	Torre-in-Pietra, level d	
Acheuleano	Torre-in-Pietra, level m	

Table 3. Prior probabilities that an end scraper on flake is associated with different archaeological cultures (based on 103 end scrapers on flakes reported in the literature).

Archaeological culture	If found on Latina level or tuff:	If found on Minturno or Borgo Ermada level:
Acheuleano	.11	-
Middle Pleistocene *Musteriano,* *Pontiniano*	.04	-
early Upper Pleistocene *Pontiniano*	.03	.04
middle Upper Pleistocene *Pontiniano*	.08	.09
Aurignaziano	.30	.35
Epigravettiano	.03	.04
Mesolithico	.41	.48

archaeological cultures and dividing each percentage by the sum to give the probabilities. The second table, to be used for artifacts found on the surfaces of other formations was constructed the same way, but only five of the archaeological cultures were used.

With this information, prior probabilities were assigned to all survey artifacts that could be put in one of the listed classes conditional upon the age of the land surface where they were found. The end scraper in figure 4 was found on soils in travertines, which developed during the Last

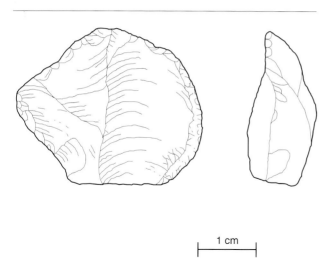

├─── 1 cm ───┤

Figure 4. An end scraper on flake collected on travertine soils in the Agro Pontino.

Interglacial, in the same period as the Minturno level, *c.* 120,000 BP. Thus, the prior probabilities for it are found in the second probability table in table 3.

3.3   TECHNOLOGICAL ATTRIBUTES OF LITHIC ARTIFACTS

The third source of potential information was technological change in lithic manufacture. Lithic specialists (e.g. Cotterell/Kamminga 1987; Crabtree 1972b; Faulkner 1973; Parry 1987) have shown that changes in such things as core platform preparation, flake profiles, flaking angles, types of fracture etc., can reflect changing techniques and tools used for lithic manufacture, which would certainly have occurred over the long period of time represented in this region. There was also reason to suspect that approaches to flaking the local raw materials changed during the Middle Palaeolithic in this region (Kuhn 1990, 1990-1991).

After selecting variables potentially relevant in a technological sense from publications by lithics specialists, I collected the data from about 900 flakes and 400 cores from four excavated collections housed in Rome. These collections were Grotta Guattari, dated from about .78 through .50 Kyr BP, level 3 of Grotta Breuil, dated to about .36 Kyr BP (both in Schwarcz *et al.* 1990-1991), part of the Aurignacian in Riparo Salvini and part of level 21 Grotta dei Fossellone (Blanc/Segre 1953; not dated radiometrically) and the *in situ* portions of Riparo Salvini (collected by A. Bietti; not dated radiometrically), dated to about 12,400 BP (Avellino *et al.* 1989). Probability tables were constructed using the chronologically significant technological variables or combinations of them that emerged from the analysis of the collections. The probabilities were derived directly from the data itself or from models that fit the data.

Unfortunately, it was not possible to study samples from all seven archaeological cultures, and it was necessary to collapse categories to middle Middle Palaeolithic and earlier, late Middle Palaeolithic, Early Upper Palaeolithic, and Late Upper Palaeolithic and later (table 4). The probabilities for tool and core types were recalculated to fit these four temporal categories. If samples from the other cultures — i.e. Lower Palaeolithic, Middle Pleistocene Middle Palaeolithic, and Mesolithic — are analysed technologically, then this will no longer be necessary.

The next step in the application was to calculate posterior probabilities for all items that had acquired a prior probability in the first step and that could be coded for the relevant technological variables listed in the technological probability tables. In doing so, it was assumed that these two sets of probabilities were independent of each other. This was necessary because I had no information about the relationship between tool types and the technological variables.

The end scraper on a flake found on soils developed in Last Interglacial travertines (fig. 4) has adjusted prior probabilities for four archaeological temporal categories as shown in table 5. Technologically, this artifact is a conchoidal tertiary flake with a smooth prepared platform, with dorsal flaking oblique to the direction from which the flake was struck, and with no ventral features, i.e. an eraillure scar or fissures, and no signs of abrasion adjacent to the butt on the dorsal side. The probabilities for a flake with these characteristics occurring per temporal category provide additional information. The posterior probabilities are calculated using Bayes's Theorem. So, the end scraper, which has prior probabilities in favour of Late Upper Palaeolithic or later changes to probabilities in favor of Early Upper Palaeolithic.

All other artifacts with technological attributes that were chronologically significant according to the analysis of excavated materials and had no prior probabilities were assigned prior probabilities on the basis of these attributes or combinations of them.

3.4   PATINA OF FLINT ARTIFACTS DEPENDENT ON AGE,
FLINT TEXTURE, AND SOIL PARENT MATERIALS

The fourth and last source of information about age of surface artifacts in the Agro Pontino region was degree of patination. That the glossy patina on many of the artifacts collected by the Agro Pontino survey might be related to age of artifacts was suggested by Dick Stapert of the University of Groningen when he first saw them. So that this might be investigated, all artifacts were coded by comparing them with four items showing different categories of glossy patina — none, slight, medium, and heavy. Theoretically, glossy patination develops as

Table 4. Probabilities that an end scraper on flake comes from four temporal categories.

Archaeological culture	Original probability	Temporal category	Adjusted probability
if found on Latina level or tuff:			
Acheuleano	.11	middle Middle Palaeolithic or earlier	
Middle Pleistocene *Must. & Pont.*	.04		.18
early Upper Pleistocene *Pontiniano*	.03		
middle Upper Pleistocene *Pontiniano*	.08	late Middle Palaeolithic	.08
Aurignaziano	.30	Early Upper Palaeolithic	.30
Epigravettiano	.03	Late Upper Paleolithic or later	
Mesolithico	.41		.44
if found on Minturno or Borgo Ermada levels:			
early Upper Pleistocene *Pontiniano*	.04	middle Middle Palaeolithic or earlier	.04
middle Upper Pleistocene *Pontiniano*	.09	late Middle Palaeolithic	.09
Aurignaziano	.35	Early Upper Palaeolithic	.35
Epigravettiano	.04	Late Upper Palaeolithic or later	
Mesolithico	.48		.52

Table 5. Effect of additional information about technological features for estimating the age of the end scraper on a tertiary flake (based on 348 tertiary flakes examined from excavated collections).

	prior probabilities	probabilities based on technical features	posterior probabilities
middle Middle Palaeolithic or earlier	.04	.11	.01
late Middle Palaeolithic	.09	.36	.13
Early Upper Palaeolithic	.35	.39	.55
late Upper Palaeolithic or later	.52	.15	.31

superficial projections of silica are dissolved by soil water and deposited in superficial depressions on the surface of a fracture of flint, creating a glassy appearance. Important properties of the soil that promote or hinder solution of silica are pH and temperature in conjunction with the amount of organic compounds and aluminum ions (Luedtke 1992; Rottländer 1975). A few years ago, a loglinear model was found incorporating degree of patination, three archaeological periods, and three different kinds of sediment showing that these variables were probably interrelated in our samples (Loving/Kamermans 1991).

In examining the materials, we had also noted that more coarsely grained flints seemed to have less patina. According to geologists, it is probable that differences in the texture of the fracture surface seen macroscopically is due to porosity and clustering of quartz crystals in the stone as well as texture and that these properties affect both rates of weathering and appearance (Luedtke 1992).

Artifacts that had acquired a .6 probability or more for one of the four temporal categories in the previous steps of the application were used to build new loglinear models predicting for degree of patination based on age, sediment,

Table 6. Probabilities derived from loglinear models predicting degree of patination from age, type of sediment and stone texture (based on 1417 artifacts collected by surface survey).

| | Materials found in soils developed in travertines, aeolian and littoral sands: | | | | | |
| | light patina | | | heavy patina | | |
	fine-grain	medium-grain	coarse-grain	fine-grain	medium-grain	coarse-grain
middle Middle Palaeolithic or earlier	.18	.23	.24	.29	.30	.31
late Middle Palaeolithic	.23	.24	.24	.27	.29	.29
Early Upper Palaeolithic	.17	.22	.24	.30	.32	.33
late Upper Palaeolithic or later	.42	.31	.27	.14	.08	.07

Table 7. Effect of additional information about patina and texture for estimating the age of the end scraper on flake example.

	prior probabilities based on tool or core type and technological features	probabilities based on patina and texture	posterior probabilities
middle Middle Palaeolithic or earlier	0.01	.30	.03
late Middle Palaeolithic	.13	.29	.19
Early Upper Palaeolithic	.55	.32	.75
late Upper Palaeolithic or later	.31	.08	.02

and texture. Incorporating texture in the models showed that it had more effect than the type of sediment and as much effect as age of the artifact on the degree of patination; furthermore, texture of raw material is associated with the age of the artifact, so we even learned something we had not known before. After selecting the models that best fit the data, probability tables for age of artifacts given, degree of patination, texture, and type of sediment on which they were found were constructed from the models. There are two models. One for soils developed in tuff and lagoonal clays and a second one for all other soils (table 6).

The end scraper on a flake (fig. 4) was found on soils developed in travertine. It has a medium texture out of three categories — fine, medium, coarse — and a heavy degree of patination out of two categories — light and heavy. Based on these properties alone, it would have about equal probabilities of coming from one of the first three categories, but a very low probability of coming from the fourth category — Late Upper Palaeolithic or later.

The next step in the application, then, was to calculate posterior probabilities for all artifacts with prior probabilities that had not been used for analysis to construct the last set of probability tables. Again, it was assumed that information for prior probabilities was independent of the

added information. The additional information for the end scraper on flake gives it a much higher probability of dating to the Early Upper Palaeolithic (table 7).

All other flint artifacts collected by the survey from older surfaces that had not acquired probabilitistic estimates of age in the previous steps were assigned probabilities deriving from each of the temporal categories using this last set of probabilities tables.

4   Computerized aspects of the application

Calculating posterior probabilities as other sources of information become available is an extremely tedious procedure. Thus, a small computer program was written by Albertus Voorrips (University of Amsterdam) that allowed probabilities to be typed in and then performed the necessary calculations. This made it easier to 'walk' a sample of artifacts through the estimation procedure to see how the application performed.

A schema was drawn up to order the decisions used in the application. The order was generally the same as presented in the preceding section, but was adjusted to accommodate certain logical and archaeological precedents. For example, artifacts used for developing the models for degree of patina retained the probabilities used before the analysis. Likewise, certain technical attributes, most of them metrical, restricted an artifact to fewer chronological categories.

The schema was the basis for Voorrips to write a computer program to route the approximately 9000 artifacts collected by the surveys through the decision pathways, identify the appropriate probability tables, do the necessary calculations, and write out the final probabilities.

5   Assignment of artifacts to temporal categories

The final step in the application was to assign individual artifacts to one of the four temporal categories on the basis of their final probabilities. Since I do not know a way to determine a significant departure from a uniform distribution, a value of .6 or more for any one category seemed reasonable to accept as a best estimate.[1] In this way, about 4000 artifacts, a little over 40%, were assigned to one of the four temporal categories. By collapsing temporally adjacent categories into General Middle Palaeolithic and General Upper Palaeolithic, an estimate of age could be made for an additional 10% of the artifacts.

6   Discussion

These results made it possible to use counts and densities, to correct for time by calculating discard rates, and thereby to begin to see some patterning in possible use of the area. Although the data are now more tractable than before, there are certain drawbacks to the application. For one, there is no independent means of checking the validity of the results. For another, many decisions were made to construct the probability tables, and other archaeologists might do it slightly differently, which would most probably alter the outcome. Just how 'stable' the results that I obtained are is a matter for future investigation incorporating information from other or new analyses in the probability tables.

The procedure is most suitable for situations where the certainty about assignment to a class is low. If prior probabilities for an artifact belonging to a class are low, they will remain low unless additional information assigns low probabilities for the other classes. If, on the other hand, probabilities for belonging to two or more classes are about equal, additional information incorporated into the procedure will either increase the certainty of assignment of an artifact to one of the classes or it will maintain the initial uncertainty, showing that for that case the additional information is irrelevant for assignment to a class.

Acknowledgements
I would like to thank Amilcare Bietti of the University of Rome and the members of the Istituto Italiano Paleontologia Umana for access to the excavated collections and the Fondi Basin survey materials housed in Rome. I am, as usual, indebted to my partner in life and work, Albertus Voorrips; without his contribution, I would be doing the calculations into the next century. Katarina Biró, Hungarian National Museum, critically reviewed the analysis on which the technological probabilities are based.

Most of the financial support for the Agro Pontino survey was provided by the Instituut voor Pre- en Protohistorische Archeologie, Universiteit van Amsterdam. Additional funding was provided by NWO (Nederlandse Organisatie voor Wetenschappelijk Onderzoek) grant nos. 280-152-024 and 280-152-033. The project would not have been possible without the cooperation of the Soprintendenze di Lazio and the Nederlands Instituut te Rome and the participation of many students from the Instituut voor Pre- en Protohistorische Archeologie, the Instituut voor Prehistorie Leiden, and the Università di Roma, who did most of the field walking for the survey.

Finally, in preparation for this article, I would like to thank Hans Kamermans and an anonymous reviewer for their comments, which helped to improve the article and correct some of my oversights.

note

1 Bob Laxton suggested that Monte Carlo techniques might be used to establish probabilities for various probabilities under different numbers of classes.

references

Arts, N.   1989   Archaeology, environment and the social evolution of later band societies in a lowland
                                                    area. In: C. Bonsall (ed.), *The Mesolithic in Europe*, 291-312, Edinburgh: J. Donald.

Attema, P.   1993   *An Archaeological Survey in the Pontine Region.* Ph.D. dissertation. Archeologisch Cen-
                                                    trum Groningen, Rijkuniversiteit Groningen.

Avellino, E.   1989   Riparo Salvini: A new Dryas II site in Southern Lazio. Thoughts on the Late Epi-
    A. Bietti   Gravettian of Middle and Southern Tyrrhenian Italy. In: C. Bonsall (ed.), *The Mesolithic
    L. Giacopini   in Europe*, 516-532, Edinburgh: J. Donald.
    A. Lo Pinto
    M. Vicari

Bamforth, D.B.   1986   Technological efficiency and tool curation, *American Antiquity* 51(1), 38-50.

Bietti, A.   1976-   Analysis and illustration of the Epigravettian industry collected during the 1955
                                        1977   excavations at Palidoro, *Quaternaria* 19.

                                        1984a   Primi resultati dello scavo nel giacimento epigravettiano finale di Riparo Salvini
                                                    (Terracina, Latina), *Atti XXIV Riunione Scientifica dell'Istituto Italiano di Preistoria e
                                                    Protostoria nel Lazio, 8-11 Ottobre 1982*, 195-205.

                                        1984b   Il Mesolitico nel Lazio, *Atti XXIV Riunione Scientifica dell'Istituto Italiano di Preistoria e
                                                    Protostoria nel Lazio, 8-11 Ottobre 1982*, 79-102.

Bietti, A.   1988   Ricognizione sistematica di superficie nella Piana di Fondi (Latina), Primi risultati,
    M. Brucchietti   *Archeologia Laziale* IX, 389-396.
    D. Mantero

Blanc, A.C.   1953   *Excursion au Mont Circé*, Guides, Rome, INQUA, IVe Congress.
    A.G. Segre

Bordes, F.   1961   *Typologie du Paléolithique Ancien et Moyen.* Bordeaux: Delmas.

Buck, C.E.   1991   Applications of the Bayesian paradigm to archaeological data analysis. In: K. Lockyear/
    C.D. Litton   R. Sebastian (eds), *Computer Applications and Quantitative Methods in Archaeology
                                                    1990*, 93-97, BAR Intenational Series 565, Oxford: Tempus Reparatum.

Cotterell, B J.   1987   The formation of flakes, *American Antiquity* 52(4), 675-708.
    J. Kamminga

Crabtree, D.   1972   *An Introduction to Flintworking*, Occasional Papers of the Idaho State University Museum,
                                                    no. 28.

Faulkner, A.   1973   Mechanics of eraillure formation, *Newsletter of Lithic Technology* II(3), 4-12.

Fornaseri, M.   1985   Geochronology of volcanic rocks from Latium (Italy), *Rendiconti della Società Italiana di
                                                    Minerologia e Petrologia* 40, 73-106.

Hearty, P.J.   1986   Aminostratigraphy of Quaternary marine deposits in the Lazio region of Central Italy,
    G. Dai Pra   *Zeitschrift für Geomorphologie N.F.* 62, 131-140.

Kamermans, H.   1993   *Archeologie en Landevaluatie in de Agro Pontino (Lazio, Italië).* Ph.D. dissertation.
                                                    Faculteit der Ruimtelijke Wetenschappen, Universiteit van Amsterdam.

Kuhn, S.L.   1990   *Diversity within Uniformity: Tool Manufacture and Use in the 'Pontinian' Mousterian of Latium (Italy)*. Ph.D dissertation, University of New Mexico, Albuquerque.

   1990-1991   Preliminary observations on tool manufacture and use histories at Grotta Breuil, *Quaternaria Nova* I, 367-378.

Loving, S.H.
   H. Kamermans   1991   Figures from flint: first analysis of lithic artifacts collected by the Agro Pontino survey. In: A. Voorrips/S.H. Loving/H. Kamermans (eds), *The Agro Pontino Survey Project*, Studies in Prae- en Protohistorie no. 6, 99-116, Amsterdam: Instituut voor Pre- en Protohistorische Archeologie Albert Egges van Giffen, Universiteit van Amsterdam.

Luedtke, B.E.   1992   *An Archaeologist's Guide to Chert and Flint, Archaeology Research Tools*, no. 7. Los Angeles: University of California, Institute of Archaeology.

Mussie, M.
   D. Zampetti   1984-1987   La presenza umana nella pianura Pontina durante il Paleolitico medio e superiore, *Origini* XIII, 7-26.

Parry, W.J.   1987   Technological change: Temporal and functional variability in chipped stone debitage. In: W.J. Parry/A.L. Christenson (eds), *Prehistoric Stone Technology of Northern Black Mesa, Arizona*, Occasional Paper no.12, 199-256, Southern Illinois University at Carbondale: Center for Archaeological Investigations .

Piperno, M.
   I. Biddittu   1978   Studio tipologico ed interpretazione dell'industria acheuleana e pre-musteriana dei livelli *m* e *d* di Torre in Pietra (Roma). *Quaternaria* XX, 441-428.

Rottländer, R.   1975   The formation of patina on flint, *Archaeometry* 17(1), 106-110.

Schwarcz, H.P.
   W. Buhay
   R. Grün
   M. Stiner
   S. Kuhn
   G.H. Miller   1990-1991   Absolute dating of Sites in Coastal Lazio, *Quaternaria Nova* I, 51-67.

Segre-Naldini, E.   1984   Il musteriano di Grotta della Cava, Sezze Romano (Latina), *Atti della XXIV Riunione Scientifica dell'Istituto Preistoria e Protohistoria nel Lazio, 8-11 Ottobre 1982*, 142-147.

Sevink, J.
   P. Vos
   W.E. Westerhoff
   A. Stierman
   H. Kamermans   1982   A sequence of marine terraces near Latina (Agro Pontino, Central Italy), *Catena* 9, 361-378.

Sevink, J.
   A. Remmelzwaal
   O.C. Spaargaren   1984   *The Soils of Southern Lazio and Adjacent Campania*. Amsterdam: Universiteit van Amsterdam Fysisch Geologisch en Bodemkundig Laboratorium Publicatie 138.

Taschini, M.   1967   Il 'Protopontiniano' rissiano di Sedia del Diavolo e di Monte delle Gioie (Roma), *Quaternaria* IX, 301-319.

   1979   L'industrie lithique de Grotta Guattari au Mont Circé (Latium): Définition culturelle, typologique et chronologique du Pontinien, *Quaternaria* XXI, 179-247.

Tozzi, C.   1970   La Grotta di S. Agostino (Gaeta), *Rivista di Scienze Preistoriche* 25, 30-87.

Vitagliano, S.
   M. Piperno   1990-1991   Lithic industry of level 27 *beta* of the Fossellone Cave (S. Felice Circeo, Latina), *Quaternaria Nova* I, 289-304.

Voorrips, A.   1991   *The Agro Pontino Survey Project.* Studies in Prae- en Protohistorie no. 6. Amsterdam:
  S.H. Loving   Instituut voor Pre- en Protohistorische Archeologie Albert Egges van Giffen, Universiteit
  H. Kamermans (eds)   van Amsterdam.

Wit, H.E. De   1987   Stratigraphy and radiometric datings of a mid-Pleistocene transgressive complex in the
  J. Sevink   Agro Pontino (Central Italy), *Geologica Romana* 26, 449-460.
  P.A.M. Andriessen
  E.H. Hebeda

Zampetti, D.   1988   Du paléolithique moyen au paléolithique supérieur dans le Latium. In: M. Otte (ed.),
  M. Mussi   *L'Homme de Néandertal.* Actes de colloque international de Liège (4-7 décembre 1986),
                                        La Mutation, vol. 8, 273-288. Études et Recherches Archéologiques de l'Université de
                                        Liège, No. 35.

Susan Holstrom Loving
Willem Beukelstraat 30
1097 CT Amsterdam
The Netherlands
e-mail: SHL@IVIP.FRW.UVA.NL

Oleg Missikoff

Application of an object-oriented approach to the formalization of qualitative (and quantitative) data

1 Introduction

'Archaeology is the discipline concerned with the recovery, systematic description and study of material culture in the past.' (Clarke 1968)

This description of the targets of archaeological research, given by David Clarke in the fundamental 'ANALYTICAL ARCHAEOLOGY', allows us to single out the three main phases of the approach to the material culture in archaeology: the recovery phase, represented by surveys and excavations; the systematic description phase, operated through the classification of the data obtained from surveys and excavations; and the study of the results deriving from the two preceding phases, in order to obtain a deeper comprehension of the social, economical, and technological development of a certain area over a certain period.

The present work is oriented towards an enhancement of the conceptual and methodological tools for the management of the second phase which, compared to the others, shows a much lower degree of maturity. The problem appears even more urgent if we think that this phase occupies a conspicuous share of the archaeological research. In fact, according to K. Chang (1967), 'it is reasonable to estimate that 80 or 90 percent of an archaeologist's time and energy is spent in classifying his material.' The acknowledged importance of this aspect of research has led, along the history of archaeological studies, to the production of a large number of publications oriented towards the design of a methodological approach which could be universally accepted. Unfortunately, unlike what happened, for example, to the techniques of archaeological excavations, any such attempt has, sofar, inevitably failed.

The target of this work is to carry forward a new proposal which, supported by advanced tools of analysis borrowed from the information technology and specifically designed to perform this task, could guarantee a reasonable chance of success. The paper is structured in two main parts: the first part shows a synthesis of the history of classification theory in archaeology, for providing a frame of reference for the problem; this synthesis is followed, in the second part, by a description of the informatic tool the use of which is proposed, together with a brief example of the implementation of this tool, to a case study.

2 A historical outline of classification in archaeology

With the benefit of hindsight it is possible to identify four main phases in the history of archaeological thought concerning classification problems. For a better understanding of the fourth phase, currently active, it is necessary to give a brief examination of the key points which have characterized the previous three.

2.1 THE 'INTUITIVE' PHASE

The first phase, defined as 'intuitive', represents the period of the history of classification in which the artifact analysis is performed on a totally empirical base. This phase, the higher expression of which is represented by the work of Oscar Montelius (1874, 1885, 1899), was characterized by the production of increasingly refined typologies, but without any need, from the archaeologists, to explain the principles on which the typologies were built: 'Montelius was not concerned in a methodology for determining types, whose existence he implicitly accepted' (Klejn 1982).

2.2 THE 'SUBJECTIVE' PHASE

The second phase is represented by the emergence, in the early thirties, of the awareness of the fundamental importance of a clearer exposition of the principles on which typologies were based (Gorodzov 1933; Kluckhohn 1939). During this phase typology is recognized as a substantially subjective operation (Brew 1946; Krieger 1944), but the lack of conceptual tools able to formalize a qualitative-based approach led to a general dissatisfaction with the traditional model and, consequently, to the search for a new paradigm which could offer a greater warranty of formalization. In fact the subjective phase, though having recognized the importance of an explicit formalization of the constituent elements of typologies, failed to provide a classificatory paradigm able to handle the problem.

2.3 THE 'POSITIVIST' PHASE

That paradigm has instead been envisaged, by the supporters of the mathematical approach to artifact study and classification, in the numerical codification of attributes to be analysed by means of statistical techniques (Bordes 1950; Brainerd 1951; Ford 1949; Robinson 1951). Imported from natural and social sciences, where they had been utilized with success, statistics seemed to offer what archaeological research needed: a tool of formal analysis which used standardized and explicit mechanisms, thus ensuring a greater comprehension of the conceptual paths followed by analysts and, consequently, a possibility of verification and replication of the single analysis.

The fifties provided a stage for harsh epistemological disputes between the supporters of the traditional approach (Ford 1954) and the proponents of the new techniques of analysis (Spaulding 1953). These disputes ended with an explosion of popularity for the quantitative approach, leitmotif of the third phase (Binford/Binford 1966). Though moving from a sound principle, for a number of reasons, this approach has proven of a little practical use in archaeological research.

2.4   THE CONTEMPORARY SCENE
Since the loss of popularity of the quantitative paradigm (Aldenderfer 1987; Christenson/Read 1977; Thomas 1978), archaeologists have become very cautious in dealing with the problems of classification (Seitzer 1978) and, consequently, very few have been the proposals of new or revolutionary approaches to classification (Kampfmeier 1986). In fact the current phase has not yet produced an algorithm which could have enough impact to characterize it.

At this stage it appears necessary to stress two key points which constitute the conceptual base on which the present research has been structured. The first point concerns the traditional approach that, if failing at a theoretical level for its poor possibilities of formalization, has shown a demonstrable empirical value and does not need any improvement at a technical level, in fact, as Thomas has put it: 'To propose a computer technique for deriving morphological types presumes that traditional methods have failed, and nobody has demonstrated that yet' (Thomas 1978). The second point refers to the need, stressed by the proponents of the quantitative approach, of a tool of analysis able to produce formal descriptions: such a need is even more impelling now than it was thirty years ago.

The conclusion drawn from these considerations is that an integrated reformulation, thus allowing the formalization of typologies operated through a traditional methodology, could offer a reasonable possibility of solving the paradigmatic disputes which have characterized more than sixty years of typological debate.

The present work represents an attempt to produce a synthesis between the two approaches. In fact the model presented hereafter agrees with the definition of typology as

a subjective task but, at the same time, believes in the necessity for a rigorous formalization of the principles on which each typology is based. The target therefore results in a subjective but formal and explicit approach to artifact typology. This paradigm is made complete by the support of a tool of analysis which has been borrowed from computer science.

3   The 'Mosaico' Project
The 'Mosaico' Project has been developed in Italy within the CNR (National Research Council), and consists of an environment for conceptual modelling according to the paradigm Object-Oriented (Coad/Yourdon 1991; Khoshafian/Abnous 1990). This modelling, performed using the formal language TQL++ (see sec. 6), has the structure of a knowledge base (KB). The system allows the formal description of any kind of entity using attributes both qualitative and quantitative, whatever the epistemological position of the user. It is however necessary to exhaustively explain the conceptual path chosen for the entity definition.

Mosaico assists the analyst in the formal and correct description of the application domain, operating a syntactical and semantical verification of given definitions. Following this procedure it is possible to avoid those little 'arrangements' performed by authors in the presence of practical inconsistencies of typologies not perfectly formulated at a theoretical level.

4   Terminological specifications
Before going any further, it is necessary to clarify some key points of this method.

To begin with a clear definition of the three key words mentioned above, Typology, Taxonomy and Classification, will be given. These terms are currently used in archaeology but their meanings vary according to the different epistemological positions of the various authors, for that reason the definitions given here are drawn from Artificial Intelligence.

– Typology: The word 'typology' specifies the definition of a conceptual entity, the 'type', which describes a group of similar phenomena, the 'class', by means of a number of attributes considered to be 'significant', together with the type and range of values that those attributes can assume in order to consider a certain phenomenon as a member of that specific group.
– Taxonomy: In the real world phenomena do not have isolated lives, rather they are organically connected with other phenomena by a network of hierarchical relationships. These relationships can be of various kinds, but for what concerns the present work, just one type will be taken into consideration: the Generalization/

Specialization relationship (also called 'ISA' relationship). The word 'Taxonomy' is used to indicate the organization of gen/spec relationships between all types within a certain application.

- Inheritance: As previously stated, the various entities are interconnected through a network-type organization of generalization/specialization relationships forming a hierarchical structure, graphically expressed by an inverted tree. This has at its root a very general type which is then refined using two mechanisms: 1) Restriction of the range of values for one or more attributes; 2) Addition of new attributes. The mechanism of inheritance simplifies and speeds up the definition of more specialized concepts further down the tree. In fact the ISA relationship requires only to show the differences from the more generalized concept as all the rest are equal by default.

- Classification: Compared with the two concepts explained above, the term 'classification' appears very easy to define. It indicates the operation of assigning a phenomenon (be it an object, a decoration, a culture, or else) to a certain class by matching the types and values of its attributes to the types and ranges given in the definition of types.

5   Description of the system

The target of Mosaico is to support the designer in the formal and correct specification of an application domain and in the rapid prototyping of the application software. The fundamental component of the Mosaico System is the 'type' intended as the abstraction of a group of objects in a particular application domain. In other words an archetypal representation describing common aspects of individuals belonging to the same group. In Artificial Intelligence types are also referred to as 'entities'.

In Mosaico, the KB is organized using a hybrid methodology: 'Frames' are used to represent concepts and a 'Semantic Network' to define relationships between frames (Colombetti 1985; Giarratano/Riley 1989).

In structuring a KB much like a database we have two main levels of organization: the schema definition and the input of actual data. In the Mosaico environment the two levels are referred to as 'intensional' and 'extensional' respectively. At the intensional level the entities are described by listing their characteristic properties and defining the hierarchical relationship between each other. At the extensional level, on the other hand, are stored the instances of the entities represented at the intensional level. The instances are entered by associating values to the properties listed in the corresponding entities.

The operation of type definition is performed by using a conceptual language specifically conceived: 'TQL++'.

6   'TQL++': a Conceptual Modelling Language

TQL++ (Type Query Language). Because of the complexity of the whole model we will present just the aspects more likely to be useful for the needs of an archaeologist attending to artifact classification.

TQL++ has been conceived for the description of the entities of specific application domains; the static definition of a type is structured in five main sets:

- Structural Specification
- Properties Typing
- Integrity Constraints
- Hierarchical Organization
- Type Specialization

6.1   STRUCTURAL SPECIFICATION

The type structural specification consists in supplying the list of properties and, for each of them, the type corresponding to the values that they can assume.

<type-name> := [<prop-name> : <prop-type>
<prop-name> : <prop-type>]

Properties can be single or compound: a single property can have just one value associated to it; a compound property can be either 'multivalued' or 'structured'. In the first case it is possible to associate more than one value to it, whereas in the second it is not possible to associate any value directly to it. Structured properties have 'subproperties' and values will be associated with them (unless they are structured themselves as well).

6.2   PROPERTIES TYPING

A property type is used to show the kind of value it can assume when ascribed to an application object. The properties of a hypothetical type of vase, for example, could be: 'id' (number for object identification), 'max_h' (for maximum height), 'max_w' (for maximum width), 'dec' (for decoration). Those properties shall be typed showing that the values for 'id' should be integer numeric values *(integer)*, those for 'max_h' and 'max_w' should be real numeric values *(real)*, whereas for 'dec' the values should be indicated through a string of characters *(string)*.

The indication of a property type *(typing)*, can either use a base type such as *integer* or *string*, or it can be more precisely specified by the user through some property typing tools. Here follows the description of the two simpler property typing tools offered by the type specification language TQL.

Listing: Through a listed set, it is possible to explicitly indicate allowed values for a given property (this construction is used mainly with categorical variables). For example to the property 'dec' we can associate the values: 'painted' or 'scratched'; this implies that for any object of the type 'vase', the property 'dec' can assume just one of the two indicated values:

vase := [..., dec: (painted, scratched), ...]

Range: Like the previous case this construction allows the indication of the values that a given property can assume, but without listing them all. The present construction can be used for continuous variables, in which case it suffices to indicate the minimum and maximum values allowed (it is also possible to use the extreme values):

vase := [max_h: (3...150), max_w: (5...80)]

Tuple: Typing through tuple is requested when a property is structured. In this case the property is defined by its subproperties, referred in the associated tuple:

vase := [..., dec: [lip_dec: string, body_dec: string, base_dec: string], ...]

Sofar the possibilities have been listed that the language TQL++ offers to type the properties that define the information structure of an entity, and consequently of the objects associated to it, which all together form the corresponding *class*. In the following paragraph, the possibilities of imposing constraints in the phase of type definition will be shown. Although those constraints may be of different sorts, they will have to be respected by all object introduced in the KB.

6.3   INTEGRITY CONSTRAINTS
TQL has been conceived with a particular consideration for integrity constraints and it appears to be very powerful in this respect. As stated above, because of the complexity of this language, many of the TQL features will not be mentioned in this exposition but, for sake of clarity, will be limited to the following:

i.   Typing constraints: As already explained, giving the type of a property implies itself a limitation to the values that the corresponding objects can assume. Thus, having indicated that, for instance, the maximum height of a vase is of type *real* provokes an automatic checking by the system and an error message in case of an attempt to input a datum inconsistent with the correspondent typing like, for example, a string of characters.
ii.   Domain constraints: these constraints are associated with either the listing or the range of a property value. Here the allowed values are explicitly indicated by the user through those two typing tools.
iii. Functional constraints: It has been previously stated that properties can be single or multivalued. It is assumed for default that a property be single, like for instance

the identification number of an object. However in the phase of typing, the property type is enclosed in curly brackets. If for instance we want to express that a vase can have multiple types of decoration or be undecorated we have:
vase := [..., dec: {string}, ...]

After having performed the structural specification, together with the properties typing and the description of integrity constraints, the type definition ends with its hierarchical allocation within the whole knowledge-base structuring which is based on a conceptual tool borrowed from semantic networks: namely the ISA relationship.

6.4   HIERARCHICAL ORGANIZATION
In a knowledge-base, and more precisely in the K-Schema, it is possible to organize the type definition within an ISA hierarchy. That is basically a generalization/specialization relationship between types. For instance we can declare that: 'cup ISA vase'. Intuitively this statement shows that all the characteristics of 'vase' are encountered in 'cup' as well, although the latter could have additional characteristics which are not necessarily encountered in all vases. This principle is often referred to as *principle of inheritance* because the type cup *inherits* all the characteristics of the type vase.

In the extensional level the ISA relationship turns into an inclusion relationship between classes. The example shows that the class of cups is contained in the class of vases. These qualitative considerations are rigorously described by the language, through strict criteria that guide the building of ISA hierarchies.

6.5   TYPE SPECIALIZATION
As already stated, the ISA relationship implies that the type being defined be a specialization of the types appearing under ISA. Moreover, the principle of *inheritance* is also used to obtain a more compact schema description. Inheritance can be single or multiple, if in the ISA construction appear one or more supertypes. We talk instead of *absolute* inheritance when the properties of the supertype are inherited without being modified.

Having given a type, the creation of a subtype is performed through specialization. The mechanisms of specialization must always be respected in defining a type using the ISA construct. Those mechanisms are explained in the following sections and are of two basic sorts: specialization by specification and specialization by restriction.

i.   Specialization by specification: This mechanism of specialization requires the addition of new properties to those already defined in the supertypes (which, as stated above, are inherited by the subtype). If the supertypes are two or more and have properties in common, inconsistencies can arise. This is a critical point in multiple inheritance, the problem has already been faced in the literature and there are different ways to solve it, but their description goes beyond the scope of this paper.

ii. Specialization by restriction: The mechanism of restriction allows to refine in the subtype one or more properties already defined in the supertype (this mechanism is called *overriding*). The overriding is performed essentially on the two property typing tools mentioned above: the explicit listing of allowed property values in the case of categorical variables and/or the range of allowed property values in the case of continuous variables.

7   Architecture of the system

The design of an application starts with the definition of the schema and proceeds by verifying its syntactic and semantic correctness. The schema contains the definition of the types of the application domain which describe the structure of objects and the relative integrity constraints. The cycle definition/verification can be iterated several times and, at each cycle, the schema is expanded progressively. Finally, a prototype for the designed application is generated. Each of these design steps corresponds to a subsystem of Mosaico: *Editor-Browser, Semantic Verifier, Code Generator, Functional Verifier, ODB Manager, and Stand Alone Prototyper*. These subsystems will now briefly be described.

1. Editor-Browser (EdiBro): This subsystem provides all the tools necessary to compose the specifications of an application domain, according to the OO paradigm (see sec. 4). As already stated a domain is described through the definition of its types. Types can be defined *ex-novo* or imported from a type library, in which case they can be refined and subtyped. New types can be inserted in the type library for future use.

2. Semantic Verifier (SemVer): By using the Semantic Verifier it is possible to check the syntactic and semantic correctness of the developed KB. The first step of the semantic verification is the parsing of the TQL++ specification. If any errors are detected at this level, the designer can go back to the *EdiBro* subsystem and change the incorrect type definitions. Otherwise the TQL++ specification is first translated into *Intercode* (an internal representation of the specification), and then semantically checked by using theorem-proving techniques. The Intercode is also used for the final, executable code generation, as described below.

3. Code Generator (CodGen): The Code Generator is devoted to the production of executable code, implementing a rapid prototype of the designed application (or part of it). This is done by mapping Intercode into a computer language (also called *object language*). The designer can generate the rapid prototype by choosing from the following languages: C++, Prolog, and O2C.

4. Functional Verifier (FunVer): This subsystem allows the user to run the prototype and monitor the execution.

5. ODB Manager (ODBman): To actually test the application it is necessary to populate the object database. This subsystem allows for the initial generation of a set of test objects (i.e. the specification of an ODB), by using the language Lobster (Missikoff/Toiati 1993). Once created, the ODB is processed to check its correctness, by matching the objects with the corresponding type definitions (declared in the schema). If no error occurs the ODB is loaded and its content can be used by the prototype during execution.

   The ODB Manager also provides a *Query Tool* to retrieve data interactively from the database. The querying is performed by using the same language conceived for the data definition: TQL++.

6. Stand Alone Prototyper (MOSAP_Gen): After the application has been semantically and functionally verified, the stand alone prototype, referred to as MOSAP (MOsaico Stand Alone Prototype), can be generated. In particular, MOSAP_Gen takes the Intercode representation of the application, generated by CodGen, as input and produces the executable prototype as output. A stand alone prototype is an autonomous executable program. It can be installed on a machine different from the one on which Mosaico runs.

In developing the specification of an application, the designer can interact with all Mosaico subsystems. The interaction is guided by the iconic interface described below. The only component implemented in the interface to date is represented by the EdiBro subsystem, through which it is possible to specify a KB using the language TQL++.

8   The iconic interface of Mosaico

The development of good user interfaces based on the iconic paradigm is a difficult task, since sound techniques, which guarantee that the interface will be easy to learn and easy to use, are still lacking. In the development of InterMos, the iconic interface of Mosaico, the methodology Iconit has been applied (Constabile/Missikoff in press). Iconit distinguishes two major design phases: (i) the design of the interface scheme and (ii) the detailed design of the windows. By interface scheme (also called dialog scheme)

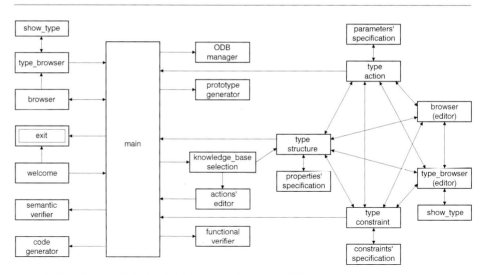

Figure 1. A partial ISTD (Interface State Transition Diagram) of Mosaico.

is meant the design of the overall interface organization, which refers to both the content and sequencing of the windows, omitting the description of each window appearance

8.1   THE INTERFACE DEVELOPMENT METHODOLOGY

Existing tools for interface design are mainly targeted at the construction of the windows and do not address explicitly the definition of the dialog scheme. Usually, the designer sketches the overall structure of the interface on paper, using some diagrammatic representation of the window organization and sequencing, and then creates and implements the interface windows, which are linked explicitly one to another. The consequence of this approach is that any modification in the interface organization, after the implementation, requires the recompilation of a certain number of windows. This is one of the reasons why we believe that it is useful to separate the two issues, thus creating the specific windows independently, and later organizing them in the interface as indicated by the dialog scheme. According to this approach, we have conceived a methodology which allows for an explicit separation of the two above design phases, in particular the first phase produces the dialog scheme (referred to as ISTD: Interface State Transition Diagram) and the second one the set of windows.

8.2   THE ISTD OF MOSAICO

Once a preliminary analysis of the entities and functions required by the target system is performed, it will be possible to start the first phase of the interface development, namely the ISTD (Interface State Transition Diagram)

definition. A partial ISTD of Mosaico is shown in figure 1. Note that the ISTD is fully specified only for the Browser and Editor components. In the diagram, it is possible to distinguish the root, corresponding to the initial WELCOME window (fig. 2), in which a password must be provided by the user. If the password is correct, there is a transition to the MAIN window (fig. 3), in which the user can choose the subsystem of interest; this choice will determine a transition to a specific window. If the user chooses the Editor subsystem, the interface prompts the user with the name of the KB to be edited, and then performs the transition to the TYPE STRUCTURE window (fig. 4). From this window the user has several options: 1) edit a type (thus remaining in the same window); 2) call the Browser (e.g. for loading a type defined in another schema); 3) go back to the MAIN window (see the links in the ISTD in fig. 1) and so forth.

Once the ISTD has been designed, the interface windows corresponding to the ISTD nodes are also created. Some functionalities of the developed interface are shown in the next section through a working example.

8.3   INTERACTING WITH THE SYSTEM

It will now be shown with an example how the EdiBro subsystem works. A prototype of Mosaico, with the interface, has already been developed on a Sun workstation and the figures included here are hard copies of the screen.

The case study is represented by the conceptual structuring of the type 'Fibula' (and of some of its specializations), using materials from the Villanovan cemetery of Quattro Fontanili near Veii, in Southern Etruria. A particular interest derives from the fact that the materials have been

WELCOME

WELCOME
TO
MOSAICO

password:

Version 3.5 - Copyright (c) IASI-CNR 1995
Development partially supported by
Progetto Finalizzato Sistemi Informatici e Calcolo Parallelo
Tel. +396-77161 - E-mail mosaico@sparca.iasi.rm.cnr.it

Figure 2. The initial WELCOME window of Mosaico.

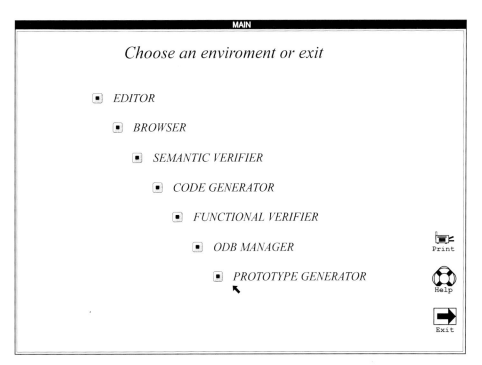

MAIN

Choose an enviroment or exit

◼ *EDITOR*

   ◼ *BROWSER*

      ◼ *SEMANTIC VERIFIER*

         ◼ *CODE GENERATOR*

            ◼ *FUNCTIONAL VERIFIER*

               ◼ *ODB MANAGER*   Print

                  ◼ *PROTOTYPE GENERATOR*

Help

Exit

Figure 3. The MAIN window of Mosaico.

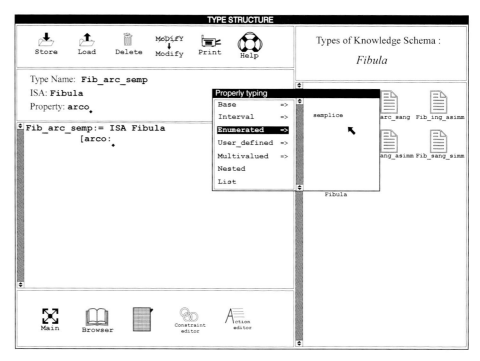

Figure 4. The TYPE STRUCTURE window of Mosaico.

previously studied by several authors (e.g. Close-Brooks 1965; Toms 1986; Kampfmeier 1986; Guidi 1993), making a comparison possible between the various approaches and results. The description of materials has been performed on the basis of *Die alteren italienischen Fibeln,* written by J. Sundwall in 1943, and the *Dizionari Terminologici,* published by the Italian Ministero dei Beni Culturali in 1980. Such a description is developed according to a hierarchy of attributes which generates, consequently, a hierarchy of types progressively more specialized. The attributes hierarchy is the following:

1. form of the arco (bow);
2. decoration
3. form of the staffa (catch).

Supposing that the user wants to define a new type for the KB, the Editor is selected from the MAIN window and the TYPE STRUCTURE window appears (fig. 4). The structure of this window, composed of several panes, is the same for all Editor windows, so that the user will keep a consistent view. On the right side, the types already defined for the current KB are shown. In our example seven types have already been defined, namely: Fibula; Fib_arc_ing (fibula ad arco ingrossato); Fib_arc_sang (fibula ad arco a sanguisuga); Fib_ing_simm (fibula ad arco ingrossato e

staffa simmetrica); Fib_ing_asimm (fibula ad arco ingrossato e staffa asimmetrica); Fib_sang_simm (fibula ad arco a sanguisuga e staffa simmetrica); Fib_sang_asimm (fibula ad arco a sanguisuga e staffa asimmetrica).

The top and bottom panes on the left side of the window contain some icons. The icons in the top pane indicate four operations: 1) *store,* for storing the current type into the KB schema; 2) *load,* for extracting an already defined type; 3) *delete,* for eliminating a type from the schema; 4) *modify,* for updating some characteristics of an existing type. The usual *help* icon is also in this pane.

In the bottom pane, the icons indicating navigational actions are included. A navigational action allows the user to move to other windows of the interface. Going from left to right, the first icon allows to go back to the MAIN window, the second one calls the Browser, the third one goes to the TYPE STRUCTURE window (in fig. 4 it is not active because the TYPE STRUCTURE window is the current one), the fourth and the fifth icons go to the other two windows of the editor, for editing constraints and actions respectively. Such icons, in the same position in all windows, are shown in reverse when not active.

Figure 4 shows the creation of the type 'Fibula'; the first operation to perform is to enter a value for the property 'type name'. According to the TQL++ syntax, one or more supertypes can be specified using the ISA construct. After that it is necessary to proceed to the properties definition; in doing this, the user is helped by the interface which translates the definitions in the TQL++ syntax, thus alleviating the user from knowing all the syntax details.

10   Conclusions

In the previous pages a new classificatory paradigm has been presented that could contribute to drawing the archaeologists' attention again to an aspect of archaeological research characterized, in recent years, by a substantially static period. The reason for this is to be found, we believe, in the climate of disillusionment which took place after the loss of popularity of the quantitative paradigm, proposed by the new archaeologists to assure a good degree of formalization in the process of typology production.

The appearance of information methodologies allowing the formalization of classifications performed on a mainly qualitative base, opens up new perspectives able to offer reasonable possibilities of solving this fundamental and aging debate.

An application of the techniques described in this paper to the material from the Villanovan cemetery of Quattro Fontanili is however in progress, and the relative results will be the subject of a further and more extensive publication.

references

Aldenderfer, M.S.   1987   Assessing the impact of Quantitative Thinking on archaeological research: Historical and Evolutionary Insights. In: M.S. Aldenderfer (ed.), *Quantitative Research in Archaeology*, 9-29, Newbury Park: Sage Publications.

Binford L.R.   1966   A preliminary analysis of functional variability in the Mousterian of the Levallois facies,
    S.R. Binford   *American Anthropologist* 68, 238-295.

Bordes, F.   1950   Principes d'une méthode d'étude des techniques de débitage et de la typologie du paléo-litique ancien et moyen, *L'Anthropologie* 54, 19-34.

Brainerd, G.W.   1951   The place of chronological ordering in archaeological analysis, *American Antiquity* 16, 301-313.

Brew, J.O.   1946   The use and abuse of taxonomy, *The archaeology of Alkali Ridge, Papers of the Peabody Museum* 21, 44-66.

Chang, K.C.   1967   *Rethinking archaeology*. New York: Academic Press.

Christenson, A.L.   1977   Numerical Taxonomy, R-Mode factor analysis, and archaeological classification,
    D.W. Read   *American Antiquity* 42, 163-179.

Clarke, D.   1968   *Analytical Archaeology*. London: Methuen.

Close-Brooks, J.   1965   Proposta per una suddivisione in fasi della necropoli veiente di Quattro Fontanili, *Notizie degli Scavi*, 53 ss.

Coad, P.   1991   *Object-Oriented analysis*. Hemel Hempstead: Prentice Hall International.
    E. Yourdon

Colombetti, M.	1985	*Le idee dell'Intelligenza Artificiale*. Milano: Arnoldo Mondadori Editore.
Costabile, M.F. M. Missikoff	in press	Iconit: An environment for Design and Prototyping of iconic interfaces, *Journal of Visual Languages and Computing*.
Ford, J.A.	1954	The Type Concept Revisited, *American Anthropologist* 56, 42-54.
Giarratano, J. G. Riley	1989	*Expert systems principles and programming*. Boston: PWS-KENT.
Gorodzov, V.A.	1933	The Typological Method in Archaeology, *American Anthropologist* 35, 95-103.
Guidi, A.	1993	*La necropoli veiente dei Quattro Fontanili*. Firenze: Leo S. Olshki.
Kampfmeier, U.	1986	ARCOS – A video-computer-documentation system for the use in archaeology and historic sciences, *Computer Applications in Archaeology*, 91-147.
Khoshafian, S. R. Abnous	1990	*Object-Orientation*. New York: John Wiley and Sons.
Klejn, L.	1982	*Archaeological Typology*. BAR International series 153, 3. Oxford: British Archaeological Reports.
Kluckhohn, C.	1939	The place of theory in anthropological studies, *Philosophy of Science* 6 (3), 328-344.
Krieger, A.D.	1944	The Typological Concept, *American Antiquity* 9 (3), 271-288.
Missikoff, M. M. Toiati	1993	*Object-Oriented Databases, the language TQL++, Usage Notes*. Leysin: EDBT Summer School.
Montelius, O.	1874	*La Suède prehistorique*. Stockholm: P.A. Norstedt.
	1885	Sur la chronologie de l'Age du Bronze, *Materiaux pour l'Histoire de l'Homme*.
	1899	*Der Orient und Europa*. Stockholm.
Robinson, W.S.	1951	A method for chronologically ordering archaeological deposits, *American Antiquity* 16, 293-301.
Seitzer, D.J.	1978	Problems and Principles of Classification in Archaeology, *Helinium* 18, 3-34.
Spaulding, A.C.	1953	Statistical Techniques for the Discovery of Artifact Types, *American Antiquity* 18 (4), 305-313.
Thomas, D.H.	1978	The awful truth about statistics in archaeology, *American Antiquity* 43, 231 244.
Toms, J.	1986	The relative chronology of the Villanovan Cemetery of Quattro Fontanili at Veii, *AION* 7, 41 ss.

Oleg Missikoff
Via di Vigna Filonardi 7
00197 Rome
Italy